W9-CKB-845

THE
TWENTY-FIFTH
AMENDMENT

ITS COMPLETE HISTORY
AND APPLICATIONS

Third Edition

JOHN D. FEERICK

MJF BOOKS
New York

Published by MJF Books
Fine Communications
589 Eighth Avenue, 6th Floor
New York, NY 10018

The Twenty-Fifth Amendment:
Its Complete History and Applications
Third Edition
LC Control Number: 2018935808
ISBN 978-1-60671-409-6

Printed in the United States of America.

MJF Books and the MJF colophon are trademarks of Fine Creative Media, Inc.

QF   10 9 8 7 6 5 4 3 2 1

With deep gratitude to my wife, Emalie, and in loving memory of my brother, Donald J. Feerick, and Leonard F. Manning, my law school professor and mentor

Contents

Introduction

The publication of the third edition of a book may attest to a degree of commercial success but is otherwise generally not a significant event. That usual rule does not apply to this new edition of John D. Feerick's work *The Twenty-Fifth Amendment: Its Complete History and Application*. Originally published in 1976 and reissued in 1992 with a lengthy new Introduction to cover subsequent developments, *The Twenty-Fifth Amendment* takes its significance in part from the constitutional amendment it discusses and from which it takes its name. The Amendment, which was ratified in 1967, addressed a range of problems dealing with presidential succession following presidential death, resignation, removal, and inability and provided procedures for filling a vice-presidential vacancy and for handling situations of presidential inability. Many of the problems the Amendment addressed had proved vexing ever since some were first raised at the Constitutional Convention in Philadelphia more than two centuries ago. Prior to 1967, they had resisted any solution, although reform efforts had been made.

These problems relating to presidential continuity, of course, present themselves episodically, rather than routinely. Yet the centrality of presidential leadership, to America and the world, mandates that reliable arrangements exist to ensure presidential continuity, particularly given America's international role in a nuclear and information age. The Twenty-Fifth Amendment to the Constitution provided such procedures to address those perils which history suggested presented the greatest jeopardy.

Section 1 of the Amendment confirmed the actions followed by Vice President John Tyler and seven successors. It established that a Vice President became, rather than simply acted as, President upon the occurrence of an event that permanently removed the prior Chief Executive. Section 2 created a new procedure to fill a vice-presidential vacancy, one that rested on the twin premises rooted in normal practice that a Vice President should be someone whom the President chose, subject to a democratic political check. Sections 3 and 4 provided procedures whereby a President, or his or her close associates in the executive branch, could initiate a temporary transfer of executive power to the Vice President in case the President was unable to discharge the powers and duties of the office.

In its first forty-five years, the Amendment has already helped ensure the continuity of presidential leadership. It provided a means whereby two Republican Presidents could fill vice-presidential vacancies in the mid-1970s, thereby ensuring that a mid-term transition would not shift party control of the White House. That contingency was not hypothetical. As Dean Feerick points out, some feared after Vice President Spiro T. Agnew resigned his office that the burgeoning effort to remove Richard M. Nixon from office could be compromised by the fact that a succession would elevate a Democrat, Speaker of the House of Representatives Carl Albert, to the presidency. Section 2, by furnishing a means of installing Gerald R. Ford as a new Vice President, obviated that concern. On three occasions, Presidents Ronald Reagan and George W. Bush followed the procedures in Section 3 for transferring power, prudent acts that are likely to create helpful precedents of their own.

The book takes its significance largely from the importance of presidential continuity and the role the Twenty-Fifth Amendment plays in ensuring it. Yet the story of the Twenty-Fifth Amendment also furnishes a marvelous case study regarding two other facets of American government. It provides a fascinating account of legislative behavior. Significant legislation generally occurs only when legislators make choices and strike compromises. That becomes particularly true for constitutional amendments, which require super-majority approval at multiple stages. Additional constraints emerge in dealing with an issue like presidential succession and inability that does not engage voters and accordingly often may not preoccupy their elected representatives. The book describes the choices Senator Birch Bayh and the Amendment's other architects needed to make to ensure its success.

The story of the Twenty-Fifth Amendment also provides insights into the process of amending and interpreting the Constitution. Regarding the former, Dean Feerick describes the way in which the Amendment was conceived and the sources from which it drew, the adjustments made to respond to various concerns, the process of mobilizing support, the challenges of drafting, and the ultimately successful ratification. Regarding ratification, the book offers extensive summaries of the framers' intent in a situation in which the presence of available comprehensive legislative records allows recourse to original intent as an interpretive guide on many questions.

Ultimately, the publication of the third edition of *The Twenty-Fifth Amendment* is a significant event because it renews and extends a book that was a seminal contribution when first published and that has retained its importance for more than three-and-one-half decades. Now, as was true then, government officials faced with a succession or inability crisis, or in structuring their contingency plans, will not proceed without consulting this work. Scholars cannot write about these topics without reading and rereading it, and we cite it frequently. Those interested in American government and the Constitution, whether scholars, students, or engaged citizens, will find their time with this book quite rewarding. I certainly have, each time I have returned to it during the life of its two previous editions.

This third edition preserves the original book, which was nominated for a Pulitzer Prize. Dean Feerick provides an account of the various crises in presidential succession and inability. Included are the numerous near-misses, culminating with the disabilities of President Dwight D. Eisenhower and assassination of President John F. Kennedy, which formed the context in which the Amendment was conceived, proposed, and ratified. (These events are recounted in even greater detail in the author's earlier book, *From Failing Hands: The Story of Presidential Succession* [Fordham, 1965].) Dean Feerick describes the deliberations that led to the drafting of the Amendment, the legislative moves that led Congress to propose it, and the events that produced ratification. He examines in detail the legislative record to bring to the surface the intentions of Senator Bayh and the other framers of the Amendment as they applied to various contingencies. Additionally, he describes the earliest applications of the Amendment's various sections. Much of the content of the Introduction to the 1992 edition, which addressed some of the earliest applications and failures to use Sections 3 and 4 during the Reagan years, now appears in expanded form in a new Chapter 13 of this volume.

The events of September 11, 2001, which affected so many aspects of American life, also gave new importance to questions regarding presidential continuity since the al Qaeda terrorists who hijacked the aircraft included government buildings in our nation's capital among their intended targets. Suppose, for instance, a terrorist attack on Washington, D.C., killed or disabled not simply the President and Vice President but also others in the line of succession. How should the line be constructed to ensure continuity of presidential leadership? That question involves not simply identifying a sufficiently long line of potential successors but also determining which officers would be well suited to follow the Vice President in case such an event occurred.

This third edition includes chapters considering developments since 1992. Dean Feerick reviews the congressional hearings and other legislative activity that occurred in the aftermath of 9/11. A new chapter summarizes many of the symposia, scholarly articles, and commissions that have considered problems of presidential inability and succession during the past quarter-century or so. These issues have also furnished a ready source of material for novels, movies, and television shows. Dean Feerick summarizes many of these works of fiction for the continuity contingencies they present. Dean Feerick also presents some new (while retaining much of the previous) material in his concluding chapters, "An Appraisal" and "Recommendations."

Many of the topics included in the new edition go well beyond the Twenty-Fifth Amendment and address issues relating to presidential continuity outside its scope. Senator Birch Bayh, the principal architect of the Amendment, and his colleagues wisely concluded in the mid-1960s that if they tried to address every problem regarding presidential continuity they would accomplish nothing. Rather than attempt a comprehensive fix that might have impressed scholars but forfeited necessary legislative support, they elected to address the most pressing gaps with achievable solutions. Nearly one-half century later, the Twenty-Fifth Amendment stands as a significant and successful contribution to our Constitution's provisions for ensuring presidential continuity. Regrettably, Congress has not returned to these subjects in the intervening time to address the remaining problems. The new material in this third edition lays out many of these problems and offers a menu of options. The hope is that its publication will help prompt needed reforms.

Ultimately, the value of this new edition inheres in the unique relationship that John Feerick has had with the subject. He has simply studied these problems longer and from more perspectives than anyone else, and his insights regarding them have singular quality and value. He began studying the topic in the early 1960s, publishing his first article on presidential inability in the *Fordham Law Review* in its October 1963 edition. His book *From Failing Hands* and many law review articles followed. He was part of the American Bar Association (ABA) group which met in the weeks following the assassination of President John F. Kennedy to arrive at a consensus proposal that largely foreshadowed the Twenty-Fifth Amendment. He worked closely, particularly with Senator Bayh, but also with other legislators, and through the ABA, in the arduous work involved in guiding the Amendment through the House of Representatives and the Senate and the subsequent ratification process. He has furnished guidance to government officials on other occasions when the Amendment's provisions were applied or reviewed. He has continued to write about the topic and to participate in public discussions on it, in a careful, intellectually honest manner, and to convene periodic symposia where those with various perspectives could study and discuss it.

This third edition provides the latest scholarly contribution to this subject by one who has added so much, here and elsewhere, as a lawyer, scholar, citizen, and friend.

Joel K. Goldstein
Vincent C. Immel Professor of Law
St. Louis University School of Law
St. Louis, Missouri

Preface to the Third Edition

It would not have been possible for me to complete this update without the enormous assistance of students at Fordham Law School. It is with great gratitude that I acknowledge the following students' dedication and superlative research efforts, drafting, source checking, suggestions, and ideas: Elizabeth Bierut, Mary Kate Brennan, Ashley Feasley, Katelynn Gray, Caitlin Polus, Caroline Saucier, and Heather Sertial. Brian Hannan, formerly a student on this work and now a practicing lawyer in New Jersey, made an important contribution in the area of presidential inability. I also wish to express my gratitude to the editors of Vol. 78 of the *Fordham Law Review*, especially Deborah Eltgroth and Daniel Hafetz, for arranging the program on presidential succession held in April 2010, and to the editors of Vol. 79, especially Alyssa L. Beaver, for producing an outstanding volume of remarks and articles relating to the subject of the program, including an oral history interview with former Senator Birch Bayh and keynote remarks by Fred Fielding and Benton Becker. The program and volume contributed greatly to this book. I thank Brandon Gershowitz, Esq., for his invaluable assistance with an article of mine appearing in Vol. 79, and Adam Sternberg, Esq., for helping with the final push toward completion of this edition. I also thank very specially Nicole Gordon and Dora Galacatos and the students we taught in Fordham's presidential succession clinic for the additional learning I received since its inception in July 2010. I acknowledge with appreciation the technical assistance of Javed Yunus.

Most appreciatively, I thank three members of the Fordham Law community for their invaluable dedication and help: Justin Ferguson, a student, who studied the congressional hearings and proposals, coordinated the work of other students, and drafted, edited, and made substantive contributions throughout the update; Derek

Hackett, my administrative assistant, for arranging meetings and conferences, typing and retyping, and in the final critical stages making certain that all my editing suggestions were reflected in the manuscript; and Katelynn Gray again for her help in the very final stages of copy editing. They all set a very special benchmark of sensitivity and excellence.

I thank Liza Talbot of the LBJ Library for locating documents for me from the files of President Lyndon B. Johnson: the President's letter agreement on presidential disability with House Speaker John W. McCormack in December 1963, and the accompanying fifteen-page explanatory memorandum; and the file surrounding President Johnson's apparent decision not to enter into a written letter agreement with Vice President Hubert H. Humphrey. I also thank Benton Becker, counsel to President Gerald R. Ford, for providing me with his insights and documents in his possession bearing on President Ford's succession to the presidency. I am very grateful to Mr. Becker for having a search made of the files of President Ford, enabling me to publish the material in Appendix J.

Finally, I thank Fordham Law School and its *Law Review* for supporting all of my work in the field of presidential succession over the past fifty years, and the law firm where I spent my first twenty-one years as a lawyer, Skadden, Arps, Slate, Meagher & Flom, for its tremendous support of my pro bono efforts in assisting committees of Congress in the areas of presidential succession and Electoral College reform. No words can adequately describe my gratitude to Fordham and Skadden for enabling me to make these areas the most meaningful and purposeful part of my professional life.

I thank Professor Joel Goldstein, our nation's outstanding authority on the Vice Presidency, for writing the Introduction to this edition. We met when he was a college senior in the 1970s and have enjoyed a lifelong series of discussions of this subject matter generally from the time he began his scholarly explorations in 1976. His 2010 article in the *Fordham Law Review* is a masterful treatment of the subject. I am deeply grateful to him for his many kindnesses and, most especially of all, his friendship. His enthusiasm for the subject has enriched my life since that lunch meeting in a Fifth Avenue restaurant in New York City in the 1970s.

I can't adequately express my thanks to Larry Bridgett of Fordham Law School for helping to assemble the materials and bringing this book project to conclusion.

I want to express my gratitude to Wilma Tamayo-Abreu for her willingness to always help. I am most grateful for the help of the staffs of Fordham University Press and the law school library.

I especially thank Prof. Gail Hollister for her exceptional contribution, dedication, and support to this project when it was most needed.

This edition brings up to date the 1992 edition, which in turn did the same for the original publication. The 1992 edition retained the chapters and pages of the 1976 version and added an extended Introduction. To add an Introduction to an Introduction was not practical, and therefore this edition incorporates in its later chapters the 1992 introductory section as well as an update covering the past twenty years as they touch on the Twenty-Fifth Amendment. Therefore, regrettably because of the citations to the 1992 edition in other works, the page numbers here do not correspond to the 1976 and 1992 editions. Chapters 14, 15, and 16 of this edition are entirely new. Chapter 13 tracks the Introduction to the 1992 edition, while Chapters 17 and 18 have many changes and additions from the earlier versions of these chapters, then appearing as 13 and 14.

I doubt there will be another update by me to this book, which builds on my first book, *From Failing Hands*, and my 1963 and 1964 *Fordham Law Review* articles on the subject of presidential inability and vice-presidential vacancy. As Senator Birch Bayh noted in a telephone conversation we had, we came at the subject together at the beginning of our careers and are going out with it, or words to that effect. The ride has been worth the effort.

Acknowledgments from the 1992 Edition

I wish to acknowledge my appreciation to Paul C. Fonseca, a member of the New York and New Jersey bars, and to the following students of Fordham Law School for their invaluable assistance in connection with this edition: Marcy Hillman, Henry Park, and Earl Wilson. I especially appreciate the help I received from Marcy Hillman in putting together a number of strands of information and in updating the bibliography.

J.D.F.
1992

Foreword to the 1976 Edition

As this nation celebrates the two-hundredth anniversary of its birth, we should take special note of one unique feature of our great constitutional experiment. Unlike almost any other Western democracy, the United States has never been faced with a serious crisis in the line of succession to office of its chief executive and head of state. Our ability to avoid such a crisis throughout much of our earlier history was, perhaps, largely a matter of luck. Fortunately, we never had to confront the prospect of a double vacancy in the offices of both President and Vice President. Thus, one of two individuals specifically designated by the voters as President and next-in-line served in the offices at all times.

The problem of the line of succession following the Vice President, however, long bothered many thoughtful Americans. But it was not until the mid-1960s, after the assassination of President Kennedy, that the Constitution was changed to provide a structural solution to the problem. As fate would have it, less than a decade after the ratification of the Twenty-Fifth Amendment, the unprecedented happened, and both offices were vacated during one presidential term. Twice, Vice Presidents were then nominated by the President and approved by both Houses of Congress under the new Amendment. When the first of these, Gerald R. Ford, became the thirty-eighth President of the United States, there was no serious question about the legitimacy of his claim to the office. One has only to imagine the divisiveness which would have been created had the White House been turned over to the opposing party in the person of the Speaker of the House to realize how significant an achievement this was.

The nation owes a great debt of gratitude to the author of this volume, John Feerick, not only for this comprehensive, scholarly, and highly readable history of the Twenty-Fifth Amendment but for his expert guiding hand throughout the process of crafting the Amendment, obtaining its approval by Congress and ratification by the states, and implementing it for the first time. Mr. Feerick, who is a distinguished attorney in private practice in New York, gave freely of his time and talents in assisting those of us in public office in providing a solution to this crucial aspect of our constitutional system. In my view, his distinguished service should serve as an example to his colleagues at the bar of a man who has fulfilled his public responsibilities in an outstanding way.

Birch Bayh
United States Senator

Preface to the 1976 Edition

This book is a sequel to my earlier book, *From Failing Hands: The Story of Presidential Succession* (Fordham, 1965). Therein, the development from 1607 to 1964 of our political and legal experiences with executive succession machinery was traced. *From Failing Hands*, among other things, constitutes a detailed account of presidential succession as reflected in the deaths and illnesses of Presidents and Vice Presidents, the crises reflected in those events, and the continuing growth in importance of the vice presidency.

This book focuses on the Twenty-Fifth Amendment—its meaning, legislative history, and applications in 1973 and 1974 following the resignations from office of Spiro T. Agnew and Richard M. Nixon. Necessarily, certain historical background material appearing in *From Failing Hands* is repeated in abbreviated form.

Here I have desired to complete to date the story of presidential succession initially undertaken in *From Failing Hands*. My present purpose has been fortified by the considerable interest shown in the Twenty-Fifth Amendment since its adoption on February 10, 1967. It has been the subject of fiction and nonfiction.* It has been criticized for being vague and undemocratic. It has been praised for making possible swift and orderly successions to the presidency and vice presidency upon the occurrence of some of the most extraordinary events in American history. Its vice-presidential selection feature has been recommended as the best method for selecting all Vice Presidents. The repeal of that feature and the abolition of the vice presidency have also been suggested. Moreover, throughout the Watergate crisis

* See F. Knebel, *Night of Camp David* (1965); B. Bayh, *One Heartbeat Away* (1968).

the Amendment was alluded to as affording a means by which a President voluntarily and temporarily could transfer presidential power during an impeachment proceeding, and it was suggested as authorizing a Vice President and Cabinet to suspend, so to speak, a President during the period of an impeachment trial before the Senate.

Judging by all the attention the Amendment has received and by the number of presidential and vice presidential vacancies and illnesses that have occurred in our history, one can expect that the Twenty-Fifth Amendment will receive frequent application in the future history of our country. I hope that this book will serve as a useful reference work and afford greater understanding of an amendment that is unique in so many ways. It is the only part of the Constitution that confers an explicit power on the President's Cabinet, places specific time limits on congressional action, empowers persons other than the President to convene a special session of Congress, and assigns the House of Representatives a role in the appointive process. It also adds to the Vice President's constitutional duties, establishes a procedure in addition to impeachment by which a President can be prevented from discharging his powers and duties, and prescribes for the first time a method of filling a vice-presidential vacancy. Finally, it is one of the longest amendments to the Constitution, and its every detail is filled with considerable meaning.*

In the writing of this book I owe my greatest debt of gratitude to my wife, Emalie, and to our children.

I wish to express special thanks to Linda Wood for editorial and substantive suggestions that greatly improved the manuscript, for invaluable assistance with the research and drafting of Part III, and for her cheerful help with numerous details. Although this book was started shortly before Agnew's resignation, I could not have finished it without Mrs. Wood's assistance since October 1974.

My debt to Gloria Frank and Linda Schurmann for typing and retyping the manuscript and for helping me in so many ways is inexpressible.

I am particularly grateful to my colleagues Joseph T.C. Hart and Kurt Koegler; to my father-in-law, William B. Platt Jr.; and to my brother-in-law, Harold K. Platt, for taking the time to read the manuscript and make suggestions that improved it. Kurt Koegler was especially helpful with Chapters 13 and 14 [now Chapters 17 and 18].

To the secretarial supervisors of my firm, Anthony Arbisi and Lorraine Meyer, I owe a debt of thanks for their understanding of my requests. I am grateful to my law partners for their encouragement in this undertaking; to Kathryn V. McCulloch and Finbarr O'Neill of the *Fordham Law Review* for their work in checking

---

* I have placed in a volume copies of correspondence and memoranda that may shed additional light on the Amendment. For the fascinating inside story of the development of the Amendment, see Bayh, *One Heartbeat Away* (1968).

the accuracy of citations and quotations; and to the staff of Fordham University Press, especially Dr. Mary Beatrice Schulte, for many helpful suggestions and painstaking attention to detail.

I wish to acknowledge my deep gratitude to the American Bar Association, especially to Donald E. Channell and Lowell R. Beck of its Washington office at the time the Amendment was developed, for making possible my participation in that development. The contributions of Channell and Beck to the Amendment's success were immeasurable.

Finally, I am honored to have Senator Birch Bayh, the chief architect of the Twenty-Fifth Amendment, write the Foreword to this book.

John D. Feerick

The Problems

Presidential Inability

What is the extent of the term "disability" & who is to be the judge of it?

JOHN DICKINSON, August 27, 1787[1]

When the framers of the Constitution met in Philadelphia in 1787, they brought with them almost two hundred years of experience with executive succession machinery.[2] Yet they did not spend much time discussing the subject at the Constitutional Convention of 1787. They seem to have thought they handled the matter adequately by providing for the office of Vice President and by inserting in the Constitution the following clause on presidential succession:

> In Case of the Removal of the President from Office, or of his Death, Resignation, or Inability to discharge the Powers and Duties of the said Office, the Same shall devolve on the Vice President, and the Congress may by Law provide for the Case of Removal, Death, Resignation or Inability, both of the President and Vice President, declaring what Officer shall then act as President, and such Officer shall act accordingly, until the Disability be removed, or a President shall be elected.[3]

The debates were silent on the meaning of "inability" and on who should determine its existence and termination.[4] Also untouched was the question of what happened when the President became disabled. Did the Vice President become President for the remainder of the term, or did he merely act as President for the duration of the inability? In the answer to this question, the antecedent of the words "the Same" became determinative. If the "Office" devolved, the Vice President presumably became President for the rest of the term; if "the Powers and Duties" devolved, he presumably would be Acting President. Moreover, since the clause did not differentiate among the covered contingencies, whatever devolved did so whether it was a case of removal, death, resignation, or inability.

This question and these fine distinctions did not surface until many years after the adoption of the Constitution. For the first fifty-two years of the existence of the presidency, our nation was remarkably fortunate. No President died in office, although three vacancies did occur in the vice presidency. In 1812 George Clinton, James Madison's first Vice President, died in office, and in the following term Madison's second Vice President, Elbridge Gerry, also died.* These deaths left the vice presidency unoccupied for a period of more than three years. Another vice-presidential vacancy occurred when John C. Calhoun resigned in 1832, less than three months before the expiration of his term, in order to accept an appointment as U.S. Senator from South Carolina.

MADISON'S ILLNESS

A little more than a year prior to Gerry's death, President Madison suffered an illness that left him unable to conduct the affairs of state for three weeks and set off widespread discussion of presidential succession. By a note of June 18, 1813, Madison postponed a meeting with a congressional delegation to discuss the nomination of Albert Gallatin, then Secretary of the Treasury, to be Envoy Extraordinary. The note read:

> James Madison is sorry that a continuance of his indisposition will not permit him to see the committee of the Senate today, nor can he at present fix a day when it will be in his power.[5]

Word traveled throughout the capital that Madison was critically ill with bilious fever, and attention focused on the possible succession of Vice President Elbridge Gerry, who was almost sixty-nine years old at the time. French Minister Louis Sérurier wrote on June 21:

> The thought of [Madison's] possible loss strikes everybody with consternation. It is certainly true that his death, in the circumstances in which the Republic is placed, would be a veritable national calamity. The President who would succeed him for three and a half years is a respectable old man, but weak and worn out. All good Americans pray for the recovery of Mr. Madison.[6]

Daniel Webster delivered some congressional resolutions to Madison but found him too ill to read them.

---

* Shortly before the vacancy caused by Gerry's death, President Madison risked death or capture by his personal involvement in the War of 1812. I. Brant, *James Madison, Commander In Chief, 1812–1836* 299–300 (1961).

There was speculation in the press that Madison might not survive. The *Alexandria Gazette* observed that the President's age (sixty-two), "added to the heavy weight with which the public burdens must bear upon his mind, in this calamitous crisis is enough to create serious doubts of his recovery."[7]

Both houses of Congress became engrossed with the possibility of the President's death and the Vice President's succession. The presidential succession statute at that time ran first to the President pro tempore of the Senate and then to the Speaker of the House. There was a vacancy in the Senate post because Madison had appointed the former President pro tempore, William H. Crawford, Minister to France. James Monroe wrote that there was plotting in the Senate to fill the post of President pro tempore because the deaths of both the President and the Vice President were presumed to be near.[8] The *Federal Republican* newspaper focused on the future of House Speaker Henry Clay. In an analogy to the Duke of Gloucester, who had murdered repeatedly to gain the throne of England, the paper obliquely suggested that Clay would murder Gerry to become President.[9]

Fortunately, Madison began a slow recovery from his illness. On July 2 Dolley Madison wrote that his fever had subsided and that he was improving. On July 7 it was announced that the President had resumed the most urgent public business,[10] and a week later he met with a Senate committee. In early August he journeyed four days from Washington to his home, Montpelier, where his health continued to improve. The *Federal Republican,* however, sought to prolong the controversy and reported on August 13 that the sickness had left Madison with only a few months or perhaps a few days to live: "We know that his mind has shared the fate of his body . . . not a few, who have recently visited him, have left his chamber under a full conviction of the derangement of his mind."[11] This account set off another series of rumors that were quelled only by further accounts of his good health. When Madison returned to Washington on October 24, 1813, it was obvious that his recovery was complete.[12]

Vice President Gerry died the next year; Madison survived until 1836, when he died at the age of eighty-five.

TYLER PRECEDENT

The luck of the first fifty-two years ended on April 4, 1841, when President William Henry Harrison, the oldest President at inauguration, died of pneumonia. It was not until early the next day that a messenger, traveling by boat and horse, reached Vice President John Tyler in Williamsburg, Virginia, to give him the news. Tyler immediately proceeded to Washington and, shortly after his arrival on April 6, took the presidential oath of office. Although he apparently held the view that he was President without the oath, Tyler took it to remove any future questions of his authority.[13] To make his view clear, Tyler had William Cranch, Chief Judge of the

United States Circuit Court for the District of Columbia, prepare an appropriate certification:

> I, William Cranch, chief judge of the circuit court of the District of Colum-
> bia, certify that the above-named John Tyler personally appeared before me
> this day, and although he deems himself qualified to perform the duties and
> exercise the powers and office of President on the death of William Henry
> Harrison, late President of the United States, without any other oath than
> that which he has taken as Vice-President, yet as doubts may arise, and for
> greater caution, took and subscribed the foregoing oath before me.[14]

After taking the oath, Tyler held his first Cabinet meeting. When asked by Secretary of State Daniel Webster whether he would continue Harrison's practice of assigning the President's vote no more weight than that of any member of the Cabinet, Tyler said: "... I can never consent to being dictated to. ... I, as president, will be responsible for my administration."[15] Several days later he delivered an inaugural address, and on April 14 moved into the White House. Declared the *New York American* on April 16: "It is impossible for an American not to feel ... great pride at the quiet, orderly, and, as it were, matter of course transition, by which so important a movement has been operated."

Tyler's ascendancy to the "office" of President was not without dispute. Protests were echoed by some newspapers, and leaders of the Whig Party referred to him as simply the "Acting President." When the Cabinet notified Tyler of Harrison's death, he was addressed as "Vice President," although the Cabinet quickly acquiesced in his assumption of the office of President. John Quincy Adams, a former President of the United States and then a member of the House of Representatives, noted in his diary for April 16, 1841:

> But it [Tyler's assumption of the title and office of the presidency] is a
> construction in direct violation both of the grammar and context of the
> Constitution, which confers upon the Vice-President, on the decease of the
> President, not the office, but the powers and duties of the said office.*

Webster, on the other hand, reportedly held the view that the powers and duties of the President were inseparable from the office itself and that any succession by a Vice President to the presidential office was a succession for the remainder of the term.[16]

Upon the convening of the special session of the Twenty-Seventh Congress on May 31, 1841, Tyler's assumption of the presidential office came under attack.[17]

---

* In his diary on April 4, 1841, Adams reported that the Constitution "makes the Vice-President of the United States, John Tyler, of Virginia, Acting President of the Union for four years less one month." 10 *The Memoirs of John Quincy Adams* 463–64 (Adams ed., 1876). Id. At 456.

When Representative Henry A. Wise of Virginia introduced a resolution calling for the formation of a committee "to wait on the President of the United States," Representative John McKeon of New York moved to strike "President" and substitute "Vice-President, now exercising the office of President." He stated that "a grave constitutional question" had been presented, which should be set "at rest for all future time." The House of Representatives rejected McKeon's suggestion and passed the Wise resolution, sending it to the Senate.

In the Senate the next day, Senator William Allen of Ohio urged that Tyler be addressed as "the Vice President, on whom by the death of the late President, the powers and duties of the office of President have devolved." Allen said that if a President were afflicted with a disease producing a temporary mental disability from which he subsequently recovered, he then could be reinstated to his powers and duties. He further stated that he had no objection to Tyler's calling himself President, provided it was understood that a person could become President only through election.

Senator Robert J. Walker of Mississippi disagreed. In his opinion, the Constitution provided for two separate contingencies. He stated that the Vice President succeeded to the "Office" of President in all cases because Article II, section 1, clause 6 was explicit: An officer appointed by Congress acts as President when both the President and the Vice President have died, resigned, been removed, or become disabled, but not so when a Vice President takes over upon the happening of any of these eventualities to the President. "This is the language and the meaning of the Constitution," Walker said. "Can there be any doubt on the subject?" Senator Allen thought there was. He hypothesized a case of temporary disability, more easily contemplated by the Founding Fathers than death, he said, when a disabled President recovered to find the Vice President in his office:

> The question would then arise, which of the two officers should continue in the chair. . . . Was it [the office] to vibrate [assume a struggle for power] between the two claimants? In what manner could a President of the United States—unimpeached, sane, and alive—cease to be President? There was none known to the Constitution. None.[18]

Senator Calhoun of South Carolina considered the entire discussion irrelevant since there was a permanent vacancy in the presidential office. The House resolution passed the Senate, without change, by a vote of 38 to 8, and the Tyler precedent became firmly established in our history.*

---

* Not everyone, of course, came to accept Tyler's succession to the office. Thus, when a Whig congressman introduced an impeachment resolution in January 1843, Tyler was referred to as "Vice President, acting as President." 12 Cong. Globe, 27th Cong., 3d Sess. 144 (1843).

More than one hundred years later, an unsuccessful challenge would be made to Lyndon B. Johnson's succession on the ground that he had assumed the "office" of President in violation of the Constitution. *From Failing Hands* 10 & n.

GARFIELD'S INABILITY

Within the next twenty-five years the Tyler precedent was followed twice—by Vice President Millard Fillmore upon the death in office on July 9, 1850, of President Zachary Taylor, and by Vice President Andrew Johnson upon the death of Abraham Lincoln on April 15, 1865. Each succession to the office of President took place swiftly and without question.

On July 2, 1881, however, when the nation was confronted with its first case of prolonged presidential inability, the Tyler precedent became a formidable obstacle to the Vice President's acting as President.[19] That day President James A. Garfield was shot by an assassin and for the next eighty days wavered between life and death. Although at times it appeared that he would recover, he suffered frequent relapses and experienced periods of hallucinations. "Hope alternated with despair and days of physical strength and mental alertness inevitably gave way to days of extreme weakness and moments of mental aberration."[20] For most of the last eighty days of his life, Garfield was confined to bed. Only toward the end was he permitted to sit in a reclining chair. When he was moved to the New Jersey shore from the White House on September 6, "those watching were shocked by the change that had come over the great, strong man who had been the President of the United States."[21]

During the period of his inability, the number of Garfield's visitors was restricted. From July 2 through July 20, only his family and physicians were permitted to see him, and although occasional visits from members of the Cabinet were permitted thereafter, at no point did Vice President Chester A. Arthur confer with him. This may have been in part because they were not good friends and were from different factions of the Republican Party. The further fact that Garfield's assassin, Charles J. Guiteau, was motivated by a desire to have Arthur succeed to the presidency also initially turned public opinion against Arthur.

Arthur was in New York when informed of the shooting of Garfield. He was unwilling to go to Washington until officially notified of the President's death. But the Cabinet requested that he take the midnight train to the capital, and he arrived at approximately 8:00 A.M. on July 3. Arthur stayed at the home of Senator John P. Jones of Nevada, and the Cabinet paid daily visits. On July 13 Garfield's physicians expressed optimism about his full recovery, and with great relief Arthur returned to his home in New York, where he remained secluded.*[22] Arthur's conduct during the entire period of Garfield's inability was such that the *New York Times* observed in late August:

---

* A full account of the medical treatment given to the President will be found in Millard, Candice, *Destiny of the Republic: A Tale of Madness, Medicine and the Murder of a President* (2011, Doubleday, New York), wherein the author concludes that the President could have been saved but for medical malpractice.

Such impending fear as there might have been early in July of the dangers to the common weal from the President's sudden taking off has passed away. If his legal successor has not disarmed criticism, he has at least done nothing to sharpen it. . . . A change of Executive eight weeks ago would have been felt as one of the most violent of the jars to which the institutions of the United States have been subjected. A change today would be effected merely amid a certain silent and watchful expectancy. . . . [23]

Garfield's only official act during the eighty days was the signing of an extradition paper on August 10. He was prevented from discharging his powers and duties by his doctors, who felt his only chance of survival lay in isolation from the burdens of public affairs. On one occasion when Garfield wanted to discuss the business of the executive department, a doctor forbade it, stating, "I told him that he must dismiss that subject from his mind until he was fully recovered. He said that it was on his mind and he had to let it off; but he obeyed me as implicitly as a school-boy would obey his teacher, and he has said hardly anything since."[24]

The members of the Cabinet tried to keep the wheels of government turning. Whenever the President's condition became critical, the Cabinet would spend long hours of vigil at the White House. But there was much the Cabinet could not do. Important matters such as the handling of foreign affairs and the prosecution of post office swindlers were neglected. Accordingly, it was not surprising that in late August Secretary of State James G. Blaine prepared a paper on presidential inability and argued that since the Constitution contained no directions for replacing a disabled President, Arthur should be called to Washington to take over the presidency. Only a few Cabinet members agreed.[25] It is reported that a majority of the Cabinet, including Attorney General Wayne MacVeagh, was of the view that any succession by Arthur would be, by virtue of the Tyler precedent, to the President's office for the rest of the term.[26] Arthur, however, fearful of being labeled a usurper and of possibly killing Garfield, made it clear that he would not assume presidential responsibility.

Following Garfield's death on September 19, 1881, and Arthur's subsequent swearing in as president in the early morning of September 20, the debate over the meaning of the succession provision continued in the press, in the legal journals of the day, and in Congress.[27] When Arthur became President there was no Vice President, President pro tempore of the Senate, or Speaker of the House—in short, no constitutional successor to the presidency. Arthur recognized the problem and, before leaving New York to accompany Garfield's body to Washington, wrote a proclamation summoning the Senate into an immediate special session so that it could elect a President pro tempore. He mailed the proclamation to the White House so that if he were struck down on his way to Washington a constitutional crisis would be averted. If he arrived in the capital safely, he planned to call the Senate into session himself and destroy the letter.[28] On October 10 the Senate convened in special session called by Arthur, and the independent David B. Davis of Illinois was ultimately selected to be President pro tempore.

In several messages to Congress, Arthur himself expressed concern over the ambiguities in the succession provision, stating in his message of December 6, 1881:

> Is the inability limited in its nature to long-continued intellectual incapacity, or has it a broader import? What must be its extent and duration? How must its existence be established? Has the President whose inability is the subject of inquiry any voice in determining whether or not it exists, or is the decision of that momentous and delicate question confided to the Vice-President, or is it contemplated by the Constitution that Congress should provide by law precisely what should constitute inability and how and by what tribunal or authority it should be ascertained? If the inability proves to be temporary in its nature, and during its continuance the Vice-President lawfully exercises the functions of the Executive, by what tenure does he hold his office? Does he continue as President for the remainder of the four years' term? Or would the elected President, if his inability should cease in the interval, be empowered to resume his office? And if, having such lawful authority, he should exercise it, would the Vice-President be thereupon empowered to resume his powers and duties as such?[29]

ARTHUR'S ILLNESS

Arthur's interest in the problem of presidential inability was not merely intellectual. In the summer of 1882 the Surgeon General examined him and found that he was suffering from Bright's disease, an almost inevitably fatal kidney affliction. Early in October an Associated Press release describing his illness appeared in newspapers across the country, but it was denied on the President's authority and labeled "pure fiction" by a "friendly" newspaper. The disease produced spasmodic nausea, mental depression, and indolence and, according to one biographer, perhaps was responsible for Arthur's early distaste for the presidency and his somewhat casual approach to the duties of his office.[30]

In April 1883, on a vacation trip to Florida, Arthur suffered a severe attack of the disease, and the newspapers described his sudden and violent illness. The President's physician told reporters that he was suffering only from overexposure to the sun and indigestion caused by seasickness. In light of the President's travels, the explanation seemed reasonable. Arthur was intent upon concealing his condition from the public lest he become the object of sympathy, and reports of his ill health were dismissed as grossly exaggerated.[31] By June, Arthur had reduced his schedule so that he would not begin work until noon or one o'clock. Administration critics complained of "the shadow of repose that has come over the Government business."[32]

By early 1884, as the next presidential election approached, Arthur enjoyed little Republican support. Each of the warring Republican factions found him objectionable, yet Arthur refused to exclude himself from contention for the nomination. He feared that suspicions about his health would be raised that would cast doubt on his ability to handle the presidency and that a withdrawal would indicate an insecurity about his record in office and his ability to be elected.[33] But Arthur did not make a serious effort to secure the nomination and asked all his Cabinet members to stay away from the Republican convention. Arthur also privately asked several supporters to abandon their efforts on his behalf because he did not wish to be elected.[34] His only stronghold in the convention balloting was the South, and on the fourth ballot James G. Blaine was selected as the Republican nominee. Arthur, by then helplessly ill, was relieved rather than disappointed by Blaine's nomination, and he played no role in the ensuing presidential campaign.

After the inauguration of Grover Cleveland as the twenty-second President, Arthur retired to private life and served briefly as counsel to his old New York law firm. He spent the last year of his life as an invalid, and died on November 18, 1886, at the age of fifty-six.

With the passing of Arthur's administration, interest in solving the problem of presidential inability faded.

CLEVELAND'S INABILITY

Twelve years after Garfield's assassination, another President of the United States suffered an inability.[35] President Grover Cleveland was a mere two months into his second, nonconsecutive term in May 1893 when he noticed a rough spot on the roof of his mouth.[36] The tumor continued to grow, and in June the family doctor, Joseph Decatur Bryant, advised, "[I]t is a bad looking tenant. Were it in my mouth I would have it removed at once."[37] Cleveland's doctors diagnosed the "particular lesion" as squamous cell carcinoma, or a malignant tumor. While Presidents have traditionally sought to conceal brushes with cancer, the disease carried a particular stigma in the nineteenth century, when cancer was referred to as the "dread disease."[38]

When Cleveland received this diagnosis, the country was in the throes of the "Panic of 1893," the worst economic crisis before the Great Depression of the 1930s.[39] Given the precarious political and economic climate, it was imperative to Cleveland that his impending operation remain a carefully guarded secret and that no visible scarring result. Bryant later recollected, "[T]he president would not under any circumstances consent to the operative removal of the disease at a time or place that would not give the best opportunity of avoiding disclosures and even a suspicion that anything of significance had happened to him."[40] Because of the sensitive state of the economy, Cleveland feared that if his diagnosis were revealed, he would lose absolutely all public confidence.[41] In turn, because he was such an animating force behind the repeal of the Sherman Act,* all efforts to do so would be lost, and instead, pro-silver forces, led by Vice President Adlai E. Stevenson, would prevail. Indeed, in August of that year, at the height of repeal efforts, the *Commercial and Financial Chronicle* wrote, "Mr. Cleveland is about all that stands between this country and absolute disaster and his death would be a great calamity."[42]

On June 30, 1893, Cleveland issued a call for a special session of Congress to repeal the silver purchase provisions of the Sherman Act, and that night he boarded the *Oneida*, a friend's yacht, in New York City.[43] This location was chosen partly because it was guaranteed that no reporters would witness an operation at sea, and because Cleveland's presence on the yacht would not be suspicious in the least since he had embarked on many fishing trips on the *Oneida* in the past. The surgical team, consisting of six doctors in total, secretly boarded the yacht before the President.[44] Each team member, sworn to secrecy, was ferried to the yacht from a different pier. For the next five days the President cruised Long Island Sound. He then visited his summer home at Gray Gables on Buzzards Bay, Massachusetts, returned to the yacht for a few more days of cruising, and then revisited his summer home. There he remained until August 5, when he returned to Washington to address a special session of Congress on August 7.

Unknown to the public, all but one member of the Cabinet, and virtually every member of the government, including Vice President Stevenson,† was the fact that during the initial cruise Cleveland had undergone an operation for the removal of the cancerous growth on the roof of his mouth. That the operation was a great success could have hardly been predicted with certainty. There were tremendous risks involved, including that of operating on a patient at sea with the attendant rough conditions and possibility of running aground. The operation took place in the ship's small, dark, poorly ventilated saloon, illuminated by a single electric bulb.[45] Cleveland was propped up by a pillow and positioned on a large chair tied to the mast in the center of the room.[46] Furthermore, Cleveland was hardly the portrait of perfect health: He was very overweight, probably suffered from high blood pressure, was exhausted, and risked losing a fatal amount of blood over the course of the operation. Likewise, administering anesthesia could trigger a heart attack or a stroke. It was also hazardous to administer ether in a small, unventilated space such as the saloon.[47] The risks involved in the operation were such that one of the doctors

---

* As Allan Nevins put it, "The whole strength of the assault upon the Sherman silver-purchase clauses lay, as everyone realized, in the grim determination of Cleveland's purpose. . . . [I]f any accident suddenly removed him from the scene, all would be lost." Allan Nevins, *Grover Cleveland* (New York, 1962), p 528.

† Stevenson would have been one of the last to be informed anyway because he did not enjoy a close relationship with Cleveland, and his views on the economy differed substantially from those of the President. M. Harwood, *In the Shadow of Presidents: The American Vice-Presidency and Succession System* 135–36 (1966).

felt compelled to joke to the captain, "If you hit a rock, hit it good and hard, so that we'll all go to the bottom!"[48] The operation itself took one-and-a-half hours, during which five teeth, about a third of the upper palate, and a large piece of the upper left jawbone were removed, leaving a two-and-a-half-inch-long and one-inch-wide cavity.[49] One of Cleveland's doctors later reflected, "Never did I feel such a deep, almost overwhelming sense of responsibility as during that operation" because of its "possible consequences for good or evil."[50]

Although normally a fifteen-hour journey, the *Oneida's* trip to Buzzards Bay took four days, during which time the nation heard no word from the President. Reporters began to suspect that something was out of the ordinary, and rumors began to circulate that the President had had a malignant tumor removed. Cleveland's team responded that "nothing but dentistry" had taken place aboard the yacht, that an ulcerated tooth had been removed and nothing more.[51] They also announced that the President was suffering an attack of rheumatism, which accounted for his inability to leave his home.[52] Subsequent official visitors to the Cleveland residence were complicit in the cover-up. After the Attorney General visited Cleveland, he proclaimed, "Mr. Cleveland was doing finely, was in good spirits, and apparently enjoying excellent health, and . . . his illness was confined to his knee and foot."[53]

While recovering at his summer home, Cleveland was fitted with an artificial jaw, without which his speech would have been wholly unintelligible. Indeed, without this device, one of his doctors noted that he suffered from "the worst imaginable case of cleft palate."[54] During a second cruise in July, Cleveland underwent a second operation for the removal of suspicious tissue that was observed after the first operation.

Despite the tremendous lengths that Cleveland and his medical team took to ensure secrecy, an eerily accurate article* appeared in the *Philadelphia Press* on August 29, 1893, written by E. J. Edwards (under the pseudonym "Holland"), entitled "The President: A Very Sick Man."[55] The article described the operations in detail and alluded to the fact that Cleveland had cancer. Thanks to Cleveland's connections at prominent newspapers, the story was denounced as a hoax; a number of newspapers claimed there had been no operations. In particular, Cleveland's friendship with the publisher of the *Philadelphia Times* also proved to be of tremendous value as the paper commenced a sustained and scathing attack against Edwards. In particular, the *Times* criticized Edwards's "exquisite heartlessness," as well as the "cruel and cold-blooded details, true and false, which his imagination could call up."[56] Cleveland's doctors and members of the government either denied or

---

* Given the precise details in the article, it was clear that someone present at the operation had provided the information about Cleveland's secret surgery. It turns out that this was Hasbrouck, the dentist/anesthesiologist, who, after missing an appointment as a result of his participation in the Cleveland operation, had confessed in full to the angry doctor he was supposed to have assisted. *Id.* 127.

refused to confirm the story. Cleveland himself seemed to belie the whole account. He went about his normal duties, making public appearances and speeches. There was no evidence of any change in his facial structure, his speech, or his general health. Eventually the clamor died, with the general feeling that the story had been a fake.[57] One of the doctors who participated in the operations subsequently stated that he did more lying during this period than in all the rest of his life put together.[58]

Not until the publication of an article in *The Saturday Evening Post* in 1917—by which time former President Cleveland had been dead for nine years—by one of Cleveland's doctors, William Williams Keen, did the public learn the facts. After conceding that the Edwards piece had been "substantially correct," Keen stated that the operations had been performed under complete secrecy because of the unstable financial situation in the country at that time.[59] He wrote that this "was by far the most responsible operation in which I ever took part" because "on it hung the life not only of a human being and an illustrious ruler, but the destiny of a nation. . . . What the consequences would have been had it become known at once we can only surmise, and shudder!"*[60]

MCKINLEY'S ASSASSINATION

Cleveland's concealed inability was followed eight years later by a case of publicized presidential inability. On September 6, 1901, while attending a reception in Buffalo, New York, President William McKinley was struck by an assassin's bullet.[61] McKinley was taken to a nearby emergency hospital where he was given ether and underwent surgery. By the next day most of the members of his Cabinet and Vice President Theodore Roosevelt had assembled in Buffalo. During the next few days McKinley, although conscious, was confined to bed and unable to perform his presidential duties. His condition appeared to improve until September 12, when he suffered a relapse. He died in the early morning hours of September 14.

WILSON'S INABILITY

On September 25, 1919, President Woodrow Wilson fell ill while on a speaking tour of the United States to gain support for the League of Nations. The tour was canceled promptly, and the presidential train was ordered to return to Washington. The public was informed that the President had suffered a nervous breakdown. His illness was attributed variously to overwork, an apparent attack of influenza the previous April, and his trips to Europe in December 1918 and March 1919.

---

* Cleveland's tumor has outlived him and to this day is on view in a glass jar at the museum of the College of Physicians of Philadelphia. *Id.* 222–23

On October 2, 1919, after his return to Washington, Wilson suffered a stroke that paralyzed the left side of his body. Dr. Cary T. Grayson, the President's close friend and physician, released a bulletin stating, "The President is a very sick man." From that time until the inauguration of Warren G. Harding on March 4, 1921, the country was without the services of an able President.[62] For more than six months after Wilson suffered the stroke, only a few people were permitted to see him. The ambiguous nature of the medical bulletins prompted wild rumors about his condition. Some stated that he had an abscess of the brain; others, that he had suffered a cerebral hemorrhage; and still others, that he had gone mad and was being kept a prisoner in the White House. "His mind was uninjured," said one historian later, "but his emotional balance was permanently upset. . . . What remained was not Woodrow Wilson but a shell and travesty of him."[63] Demands that the people be informed of his true health were ignored.

The facts were concealed from not only the public but also from the Congress and members of the Cabinet. Vice President Thomas R. Marshall, whom Wilson reportedly had described earlier as a "small-caliber man,"[64] was kept almost completely ignorant and was forced to depend upon the newspapers and second-hand accounts for his information. He resented this and said that it would be tragic for the country if he ever had to act as President under such circumstances. A few members of the Cabinet, including Secretary of State Robert Lansing, were told about the President's true condition, but only in the strictest of confidence. The President's wife, Dr. Cary Grayson, and Joseph Tumulty controlled the flow of information.

While Wilson lay ill, unable to discharge the powers and duties of office, attempts were made to provide executive leadership. The day after the stroke, Lansing suggested to Tumulty that the Vice President be called upon to act as President. Lansing read the succession provision to Tumulty, who responded, "I have read the Constitution and do not find myself in need of any tutoring at your hands of the provision you have just read." When Lansing said that either Dr. Grayson or Tumulty should certify the President disabled, Tumulty declared, "You may rest assured that while Woodrow Wilson is lying in the White House on the broad of his back I will not be a party to ousting him."[65] Grayson made it clear to Lansing that he would also oppose any attempt to have Wilson declared disabled.

A Cabinet meeting on October 6 was called at Lansing's initiative, and the subject of Marshall's acting as President was discussed.[66] Lansing noted that the Constitution was unclear on the meaning of "inability" and on who should determine its existence. He expressed the view that if Wilson were unable to attend to public matters, Marshall should act as President. Grayson and Tumulty arrived at the meeting and voiced Wilson's irritation over the fact that the meeting had been called without his authority. Predictably, the possibility of Marshall's acting as President was quickly dropped.

In the days and weeks that followed, there were repeated demands for Marshall to act as President. The confusion surrounding the succession provision, coupled with Marshall's strong reluctance to appear as a usurper and to incur the wrath of the President and Mrs. Wilson, all combined to prevent him from so acting. Marshall reportedly stated, "I am not going to get myself entangled with Mrs. Wilson. No politician ever exposes himself to the hatred of a woman, particularly if she's the wife of the President of the United States."[67]

As a result of the vacuum at the top, presidential leadership was assumed for all practical purposes by Mrs. Wilson, Grayson, and Tumulty. They decided who saw the President and what matters, documents, and notes were forwarded to him. Said Mrs. Wilson: "Woodrow Wilson was first my beloved husband whose life I was trying to save, fighting with my back to the wall—after that he was the President of the United States."[68] The possibility of Wilson's resigning seems to have been discussed and rejected, partly because it would have removed his main incentive to recovery.[69] One doctor, Francis X. Dercum, strongly opposed resignation, believing it would be bad not only for Wilson but for the country, because of his view that Wilson's leadership was necessary for the establishment of the League of Nations.

Meanwhile, Secretary Lansing took the initiative in convening the Cabinet more than twenty times between October 1919 and February 1920. At these meetings governmental problems were discussed and actions recommended. Prompted by his distress over Lansing's earlier suggestion that Marshall act as President and the convening of the Cabinet without his approval, Wilson dismissed Lansing as Secretary of State in February 1920. Wilson is reported to have said to Tumulty upon the dismissal, "Tumulty, it is never the wrong time to spike disloyalty. When Lansing sought to oust me, I was upon my back. I am on my feet now and I will not have disloyalty about me!"[70]

As a result of the lack of presidential leadership by Wilson or by an Acting President, U.S. participation in the League of Nations was defeated in the Senate; numerous governmental vacancies went unfilled; twenty-eight bills became law by default of any action by the President; foreign diplomats were prevented from submitting their credentials to the President; letters and notes to the White House either went unanswered or were answered by Mrs. Wilson, or by the President in illegible handwriting; and, in many other ways the business of government was brought to a standstill in 1919 and 1920.

Throughout the Wilson inability period, varying interpretations of the Constitution's succession provision were offered. Numerous proposals for dealing with the constitutional problem were introduced in Congress, and hearings were conducted by the House Judiciary Committee.[71] But the installation of a new administration once again pushed the matter aside.

HARDING'S DEATH

While on a speechmaking tour in July 1923, President Warren G. Harding became ill. His ailment was initially diagnosed as acute indigestion. "There is every indication," said the *New York Times* on August 2, "that he ultimately will recover his health and strength. It may as well be understood by the country, however, that Mr. Harding will be an invalid for a considerable period, during which he will be unable to attend actively to important public business." Several hours later Harding was dead. His death was probably caused by a cerebral thrombosis, but since Mrs. Harding refused to permit an autopsy, the exact cause remains undetermined.[72]

ROOSEVELT'S "INABILITY"

The extent to which President Franklin D. Roosevelt was disabled, if at all, during the last year of his life is unclear. Also unclear is whether the outcome of the 1944 election would have been different had the American people had the relevant medical information. What is clear is that the President refused to acknowledge his medical condition lest his goals of ending World War II and of establishing an organization for world peace be thwarted.[73]

In early 1944 President Roosevelt underwent a physical examination that revealed hypertensive heart disease, accompanied by hardening of the arteries, hypertension, and acute bronchitis. Dr. Ross McIntire, the President's personal physician, and Dr. Howard Bruenn, the cardiologist who conducted the examination, agreed to keep the findings private and not to discuss them with either the President or his family. Bruenn also agreed to serve from that time on as the President's physician-in-attendance.

It appears that Roosevelt and McIntire previously had reached a tacit understanding under which Roosevelt would not question, and McIntire would not describe, the condition of his health. Thus, from April 1944 until his death a year later, Roosevelt did not ask Bruenn about his condition or treatment, or even about the need for a cardiologist.[74]

In May 1944, Roosevelt decided to seek a fourth term as President. Although he expressed his support for a number of vice-presidential candidates, including incumbent Vice President Henry A. Wallace, Senator Harry S. Truman of Missouri, Associate Justice William O. Douglas, and former Associate Justice James F. Byrnes, he allowed the Democratic Party leaders to select the nominee. Following the Democratic Convention of 1944, which he did not attend, Roosevelt met with Truman only once prior to election day. At that meeting he asked Truman about his campaign plans. When Truman replied that he would travel by airplane, Roosevelt said, "No. Make it by train all the way. This time we may need you."[75]

In September and October 1944, rumors circulated about the President's health, and to offset their impact, Roosevelt took to the campaign trail in the two weeks before the election, delivering major speeches in New York, Philadelphia, Chicago, and Boston. After the excitement of his fourth election victory, Roosevelt relapsed into physical and mental fatigue. Duties that had never been troublesome now required his utmost concentration. He was beset with indecision about simple problems. His attention span was short, and his signature became an illegible scrawl. He lost weight, his appetite disappeared, and his blood pressure rose. McIntire, however, continued to conceal the true situation, maintaining that Roosevelt was in good health.

Former Secretary of State Dean Acheson wrote of Roosevelt's appearance at a meeting held a few days before his fourth inauguration: "We were all shocked by the President's appearance. Thin, gaunt, with sunken and darkly circled eyes, only the jaunty cigarette holder and his light-hearted brushing aside of difficulties recalled the FDR of former days."[76] Of Roosevelt on the day of his inauguration, John Gunther said, "I was terrified when I saw his face. I felt certain that he was going to die. All the light had gone out underneath the skin. It was like a parchment shade on a bulb that had been dimmed. . . . I could not get over the ravaged expression on his face. It was gray, gaunt, and sagging, and the muscles controlling the lips seemed to have lost part of their function."[77]

At his inauguration* in January 1945 Roosevelt suffered severe chest pains, but neither of his physicians was called to render assistance or was even informed of the incident. The following month on the journey to Yalta, Roosevelt's fatigue was noted by his entire staff. Lord Moran, Winston Churchill's personal physician, observed that the President had symptoms of hardening of the arteries of the brain, which can cause insufficient blood supply to the brain and result in impaired powers of reasoning and concentration.[78] Secretary of State Edward R. Stettinius Jr. observed that the attainment of world peace and the formation of the United Nations were Roosevelt's primary goals at Yalta, while his other positions were negotiable.[79] Immediately upon his return from Yalta, where the emotional and intellectual demands had been exhausting, Roosevelt insisted on a personal report to Congress. His speech, delivered in a hoarse, weak voice, with trembling hands and frequent departures from the text, convinced many members of Congress that he was gravely ill.

Despite long rests at Hyde Park and Warm Springs, Roosevelt's health continued to decline. Occasionally, he had active days when he appeared to regain his strength. At other times advisers found him unable to discuss serious matters. He vacillated between intellectual acumen and a vacuous attitude that seemed impossible to penetrate. By March, he no longer could bathe or shave himself. His mind wandered and he awoke exhausted. His staff was forced to limit his appointments and shield him from routine problems.

As his dreams of peace dissolved with the continued controversy over a new Polish government, Roosevelt became depressed and saw fewer people. In increas-

---

* The inauguration took place on the South Portico of the White House instead of at the Capitol. The reason given was that an ostentatious ceremony would be unseemly during a time of war, but the President's failing health may have been the actual reason for the change.

ing numbers, he signed messages written by others. Somehow he found the energy to involve himself in planning the United Nations organizational meeting in San Francisco, laboring over the smallest detail. Yet even here he vacillated, at one time planning to open the conference, later stating that he would not attend, and on the morning of his death suggesting that he might resign the presidency to head up the United Nations.

On April 12, less than three months into his fourth term, Roosevelt died of a massive cerebral hemorrhage, and Vice President Truman was sworn in as President. Truman had had only two conversations with Roosevelt since Inauguration Day, both dealing with legislative matters. The development of the atom bomb was one of many matters not disclosed to Truman.[80] Fortunately, Truman was able to provide the country with effective leadership during the remainder of the term. As Winston Churchill told Truman in 1952, "I must confess, sir, I held you in very low regard then. I loathed your taking the place of Franklin Roosevelt. . . . I misjudged you badly. Since that time, you, more than any other man, have saved Western civilization."[81]

EISENHOWER'S INABILITIES

On September 24, 1955, while vacationing in Colorado, President Dwight D. Eisenhower suffered a heart attack, thus confronting the nation once again with a case of presidential inability.[82] The initial medical announcement said that the President had suffered "a digestive upset." After the President had been removed to a hospital and placed under oxygen, the public was advised that he had suffered a coronary thrombosis that would require complete rest for about a month. Fortunately, the heart attack occurred at a time when no emergencies existed in either the foreign or the domestic area. Congress, too, was out of session.

On the evening of September 24, Vice President Richard M. Nixon, Acting Attorney General William P. Rogers, and White House assistant Wilton Persons met to discuss arrangements for the operation of the executive branch during Eisenhower's inability. Among those consulted were Secretary of State John Foster Dulles and Treasury Secretary George M. Humphrey. It was decided that the Cabinet and White House staff should continue the administration of the government. The next day Nixon announced that "the President's well-defined policies and Government business would be carried out without delay."[83] After conferring with Rogers, Persons, presidential assistant Sherman Adams, and others, Nixon announced on the following day that the Cabinet would meet on Friday, September 30. An initial White House request for the Attorney General's opinion on the legality of a temporary delegation of presidential power was not acted upon, according to Attorney General Herbert Brownell, because there were "sufficient legal arrangements to carry on 'the day-to-day operations of the Government.'"[84] Consequently, no opinion was ever delivered.

On September 28, Nixon signed some ceremonial papers on the President's behalf. The National Security Council met the next day, with Nixon presiding for the first time; the Cabinet, the day after. The Cabinet accepted a recommendation of the National Security Council that Sherman Adams go to Denver to serve as liaison and administrative assistant to the President. Nixon initially thought that Adams should remain in Washington but was persuaded by Dulles that one person closely identified with the President should act as his official spokesman.[85] Dulles was influenced by the Wilson inability and by the apprehensions that had been created by the Cabinet meetings for which his uncle Robert Lansing had been dismissed. The Cabinet agreed on the following procedure:

> On actions which Cabinet members would normally take without consulting either the Cabinet or the President, there would be no change in procedure from the normal.
>
> Questions which would normally be brought before the Cabinet for discussion before decision should continue to be discussed there.
>
> *Decisions* which would require consultation with [the President] should go first to the Cabinet or the National Security Council for thorough discussion and possible recommendation and then go to Denver for . . . [the President's] consideration.
>
> The proper channel for submission to . . . [the President] of matters requiring presidential decisions should be to General Persons in the White House and then through Governor Adams to . . . [the President] in Denver.[86]

After the meeting, the following statement was released to the press:

> After full discussion of pending matters, it was concluded that there are no obstacles to the orderly and uninterrupted conduct of the foreign and domestic affairs of the nation during the period of rest ordered by the President's physicians.
>
> Governor Sherman Adams, the Assistant to the President, will leave for Denver today and will be available there, in consultation with the President's physicians, whenever it may later become appropriate to present any matters to the President.
>
> The policies and programs of the administration as determined and approved by the President are well established along definite lines and are well known. Co-ordination of the activities of the several departments of the government within the framework of these policies will be continued by full co-operation among the responsible officers of these departments so that the functions of the government will be carried forward in an effective manner during the absence of the President.[87]

On the day of the Cabinet meeting, Eisenhower, who had been kept practically incommunicado during the prior week and in an oxygen tent for most of it, performed his first official act by signing lists of foreign service officer appointments. Adams journeyed to Denver and reported the developments at the Cabinet meeting to the President. Several days later Eisenhower directed that all regularly scheduled meetings of the Cabinet and of the National Security Council be held under the chairmanship of the Vice President.[88] He wrote Nixon as follows, "I hope you will continue to have meetings of the National Security Council and of the Cabinet over which you will preside in accordance with procedures which you have followed at my request in the past during my absence from Washington."[89] In the next few weeks a number of such meetings took place, with Adams usually traveling in from Denver and then returning to report to the President. Said Secretary of Agriculture Ezra Taft Benson:

> [I]t had seemed to me that Nixon deferred too much to Sherman Adams; sometimes you wondered whether Sherm or Dick was running the meeting. On the one hand most major policy matters were held over until later. But there also was a spreading tendency for Cabinet officials to go ahead on their own—on things that before the heart attack would have been checked out with the President.[90]

Eisenhower began to receive visitors during the second and third weeks of his illness and saw Nixon on October 8. He was allowed to walk on October 25 and was discharged from the hospital on November 11. He met with his Cabinet for the first time on November 22 at his Camp David retreat in the Catoctin Mountains. After convalescing in Georgia and Florida, the fully recovered President returned to Washington during the week of January 16, 1956, thereby ending this period of uncertainty.

Although the "committee system" worked well during Eisenhower's illness, Adams noted that it left everyone "uncomfortably aware of the Constitution's failure to provide for the direction of the government by an acting President when the President is temporarily disabled and unable to perform his functions."[91] Said Eisenhower of this period:

> I was not required to make any immediate operational decisions involving the use of the armed forces of the United States. Certainly, had there been an emergency such as the detection of incoming enemy bombers, on which I would have had to make a rapid decision regarding the use of United States retaliatory might, there could have been no question, *after* the first forty-eight hours of my heart attack, of my capacity to act according to my own judgment. *However*, had a situation arisen such as occurred in 1958 in which I eventually sent troops ashore in Lebanon, the concentration, the weighing of the pros and cons, and the final determination would have represented a burden, during the *first week* of my illness, which the doctors

would likely have found unacceptable for a new cardiac patient to bear. As it was, with a period of rest, I was able to keep my mind clear, to talk to members of the government on matters of long-range interest, and to experience a satisfactory recovery [emphasis added].[92]

Nixon noted that:

[The committee system] worked during the period of President Eisenhower's heart attack mainly because . . . there was no serious international crisis at that time. But had there been a serious international crisis requiring Presidential decisions, then . . . the committee system might not have worked.[93]

Nixon described his personal dilemma in these words:

[A]side from the President, I was the only person in government elected by all the people; they had a right to expect leadership, if it were needed, rather than a vacuum. But any move on my part which could be interpreted, even incorrectly, as an attempt to usurp the powers of the presidency would disrupt the Eisenhower team, cause dissension in the nation, and disturb the President and his family.[94]

To avoid misunderstandings, Nixon abstained from using the President's office in the White House and declined to sit in the President's chair at Cabinet meetings.

On two other occasions during the Eisenhower administration, the question of presidential inability was forcibly revived. On the morning of June 8, 1956, the public was advised that the President had "an upset stomach and headache" which required a postponement of his schedule for the day. Several hours later the President was removed from the White House on a stretcher and taken to Walter Reed Hospital. The public was told that he had had an attack of ileitis and was being taken to Walter Reed as a precautionary measure.

There, at 2:59 A.M. on June 9, the President underwent an operation for the removal of a nonmalignant obstruction of the small intestine. The operation lasted for two hours, during which the President was unconscious. At a press conference later in the day, Dr. Leonard Dudley Heaton, the commanding officer at Walter Reed Hospital, stated:

We look for a rapid and complete recovery. . . . During the coming week he should be able to sign official papers and carry on those functions of the Government which are necessary. We should like to establish here that his cardiac condition had no relationship to this present illness. We do not expect his heart in any way to affect his convalescence. . . . I want you to know that there was nothing suggesting a malignant disease found at operation.[95]

By June 10 the President was up walking, and the following day he began performing official acts. By August 1 he was said to be in "fine shape" and on August 27 "completely recovered."

During his stay at Walter Reed, President Eisenhower said that he would resign if another illness should occur. He was profoundly disturbed about the operation and its significance for the nation. Said Nixon:

> On several occasions afterwards, he [President Eisenhower] pointed out to me that for the two hours he was under anesthesia the country was without a Chief Executive, the armed forces without a Commander-in-Chief. In the event of a national emergency during those two hours, who would have had the undisputed authority to act for a completely disabled President?[96]

On November 25, 1957, another inability crisis struck when the President sustained a stroke that affected his ability to speak. The stroke occurred at "the worst time possible, short of outright war," according to Nixon, since the Soviet Union had just launched its first *Sputnik* satellite and the country's military and scientific programs were under critical review.

The stroke, which was described initially to the public as a clot or spasm, prevented Eisenhower from attending a state dinner that night in honor of King Mohammed V of Morocco. He became very distressed and reportedly stated to a group of confidants, including Adams, "If I cannot attend to my duties, I am simply going to give up this job. Now that is all there is to it." Adams notified Nixon, stating, "You may be President in the next twenty-four hours."[97]

The next day, Adams met with Brownell, Nixon, and Persons to discuss Eisenhower's condition. At the same time the medical bulletins indicated that the President's condition had improved. By December 2 he was back at work in the White House.

Eisenhower's inabilities focused attention on the Constitution's succession provision and its lack of clarity. In 1956 Eisenhower asked the Department of Justice to study the problem and recommend a solution. On February 8, 1957, the entire matter was reviewed at a Cabinet meeting. Attorney General Brownell informed the Cabinet that his staff could not reach a conclusion on what procedure should be followed if the President were unable to declare his own inability. Brownell himself and Adams favored the Vice President's making the determination, checked by the Cabinet, while Eisenhower expressed a preference for a commission consisting of the Chief Justice and some medical experts. A President, asserted Eisenhower, should be allowed to declare his own inability and its termination. He also believed that the 1947 succession law should be revised in favor of a Cabinet line of succession. Brownell and Nixon pointed out that an attempt to change the line of succession would cause a political controversy that might obfuscate the important problem of presidential inability. Thus, it was decided to propose a constitutional amendment of the type favored by Brownell.[98]

A meeting was held with legislative leaders on March 29, 1957, during which opposition to such an amendment was voiced. Speaker Sam Rayburn of Texas said that the public would be suspicious of any attempt by Eisenhower to turn over the government to another. Senator William Knowland of California, the Republican leader in the Senate, felt that a President's competency should be decided by a committee having congressional representatation. "There being no unanimity and little enthusiasm among the Republican leaders, and strong opposition from Rayburn, it was apparent that the proposal would not get far and it didn't."[99]

Following Eisenhower's stroke, another attempt was made to get Congress to act on the problem. It, too, met with failure. According to Nixon, "the reason was purely political and obvious. The Democratic congressional leaders would not approve any plan which might put Richard Nixon in the White House before the 1960 election."[100] As a result of these failures, Eisenhower developed an ad hoc solution for any further cases of inability during his administration.*

KENNEDY'S ASSASSINATION

On November 22, 1963, the nation experienced one of its greatest tragedies when President John F. Kennedy, the youngest elected Chief Executive, was assassinated. Although the efforts made to save the President did not succeed, they underscored the absence of procedures to deal with the case in which a President might linger on unconscious for days, weeks, or months. As noted in the November 23, 1963, issue of the *New York Times*:

> For an all too brief hour today, it was not clear again what would have happened if the young President, instead of being mortally wounded, had lingered for a long time between life and death, strong enough to survive but too weak to govern.[101]

Succession beyond the vice presidency also was highlighted because, shortly after Kennedy had been shot, rumors circulated that Vice President Lyndon B. Johnson had suffered a heart attack. Fortunately, these rumors were false, and the nation did not have to test the adequacy of the 1947 succession law.

* See pp. 55–56, infra.

2

Vice-Presidential Vacancy

[M]y country has in its wisdom contrived for me the most insignificant office that ever the invention of man contrived or his imagination conceived. . . . I can do neither good nor evil. . . .

    JOHN ADAMS, December 19, 1793[1]

From May 29 through September 4, 1787, the framers of the Constitution spent a considerable amount of time on the executive article.[2] A consensus on a single executive developed early in the Convention, but the method of selecting that executive was not so easily settled. Numerous proposals were advanced, including election by Congress, by the people, and by electors chosen either by the state legislatures or by the people from districts in each state. An election by Congress, for which both the Virginia and the New Jersey Plans of government had provided, was approved by the Convention on a number of occasions between June 1 and August 24, unanimously on July 17. Direct popular election, on the other hand, was rejected by substantial margins on July 17* and August 24, and a proposal that the President be selected by electors chosen by the people was also defeated on August 24. Since the method of election had not been finally approved at the end of August, the Convention appointed a Committee of Eleven to resolve this and a number of other items.

---

* Said delegate George Mason of Virginia: "[I]t would be as unnatural to refer the choice of a proper character for chief Magistrate to the people, as it would, to refer a trial of colours to a blind man. The extent of the Country renders it impossible that the people can have the requisite capacity to judge of the respective pretentions of the Candidates." 2 *The Records of the Federal Convention of 1787* 31 (Farrand ed., 1911 & 1937).

In a partial report delivered on September 4, the committee proposed that the President be selected by an electoral college system under which the state legislatures would appoint, in such manner as they should decide, presidential electors to make the choice. On the following day a congressional election of the President was rejected, in a vote of 8 to 2, and on September 6 and 7 the Convention approved the committee's proposal. Although an electoral college method of election was adopted, many delegates believed that Congress nevertheless would often make the final decision, since it would be difficult for any candidate to receive a majority of the electoral votes. Thus, delegate George Mason predicted, it would not be "once out of fifty" elections when the President would receive a majority of the electoral votes.[3]

In view of the controversy over the executive article throughout the debates, it is not surprising that the vice presidency was created in the closing days of the Constitutional Convention of 1787. The need for a successor to the President, however, had been recognized from the beginning of the Convention. Both Alexander Hamilton's plan of government of June 18, 1787, and the August 6 report of the Committee on Detail provided that the President of the Senate, who was to be elected from among its members, should discharge the powers and duties of the President in the event of the President's death, resignation, removal, or disability.[4] On August 27, when election of the President by Congress was still the favored method at the Convention, Gouverneur Morris of Pennsylvania objected to the President of the Senate's being the "provisional successor" and suggested the Chief Justice.[5] James Madison of Virginia also objected to the President of the Senate, fearing that the Senate might delay the appointment of a President if its presiding officer were the immediate successor. He suggested that during a presidential vacancy the executive powers be administered by a council to the President.* Hugh Williamson of North Carolina suggested that Congress be empowered to provide for occasional successors and then successfully moved that the entire subject be postponed.

On September 4, the Convention's Committee of Eleven recommended an office of Vice President and an electoral college selection of both the President and the Vice President.[6] These proposals were favorably acted upon on September 6 and 7.

The discussion of September 7 on the office of Vice President focused almost entirely on the Vice President's position as President of the Senate. Elbridge Gerry of Massachusetts, the only framer to become a Vice President, thought that the proposed office, which combined the functions of presidential successor and presiding officer of the Senate, violated the principle of separation of powers since it allowed for executive interference in the legislature.[7] Gouverneur Morris dismissed this notion, arguing that the Vice President could be expected to be independent of the

---

* Current at the time was a suggestion of a council to the President consisting of the Speaker, the President of the Senate, the Chief Justice, and the heads of certain executive departments.

President ("the vice president then will be the first heir apparent that ever loved his father") and that it mattered little whether the successor was a Vice President who was also President of the Senate or a senator who was elected President of the Senate.[8] Roger Sherman of Connecticut voiced concern that, unless there was a Vice President, some senator would frequently be deprived of his vote by being made President of the Senate, with the right to vote only when the Senate was deadlocked. Sherman also feared that the Vice President "would be without employment" if he were not also President of the Senate.[9] Hugh Williamson stated that "such an officer as vice-President was not wanted."[10] At the conclusion of this discussion the delegates, by a vote of 8 to 2, decided that the Vice President should be *ex officio* President of the Senate.

The Convention paid little attention to the Vice President's role as a presidential successor. Similarly, scant attention was paid to the office in the state ratifying conventions.[11] The limited discussion of the post-Convention period centered principally on the office's blending of legislative and executive functions. Some objected to the Vice President as unnecessary and useless. George Clinton of New York, later to be Vice President, referred to the office as dangerous and unnecessary, because it blended executive and legislative powers.[12] Only oblique references were made in the state ratifying convention debates to the succession provision. The weight of the available evidence indicates that the framers contemplated that the Vice President would not become President but would act as President in the event of the President's death, resignation, removal, or inability.*[13] In that way, a President would not be ousted from office in a case where he recovered from an inability.

The Vice President was given only two duties by the Constitution: (1) to preside over the Senate, in which capacity he could vote only when the Senate was "equally divided," and also open the certificates containing the votes of the presidential electors, and (2) to discharge the powers and duties of the President in case of his death, resignation, removal, or inability. What his actual role would be was clouded in such mystery that Alexander Hamilton was impelled to declare in Number 68 of *The Federalist*:

> The appointment of an extraordinary person as Vice President has been objected to as superfluous, if not mischievous. It has been alleged that it would have been preferable to have authorized the Senate to elect out of their own body an officer answering that description. But two considerations seem to justify the ideas of the convention in this respect. One is that, to secure at all times the possibility of a definite resolution of the body, it is necessary that the President should have only a casting vote. And to take the senator of any State from his seat as senator, to place him in that

---

* The author explains this conclusion in detail in *From Failing Hands* 40–51.

of President of the Senate, would be to exchange, in regard to the
State from which he came, a constant for a contingent vote. The other
consideration is that, as the Vice President may occasionally become a
substitute for the President in the supreme executive magistracy, all the
reasons which recommend the mode of election prescribed for the one
apply with great if not with equal force to the manner of appointing the
other.[14]

The Vice President, like the President, was to serve for four years. He was to be
elected at the same time and generally in the same manner and was to be subject to
impeachment. While the Constitution provided that the Chief Justice would preside at an impeachment trial of the President, no presiding officer was specified for
a trial of the Vice President. Presumably, the President pro tempore of the Senate
would preside, since it would be incongruous for an impeached Vice President to
preside over his own trial and since the Constitution provides for the President pro
tempore to serve as President of the Senate in the absence of the Vice President.

In contrast to its prescribed oath of office for the President, the Constitution
prescribed no oath for the Vice President; one had to be created by an act of Congress of June 1, 1789.[15] Similarly, the Constitution failed to mention any qualifications for the vice presidency, but not through oversight or lack of deliberation. The
Vice President would necessarily have the same qualifications as the President (i.e.,
be a natural-born citizen, at least thirty-five years of age, and for fourteen years a
resident within the United States) because, under the original method of election,
presidential electors would vote for two persons for President, and the person obtaining the second-highest number of votes for President would be Vice President.
This method was designed to place in the office of Vice President a person equal in
stature to the President.[16]

Its purpose was frustrated early, however, because the electors began to distin-
guish the two votes in their own minds, casting the first for the candidate they
considered suitable for the presidency and the second for their vice-presidential
choice. This practice surfaced in 1800 when most of the Republican electors voted
for Aaron Burr and Thomas Jefferson, intending Burr for Vice President and
Jefferson for President. Burr received as many votes as did Jefferson, so the election
of the President fell to the House of Representatives pursuant to Article I, Section
1, Clause 3 of the Constitution.[17]

The election of 1800, coupled with the 1796 election of a President and Vice
President of different parties, led to the adoption in 1804 of the Twelfth Amendment, providing that henceforth electors would cast distinct votes for President
and Vice President. The candidate who received a majority of the electoral votes
for each office would be elected. If no candidate obtained a majority, the House of
Representatives would choose a President "from the persons having the highest
numbers not exceeding three on the list of those voted for as President . . ."; and

the Senate would choose a Vice President from "the two highest numbers on the list" of those voted for as Vice President. If it happened that the election of a President fell to the House of Representatives and the House failed to elect a President by the date set for his term to begin, the Twelfth Amendment provided that the Vice President–elect would "act" as President. Ironically, there is evidence indicating that the framers of the amendment believed that under this language the Vice President would, if he so acted, become President for the full term.*[18] In order to ensure that the Vice President would have the same qualifications as the President, the Twelfth Amendment provided that "no person constitutionally ineligible to the office of President shall be eligible to that of Vice-President. . . ."

DECLINE AND RISE OF OFFICE

Shortly after the ratification of the Constitution, a number of matters concerning the vice presidency came under discussion in Congress that revealed the low opinion most congressmen held for the office. In a discussion regarding titles, one senator reportedly suggested that the Vice President be referred to as "his Superfluous Excellency."[19] In the debates over an annual salary for the Vice President, some members of the House of Representatives felt that his work would be so sporadic that he should be paid only on a per diem basis.[20] Others, including James Madison, believed that to withhold an annual salary would be offensive to the dignity of the second officer of the government. Said Madison:

> If he is to be considered as the apparent successor of the President, to qualify himself the better for that office, he must withdraw from his other avocations, and direct his attention to the obtaining a perfect knowledge of his intended business. . . . [I]f we mean to carry the constitution into full effect, we ought to make provision for his support, adequate to the merits and nature of the office.[21]

The Congress finally agreed upon an annual salary of $5,000, which was to remain the Vice President's salary for the next sixty-five years. The President's salary was fixed at $25,000.

The paradox that became evident in these debates was the tremendous gap between what the Vice President was and what he could be. As Vice President John Adams declared:

> I am possessed of two separate powers, the one in *esse* and the other in *posse*. I am Vice-President. In this I am nothing, but I may be everything. But I am president also of the Senate.[22]

---

* The Twentieth Amendment, which modified the Twelfth, makes clear that the Vice President serves only until a President shall qualify. See Appendix B.

Although two of the first three Vice Presidents became President in their own right (Adams and Jefferson), the notion that the vice presidency was a sure spring-board to the presidency ceased with the adoption of the Twelfth Amendment and the rise of political parties. It was not until 1836 that a third Vice President, Martin Van Buren, was elected President directly from the vice presidency, and then not again until the twentieth century, when George H.W. Bush was elected in 1988. As a result of the Twelfth Amendment, political considerations rather than ability became paramount in the selection of a Vice President. Senator Alexander White of Virginia was remarkably perceptive when he said during the debates on the amendment:

[C]haracter, talents, virtue, and merit, will not be sought after, in the candidate. The question will not be asked, is he capable? Is he honest? But can he by his name, by his connexions, by his wealth, by his local situation, by his influence, or by his intrigues, best promote the election of a President?[23]

Other members of Congress went so far as to advocate the abolition of the office itself. Indeed, on November 23, 1803, a vote on such a motion was defeated in the Senate 19 to 12, and in the House of Representatives on December 7, 1803, by 85 to 27.[24]

As predicted, in ensuing years the vice presidency became a very limited and often disparaged office:

The adoption of the Twelfth Amendment in 1804 marks a great turning point in the history of the Vice Presidency, and the turn was definitely for the worse. . . . Even without the Twelfth Amendment political party practice was pointing the Vice Presidency toward a decline. But by specifying that each elector would cast one ballot for President and a separate ballot for Vice President the amendment made the descent of the Vice Presidency clearer and more understandable.[25]

Thus, Vice Presidents in the nineteenth century rarely were given any executive responsibilities. They did not take part in meetings of the President's Cabinet, and their role as President of the Senate became little more than a diversion. No longer followed were such pre–Twelfth Amendment precedents as the Vice President's deciding disputed questions regarding the certificates of the presidential electors and participating in Senate debates. Few nineteenth-century Vice Presidents left any legacy for future occupants of their office. In 1840, because of a two-thirds-vote requirement, the Democratic National Convention was unable to select any vice presidential candidate to run with its presidential candidate, Martin Van Buren. The incumbent Vice President, Richard M. Johnson, failed to secure his party's re-nomination. Four years later, though, provided an opportunity to be the democratic nominee for Vice President, Senator Wright declined, choosing instead to run for governor of New York.

In general, it may be said that the names of the nineteenth-century Vice Presidents—for example, Richard M. Johnson, George M. Dallas, William R. King, Hannibal Hamlin, Schuyler Colfax, Henry Wilson, William A. Wheeler, Thomas A. Hendricks, and Levi P. Morton—are wholly unfamiliar to most Americans. Although Vice Presidents John Tyler, Millard Fillmore, Andrew Johnson, and Chester A. Arthur succeeded to the presidency upon the deaths of Presidents, none subsequently was nominated by his party to run for President in his own right.

The vice presidency did not experience a "renaissance" until the twentieth century. For more than fifty years, the role of the Vice President has steadily grown. He has become a regular member of the President's Cabinet,[26] a member of the National Security Council, the head of some executive agencies, a presidential representative on good will and diplomatic tours around the world, and a participant in some of the ceremonial political functions of the President.[27] And, in the twentieth century, the four Vice Presidents who succeeded to the presidency upon the death of a President subsequently were elected President, and five other Vice Presidents secured the presidential nominations of their party.*

While the Vice President's duties have been minimal during much of our history and his effectiveness has depended almost completely on his relationship with the President, the office proved to be of vital importance on numerous occasions in the period between 1841 and 1964. Eight times during that period Vice Presidents succeeded to the presidency upon the death of the President; eight times the country was led successfully through the trauma caused by the loss of the President.

Yet the vice presidency had been vacant often in the period prior to 1965.† In addition to the eight vacancies created by a Vice President's succession to the presidency, the office also was vacant when Vice Presidents George Clinton, Elbridge Gerry, William R. King, Henry Wilson, Thomas A. Hendricks, Garret A. Hobart, and James S. Sherman died in office, and when John C. Calhoun resigned to become a U.S. senator. Between July 9, 1850, and March 4, 1857, the office was occupied for less than two months; and between September 19, 1881, and March 4, 1889, for less than nine months. In each of James Madison's two terms as President, the Vice

---

* The four who succeeded were Theodore Roosevelt, upon President McKinley's assassination; Calvin Coolidge, upon President Harding's death; Harry S. Truman, upon President Franklin D. Roosevelt's death; and Lyndon B. Johnson, upon President Kennedy's assassination. Former Vice Presidents Hubert Humphrey and Richard Nixon were chosen as the presidential candidates of their respective parties in 1968. Robert Dole, Ford's vice-presidential candidate in 1976, led his party's ticket some twenty years later. Former Vice President Walter Mondale and incumbent Vice President Albert Gore were their party's presidential candidates in 1984 and 2000, respectively. Even the role of losing vice-presidential candidates has significantly increased in the last half century.
† Appendix D.

President died. Gaps of more than three years each occurred following the successions to the presidency of Tyler, Andrew Johnson, Arthur, Theodore Roosevelt,
and Truman.

Despite vacancies totaling more than thirty-seven years, no serious effort was
made to devise a means for filling a vice-presidential vacancy until after the assassination of President Kennedy. It was then that politicians and scholars alike finally
concluded that the nation required a Vice President at all times.

3

Succession Beyond the Vice Presidency

Mr. Burke said, that he had consulted a gentleman skilled in the doctrine of chances, who, after considering the subject, had informed him, that there was an equal chance that such a contingency would not happen more than once in eight hundred and forty years.

ANNALS OF CONG., 1st Cong., 3d Sess. 1914 (1791)

As the framers debated the executive article, they realized that a vacancy could occur in the presidency during the course of a term. Indeed, they remembered situations in America's past involving the death, resignation, absence, and removal of colonial governors. Fortunately, there had been procedures to handle such contingencies.[1] In the royal colonies there was an office of lieutenant governor, and a provision was made for either the governor's council or the senior councilor to assume the reins of government in the event that there was no governor or lieutenant governor. In the early history of the proprietary colonies, the governor was given the power to deputize a successor and at times exercised the power from his deathbed; later, the senior councilor was designated to act as governor in the event of a vacancy. It is of interest that the charters of Connecticut and Rhode Island provided for a governor and deputy governor elected by the people and authorized the legislature to fill a vacancy occurring in either of these offices—a power that was used on numerous occasions.

The first state constitutions adopted after the Declaration of Independence all contained provisions for dealing with executive succession. A lieutenant governor was the immediate successor in several of the colonies, the president of the governor's council in a few, and the presiding officer of the upper house of the legislature in others. Several colonies continued the line of succession beyond the immediate successor. For example, New York ran the line of succession from the lieutenant governor to the legislative officers, and Delaware and North Carolina from the presiding officer of the upper house to the speaker of the lower house.

This pre-Convention experience undoubtedly shaped the provisions of Article II, section 1, clause 6 of the Constitution with respect to a line of succession beyond the vice presidency. It was late in the Constitutional Convention of 1787 when Hugh Williamson declared that Congress "ought to have power to provide for occasional successors . . ." to the President. Accepting his suggestion, Edmund Randolph of Virginia on September 7 moved to expand the provision providing for a Vice President's succession in the event of a President's death, resignation, removal, absence, or inability.* At the time of Randolph's proposal the provision simply stated:

> [I]n case of his [the President's] removal as aforesaid, death, absence, resignation or inability to discharge the powers or duties of his office, the vice-president shall exercise those powers and duties until another President be chosen, or until the inability of the President be removed.

Randolph's suggested addition was:

> The Legislature may declare by law what officer of the U.S. shall act as President in case of the death, resignation, or disability of the President and Vice-President; and such officer shall act accordingly *until the time of electing a President shall arrive* [emphasis added].[2]

James Madison objected that the last nine words (italicized above) would prevent the filling of a vacancy by means of a special election of the President. He suggested as an alternative the expression "until such disability be removed, or a President shall be elected." A few delegates opposed Madison's proposed change, believing that it would be difficult to schedule a special election. Other delegates objected to the limitation that Congress could appoint only officers of the United States. Notwithstanding these objections, Randolph's suggestion with Madison's amendment was accepted by a vote of 6 to 4. The debates at the Virginia ratifying convention clearly show that the intent was to allow for a special election, at least in the event of a double vacancy. There, George Mason objected to the succession provision on

---

* The "absence" contingency was subsequently deleted from the succession provision by the Committee on Style. No doubt, it had been included initially because of the colonial practice under which a governor's absence from the colony resulted in the assumption of his powers and duties by the person next in line. *See* Feerick, *From Failing Hands* 23–38. The intent in using it seems to have been to cover situations when a President might be absent from the seat of government. It was dropped by the Committee on Style probably because of the belief that the term "inability" was broad enough to cover such situations. The term "disability," which seems to have been used interchangeably with "inability," was dropped only from the first part of the provision, *id*. at 48–50.

the ground that it did not provide for an immediate election in case of a presidential vacancy. In reply, Madison stated that if both the President and the Vice President should die, another election would take place immediately, but that in default of such election the successor appointed by Congress could serve only for the remainder of the term.[3]

Unfortunately, the various congressional enactments prescribing a line of succession beyond the vice presidency have never been very satisfactory. Each reflected considerations of the personalities occupying the particular offices at the time, and each assigned the responsibility of succession to an official who had been chosen for his office for reasons other than his qualifications as a potential President.

THE 1792 LAW

The first succession law was formulated at the time when Thomas Jefferson was serving as Secretary of State (1790–93).[4] His political foe Alexander Hamilton was serving both as Secretary of the Treasury and as leader of the Federalist Party, which then controlled the U.S. Senate. The view was very much current that should the Secretary of State be placed first in the statutory line of succession, Hamilton's pretense as head of the Cabinet would be exposed and Jefferson's potential as a future President enhanced.

A bill was presented in the First Congress providing that some officer, whose designation was left blank, should act as President whenever there were vacancies in the offices of President and Vice President.[5] Suggestions subsequently were made to name the officer variously as the Secretary of State, the Secretary of the Treasury, the Chief Justice, the President pro tempore of the Senate, and the Speaker of the House. One of those objecting to the Chief Justice was James Madison, who felt that this would be an excessive merging of the executive and the judiciary. Madison was also opposed to the selection of the President pro tempore because he would be holding two offices simultaneously—those of senator and of Acting President— and that as a senator he would be subject to instruction by his state. In Madison's view, the Secretary of State was the preferable successor, but others felt that the designation of the Secretary of State would give too much power to the President in the selection of a potential successor. It is not surprising, then, that no consensus developed in the First Congress and that the entire subject was dropped—but not until after some delegates had expressed their views concerning the need for immediate action. One member of Congress observed that dual vacancies would not happen once in 100 years; another, that there was an equal chance that the situation would not happen more than once in 840 years. In contrast, Representative William B. Giles of Virginia urged that the matter be dealt with promptly before any such calamity occurred. "Suppose," he said, "the Vice President should die, then the fate of this Government would remain in the hands of the President who, by resigning, would destroy its organization, without leaving a constitutional mode of filling the vacancy."[6]

In the Second Congress, on November 30, 1791, the Senate passed a bill dealing with the selection of presidential electors. Section 9 of the bill named the President pro tempore and the Speaker successively as the persons to administer the government in the event of vacancies in the offices of both President and Vice President. When the bill came under scrutiny in the House by the Committee of the Whole, a motion to eliminate Section 9 entirely was made and defeated. Also made and defeated was a motion to remove the President pro tempore and the Speaker from the line of succession.

At the committee stage, a number of representatives expressed the view that neither the President pro tempore nor the Speaker was an officer in the sense contemplated by the Constitution.* Thus, Representative Giles declared, "if they had been considered as such, it is probable they would have been designated in the Constitution; the Constitution refers to some permanent officer to be created pursuant to the provisions therein contained."[7] Said Representative Hugh Williamson, "this extensive construction of the meaning of the word officer, would render it proper to point out any person in the United States, whether connected with the Government or not, as a proper person to fill the vacancy contemplated."[8] Other representatives, however, felt that they were officers. "If [the Speaker] is not an officer," said Representative Elbridge Gerry of Massachusetts, "what is he?"[9] Gerry, however, objected to Section 9 on the ground that it blended the executive and legislative branches. Representative James Hillhouse of Connecticut preferred a legislative succession and registered a general objection to any provision by which the President could appoint his own successor, since it would take "away the choice from the people . . . violating the first principle of a free elective Government."[10]

When on January 2, 1792, the Committee of the Whole reported the bill to the House, a motion to strike out the President pro tempore was defeated narrowly while one to eliminate the Speaker was carried. Voting in favor of these motions were a number of framers, including Madison, Williamson, Abraham Baldwin of Georgia, and Thomas Fitzsimmons of Pennsylvania. Elbridge Gerry joined in the motion to eliminate the Speaker but not the President pro tempore. Thereupon, the bill was returned to the committee, which removed the President pro tempore from the line of succession and substituted the Secretary of State. The House then passed the bill and forwarded it to the Senate.[11]

---

* In the First Congress, Representative Alexander White of Virginia had advanced this argument, with which Representative Roger Sherman of Connecticut had disagreed. Annals of Cong., 1st Cong., 3d Sess. 1902–03 (1791). Representative William L. Smith of South Carolina also questioned whether Congress could provide for an officer to serve only until a special presidential election were held to elect a new President and Vice President. In his view, the Constitution provided only for a regular quadrennial election *id.* at 1902.

In the Senate—the result in no small measure of Hamilton's influence and the opposition to Jefferson—the House amendment was rejected, and the President pro tempore and the Speaker were again inserted. On February 21, 1792, the bill was returned to the House, which withdrew its amendment, 31 to 24. The bill became law on March 1, 1792, when it was signed by President George Washington.[12]

Section 10 of the act provided that whenever the offices of President and Vice President became vacant, the Secretary of State was to notify the governor of every state that electors were to be appointed within thirty-four days prior to the first Wednesday of the ensuing December. If less than two months remained before that date and if the term of the last President and Vice President was not to end in the following March, the election would take place in December in the year next ensuing, with the newly elected President and Vice President taking office in the following March.* If the term was to end in March, no election at all would take place. The bill seems to have contemplated a four-year term for a specially elected President and Vice President.

Shortly after the law of 1792 was passed, James Madison expressed his opposition to it, in a letter to Edmund Pendleton, a prominent lawyer in the state. He questioned the constitutionality of placing the legislative officers in the line of succession, stating,

> It may be questioned whether these [the President pro tempore and the Speaker] are officers in the Constitutional sense. . . . If officers, whether both could be introduced. . . . As they are created by the Constitution, they would probably have been there designated if contemplated for such service, instead of being left to the legislative selection.[13]

He also stated that the Speaker and the President pro tempore

> will retain their Legislative stations, and then incompatible functions will be blended; or the incompatibility will supersede those stations, & then those being the substratum of the adventitious functions, these must fail also. The Constitution says Congress may declare what officers, &c., which seems to make it not an appointment or a translation, but an annexation of one office or trust to another office.†[14]

For the next ninety-four years, the President pro tempore and the Speaker were the only successors after the Vice President. Although four Presidents and five Vice

---

* Hence, depending on when the dual vacancies occurred, the 1792 law left open the possibility of the statutory successors' serving for a period of up to seventeen months.

† In her pioneering work on presidential succession, Ruth Silva argues persuasively that the framers intended the Vice President and the officer designated by Congress to serve only as an Acting President, while continuing to occupy the position they held at the commencement of such service. R. Silva, *Presidential Succession* (1951).

Presidents died in office during this period, a double vacancy did not occur. Accordingly, the 1792 law was never implemented. Close calls did occur. In 1844, President Tyler's life was endangered by an explosion, and in 1853, President Franklin Pierce suffered a serious case of malaria. Had anything happened to these Presidents, there would have been no Vice Presidents to serve in their places.*

THE 1886 LAW

Dissatisfaction with the act of 1792 reached a peak in the 1880s.† Of major importance was the fact that when Chester A. Arthur succeeded to the presidency upon James A. Garfield's death there was neither a President pro tempore nor a Speaker to act as President in the event that something happened to Arthur. Both positions remained unfilled for a period of several weeks. Similarly, when Vice President Thomas A. Hendricks died in November 1885, there was no President pro tempore or Speaker to succeed if the President were to die.

These events generated considerable discussion in Congress on the problems of presidential succession and presidential inability.[15] Numerous objections to the act of 1792 were voiced. It was argued time and again during this period—particularly by Senators George F. Hoar of Massachusetts, Samuel B. Maxey of Texas, James B. Beck of Kentucky, and Augustus H. Garland of Massachusetts—that the President pro tempore and the Speaker were not officers of the United States within the meaning of the succession provision. James Madison was cited as authority for this proposition, as was the Blount impeachment, which had been interpreted as deciding that a member of Congress is not an officer of the United States.‡[16] Parts of the Constitution itself were cited in support of this position.§ An officer under the

* These events are described in *From Failing Hands* 97, 105.
† Prior to the 1880s, various suggestions for reform had been voiced. For example, in 1856 the Senate Judiciary Committee recommended that the line of succession be extended to the Chief Justice of the United States and then the associate justices according to seniority. S. Rep. No. 260, 34th Cong., 1st Sess. 5 (1856). The committee also expressed the view that the special election feature of the 1792 law was constitutional and that any specially elected President would serve a full four-year term. Eleven years later, a unanimous House Judiciary Committee said that Congress had no power to provide for a special presidential election. Cong. Globe, 39th Cong., 2d Sess. 691 (1867). In 1868, shortly after his impeachment trial, President Andrew Johnson recommended changing the line of succession to the members of the Cabinet, stating that the legislative officers had a stake in removing the President by resorting to the impeachment process.
‡ Senator William Blount of Tennessee was impeached by the House in 1797. When he was tried in the Senate, his lawyers pleaded lack of jurisdiction on the ground, among others, that a senator was not a civil officer and thus not subject to impeachment. The Senate dismissed the case, giving no reason for its decision. Since Blount had been expelled before the dismissal, another interpretation is that a member of Congress loses his status as a civil officer, and therefore may not be impeached, after he is expelled from Congress. See U.S. Const. art. II, §4.
§ See U.S. Const. art. II, §1, cl. 2, where a distinction is made between senators and representatives, on the one hand, and "officers," on the other: "[N]o Senator or Representative, or Person holding an Office of Trust or Profit under the United States . . ."; and U.S. Const. amend. XIV, §3: "No Person shall be a Senator or Representative in Congress . . . or hold any office, civil or military, under the

succession provision, the senators said, was a permanent officer, who receives his commission from the President and remains in that office while acting as President.[17] As Senator Hoar stated,

> [T]he Presidency is annexed by law to an office. It is not a person holding an office at the time succeeding to the Presidency, but it is an officer continuing in that office who is to perform as an annex or incident merely to another office the great duties of the Presidency itself. The moment he lays down or becomes incapable to perform the duties of the principal office to which the Presidency is annexed, that moment he must lay down or be incapable of performing the duties of the Presidency itself. . . .[18]

It was urged that the Speaker and the President pro tempore as members of Congress could not be "officers of the United States" in the constitutional sense because Article I, section 6 provided that "no Person holding any Office under the United States, shall be a Member of either House during his Continuance in Office." It also was pointed out that if either became Acting President while continuing to serve as a presiding officer and member of Congress, his tenure as Acting President would be subject to the will of his respective House and it could be ended abruptly if he was replaced as a presiding officer or lost his legislative seat at the polls. This objection to the 1792 law was more than academic since the law was predicated on the premise that the President pro tempore and the Speaker were not eligible to act as President unless they retained their offices while so acting. This prompted the additional objection that the law violated the principle of separation of powers, since the President pro tempore or the Speaker, as presiding officer of his House, was entitled to vote and participate in congressional debates. A further objection was voiced about the President pro tempore on the ground that in the case of an impeachment trial of the President when there was no Vice President, as in 1868, he would be placed in a difficult position, raising questions of propriety and legitimacy. Thus, Senator William M. Evarts of New York argued that the Constitution did not contemplate that the House could impeach and the Senate convict and then replace the President with one of their own members.[19] Another criticism of the 1792 law was that it rendered possible a political transfer of the administration when the opposition party controlled Congress.

Most of the critics of the 1792 law favored a Cabinet line of succession, believing that there was no doubt about a Cabinet member's status as an "officer" and that such a line would produce continuity of administration and policy. It also was asserted that the Secretary of State usually would be better qualified for the discharge

---

United States. . . ." It also was argued that a President pro tempore is not even an officer of the Senate, since U.S. Const. art. I, §3, cl. 5, provides: "The Senate shall chuse their other Officers, and also a President pro tempore. . . ." See 14 Cong. Rec. 913 (1883).

President pro tempore ahead of the Cabinet in the line of succession.[26] It was debated briefly in the House on June 29, with supporting statements made by Representatives Estes Kefauver of Tennessee, John M. Robsion of Kentucky, Sumners, Chauncey W. Reed of Illinois, Earl C. Michener of Michigan, and A. S. Mike Monroney of Oklahoma.[27] The enactment of the first succession law and its long acceptance, the Supreme Court decision in *Lamar v. United* States,*[28] and parts of the Constitution itself were referred to in support of the contention that a law placing the Speaker and the President pro tempore in the line of succession would be constitutional. Representative Kefauver argued that Article I, section 2, clause 5 of the Constitution, which provides that the "House of Representatives shall chuse their Speaker and other Officers . . . ," shows that the Speaker is an officer. Representatives John W. Gwynne of Iowa, Charles E. Hancock of New York, and Raymond S. Springer of Indiana reiterated the arguments of others from past Congresses that the Speaker and President pro tempore were not officers within the meaning of the succession clause. The special election feature of the Summers bill was attacked by Representative Robsion, who stated that it would require conforming changes in state election laws and constitutions.† He was joined by others. Kefauver observed: "[I]t probably would upset things too much within a period of four years to have four people fill the office of President—the President, the Vice President, the Speaker of the House—and then have an election to get the fourth person."[29] Said Representative Monroney: "I feel that the Speaker should continue to fill that unexpired term of the Presidency in order to avoid creating disunity and division which always occurs in a national election at a time when we would need the greatest unity in our country."[30] These representatives succeeded in eliminating the election provision altogether. As amended, the Summers bill passed the House and was forwarded to the Senate, where it became pigeonholed in committee.

The 1946 congressional elections placed the opposition party in the majority in Congress. Yet President Truman still asked for action on his succession recommendations, in spite of the fact that their enactment would place a Republican Speaker, Joseph W. Martin of Massachusetts, first in the line of succession. In June 1947 the Senate gave serious consideration to a bill (similar to the Summers bill) that had been introduced several months before by Senator Kenneth S. Wherry of Nebraska.

---

* In *Lamar v. United States*, the Court held that a member of the House of Representatives was an officer within the meaning of a penal statute making it a crime for one to impersonate an officer of the government. The Court was careful to note that the issue presented was not a constitutional one. In the course of its opinion, the Court stated, "[W]hen the relations of members of the House of Representatives to the Government of the United States are borne in mind and the nature and character of their duties and responsibilities are considered, we are clearly of the opinion that such members are embraced by the comprehensive terms of the statute." 241 U.S. 103, 112 (1916).

† As reported from committee, the bill provided for a special election to fill vacancies in the offices of President and Vice President if such should occur ninety days or more before the mid-term congressional elections.

Unlike the Sumners bill, it contained no special election provision and expressly required the Speaker and the President pro tempore to resign from Congress before they could act as President.[31] The Senate debate on the Wherry bill was similar to the debate on the Sumners bill. Thus, during the debates of June 1947, objections were voiced that the Speaker and the President pro tempore are not officers; that if an officer resigns his office he cannot act as President; that it would violate the principle of separation of powers for a member of Congress to act as President; that it was unlikely the Speaker and the President pro tempore would act in a case of a presidential inability, and that they are not elected on the basis of their qualifications for the presidency.[32] An amendment to place the President pro tempore ahead of the Speaker was proposed by Senator Richard B. Russell of Georgia. It was narrowly defeated, largely because Senator Arthur Vandenberg of Michigan, the then President pro tempore, argued that the Speaker was "the officer reflecting the largest measure of popular and representative expression at the instant moment of his succession."[33] An amendment proposed by Senator Brien McMahon of Connecticut for a special election provision was defeated. McMahon's proposal provided for the last Electoral College to select a new President and Vice President whenever vacancies in both offices occurred 120 or more days before the end of the term. Senator Wherry objected to this amendment on the grounds that Congress lacked the power to legislate a special election, that the Constitution provided only for four-year terms, and that it would interfere with the power of the states to say how their electors are to be chosen.[34] Also defeated was a proposal by Senator Alexander Wiley of Wisconsin to add the highest-ranking military or naval officers to the line of succession after the Cabinet heads. The bill finally was put to a vote and was passed, 50 to 35. On July 10 it passed the House, 365 to 11, and on July 18 it became law with President Truman's signature.*[35]

The 1947 law provides that:

> If, by reason of death, resignation, removal from office, inability, or failure to qualify, there is neither a President nor Vice-President to discharge the powers and duties of the office of President, then the Speaker . . . shall, upon his resignation as Speaker and as Representative in Congress, act as President.

If there is no Speaker at the time, then the President pro tempore acts as President, upon his resignation as President pro tempore and as senator. If either the Speaker or the President pro tempore acts, he does so until the end of the presidential term except in cases of failure to qualify or of inability, in which case he acts until a President or Vice President qualifies or recovers from an inability. If the President pro tempore acts, he cannot be replaced by a new Speaker. If a President pro tempore

* See Appendix C.

acting as President should die while in office, he would be replaced by the new Speaker, or in the absence of a Speaker, by the new President pro tempore. The act is not clear on whether a new Speaker, elected after a Speaker had resigned to act as President, is next in line. The legislative history of the act suggests that he would be.[36] Furthermore, the act does not state that the Speaker or the President pro tempore must take the presidential oath, although the legislative history indicates that such was intended.[37] His resigning from Congress and taking the oath would probably be simultaneous so that, it may be argued, at the time at which he acts as President, he would still be an "officer."

If there should be no Speaker or President pro tempore at the time of an emergency, then the line of succession runs to the highest on the following list who is not under a disability which precludes his discharging the powers and duties of the President: Secretary of State, Secretary of the Treasury, Secretary of Defense, Attorney General, Postmaster General, Secretary of the Interior, Secretary of Agriculture, Secretary of Commerce, Secretary of Labor.* The act provides that a Cabinet officer automatically resigns his departmental position upon taking the presidential oath of office. He acts as President for the rest of the term or until a President, Vice President, Speaker, or President pro tempore is available. The 1947 law makes it clear that no one may act as President who does not have the constitutional requirements for the presidency.†

Although the 1947 act has never been applied, the act's imperfections were highlighted on several occasions when the Speaker became the heir apparent. From President Kennedy's assassination until January 20, 1965, Speaker John W. McCormack, more than seventy years of age, stood at the top of the line and lamented that circumstance:

> I have lived for 14 months in the position of the man who, in the event
> of an unfortunate event happening to the occupant of the White House,
> under the law then would have assumed the Office of Chief Executive of
> our country.[38]

Shortly after the assassination, when a reporter asked McCormack whether he might resign as Speaker to permit a younger person to become next in line, he declared, "I was elected Speaker and I'm staying Speaker. I'm amazed, just amazed, that you can ask that. Are there no limits to decency?"[39] McCormack, at least, was of the same political party as President Johnson. Similarly, following the resignations from

---

* The Secretaries of Health and Human Services, of Housing and Urban Development, of Transportation, of Energy, of Education, of Veterans Affairs, and of Homeland Security have been added to the line of succession since 1947. The Postmaster General was removed from the line at the creation of the U.S. Postal Service in 1970.
† The 1792 law was unclear on this point, thereby giving rise to a view that an Acting President did not have to possess the presidential qualifications specified in U.S. Const. art. II, §1, cl. 5, which refers to eligibility to the "office" of President.

office of Spiro T. Agnew and Richard M. Nixon, there were long periods of time during which Speaker Carl Albert—a Democrat, whereas Agnew and Nixon were Republicans—stood first in line under extraordinary circumstances. After Agnew's resignation, the problem of Albert's position as potential successor was compounded since the House of Representatives had almost concurrently begun an impeachment inquiry into President Nixon's conduct in office. Albert's succession during either of these periods would have shifted control of the White House to a different political party. Of the possibility of such succession, Albert reportedly said to a friend, "Lord help me. I pray every night it doesn't happen."[40]

II

The Solution

4

Early Steps to Solve the Inability Problem

We are very fortunate that this country now has a young, vigorous and obviously healthy President. This will allow us to explore these problems in detail without any implication that the present holder of that high office is not in good health.

ESTES KEFAUVER, June 11, 1963[1]

During and immediately after the inabilities of Presidents James Garfield and Woodrow Wilson, proposals were introduced in Congress to combat the inability problem.

In the Garfield period, debate raged over the meaning of "inability," the status of a Vice President who succeeded in the event of a presidential inability, and the question of who had the power to determine whether an inability existed.[2] Professor Theodore W. Dwight of Columbia Law School argued that inability was limited to mental incapacity; others said that it applied to any kind of inability, of the body or mind, temporary or permanent, which prevented the discharge of the powers and duties of President; and others said that it must be of an obvious nature and that there must be an urgent need for executive action. Senators Charles W. Jones of Florida and George F. Hoar of Massachusetts argued that a Vice President who succeeded in a case of inability would serve for the rest of the term regardless of whether the President recovered. The framers of the Constitution, said Jones, had deliberately substituted the word "devolve" for "exercise" and had intended the so-called special election clause ("until . . . a President shall be elected") as a limitation on the tenure of an officer appointed by Congress but not on a Vice President, who was elected for a period of four years.[3] The predominant view, however, was to the contrary—namely, that in a case of inability, the Vice President acted temporarily until the President recovered. On the question of who had the power to declare a

President disabled, a number of persons contended that the "necessary and proper" clause of Article I, section 8 gave Congress the power to adopt legislation on the subject. One point of view held that Congress itself was the only tribunal for deciding when an inability existed; another, that Congress could only provide by law the definition of an inability but could not declare of itself that an inability actually existed. Others contended that the Constitution gave the Vice President the power to determine when a President was disabled. Yet another position was that the Constitution left the question to the President and Vice President. A further view was that the Vice President could act only at the request of the Cabinet or President.

In the Wilson period one group of proposals introduced in Congress gave the Supreme Court the power to declare a President disabled whenever it was authorized so to act by resolution of Congress; another proposal authorized the Secretary of State to convene the Cabinet to inquire into a President's ability to discharge his powers and duties whenever the President had been unable to do so for a period of six consecutive weeks, with a majority of the Cabinet empowered to declare him disabled.[4] These proposals were considered at hearings of the House Judiciary Committee, but considerable disagreement arose concerning the status of a Vice President who succeeded in a case of inability—that is, whether he replaced the President for the rest of the term.

These efforts at reform failed, in large part because of the varying views on the subject and the lack of any consensus on a single proposal. From 1921 to 1955 practically no attention was given to the problem, apart from an isolated speech or article about the importance of finding a solution.[5] In September 1955, shortly before President Eisenhower's heart attack, the chairman of the House Judiciary Committee, Emanuel Celler of New York, ordered the committee staff to undertake a study of presidential inability. The staff subsequently distributed to a number of jurists, political scientists, and public officials a questionnaire seeking their views on such questions as: What was intended by the term "inability"? Should a definition be enacted into law? Who should initiate and make the determination of inability? Of cessation of inability? Is a constitutional amendment necessary?[6]

The replies were extremely varied. Although a substantial majority of those who responded suggested that no definition of inability be enacted into law, and that in the event of a temporary inability the Vice President would succeed only to the powers and duties of President, there was little agreement on the remaining areas.[7] Thus, a wide variety of proposals were advanced on who should initiate the question of inability. Many felt that the agency for initiation should be different from that of determination. Among the agencies proposed for the functions of initiation and determination were Congress, the Cabinet, the Vice President, the Supreme Court, a permanent commission of private citizens appointed by the Supreme Court, a panel of medical specialists appointed by the Chief Justice, a council consisting of Cabinet members and congressional leaders, a commission consisting of Supreme

Court justices and other federal judges, a special body created by Congress, and combinations of these agencies. There was a similar variance of views with respect to the method of ascertaining the end of an inability.

From the replies, the Judiciary Committee staff formulated five proposals—one in the form of a bill, one a joint resolution, and the others as constitutional amendments.[8] All permitted the President to declare his own inability, and four provided that he could declare the end of his inability whether he had made the initial determination or not. In the case of a President who could not declare his own inability, two proposals empowered the Vice President to make the determination of inability; two, the Cabinet; and one, a medical panel appointed by the Chief Justice.

Against the backdrop of Eisenhower's first heart attack, a subcommittee of the House Judiciary Committee held hearings on the subject in 1956. Following the hearings, its members met in executive session to attempt to reach agreement on a single proposal, but without success. In the following year, Attorney General Herbert Brownell presented to the subcommittee on behalf of the administration a proposed constitutional amendment containing the following provisions: The President could declare his own inability, and the Vice President would discharge the powers and duties of President. If the President failed to declare his inability or was unable to do so, the Vice President, "if satisfied of the President's inability, and upon approval in writing of a majority of the heads of executive departments who are members of the President's Cabinet . . . ," would act as President. In either case, the President would resume his powers and duties upon his written declaration of recovery.[9]

The feature of the administration's proposal that came under particularly heavy criticism was the provision permitting the President to declare the end to his inability. Representative Kenneth B. Keating of New York leveled the sharpest attack, stating, "I can see . . . the danger of a chaotic condition by having the Vice President say the President was unable, and the next day the President saying, 'I am able,' and then the Vice President the next day saying he is unable, so that you would have a day-by-day President."[10] In response, Brownell argued that public opinion would ultimately decide the matter since the Vice President would not act without the support of the nation and could not act without the Cabinet's approval. Brownell stated that since the President was elected by the people, there should be no obstruction to his resuming his powers and duties. If either the President or Vice President should act arbitrarily or irresponsibly, said Brownell, then the remedy of impeachment would be available.[11] But the impeachment alternative was generally regarded as unsatisfactory because there was doubt that a President could be impeached for an inability, and the process itself would be lengthy and effect a permanent removal from office.

Various other proposals were presented to the subcommittee, involving either separately or in combination the Vice President, Cabinet, Congress, Supreme Court, or an inability commission. One member of the subcommittee, Representative Keating, favored a ten-member inability commission, consisting of the Vice President as a nonvoting member, the Chief Justice, the senior Associate Justice, the Speaker and minority leader of the House, the majority and minority leaders of the Senate, the Attorney General, and the Secretaries of State and of the Treasury. The concurrence of six would be necessary for determination of inability. But Chairman Celler preferred leaving the entire process in the hands of the President and Vice President, with the President empowered to declare the end of any inability.

While the House Judiciary Committee was reviewing the matter, former President Truman set forth a proposal of his own in a copyrighted article for the *New York Times*. He suggested a commission of seven, consisting of the Vice President, the Chief Justice of the Supreme Court, the Speaker of the House, and the majority and minority leaders of the House and Senate. Truman's commission would be empowered to select a group of medical authorities from the top medical schools in the country and to call a special session of Congress if it was in recess. If the medical group found the President "truly incapacitated," the commission would so inform Congress. If Congress agreed by a two-thirds vote of its membership, the Vice President would become President for the remainder of the term.[12]

In the light of these differing views, it is not surprising that the House Judiciary Committee failed to reach any agreement, and as a result the efforts at reform came to a halt in the House.

In early 1958, after Eisenhower's third illness, the Subcommittee on Constitutional Amendments of the Senate Judiciary Committee, under the chairmanship of Estes Kefauver, took up the cudgels.[13] Hearings were held,* and the administration proposal was reintroduced, with a new provision to cover the case of a President's disagreeing with a determination of inability made by the Vice President and Cabinet. This change provided that when the President declared his inability ended, he would not resume his powers and duties for seven days, unless he and the Vice President agreed to an earlier resumption. If the Vice President, with the approval of a majority of the Cabinet, disagreed with the President's declaration of recovery, he could bring the issue before Congress for decision. If a majority of the House found that the President was still disabled and the Senate concurred by a two-thirds vote, the Vice President then would discharge the powers and duties of President until the Vice President proclaimed the end of the

---

* During the course of these hearings Senator Keating released a letter from Chief Justice Earl Warren concerning the undesirability of having the Supreme Court participate in the determination of a President's inability: "It has been the belief of all of us that because of the separation of powers in our Government, the nature of the judicial process, the possibility of a controversy of this character coming to the Court, and the danger of disqualification which might result in lack of a quorum, it would be inadvisable for any member of the Court to serve on such a Commission." Hearings on Presidential Inability Before the Subcomm. on Constitutional Amendments of the Senate Comm. on the Judiciary, 85th Cong., 2d Sess. 14 (1958).

inability, or a majority of both Houses decided that the inability had ended, or until the end of the term.

On March 12, 1958, the subcommittee approved a resolution essentially the same as the administration's revised proposal, but Congress subsequently adjourned without acting on the proposal. In the following year the proposal again was favorably reported by the subcommittee, but again neither its parent committee nor the Senate took any action.[14]

Although during the hearings there had been general agreement on the need for a constitutional amendment to confirm the Tyler precedent with respect to cases of death, resignation, and removal, and to provide for an Acting President in a case of inability, considerable disagreement arose over the mechanics of determining the beginning and ending of an inability. Each of the numerous proposals advanced had its adherents and critics. None had sufficient support for passage.

As Congress pondered the problem, with no foreseeable solution, President Eisenhower became increasingly concerned about the recurrence of another case of inability during his administration. He therefore conceived and drafted an informal agreement that offered an imaginative and practical approach to the problem. He showed it to Vice President Nixon and Attorney General Rogers and, after incorporating their suggestions, set forth this approach in a letter, copies of which were sent to Nixon, Rogers, and Secretary of State John Foster Dulles. Said Eisenhower of this agreement:

> We decided and this was the thing that frightened me: suppose something happens to you in the turn of a stroke that might incapacitate you mentally and you wouldn't know it, and the people around you, wanting to protect you, would probably keep this away from the public. So I decided that what we must do is make the Vice President decide when the President can no longer carry on, and then he should take over the duties, and when the President became convinced that he could take back his duties, he would be the one to decide.[15]

The letter was released to the public on March 3, 1958, and provided as follows:

1. In the event of inability the President would—if possible—so inform the Vice President, and the Vice President would serve as Acting President, exercising the powers and duties of the office until the inability had ended.

2. In the event of an inability which would prevent the President from so communicating with the Vice President, the Vice President, after such consultation as seems to him appropriate under the circumstances, would decide upon the devolution of the powers and duties of the Office and would serve as Acting President until the inability had ended.

3. The President, in either event, would determine when the inability had ended and at that time would resume the full exercise of the powers and duties of the Office.[16]

This informal understanding was later adopted by President Kennedy and Vice President Johnson,* President Johnson and House Speaker McCormack, and President Johnson and Vice President Humphrey.[17] Though it did not have the force of law and depended entirely on the good will of the incumbent President and Vice President, the agreement nevertheless constituted the first significant step toward solving the inability problem.

1961–63

The end of the Eisenhower administration and the election of a young, vigorous President reduced the problem of presidential inability to a low priority. Only a few members of Congress continued to press for action. Two of these, Senators Kefauver and Keating, put aside their previous proposals and joined in sponsoring a proposed constitutional amendment, known as S. J. Res. 35, which authorized Congress to adopt by statute specific procedures for determining the beginning and ending of an inability.† The proposal had actually been formulated in 1958 by the Committee on the Federal Constitution of the New York State Bar Association and was subsequently endorsed by the New York State Bar Association, the American Bar Association, and The Association of the Bar of the City of New York.[18] Said Keating about his sponsorship of S. J. Res. 35,

> . . . Senator Kefauver and I . . . agreed that if anything was going to be done, all of the detailed procedures which had been productive of delay and controversy had best be scrapped for the time being in favor of merely authorizing Congress in a constitutional amendment to deal with particular methods by ordinary legislation. This, we agreed, would later allow Congress to pick and choose the best form among all the proposals without

---

* Released at the time of such adoption was an opinion of Attorney General Robert F. Kennedy's that declared the agreement to be "clearly constitutional and as close to spelling out a practical solution to the problem as is possible." According to the opinion, the Constitution empowered the Vice President to determine the existence of an inability and authorized the President to declare its end. 42 Op. Att'y Gen. No. 5 (1961).

† S. J. Res. 35 provided that "In case of the removal of the President from office or of his death or resignation, the said office shall devolve on the Vice President. In case of the inability of the President to discharge the powers and duties of the said office, the said powers and duties shall devolve on the Vice President, until the inability be removed. The Congress may by law provide for the case of removal, death, resignation or inability, both of the President and Vice President, declaring what officer shall then be President, or in case of inability, act as President, and such officer shall be or act as President accordingly, until a President shall be elected or, in case of inability, until the inability shall be earlier removed. The commencement and termination of any inability shall be determined by such method as Congress shall by law provide."

suffering the handicap of having to rally a two-thirds majority in each House to do it.[19]

Thereupon, in June 1963 Senator Kefauver convened hearings of his Subcommittee on Constitutional Amendments. At the outset Kefauver remarked that "the essence of statesmanship is to act in advance to eliminate situations of potential danger. . . . [We should] take advantage of our present good fortune to prepare now for the possible crises of the future!"[20] At these hearings Deputy Attorney General Nicholas deB. Katzenbach; Lewis F. Powell Jr., who was soon to become president of the American Bar Association and later a justice of the Supreme Court; and representatives from the New York bar associations expressed their support for S. J. Res. 35. One witness, attorney Richard Hansen of Nebraska, advocated a limitation on S. J. Res. 35's blanket power to Congress to the effect that any method legislated by Congress must be compatible with the principle of separation of powers.

On June 25, 1963, the subcommittee favorably reported S. J. Res. 35 to the full committee. The sudden death of Senator Kefauver in August 1963 brought progress to a halt, but three months later the tragic death of President Kennedy forcefully catapulted the problem into full national concern. As Senator Keating stated,

> As distasteful as it is to entertain the thought, a matter of inches spelled the difference between the painless death of John F. Kennedy and the possibility of his permanent incapacity to exercise the duties of the highest office of the land.[21]

Keating added,

> The death of Estes Kefauver and John F. Kennedy provides a dual lesson for us. First, it is a grim reminder of the universality of tragedy, that no man, no matter his station, is immune from the accidents of fate that befall ordinary mortals.
>
> Secondly, however, it cautions those who survive of the difficulty of clearly foreseeing the absolutely incredible. Human legislation partakes always of human fallibility. No act of lawmaking, no matter how carefully conceived and executed, can possibly safeguard against all the freak contingencies of our existence. The best we can hope to achieve is the best practical solution which will meet the needs of crises we can readily envision.[22]

5

Senate Passage of S. J. Res. 139

[T]he problems of Presidential succession and Presidential inability . . . have a ringing urgency today with the tragedy of our martyred President so fresh in our memory.

BIRCH BAYH, January 22, 1964[1]

Following President Kennedy's death,* there descended on Congress a flurry of proposals dealing with the problem of presidential inability, most of which also sought to deal with the related problem of presidential succession. The presence of a seventy-two-year-old Speaker (John W. McCormack) and an eighty-six-year-old President pro tempore (Carl Hayden) at the top of the line of succession underscored the imperfections of the 1947 succession law. Neither man had been chosen for his position with an eye toward possible succession to the presidency, and neither was viewed by the public as a person of presidential stature.

Senator Birch Bayh of Indiana, Kefauver's successor as chairman of the Subcommittee on Constitutional Amendments, announced in December 1963 that the subcommittee would hold hearings on both problems early in 1964. Almost simultaneously with this announcement, Bayh and several other senators proposed a constitutional amendment (S. J. Res. 139) containing provisions on inability, filling a vice-presidential vacancy, and succession beyond the vice presidency.†[2] The

---

* See Chapter 1, "A President Dies in Office," in *From Failing Hands* 1–20, for my account of his death at the time.

† At a meeting of the Senate Judiciary Committee on December 4, 1963, before introducing the proposal, Senator Bayh and Senator Sam J. Ervin of North Carolina pointed out critically that under S. J. Res. 35 a President could be declared disabled by a simple majority of both Houses, since that is the required vote for passage of a law, and S. J. Res. 35 left it to Congress to establish by law the procedures for determining a case of presidential inability. Bayh, *One Heartbeat Away* 30 (1968). Of course, the

inability provisions were essentially the same as those in the revised Eisenhower administration approach. The vice-presidential vacancy feature specified that the President must nominate within thirty days a new Vice President, who would take office upon confirmation by a majority of both Houses of Congress. The Bayh proposal also provided for a Cabinet line of succession (starting with the Secretary of State) in the event of double vacancies in the offices of President and Vice President.

At the same time and in coordination with Bayh's initiatives, the American Bar Association (ABA) called a special conference of twelve lawyers to examine the problems and offer recommendations. The attending lawyers were former Attorney General Brownell; President Walter E. Craig of the ABA; Professor Paul A. Freund of Harvard Law School, one of the nation's foremost authorities on the Constitution; Jonathan C. Gibson of Chicago, chairman of the Committee on Jurisprudence and Law Reform of the ABA; Richard Hansen, author of *The Year We Had No President*; James C. Kirby Jr., a former chief counsel to the Subcommittee on Constitutional Amendments; former Deputy Attorney General Ross L. Malone; Dean Charles B. Nutting of the George Washington University Law Center; President-elect Lewis F. Powell Jr. of the ABA; Martin Taylor of New York, chairman of the Committee on the Federal Constitution of the New York State Bar Association; Edward L. Wright of Arkansas, chairman of the House of Delegates of the ABA; and this author.

From this two-day conference on January 20 and 21, 1964, the following consensus developed:

1. Agreements between the President and Vice President or person next in line of succession provide a partial solution, but not an acceptable permanent solution, to the problem.

2. An amendment to the Constitution of the United States should be adopted to resolve the problems which would arise in the event of the inability of the President to discharge the powers and duties of his office.

3. The amendment should provide that in the event of the inability of the President to discharge the powers and duties, but not the office, shall devolve upon the Vice President or person next in line of succession for the duration of the inability of the President or until expiration of his term of office.

4. The amendment should provide that the inability of the President may be established by declaration in writing of the President. In the event that the

---

any bill passed by Congress is subject to a presidential veto, which requires a two-thirds vote of each House of Congress to be overridden.

President does not make known his inability, it may be established by action of the Vice President or person next in line of succession with concurrence of a majority of the Cabinet or by action of such other body as the Congress may by law provide.

5. The amendment should provide that the ability of the President to resume the powers and duties of his office shall be established by his declaration in writing. In the event that the Vice President and a majority of the Cabinet or such other body as Congress may by law provide shall not concur in the declaration of the President, the continuing inability of the President may then be determined by the vote of two-thirds of the elected members of each House of the Congress.

The conference also considered the related question of Presidential succession. It was the consensus that:

1. The Constitution should be amended to provide that in the event of the death, resignation, or removal of the President, the Vice President or the person next in line of succession shall succeed to the office for the unexpired term.

2. It is highly desirable that the office of Vice President be filled at all times. An amendment to the Constitution should be adopted providing that when a vacancy occurs in the office of Vice President, the President shall nominate a person who, upon approval by a majority of the elected members of Congress meeting in joint session, shall then become Vice President for the unexpired term.[3]

The consensus was released immediately to the press, endorsed by the ABA on February 17, and formally presented to the Subcommittee on Constitutional Amendments on February 24, 1964, by ABA President Craig and Lewis F. Powell. The author was a member of this team.

SENATE HEARINGS

At the hearings of the Subcommittee on Constitutional Amendments held during the months of January, February, and March 1964, a majority of the witnesses expressed their support for the inability provisions of the ABA consensus, which closely followed those of the Eisenhower administration.[4] These included Brownell; Professor Freund; Ruth Silva, a noted scholar on presidential succession; former Vice President Richard M. Nixon; and Powell. Although some of the proponents felt that Congress had the power to legislate procedures, there was wide agreement that a constitutional amendment was necessary and desirable to remove all doubts.[5]

The witnesses who favored the involvement of the Vice President and Cabinet in determining cases of presidential inability gave various reasons for the combination. The Vice President, it was said, should have a voice in the process because it would be his duty to act as President once the determination had been made. Consequently, he should not be forced to take over under circumstances that he felt to be improper. On the other hand, it was urged that he not have the sole power of determination since he would be an interested party and therefore possibly reluctant to make a determination. Said Professor Freund:

> [T]hat officer should be spared the task of shouldering the responsibility alone. Leaving aside actual self-interest, the very appearance of self-interest might impel him to refrain from a decision which by objective standards ought to be taken.[6]

For this very reason, Professor James MacGregor Burns of Williams College testified that "[t]he Vice President is the worst person to decide Presidential inability," adding, "[n]ot because he would want to make a grab for power—though this is always possible—but the opposite: he would hesitate to take any action that would give an appearance of over-eagerness or that might be used against him in the next election."[7]

The Cabinet was said to be the best possible body to assist the Vice President in making his determination because its members are close to the President and likely to be aware of any inability and to know whether the circumstances require that the Vice President act as President. Furthermore, the use of the Cabinet would be consistent with the principle of separation of powers and would inspire public confidence. Brownell considered that the Cabinet's basic loyalty would be to the President, and he observed, "I believe that this system would guard against any such rash action or any danger that the decision might be made by persons who are unfriendly to the President."[8] Drawing on his experience, Brownell remarked that the performance of the Vice President and Cabinet during the period following Eisenhower's heart attack had met with public approval. In contrast, Burns argued that the use of the Cabinet was not desirable since its members would want to support either the President or the Vice President and therefore would be incapable of making an objective decision.

As for the ABA's recommendation that any constitutional amendment authorize Congress to substitute another body for the Cabinet,* Powell testified that such a provision would lend flexibility should subsequent experience indicate that

---

* This joining of a key feature of S. J. Res. 35 was suggested at the ABA Conference by Vincent Doyle, then of the American Law Division of the Library of Congress. The feature from S. J. Res. 35 provided that "The commencement and termination of any inability shall be determined by such method as Congress shall by law provide."

a different procedure would be more desirable. In such an event, that new body could be established by statute.[9]

With respect to the ABA recommendation that a disagreement about the President's recovery be resolved by Congress, with a two-thirds vote of each House necessary to prevent the President's return, Powell stated:

> Obviously, vital principles of government are involved. The independence of the executive branch must be preserved, and a President who has regained his health should not be harassed by a possibly hostile Congress. Yet, there must be a means to protect the country from the situation (however remote) where a disabled President seeks to resume office. It is believed that the recommendation provides appropriate safeguards for and a proper balancing of the interests involved.[10]

By having the Vice President continue to act as President pending Congress's decision, Freund said, the ABA recommendation would guard against the return of the powers and duties of the presidency to "one whose capacity was in serious doubt."[11]

In a letter to Senator Bayh dated March 2, 1964, former President Eisenhower indicated his basic agreement with the ABA recommendations, stating:

> Many systems have been proposed but each seems to be so cumbersome in character as to preclude prompt action in emergency. My personal conclusion is that the matter should be left strictly to the two individuals concerned, the President and the Vice President, subject possibly to a concurring majority opinion of the President's Cabinet.[12]

Eisenhower further suggested that if there were a disagreement between the President and the Vice President and Cabinet, the issue should be referred to a commission consisting of the three ranking Cabinet officials, the Speaker and minority leader of the House, the President pro tempore and minority leader of the Senate, and four medical persons who would be selected by the Cabinet and whose credentials were recognized by the American Medical Association. The findings of this commission would then be submitted to Congress for approval.* Eisenhower concluded:

> There is, of course, no completely foolproof method covering every contingency and every possibility that could arise in the circumstances now under discussion. We must trust that men of good will and common sense, operating within constitutional guidelines governing these matters,

---

* On May 25, 1964, at a conference convened by the ABA, Eisenhower moved away from the idea of a commission and expressed his confidence in the ability of Congress, on its own, to resolve such an issue. *See* Bayh, *One Heartbeat Away* 119–24 (1968).

will make such decisions that their actions will gain and hold the approval of the mainstream of American thinking.

Professor Silva, however, thought it unnecessary to make provision for a disagreement, considering such an eventuality to be remote. In her opinion there should be no check on the President's resumption of his powers and duties; still, she felt that the "two-thirds vote" was a "sufficiently heavy majority to protect the integrity of the office" of President. Silva further urged on grounds of separation of powers and protection of the integrity of the presidency that Congress not be given the power to change the Cabinet as the body to act with the Vice President.[13] She, like Brownell, argued that an inability commission would be undesirable, because the question of inability is more than a medical problem. Brownell had also observed that a commission composed of persons outside the executive branch "runs a good chance of coming out with a split decision," with possible catastrophic effects on the country.[14]

Senator Roman L. Hruska of Nebraska submitted his own proposal, which required that the determination of a President's inability be kept within the executive branch. In his view the Cabinet was the best possible body to make the determination. Instead of giving Congress carte blanche authority to designate another body as a replacement for the Cabinet, as did S. J. Res. 139, Hruska strongly urged that any constitutional amendment limit Congress to designating only another body within the executive branch as a replacement for the Cabinet. In that way, he said, the doctrine of separation of powers would be respected, and the President would be accorded "every fair intendment for continuation" as President and "for his restoration to full Presidential powers . . . ."[15] "[T]he people have a right," declared Hruska, that the President "serve the full term to which he was elected, except if there is some very grave disability visited upon him, nervous, mental, or physical."[16] Hruska observed that his proposal guarded against such potential abuses as Congress's using the inability procedures as a pretext to oust a healthy President rather than resort to the impeachment process, Congress's impairing the independence of the presidency, and the judiciary's being injected into the process in such a way as to impair its independence and preclude an impartial decision should an inability issue later reach the courts.[17]

A number of other witnesses expressed contrary views about the desirability of a constitutional amendment empowering the Vice President and Cabinet to declare a President disabled. Professors Clinton Rossiter of Cornell University and Richard Neustadt of Columbia University suggested merely the passage of a joint resolution by Congress endorsing the informal letter agreement approach originally adopted by Eisenhower.[18] In response to Bayh's observation that the informal arrangement did not deal with a disagreement, Neustadt asserted, "I don't know that constitutions can protect you against madmen. The people on the scene at the time have to do that. . . . . So, I would leave it alone and assume that there are going to be a lot of sensible and responsible people around to work something out pragmatically."[19] If any group had authority to remove the President, he said, it would hang "over the head of every incoming President."[20] In Rossiter's view, the disability problem was "insoluble" because "a period of clearly established Presidential disability in any case is going to be a messy situation, one in which caution, perhaps even timidity, must mark the posture of an Acting President. . . ."[21]

On the other hand, Professor Burns favored a constitutional amendment allowing Congress to establish an inability commission composed of the Chief Justice, who would represent the political neutrality of the Supreme Court; two ranking Cabinet members, representing the interests of the disabled President; and the Speaker and President pro tempore, representing both Houses of Congress.[22] Each member would have the power to appoint a doctor to gather the facts, and the commission would have the power to certify the Vice President as Acting President or, in the case of a continuing inability, as President. Burns predicted that such a group could act quickly and authoritatively. Other witnesses also preferred the inability commission approach. Francis Biddle, Attorney General under Franklin D. Roosevelt, recommended a commission of three Cabinet officials with the power to declare an inability temporary or permanent.[23] If the inability should be declared permanent, the commission's findings would have to be approved by Congress. In addition to supporting the use of the Cabinet, Professor Freund suggested the creation by statute of a disability commission appointed by the President at the beginning of his term, including in its membership former Presidents, members of the Cabinet and of Congress, and a medical expert.[24] Such a commission, said Freund, "would have the advantage of being a disinterested group, designated by the President himself, and prepared to take action without any hint of extraneous motivations."

Senator Keating and New York lawyer Martin Taylor urged that a constitutional amendment along the lines of S. J. Res. 35 be adopted.[25] They argued that the Constitution should not contain the detail in S. J. Res. 139, stating that an amendment with so much detail would be hard to ratify. Although they conceded that S. J. Res. 35 itself did not solve the inability problem since procedures would have to be adopted by Congress after its ratification, they asserted that the approach gave Congress flexibility to adopt procedures that could be easily changed if unforeseen defects appeared.[26] Sidney Hyman, noted author of books on the presidency, offered another choice. He suggested that the Vice President be given the power to declare a President disabled, stating:

> Furthermore, I would prefer vesting that discretionary power in one man who would always be the object of jealous watchfulness, than to vest it in any committee of men whose chief actors could not be singled out and called to account for what they did.[27]

Although there were varied views on the inability problem, most of the witnesses who testified at the 1964 hearings emphasized the need for finding a solution. As Senator Bayh stated:

> Here we have a constitutional gap—a blind spot, if you will. We must fill this gap if we are to protect our Nation from the possibility of floundering in the sea of public confusion and uncertainty, which ofttimes exists at times of national peril and tragedy.[28]

As a national consensus on the inability problem gradually began to take shape along the lines of the ABA approach, widespread agreement manifested itself at the hearings on the need for a Vice President at all times. Said Senator Bayh, "It is significant that every measure placed before this committee since President Kennedy's assassination agrees on one vital point—that we shall have a Vice President."[29] A Vice President, he said, "would provide for an orderly transfer of Executive authority in the event of the death of a President—a transfer that would win popular consent and inspire national confidence. . . ."[30] The need was underscored by President Johnson, then serving without a Vice President, in a press interview in March 1964,[31] and by a number of leading scholars in response to a questionnaire that Senator Hubert H. Humphrey of Minnesota had circulated.[32] Bayh had expressed the basic rationale for keeping the vice presidency filled when he introduced his proposal on December 12, 1963:

> Mr. President, there have been a number of instances of succession to the Presidency on the part of the Vice President. Each case has demonstrated the weakness of a system whereby there is no replacement of the Vice President.
>
> The accelerated pace of international affairs, plus the overwhelming problems of modern military security, make it almost imperative that we change our system to provide for not only a President but a Vice President at all times.
>
> The modern concept of the Vice Presidency is that of a man "standing in the wings"—even if reluctantly—ready at all times to take the burden. He must know the job of the President. He must keep current on all national and international developments. He must, in fact, be something of an "assistant President," such as Vice President Johnson was in the fields of space and civil rights and in carrying the flag of the United States to foreign countries on good will missions and on matters of great diplomatic concern.[33]

The measures and recommendations presented to Bayh's subcommittee differed on the means of filling a vice-presidential vacancy.

PRESIDENTIAL NOMINATION

In the hearings a number of witnesses expressed the view that the best way to fill a vice-presidential vacancy was to give the President the power to nominate a replacement who would take office if approved by Congress. Bayh emphasized that such a procedure would ensure the selection of a person with whom the President could work, and a reasonable continuity of executive policy should the Vice President succeed to the presidency.[34] Said Powell on behalf of the ABA's recommendation in favor of this approach:

> It is true that this procedure would give the President the power to choose his potential successor. But with the safeguard of congressional approval, it is believed that this is sound in theory and in substantial conformity with current nominating practice. It is desirable that the President and Vice President enjoy harmonious relations and mutual confidence. The importance of this compatibility is recognized in the modern practice of both major parties in according the presidential candidate the privilege of choosing his running mate subject to convention approval. In the proposed amendment, the President would choose his Vice President subject to congressional approval.[35]

Freund testified:

> The Vice Presidency should have a popular base and at the same time be in harmony with the Presidency. These objectives can best be achieved by associating the Congress and the President in the selection, with the opportunity for informal consultation to be expected in such a process.[36]

Under this procedure, said the political scientist Clinton Rossiter:

> [T]he three great political branches of our Government—President, Senate, and House—[would be joined] in a solemn and responsible act which strikes me as much the most sensible and convenient way to handle this delicate and vital problem.[37]

Favoring such a proposal, Senator Frank E. Moss of Utah stated:

> [I]t is foolhardy in these days of instant crisis to have a Presidential succession law which could place a member of the opposite political party in the White House, with perhaps only an hour or two in which to become acquainted with all of the details of an explosive situation and be required to act.[38]

Moss added that if inquiry revealed that a nominee had a weakness or disability, Congress, as the representative of the will and views of the people, could reject the choice.

One major criticism of the proposal was that Congress's confirmatory role would be illusory, because Congress would be reluctant to reject a presidential nomination that was made after an incumbent President's death in office and a Vice President's succession. Hence, it was reasoned, the President actually would be picking his successor. Said Senator Jacob K. Javits of New York:

> [T]here is a great difference between an informal practice at conventions which can always be overturned, which is not law, but is practice, and the cementing of an idea into the Constitution. I do not think it is a good idea for the law to say that the President chooses his successor . . . whatever may be the practice in party conventions.[39]

Another objection voiced against the proposal was that the advantage of speed said to be inherent in it could be overcome by congressional opposition to the nominee and resulting congressional "foot dragging."[40] A presidential nomination approach, others argued, would present a controversial political issue at a time when unity in the nation was most needed. Senator Mike Monroney of Oklahoma said that an election in Congress would not be "wise during a period where the country is in mourning over the loss of its Chief Executive."[41] Keating concisely summarized the major objections:

> [C]ongressional confirmation is likely to be meaningless at best and divisive at worst.
>
> Meaningless, if the country is in its usual mood of rallying behind the new President and giving him his way during more or less of a "honeymoon" period, in which case confirmation would be expected as a matter of rote. Or divisive, if the Presidential nomination of a potential successor is looked upon by his opposition as an opportunity to make real trouble from the start.[42]

Thus, it was suggested by some that the President be required to submit to Congress a list of names (between two and five) from which Congress would choose the Vice President. Senator Frank Church of Idaho proposed that the President submit a list of several names to the Senate and that those ratified by the Senate be presented to the House for final selection.[43] These proposals were criticized because the President might not get the person with whom he could best work, and because no one person might be able to obtain the necessary number of votes for selection.

Those inclined toward a presidential nomination approach differed on whether the name or names should be submitted to one or both Houses of Congress. A few preferred the Senate on the grounds that it could be assembled more quickly than the House of Representatives, and, further, that it already had the constitutional role of confirming presidential nominations such as those of ambassadors, Cabinet members, and Supreme Court justices.[44] It was noted further that, under the Constitution, the Senate was assigned the role of choosing the Vice President when no candidate for that office received a majority of the electoral votes. Other witnesses preferred using the House alone because it was the more representative body. A greater number, however, favored participation by both Houses because that method would elevate the selection of a Vice President above other presidential nominations. Moreover, it was observed that the membership of the two Houses together approximates the number of members of the Electoral College.[45]

In the group that favored the participation of both Houses, there was a difference of opinion on whether the Houses should meet separately or jointly. If they met separately, it was argued, there could be considerable delay in the confirmation process and either House could reject the nominee or prevent any action at all. If they met jointly, on the other hand, delay would be minimized and a majority of those present could be in a position to approve the President's choice. It was noted, however, that if every member had an equal vote in the joint session, the voice of the House would be more than four times greater than that of the Senate. Action by a joint session also would require the adoption of a new set of congressional rules, since there existed no established rules of procedure for such a session.

CONGRESSIONAL SELECTION

Senators Sam J. Ervin of North Carolina and Javits urged that Congress alone fill any vice-presidential vacancy. Ervin listed three reasons why such a plan "best meets the country's needs":

> It satisfies our requirement, ably voiced by President Truman, that the potential President should be democratically selected. For under this system, he will be selected by the people's representatives.
>
> Second, the need for continuity is met. There will always be a Vice President who can participate in the making of and be briefed on the policies of the existing administration.
>
> Finally, the successor to the Presidency will be chosen at a time when attention can be focused on the qualities necessary to make a good President, not those necessary for some other office, and the Congress will be able to select from among all our great men, public and private, in making their choice.[46]

Ervin also proposed that, in the event that both the presidency and the vice presidency become vacant at the same time, Congress should select both a new President and a new Vice President within ten days. In the interim the presidency would temporarily be filled according to the statutory succession law.

When Bayh asked Ervin if he had any objection to a presidential nomination approach, in order to guarantee continuity of party and administration, Ervin indicated that he had no serious objection, although he felt that a uniform rule should apply to both single and dual vacancies.[47] James C. Kirby Jr., former chief counsel to the subcommittee, noted with respect to S. J. Res. 139:

> If both offices become vacant then the existing line of succession established by Congress would give us a President, and then he would nominate and Congress would elect a new Vice President to join him. . . . We would fill both offices.
>
> The obvious disadvantage is that both could be nonelected officials, but we wrestle in an area here where there are no good solutions. The nature of the problem is such that any solution is going to be partially undesirable, and one must choose between conflicting considerations and accept the fact that any proposal is going to be subject to some disadvantage and criticism.[48]

To ensure that the views of the President would not be excluded, and to meet the objection that Congress might select a person of the other party,[49] Javits offered an amendment to his proposal that would give the President a veto over any congressional selection.[50] He said that a veto power was particularly important because Congress might be "organized by the party of which the President is not a member." He argued that giving Congress the primary role would maximize public participation, whereas a system of presidential initiative would make Congress's role in a period of crisis perfunctory and thereby allow the President to choose his successor. Javits also suggested that the new Vice President be chosen from the groups named in the 1947 succession law—that is, the members of Congress and the President's Cabinet—so that Congress could act quickly, adding that the selection of a person already holding a high position of trust would ensure public confidence in the result.[51]

Senator Moss observed that if Congress chose the nominee,

> the President then is under the pressure . . . to take the choice of the Congress and he would be inclined to do that. But yet this might not accord with what he would think could be a smooth-working team. . . . If he turned it down . . . [m]any would be incensed with the President. He turned down something that the Congress had all agreed upon. Rather than get this smooth, effectual transfer we are talking about, I think you might precipitate a greater internal crisis here. . . . [52]

TWO ELECTED VICE PRESIDENTS

Senator Keating became the principal sponsor of a proposal to provide for the election of a President and two Vice Presidents every four years. One would be an Executive Vice President and the other a Legislative Vice President.[53] The Executive Vice President would be available to undertake assignments for the President and be first in the line of succession. The other would be President of the Senate, second in line, and also available for executive assignments. Critics argued that the proposal would aggravate the ticket-balancing tendency in selecting Vice Presidents and that few people would be interested in being a Vice President under such a plan. Keating replied that the parties would act responsibly in picking the two; that most senators, representatives, and governors would be interested in either office, if the opportunity were presented; and that there is an abundance of work that the President could delegate to the two.[54] Former Vice President Nixon, however, argued that

> by dividing the already limited functions of the office, we would be downgrading the vice presidency at a time when it is imperative that we add to its prestige and importance.[55]

Richard Neustadt commented that the vice presidency is a "very frustrating position," and that it is difficult for a President and Vice President to develop a graceful relationship. "[T]o complicate that with a third man," said Neustadt, would "multiply the difficulties inherent in the relationship."[56]

The Keating proposal gained little support.*[57]

THE ELECTORAL COLLEGE

During these hearings Nixon urged that the most recent Electoral College be reconvened and, with the President's recommendation, it select a new Vice President.† In advancing this proposal, Nixon reasoned that the procedures of S. J. Res. 139 might not work when Congress is controlled by the opposition party. He said:

> The Congress 20 per cent of the time during the history of our country has been under the control of a party other than that of the President of the United States. It seems to me then that the electoral college has that advantage over the Congress as the elective body which will select or approve the selection of the new Vice President.[58]

In contrast, the most recent Electoral College would always contain a majority from the President's own party. It would also ensure, said Nixon, that the Vice President would be chosen through the elective process: "[W]hoever is to hold the Executive power in this Nation should be one who represents and has come from and has

---

* A somewhat related suggestion was advanced by Professor Ruth Miner of Wisconsin State College, who proposed that the political parties name a second Vice President at convention time and that Congress provide by statute that the person so designated by the incoming party shall serve as President in the event the elected President and Vice President were unable to complete their terms, or as Vice President if a vacancy occurred in that office. 1964 Senate Hearings 265–68.

† A similar proposal was advanced in the First Congress. Annals of Cong., 1st Cong., 3d Sess. 1911–12 (1791).

been approved by the electoral process rather than the appointive process." Nixon added that the hearings should make clear that the President has a right to a Vice President "who is compatible with his views."*

But other witnesses criticized use of the Electoral College. Kirby testified that to revitalize and dignify the college "would be a great mistake," recalling Senator Kefauver's observation: "The electoral college is a loaded pistol pointed at our system of government. Its continued existence is a game of Russian roulette."[59] Silva argued that the use of the Electoral College "would be a step away from democratic control" since it would have no current mandate from the voters[60] and would encourage discretion in a body that should have none. Brownell observed that the person chosen by the Electoral College might not be compatible with the President.[61] Bayh succinctly summarized the principal criticisms, stating that "[t]he electoral college is not chosen, as is Congress, to exercise any considered judgment or reasoning"; that it is not "equipped . . . to conduct hearings on the qualifications" of a nominee for Vice President; that it "would be a cumbersome body to try to assemble quickly"; and that the people would hesitate to have electors unknown to them decide on the confirmation of a Vice President.[62]

As a consequence of these and other criticisms, the Electoral College proposal garnered little support.

NEW ELECTION

No witness before the subcommittee advocated a special election to fill a vice-presidential vacancy. Javits, noting that theoretically it would be the best idea, stated that he did "not think it is practically feasible in short enough time to provide the rapid continuity of both the Nation's highest offices which is so vitally necessary."[63] Rossiter stated that there "would be simply too much turmoil and chaos and expense to have a special nationwide election to choose a new Vice President."[64] Bayh noted that "a time of traumatic shock . . . is hardly conducive to a well-reasoned selection by popular vote."[65] It would represent, said Lewis Powell, "a new and drastic departure from our historic system of quadrennial presidential elections and would introduce various complications into our political structure."[66] Similar views were expressed by other witnesses,[67] with the result that no support developed for the idea.

OTHER PROPOSALS

While most proposals for filling a vacancy in the vice presidency contemplated a constitutional amendment, some did not. Governor Nelson A. Rockefeller of New

---

* Another proponent of this proposal at the time of the hearings was former President Harry S. Truman.

York expressed a preference for a statutory office of First Secretary.* The First Secretary would be appointed by the President, by and with the advice and consent of the Senate, would be a member of the Cabinet and of the National Security Council, and would assist the President in the areas of national security and international affairs. Said the governor:

> An individual with the knowledge and experience gained from this position would be well suited to succeed to the Presidency in the absence of a Vice President. He would provide the essential continuity of Government in our international relations and leadership of the machinery of Government.[68]

This proposal was criticized by Richard Nixon, who alleged that it would downgrade the office of Vice President and make it possible for an appointed official to succeed to the presidency.[69]

Senator Eugene J. McCarthy of Minnesota proposed the creation of a statutory office of Deputy President to be filled within thirty days after a vacancy had occurred in the vice presidency. The President would appoint, subject to Senate confirmation, a person from among the members of Congress, the Cabinet, the justices of the Supreme Court, and the governors of the states. The Deputy President would be placed first in the line of succession. According to Senator McCarthy,

> the choice of the Deputy President would be made under politically realistic conditions. A weakness of our previous succession laws has been that the designated successor often attained his position for reasons and considerations quite apart from the possibility of succession.[70]

Added McCarthy:

> The succession law should respect the mandate of the people, who vote not only for a man but also, in a broad way, for his party and his program. The elevation of a leader of another party in midterm is undesirable in principle and could have most unfortunate practical effects.

Neustadt suggested that the 1947 law be amended to provide for an office of Acting Vice President to be filled by the President, by and with the advice and consent of the Senate, in case of a vice-presidential vacancy. Said Neustadt:

> [T]his appeals to me because it is the nearest thing I can envisage to contemporary practice . . . to the common law of the Constitution as it has operated.[71]

---

* The interesting story of why Rockefeller was not called to testify is described in Bayh, *One Heartbeat Away* 73–74.

He argued that a case of succession should produce

> no break, no sharp break, in the continuity of the administration and party installed in the Executive by the last national election.[72]

Throughout the hearings numerous witnesses expressed their opposition to the statutory line of succession and suggested instead a Cabinet line of succession after the Vice President.[73] Rossiter declared that "the act of 1947 is a poor one, in many ways one of the poorest ever to emerge from this stately and distinguished body."[74] One proposal advanced was that in the event of succession by a Cabinet member, he should serve as Acting President until a new election could be held at midterm or at the end of the four-year term.[75] Another provided that whenever the Vice President or statutory successor succeeded, a new President and Vice President would be chosen by special election to fill out the existing term.[76] There was general recognition, however, that the problem of succession beyond the vice presidency would be minimized if a procedure for filling a vice-presidential vacancy were established.

COMMITTEE ACTION

Following the completion of the Senate hearings and after consideration of the various proposals pending before it, the subcommittee, on May 27, 1964,* reported favorably on S. J. Res. 139, with amendments, and recommended its submission to the state legislatures.[77] The amendments completely eliminated the provision for a Cabinet line of succession beyond the vice presidency. This was done partly because of the concern that the presence of such a provision would be viewed as a criticism of Speaker McCormack and therefore would jeopardize passage of the proposal in the House of Representatives, and partly because of the belief that the provisions designed to keep the vice presidency filled at all times would minimize the importance of the statutory line of succession.

The amendments also conformed the provisions of S. J. Res. 139 to the consensus recommendations of the ABA.

The committee amendments to S. J. Res. 139 are as follows. Provisions of the initial resolution that were omitted are enclosed in brackets, new matter is italicized, and provisions that remained unchanged are shown in regular text:

> SECTION 1. In case of the removal of the President from office[,] or of his death or resignation, the Vice President shall become President [for the unexpired portion of the then current term]. [Within a period of thirty

* This was two days after a national forum on the problem convened by the ABA. At that forum Emanuel Celler, then Chairman of the House Judiciary Committee; Eisenhower; and others expressed their support for the ABA consensus.

days thereafter, the new President shall nominate a Vice President who shall take office upon confirmation by both Houses of Congress by a majority of those present and voting.]

SEC. 2. [In case of the removal of the Vice President from office, or of his death or resignation,] *Whenever there is a vacancy in the office of the Vice President,* the President [within a period of thirty days thereafter,] shall nominate a Vice President who shall take office upon confirmation by *a majority vote* of both Houses of Congress [by a majority vote of those present and voting].

SEC. 3. If the President [shall declare] declare*s* in writing that he is unable to discharge the powers and duties of his office, such powers and duties shall be discharged by the Vice President as Acting President.

SEC. 4. If the President does not so declare, *and* the Vice President [, if satisfied that such inability exists, shall, upon the written approval] *with the written concurrence* of a majority of the heads of the executive departments [in office,] *or such other body as Congress may by law provide, transmits to the Congress his written declaration that the President is unable to discharge the powers and duties of his office, the Vice President shall immediately* assume the [discharge of the] powers and duties *of the office* as Acting President.

SEC. 5. [Whenever the President makes public announcement in writing that his inability has terminated, he shall resume the discharge of the powers and duties of his office on the seventh day after making such announcement, or at such earlier time after such announcement as he and the Vice President may determine. But if the Vice President, with the written approval of a majority of the heads of executive departments in office at the time of such announcement, transmits to the Congress his written declaration that in his opinion the President's inability has not terminated, the Congress shall thereupon consider the issue. If the Congress is not then in session, it shall assemble in special session on the call of the Vice President. If the Congress determines by concurrent resolution, adopted with the approval of two-thirds of the Members present in each House, that the inability of the President has not termi-nated, thereupon, notwithstanding any further announcement by the President, the Vice President shall discharge such powers and duties as Acting President until the occurrence of the earliest of the following events: (1) the Acting President proclaims that the President's inability has ended, (2) the Congress determines by concurrent resolution, adopted with the approval of a majority of the Members present in each House, that the President's inability has ended, or (3) the President's term ends.] *Whenever the President transmits to the Congress his written declaration that no inability exists, he shall resume the powers and duties of his office unless the Vice President, with the written concurrence of a majority of the heads of the executive departments or such other body as Congress may by law provide, transmits within two days to the Congress his written declaration that the President is unable to discharge the powers and duties of his office. Thereupon Congress shall immediately decide the issue. If the Congress determines by two-thirds vote of both Houses that the President is unable to discharge the powers and duties of the office, the Vice President shall continue to discharge the same as Acting President; otherwise the President shall resume the powers and duties of his office.*

[SEC. 6. (a) (1) If, by reason of death, resignation, removal from office, inability, or failure to qualify, there is neither a President nor Vice President to discharge the powers and duties of the office of President, then the officer of the United States who is highest on the following list, and who is not under disability to discharge the powers and duties of the office of President, shall act as President: Secretary of State, Secretary of Treasury, Secretary of Defense, Attorney General, Postmaster General, Secretary of Interior, Secretary of Agriculture, Secretary of Commerce, Secretary of Labor, Secretary of Health, Education and Welfare, and such other heads of executive departments as may be established hereafter and in order of their establishment.

(2) The same rule shall apply in the case of the death, resignation, removal from office, or inability of an individual acting as President under this section.

(3) To qualify under this section, an individual must have been appointed, by and with the advice and consent of the Senate, prior to the time of the death, resignation, removal from office, or inability of the President and Vice President, and must not be under impeachment by the House of Representatives at the time the powers and duties of the office of President devolve upon him.

(b) In case of the death, resignation, or removal of both the President and Vice President, his successor shall be President until the expiration of the then current presidential term. In case of the inability of the President and Vice President to discharge the powers and duties of the office of President, his successor, as designated in this section, shall be subject to the provisions of sections 3, 4, and 5 of this article as if he were a Vice President acting in case of disability of the President.

(c) The taking of the oath of office by an individual specified in the list of paragraph (1) of subsection (a) shall be held to constitute his resignation from the office by virtue of the holding of which he qualifies to act as President.

(d) During the period that any individual acts as President under this section, his compensation shall be at the rate then provided by law in the case of the President.]

[SEC. 7. This article shall be inoperative unless it shall have been ratified as an amendment to the Constitution by the legislatures of three-fourths of the several States within seven years from the date of its submission.]

In summary:

1. The words in Section 1 "for the unexpired portion of the then current term" were dropped as redundant.

2. The second sentence of Section 1 was placed in Section 2 and the term "vacancy" was substituted for the specific contingencies of death, removal, and resignation. Also the terminology "a majority vote of those present and voting" was changed in favor of the expression "a majority vote of both Houses of Congress." These changes were not intended to alter the substance of S. J. Res. 139 but rather either to simplify the language or to bring it into harmony with other provisions of the Constitution. One substantive change was the deletion from S. J. Res. 139 of the provision calling for a presidential nomination of a new Vice President "within thirty days."

3. Only minor word changes were made in Section 3.

4. A number of changes were made in Section 4, including the incorporation of the "such other body" and "concurrence" terminology from the ABA consensus and the inclusion of a requirement that Congress be notified of an inability determination.

5. Section 5 was considerably shortened by the amendments to follow the recommendations of the ABA consensus. The reference to Congress's being out of session was dropped; the Vice President was required to notify Congress within two days, instead of seven, of a determination that the President had not recovered from the inability; and the language listing the events that would end a Vice President's service as Acting President was eliminated.

Although the amendments closely followed the ABA recommendations, there were exceptions. For example, the amended S. J. Res. 139 made no reference to the manner in which a President's inability was to be determined when there was no Vice President. The ABA had proposed that the person next in succession would act in place of the Vice President. Apparently, the committee considered that this contingency would be remote if the provisions on the vice-presidential vacancy were adopted. The use of a statutory successor also opened the possibility of Congress's controlling a case of presidential inability, since S. J. Res. 139 gave it the power to substitute another body for the Cabinet.

S. J. Res. 139 also did not cover the case of a vice-presidential inability occurring either alone or concurrently with a presidential inability. Nor did it deal with simultaneous vacancies in the offices of President and Vice President. But these omissions were the result of a policy judgment, not of oversight. Said Senator Ervin:

> There was a consensus . . . that amending the Constitution is a rather difficult task, and that proposals for changes should be held to a minimum rather than expanded. The underlying thought, which I believe to be absolutely sound, was that every proposal additional to filling vacancies in the Vice-Presidency and coping with Presidential inability would cause some loss of support in the subcommittee, the full committee, the Congress, or the country at large, and thus endanger the prospect of any accomplishment.[78]

The full Judiciary Committee approved the revised S. J. Res. 139 on August 4 and issued a supporting report on August 13, 1964,*[79] thereby setting the stage for action by the Senate.

SENATE ACTION

On Monday, September 28, 1964, Senator Bayh, as principal sponsor of the proposal, opened the floor debate on S. J. Res. 139. In urging the adoption of its provision to keep the vice presidency filled at all times, Bayh stated:

> We pray that we may never be faced with the supreme test—the loss of a President and a Vice President within the same 4-year term of office. But in the event that history does not treat us so kindly in the future as it has in the past, we must be prepared for such an eventuality. For, whatever tragedy may befall our national leaders, the Nation must continue in stability, functioning to preserve a society in which freedom may prosper.[80]

Bayh reviewed the history of the vice presidency, showing that it had developed from an object of satire to an integral part of the executive machinery. The procedure of Section 2 allowing the President to nominate, he said, was designed to give the President someone with whom he could work closely and to provide for continuity

---

* Accompanying the report were individual views by Senators Roman Hruska and Kenneth Keating. Hruska stated his preference for a constitutional amendment that did not set forth a specific inability procedure and limited the determination to the executive branch. Keating expressed his continuing support for S. J. Res. 35 but said he would vote for S. J. Res. 139 if his proposal was not accepted.

of authority, direction, and program. The requirement of confirmation by Congress, he said, would assure that the representatives of the people would "act as the voice of the people" and "have the final determination as to who the Vice President should be."[81] Bayh also pointed out that, by taking the votes of members of both Houses, "we would arrive at a number identical with that now composing the electoral college."

Reviewing the course that S. J. Res. 139 had run, Senator Ervin recalled that one group of senators feared that vesting the power of selection solely in Congress could result in friction between the person designated as Vice President and the President, as well as interrupt continuity if a Congress of the opposition party were to select a member of its party to be Vice President.[82] Bayh concurred:

> The people, by voting in an election, should be the ones to decide a change of policy and a change of direction in our Government, and not some illness, some assassin's bullet, or some other unfortunate situation which would remove a President from the scene.[83]

Bayh observed that one of the major problems under Section 2 was the possibility that the President and Congress would be of different parties. Under such circumstances, the majority party might tend "to delay or play politics" with a nomination, but, Bayh affirmed, "I believe . . . that at a time of national crisis the public would not tolerate the playing of politics in the choice of a Vice President."[84]

Little opposition to S. J. Res. 139 developed during the debate of September 28. Senator Monroney, however, questioned the philosophy of allowing the President to pick his successor. He said that he could think of nothing worse for a newly installed President than to have his nomination for Vice President

> tied up in a long confirmation fight, with the ultimate possibility of rejection; and with a rival party in the majority in both Houses, or even rivalry in the majority party, over the choice of the nominee, with perhaps leading Members in either House being anxious to come in the line of authority, and one or the other Houses refusing to confirm.[85]

In Monroney's opinion, the selection of two Vice Presidents by the people in the regular quadrennial election was the best solution.

> [T]his would be an expression of the entire electorate of the United States, and thus bless the office or ratify the offices of first Vice President and second Vice President with the vote and the acceptance of the entire electorate.
>
> I recognize the fact that the joint resolution must be a compromise; but I question one bit of the philosophy in the selection of the successor by the nomination of one man, placing in the supreme line of authority over 180 million Americans one man chosen absolutely by the President, by

sending the nomination to Congress, and saying, "This is my man. I choose him for my successor."[86]

In response, Bayh pointed out that the two Vice Presidents proposal was not accepted in committee because of the feeling that it might reverse the trend of making the Vice President a full-fledged working member of the executive branch, that it might cause friction between the President and his Vice Presidents as well as between the two Vice Presidents, and that it might accentuate the ticket-balancing rather than the "best man" criterion in the selection process.[87] Bayh also said that the committee did not adopt the proposal requiring the nomination of several names because of its belief that, if the President had to choose from many possibilities, he would be put on the spot in selecting the several to be presented to Congress. The selection of his first choice, it was reasoned, would lead to a more peaceful transition.[88] "What better opportunity is there," asked Bayh, "for the people to express their wishes than through those who serve in Congress?"[89]

In contrast to the vice-presidential vacancy procedure, no opposition surfaced with respect to the procedures on presidential inability. Bayh reviewed the inability problem in detail, pointing out the unsettled questions raised by Article II, section 1, clause 6 of the Constitution and the cases of inability that had occurred since the adoption of the Constitution. Regarding the private agreement approach first entered into between Eisenhower and Nixon, Bayh observed that it could be subject to serious constitutional challenge, open the door to usurpation, and would not enjoy the confidence of the public as would a constitutional amendment. He emphasized the national consensus that had developed in support of S. J. Res. 139 and was joined in his support of the proposal by Senators Alan Bible of Nevada, Ervin, Philip A. Hart of Michigan, James Pearson of Kansas, and Leverett Saltonstall of Massachusetts, as well as by some senators who had expressed different views on the means of filling a vice-presidential vacancy, such as Church and Javits. Senator Ervin praised Section 1 of the proposal "because it would lay to rest the constitutional ghost that has been stalking to and fro in America ever since that time [i.e., John Tyler's succession in 1841]."[90] "Although we cannot foresee every eventuality that might befall our Government," said Saltonstall, "this makes adequate provision for the uninterrupted conduct of our Nation's affairs."[91] Said Bible, "I know that no single proposal will ever satisfy everyone. But I believe we have at last confronted and met the problem."[92] Concluded Senate Majority Leader Mike Mansfield of Montana: "I believe this is a momentous and historic occasion. . . . [T]he proposed joint resolution . . . is a foundation which will set well in the building which is this Republic."[93]

At the conclusion of the remarks of the nine senators who participated in the discussion, S. J. Res. 139 was passed without dissent. On the following day, however, Senator John Stennis of Mississippi said that he intended to move to reconsider the vote on the ground that it would be setting a dangerous precedent to have a proposed constitutional amendment approved by a voice vote and without at least a quorum present.[94] After a brief discussion, a roll call vote was taken, and the sixty-five senators present on September 29 all voted in favor. This marked the first time in U.S. history that a House of Congress approved a proposal dealing with presidential inability.[95] Although the year ended without any affirmative action in the House of Representatives, the momentum for a solution had clearly been established.

6

Congress Acts

The provisions of these measures have been carefully considered and are the product of
many of our finest constitutional and legal minds. . . . I urge the Congress to approve
them forthwith for submission to ratification by the States.

LYNDON B. JOHNSON, January 28, 1965[1]

The failure of the House of Representatives to take any action in 1964 is not surprising, since it was anxious not to do anything that might be interpreted as a slap at its
Speaker. With the election of President Johnson and Vice President Humphrey, this
possibility, for all practical purposes, no longer existed.* The momentum for a solution was quickly reinforced by Johnson himself in his State of the Union message of
January 4, 1965, in which he promised to "propose laws to insure the necessary continuity of leadership should the President become disabled or die."[2] Two days later
S. J. Res. 1, which was identical to S. J. Res. 139 as passed by the Senate in September
1964, was introduced by Senator Bayh and co-sponsored by more than seventy other
senators. An identical measure was introduced in the House as H. R. J. Res. 1 by

---

* A search of records of the LBJ Library in Austin, Texas, reveals that a draft letter along the lines of
the Kennedy–Johnson letter was prepared and signed by one party but for reasons unexplainable
from the papers in the relevant file it was not fully executed. Possibly the fact that the President supported S. J. Res. 139 at the time, with a different mechanism for declaring a Section 4 disability, was the
reason. Indeed, the file reflects an actual draft of a letter agreement, modified from the earlier letter
agreements, to reflect a version of the provisions in Section 4 pertaining to a determination of an involuntary inability. Whether the President's heart condition bore on it is not known. The Library's
staff was most helpful, however, in providing the author with information pursuant to his requests.
Interestingly enough, when President Johnson had his gall bladder surgery, he released a written set of
procedures descriptive of his verbal agreement with Humphrey, which were exactly the same as those
in the earlier letter agreements by Eisenhower and Kennedy. See Appendix H.

Representative Emanuel Celler, Chairman of the House Judiciary Committee. Representatives William M. McCulloch of Ohio and Richard H. Poff of Virginia, senior Republican members of the Judiciary Committee, introduced similar proposals, but with the difference that if the President on the one hand and the Vice President and Cabinet on the other disagreed on whether a President had recovered from an inability, Congress would have ten days in which to decide the issue. If it failed to do so within such period, the President would automatically resume his powers and duties. In contrast, S. J. Res. 1 and H. R. J. Res. 1 merely required Congress to decide the issue "immediately."

On January 28, 1965, President Johnson sent a special message to Congress endorsing S. J. Res. 1 and H. R. J. Res. 1 and urging prompt action on these resolutions. Said the President:

> Favorable action by the Congress on the measures here recommended will, I believe, assure the orderly continuity in the Presidency that is imperative to the success and stability of our system. Action on these measures now will allay future anxiety among our own people, and among the peoples of the world, in the event senseless tragedy or unforeseeable disability should strike again at either or both of the principal Offices of our constitutional system. If we act now, without undue delay, we shall have moved closer to achieving perfection of the great constitutional document on which the strength and success of our system have rested for nearly two centuries.[3]

ACTION IN THE SENATE

On January 29, 1965, the Senate Subcommittee on Constitutional Amendments held a one-day hearing at which Attorney General–designate Nicholas deB. Katzenbach, former Attorney General Herbert Brownell, President Lewis F. Powell of the ABA, and others testified in support of S. J. Res. 1. Katzenbach presented his interpretations of the proposed amendment in several vital areas, offered a number of suggestions, and concluded by stating:

> Senate Joint Resolution 1 represents as formidable a consensus of considered opinion on any proposed amendment to the Constitution as one is likely to find. It may not satisfy in every respect the views of all scholars and statesmen who have studied the problem . . . . But, it . . . "would responsibly meet the pressing need . . . ."[4]

In view of the widespread sentiment that the procedures should be written into the Constitution, Katzenbach stated that he saw no reason why he should insist upon the preference he had expressed in 1963 for a constitutional amendment empowering Congress to establish procedures for handling cases of inability by statute. He added, "The debate has already gone on much too long. Above all, we should be concerned with substance, not form. It is to the credit of Senate Joint Resolution 1 that it provides for immediate, self-implementing procedures that are not dependent on further congressional or Presidential action."[5]

Among the suggestions* made by Katzenbach in his testimony was the addition of language to Section 3 to ensure that the recovery procedures of Section 5 applied only to instances in which the President had been declared disabled without his consent. A President thereby would be encouraged, said Katzenbach, to declare his own inability, since he would be permitted to resume his powers and duties upon his own written declaration of recovery. Katzenbach also stated that the language used in Section 5 to the effect that "Congress will immediately decide" an issue of disagreement was so vague that more precise language should be found or appropriate provisions made in the congressional rules for the speedy handling of such an issue. He stated that he understood the language "immediately decide" to mean that "if a decision were not reached by the Congress immediately, the powers and duties of the Office would revert to the President."[6] Recognizing that there could be debate on whether Congress had acted soon enough, he added, "There is no word that you can use that completely resolves that problem. I do not know what 'immediately' means, except it means as soon as you can darn well do it."[7] On balance, however, Katzenbach thought it unwise to specify a time limit in the Constitution itself, since different circumstances might require different time periods.

Katzenbach also established important legislative history concerning the voting requirement terminology used in Sections 2 and 5, stating that it meant to him a majority and two-thirds, respectively, of the members of each House present at the time of the vote, providing there existed a quorum. Focusing on Section 5 of S. J. Res. 1, he said he assumed that, with the concurrence of the Vice President acting as President, the President could resume his powers and duties before the expiration of the two days specified. Katzenbach raised a further question concerning

* See the Report of the Senate Judiciary Committee of February 10, 1965 (Rep. No. 66), which sets forth the changes it made to S. J. Res. 1 as a result of these hearings. Its changes covered Sections 3, 4, and 5, as they appeared in S. J. Res. 1 when introduced by Senator Bayh and others in January 1965. S. J. Res. 1 became the successor to S. J. Res. 139. The committee amendments are detailed in its report at pages 36 and 37. Sections 4 and 5 would eventually be combined into one section (4) after the conference committee issued its report in June 1965. See Appendix A to this book, which tracks the development of the Twenty-Fifth Amendment from 1963 through its approval by a two-thirds vote in each House of Congress: the House on June 30, 1965, and the Senate on July 6, 1965. As reflected in a note to Appendix A, the Amendment built on proposals introduced in Congress during the period from 1958 to 1962. It benefited greatly as well from the work done by the House and Senate Judiciary committees beginning in 1955, and from the leadership of the Eisenhower administration, as detailed in Chapter 4, *supra*.

a situation in which there is disagreement about the President's recovery at a time when Congress is out of session. He suggested that additional language be considered to ensure that the Vice President could not delay the process by his failure to call Congress into session.

During the course of his testimony Katzenbach engaged in significant colloquies with Senators Bayh and Hruska on the rationale for Section 5's involving Congress in the inability process. He emphasized that Congress could not initiate but only affirm a decision that had been made in the executive branch. The inclusion of Congress, he noted, was a safeguard against usurpation by the Vice President and the Cabinet. He further stated:

I continue to believe that it would be important that that decision would be affirmed as overwhelmingly as this contemplates by elected representatives and that we would get an additional measure of security out of that. I do not say that from any lack of confidence in the integrity of the Cabinet, or in the decision that they would make. I say it as I said before, because I do believe that in that kind of a crisis, which, thank God, we have never had in this country and I hope never will, it would be so important to join ranks on both sides of the aisle and to create that kind of confidence among the public of the United States by their elected representatives joining in this very unpleasant and terribly important determination so that as we have in the past, this country could indicate that in such crisis, it can and will unite.[8]

As for the possibility of confusion and chaos if a majority but less than two-thirds of the Senate believed the President to be disabled, Katzenbach stated:

On this, it would be my hope that if that situation ever evolved, you would have 100 Senators who would agree. Because it simply becomes an impossible situation, and if it is a close question and a difficult one, it is in that situation where I think the Vice President would not act, the Cabinet would not support him, and they would want to know that they had the support, whether or not, whatever system it [was] done under, they would surely want to know they had the overwhelming support of both Houses of Congress if they were determined to act in this totally unprecedented way.[9]

Bayh then added that congressional action was the closest substitute for action by the people:

The final determination, we feel, must be made by the representatives of the people. If there were some way we could get the people themselves to make this decision, I would say more power to this. But we have found no practical way of doing this.

Katzenbach also pointed out that a Vice President acting as President had the power to remove a Cabinet officer to gain support or even to change a member in the event of a Cabinet evenly divided on the question of the President's recovery. Said Katzenbach:

> Certainly, if [the Vice President] were discharging the powers of the Presidency, he could remove a Cabinet officer. There is no question about that, Senator. He could only effectively appoint one if Congress happened to be out of session at that time.[10]

These possibilities, he argued, represented a further reason for allowing Congress to make the final determination.

On the vice-presidential vacancy feature of the proposed amendment, Katzenbach rejected the suggestion that the President's choice be limited to certain public officials because it would alter the long tradition that the President can choose his running mate. He added that a requirement of a two-thirds vote for confirmation would give too much power to the opposition party in the selection of a Vice President and possibly delay the filling of the vacancy.[11]

Following Katzenbach's testimony, Senator Hruska testified in favor of his S. J. Res. 28 and strongly urged that Congress be prohibited from substituting for the Cabinet a procedure for determining a President's inability that involved either the judicial or the legislative branch of government. He urged:

> The determination of presidential inability and its termination is obviously a factual matter. No policy is involved. The issue is simply whether a specific individual with certain physical, mental, or emotional impairments possesses the ability to continue as the Chief Executive or whether his infirmity is so serious and severe as to render him incapable of executing the duties of his office.
>
> To inject Congress into the factual question of inability would be to create a secondary impeachment procedure in which the conduct of the President would not be the test.[12]

The involvement of Congress, he said, would also delay the process, and he added:

> Obviously, such a decision must rest on the relevant and reliable facts regarding the President's physical or mental faculties. It must be divorced from any thoughts of political advantage, personal prejudice, or other extraneous factors. Those possessing such firsthand information about the Chief Executive, or most accessible to it on a personal basis, are found within the executive branch and not elsewhere.[13]

Hruska further noted that difficulties would be encountered in construing the term "immediately" in Section 5. It could be interpreted, he said, so as to limit debate in Congress, as well as to preclude hearings seeking evidence with regard to a disagreement issue. Earlier Katzenbach had testified that he felt the expression was broad enough to permit reasonable debate, and to enable Congress to inquire of psychiatrists and physicians and of members of the President's family and of the Cabinet.[14]

Speaking on behalf of the Committee for Economic Development (CED), Marion B. Folsom, who had served as Secretary of Health, Education and Welfare under President Eisenhower, urged that a vice-presidential nominee be subject to confirmation by a joint session of Congress. He said that such a procedure would correspond to the voting strength of each state in the Electoral College, would be more expeditious, and would avoid the difficulties that would arise if the House and Senate disagreed.[15] He also suggested that the Cabinet initiate the question of inability and that the Vice President's role be limited to one of concurrence. Folsom's reasoning was that a Vice President would be most reluctant to initiate such a question, "no matter how urgent or obvious the necessity." Folsom stated that the Vice President should "never be forced to accept authority under conditions permitting unfair charges of usurpation against him, nor should his natural feelings of deference and loyalty to a disabled Chief Executive be allowed to absolve him from his proper responsibility."[16] Folsom also expressed the CED's opposition to the "such other body" provision of Section 5 on the ground of separation of powers and said that the Cabinet, through its knowledge of major issues and association with the President, was best situated to judge a case of presidential inability. Accordingly, in the view of the CED the issue of termination of an inability should be decided by the Cabinet alone, subject only to presidential concurrence. Folsom noted that S. J. Res. 1 allowed for the possibility of the President's terminating his inability despite the contrary judgment of the Vice President, the entire Cabinet, and the unanimous vote of the Senate, since all he needed was a one-third vote of either House.[17] In his concluding remarks, Folsom quoted the following paragraph from the CED's policy statement concerning the disadvantage of bringing Congress into the picture:

> [A] Congress with a hostile two-thirds majority such as existed during the Presidency of Andrew Johnson . . . could be used to deprive the President of his powers and duties, without resorting to the circumscribed impeachment procedures.[18]

The CED concluded therefore that Congress should play no role in the area of presidential inability.

In his testimony before the subcommittee, Brownell expressed the view that public opinion and the patriotism of our public officials would assure the proper and speedy application of the amendment. "I think our public officials always rise to their best heights at a time of crisis . . . ," he said, and "with the overwhelming backing of public opinion for a solution of any crisis to having an orderly government, the Congress could be counted upon . . . to do its part."[19] He added that "the men who are involved here, both in the executive branch and the congressional branch, in time of crisis will act not as rogues and rascals, but as patriotic Americans, as they always do and have done in time of crisis . . . ."[20] Specifically, Brownell said that the use of separate sessions of each House would speed consideration and eliminate the procedural difficulties that might arise with a joint session. He also regarded the term "immediately" as sufficient, since, if the extraordinary case of a disagreement occurred, an overwhelming opinion on one side or the other would demand immediate action. He expressed the view that a case of disagreement would be one in which the President "was mentally unbalanced," which "would be very obvious to everyone when you consider the white heat of publicity that beats upon the White House."[21] Congressional involvement, he said, would promote "greater confidence on the part of the public that the right solution had been reached" and would provide "safeguards against cabals, against charges, however ridiculous they might be, that certain public officials within the executive branch were acting for personal selfish gains rather than for the public interest."[22]

Among other witnesses who testified was Martin Taylor, who continued to oppose S. J. Res. 1 and to support the broad inability language of S. J. Res. 35.* "Everyone," he said, approved of the vice-presidential vacancy provision of S. J. Res. 1, but other features of the amendment were objectionable. Criticizing the machinery for resolving a disagreement issue, Taylor said:

> First, the President has to transmit his own conviction that he is well. Then the Vice President has to say, "No, I do not agree with you, you are not well." Then the Vice President has to have a talk with a majority of the members of the Cabinet. They do not agree. Then he has to agree with this other body created by statute, and they do not agree. Meanwhile, airplanes are flying over the Potomac. Then Congress, with no other guide as to urgency, imminence, or time, has to meet and make this executive decision that three other tribunals and individuals have been unable to make.[23]

Taylor also raised questions about the effect of the "such other body" provision. His so doing established the important legislative history that if Congress created another body, that body would replace the Cabinet in the determination of a President's inability.[24] Prophetically, Taylor, who was the last witness to testify at

---

* Others who testified were Representative Willard S. Curtin of Pennsylvania, who favored a presidential inability commission headed by the Chief Justice; Justice Michael Musmanno of the Pennsylvania Supreme Court, who suggested that the term "forthwith" be substituted for "immediately" in Section 5 and that the Vice President be transferred from the legislative to the executive branch; Professor Robert Deasy, who favored the ad hoc letter arrangement of Eisenhower and the election of a second Vice President; and Senator Jack Miller of Iowa, who recommended that the President be required to nominate a person of his own party for Vice President and that the nomination be confirmed by a joint session.

the one-day hearing, concluded, "Instead of arguing your questions, let me congratulate you [Bayh] on your success to this point and hope that you have further success."[25]

Three days later the subcommittee unanimously approved S. J. Res. 1 and reported it to the full Judiciary Committee, where it was approved on February 10, 1965, with amendments.[26] In individual views accompanying the committee's report, Senator Hruska suggested that Section 5 be amended by the full Senate to enlarge the two-day period in which to challenge a President's declaration of recovery. He said that the two-day period did not take into account the fact that Cabinet members often travel and that there may be long periods of time during which they do not observe and meet with the President.

Among the amendments made by the full Judiciary Committee was the specification in Section 3 of a requirement that a declaration of inability be sent to the Speaker of the House and the President pro tempore. S. J. Res. 139 as passed by the Senate, and S. J. Res. 1 as introduced, had included no public notice to Congress in Section 3, simply stating that "if the President declares in writing that he is unable to discharge the powers and duties of his office, such powers and duties shall be discharged by the Vice President as Acting President." Concern was expressed in committee over the absence of a provision for the transmittal of a declaration of inability. As Hruska speculated, a Vice President might produce a letter from the President at a critical point in history, and a question could be raised whether the letter actually was genuine.[27]

Similarly, while Sections 4 and 5 provided that declarations of inability and recovery be sent to "Congress," the committee decided instead that the transmittal should be to the Speaker and the President pro tempore. It felt that notice to these officials, even if they were not in their "offices" at the time of transmittal, would guarantee "notice to the entire country" and would provide a basis for Congress's being called into session, if then out of session, to consider a disagreement issue. With this change, the committee believed that Congress would be empowered to reconvene in special session and that the presiding officers would then be required to call a special session to consider a Section 5 issue, if Congress were also in recess. The committee noted, however, that nothing would limit the President's power under Article II, section 3 of the Constitution to call a special session.

Another change made by the committee was to substitute the expression "principal officers of the executive departments" for "heads of the executive departments." This change was meant to clarify that only those who are members of the Cabinet would be permitted to participate in any decision regarding inability, as well as conform the terminology to that used in Article II, section 2, clause 1 of the Constitution.* In

---

* "[The President] may require the Opinion, in writing, of the principal Officer in each of the executive Departments . . . ."

response to the concern expressed by Senator Robert F. Kennedy of New York over a possible Cabinet coup, Judiciary Committee Chairman James O. Eastland of Mississippi moved unsuccessfully to require a vote of two-thirds of the Cabinet.[28]

Finally, the "immediately decide" language of Section 5 was changed to "immediately proceed to decide." The committee stated that the new expression would connote great urgency while at the same time allowing Congress "to collect all necessary evidence and to participate in the debate needed to make a considered judgment."[29] The committee opposed a specific time limitation "because of the complexities involved in determining different types of disability" but noted that, "the proceedings in the Congress prescribed in Section 5 would be pursued under rules prescribed, or to be prescribed, by the Congress itself."[30]

A little more than a week later, on February 19, 1965, S. J. Res. 1 was debated in the Senate. There was almost unanimous agreement on the need for a constitutional amendment to address the inability and vice-presidential vacancy problems, but Senator Allen J. Ellender of Louisiana expressed the view that Article II gave Congress the power to legislate all the procedures of S. J. Res. 1 except the method of selecting a new Vice President.[31] Disagreeing, Bayh reflected the dominant view when he said, "Dealing with the problem in statutory form alone would create all the uncertainty of a court test of the constitutionality of the statute. That, we believe, should be avoided, if at all possible."[32]

One area in which there was substantial disagreement during the debate was whether the amendment should set forth specific procedures for handling a case of inability, as did S. J. Res. 1, or merely empower Congress to enact procedures by legislation, as S. J. Res. 35 had done. Senator Everett M. Dirksen of Illinois, a leading proponent of the latter approach, argued that "it has been pretty much of a rule in our constitutional history that we do not legislate in the Constitution. We try to keep the language simple. We . . . offer some latitude for statutory implementation thereafter, depending upon the events and circumstances that might arise."[33]

Therefore, Dirksen offered a substitute amendment providing: "The commencement and termination of any inability shall be determined by such method as Congress may by law provide."[34] He noted that, under his proposal, Congress could deal with such situations as the simultaneous inabilities of both the President and the Vice President as well as the inability of either of them. Dirksen observed that S. J. Res. 1 did not treat the inability of a Vice President or an Acting President, and if there were no Vice President, the inability procedures for a President could not be invoked. He also raised questions about a situation when Congress was not in session. He further stated that S. J. Res. 1 was not clear on whether the recovery mechanism of Section 5 applied to instances in which the President had declared his own inability under Section 3, whether under Section 5 the President had to wait two days to see if the Vice President and Cabinet challenged his declaration of recovery, and how a President who was physically unable to write or sign his name would make a declaration of inability under Section 3. "My interest," concluded Dirksen, "is that there be no ambiguities and no rigidities written into the Constitution that could be modified only by another constitutional amendment."[35]

Senator Ervin opposed Dirksen's substitute amendment, declaring that it "totally ignores one of the crucial questions which has brought this matter to the floor of the Senate. That is the fact that vacancies occur in the office of Vice President." He added that the Dirksen proposal "would place dangerous power in the hands of Congress," since it would give Congress a new power over the President by which "any time that power-hungry men in Congress were willing to go to the extremes that men were willing to go to in those days [i.e., when the Radical Republicans sought to remove President Andrew Johnson], they could take charge of the Presidency."[36] Only if specifics were set out in the Constitution, said Ervin, would the presidency be sufficiently protected. Ervin observed, "[W]hen we try to protect somebody, we had better write specifics into the Constitution if we do not want to run the risk of converting the United States into what I would call a banana republic."[37] Senator Bayh, agreeing with Ervin, pointed out that the Constitution was quite specific in its provisions for the election and impeachment of the President. If this specificity were not maintained for the case of inability, Bayh argued, there would be a violation of the principle of separation of powers, and the state legislatures might hesitate to ratify a general amendment. Finally, unless the amendment were specific, Congress might never settle on procedures for determining inability since interest in the subject would wane once the amendment had been ratified. In answer to Dirksen's technical objections to S. J. Res. 1, Bayh observed that the legislative history was quite clear on the meaning and intent of Sections 3, 4, and 5,[38] and that Section 5 applied only to declarations of inability by a Vice President and Cabinet under Section 4. At the conclusion of this debate, a vote was taken on the Dirksen substitute amendment, and it was defeated 60 to 12.

Senator Strom Thurmond of South Carolina then proposed an amendment to empower the most recent Electoral College to fill a vacancy in the vice presidency. He argued that the College had the advantage of retaining the general election process, and that its use would generate "a greater degree of public confidence and a broader base of support for the individual chosen." In response to the objections that this method would be time-consuming and would not allow for hearings on the qualifications of a candidate, Thurmond said that the College could act within a month and that formal hearings were not necessary since the views of any serious candidate would be well known. Thurmond added that the electors most likely would select the person desired by the President.[39] In reply, Bayh argued that the people of the country "would wonder what in the world was being perpetrated upon them if we brought in members of the Electoral College whom they did not know from Adam."[40] He said that the people would accept a judgment made by Congress. Thurmond's proposal was rejected by voice vote.

Senator Hruska then offered his promised amendment to change from two to seven the number of days the President might be required to wait before resuming his powers and duties after his declaration of recovery. Said Hruska:

> In these days when much traveling is done by members of our Cabinet, and when on occasion the Vice President also travels frequently, if there would be . . . a declaration by the President in the absence of these parties the 48-hour period would obviously prove to be much too small . . . .
>
> I feel that 7 days would be an appropriate and adequate time for the members of the Cabinet to . . . inform themselves of the actual condition of the President, perhaps visit with him, perhaps visit with his personal physician.[41]

The amendment was accepted.[42]

Senator John O. Pastore of Rhode Island moved to amend Section 5 of S. J. Res. 1 to require Congress to decide an inability disagreement without transacting any other business in the interim. "[W]e ought to stay here," said Pastore, "until we decide that question, even if we must sit around the clock, or around the calendar, because this problem involves the Presidency of the United States."[43] Pastore noted that a filibuster or hearings could unduly delay a decision. Senators Bayh, Hruska, and Ervin opposed Pastore's suggestion, arguing that such a restriction would be unwise as evidence might have to be taken in committee or the President examined before a decision could be reached. Said Hruska:

> Suppose the question should relate to the mental ability of the President. An examination would be necessary. Psychiatrists would not be able to go into the President's office, look him over, and say, "The man is insane," or, "the man is not insane." They would need time in which to observe and conduct tests. Congress would need time to hear the reasons why the members of the Cabinet had said, "Mr. President, you are not able to resume the duties and powers of your office."[44]

Bayh and Hruska argued that the use of the word "immediately," which also appeared in the Twelfth Amendment, would connote the needed urgency, and Hruska added that while hearings were proceeding, Congress would and should be free to deal with any other urgent situation. Unpersuaded, Pastore retorted, "I can conceive of nothing more important to the people of our country and the peace of the world than to determine the question as to who is the President of the United States."[45] In the course of the debate Senator Philip Hart suggested that a time limit such as three days might be appropriate, to which Ervin replied, "If we cannot trust Members of the Senate and House to exercise intelligence and patriotism in a time of national crisis, we might as well not do anything." He then declared, "This is essentially a subject . . . which will require the taking of testimony. We cannot put a time limit on the search for truth, especially when it concerns the intelligence of the President."[46]

As the Senate debated Pastore's proposal, Senator Ross Bass of Tennessee offered an amendment adding the word "immediately" to Section 2 so that whenever a vacancy arose in the vice presidency and the President nominated a replacement, Congress would be required to act with dispatch.[47] Without such a direction, Bass feared, Congress might delay filling a vacancy to keep the Speaker first in line of succession, Said Bass: "If Vice President Nixon had succeeded to the Office of the Presidency, his nomination [of a new Vice President], from my own experience in the House, would have been delayed and stalled, because Members of the House had a deep respect for [then-Speaker] Sam Rayburn."[48] The possibility of delay would be especially real, said Bass, when Congress was controlled by the opposition party. Bayh responded, "I have more faith in the Congress acting in an emergency in the white heat of publicity, with the American people looking on. The last thing Congress would dare to do would be to become involved in a purely political move."[49]

And Ervin, referring to the possibility that Congress might stall to keep the Speaker first in the line of succession, remarked, "God help this Nation if we ever get a House of Representatives, or a Senate, which will wait for a President to die so someone whom they love more than their country will succeed to the Presidency."[50]

Bayh and Hruska argued that under Bass's proposal Congress might be required to act more quickly than the circumstances required. Said Bayh, "I do not believe we need to grind everything to a halt to decide who the Vice President is."[51] Both senators felt that the urgency was greater when the President's recovery from an inability was at issue, hence the use of the word "immediately" in Section 5 and not in Section 2. Hruska remarked that the use of "immediately" in Section 2 would raise such questions as: "Does it mean that there will be no hearings? Does it mean that there will be no debate? Does it mean that there will be no consideration of any kind to determine what kind of person the nominee is?"[52]

Following the discussion, both the Bass and Pastore proposals were rejected by voice votes. Initially, Bayh had been willing to accept Pastore's amendment, but he rejected the change when he realized that if it should be accepted, the entire proposed amendment would likely be sent back to committee for further study.* As Bayh said, "Later, thinking it over, I was to see that point as a turning point. If I had given ground on the Pastore amendment, all would have been lost: the resolution would have gone back to committee and might never have seen the light of the Senate Chamber again."[53]

---

* This was because of the view that each provision of a constitutional amendment should first be considered in committee.

After the rejection of these proposals, Bayh proceeded to clarify the legislative intent behind various provisions of the amendment. As for definitions of the words "inability" and "unable" as used in Sections 4 and 5, he said, "[They] refer to an impairment of the President's faculties, [and] mean that he is unable either to make or communicate his decisions as to his own competency to execute the powers and duties of his office." Added Bayh, "[We] are not dealing with an unpopular decision that must be made in time of trial and which might render the President unpopular."[54] Bayh also stated his interpretation of the meaning of the expression "heads of the executive departments," used in Sections 3, 4, and 5, and discussed the effect of a Cabinet vacancy. It also was made clear that the Vice President would continue to serve as Acting President during the seven-day challenge period mentioned in Section 5, since there likely would be a serious question about the President's mental capacity; however, the Vice President could agree to the President's resuming his powers and duties immediately upon his declaration of recovery. Bayh also stated that a Vice President acting as President could replace a Cabinet member who died or resigned. A usurping Vice President, Bayh said, would be checked by Section 5, which enabled the President to refer the issue to Congress.

At the conclusion of this legislative history-making, the Senate unanimously approved S. J. Res. 1, as amended, by a vote of 72 to 0.[55]

ACTION IN THE HOUSE

As the Senate was preparing to debate S. J. Res. 1, the full House Judiciary Committee, on February 9, 1965, commenced hearings on H. R. J. Res. 1 and more than thirty proposals dealing with presidential inability and vice-presidential vacancy. At the outset, Representative William M. McCulloch of Ohio, the ranking Republican committee member, expressed his strong support for a provision requiring congressional action within a period of ten days on a challenge to a President's declaration of recovery, stating, "For, right or wrong, we are providing a means for taking away the President's office. The burden should thereby be placed upon the Vice President and, indirectly, the Congress to have the issue decided without unnecessary delay."[56] McCulloch said that he was influenced by the fact that Congress at times has been hostile to the President, and at times the Vice President and President have not been on friendly terms. Without a time limitation, he feared, Congress might delay reaching a decision or a Vice President acting as President might fail to reconvene an adjourned Congress.

Considerable discussion followed at these hearings on the advisability of a time provision. Brownell, Powell, Katzenbach, and Bayh all expressed their preference for no such provision, believing that Congress would act quickly if a disagreement occurred. Brownell thought that the possibility of a disagreement was remote but felt that if such a situation should arise, "public opinion would force speedy action, as speedy as was wise under the circumstances, assuming that Congress was obviously filibustering or delaying for some non-public reason . . . ."[57] He added, "I have always found in my experience that men under the pressure of national or international crises do act responsibly, but if the occasion arose when they didn't, I think public opinion would force them to do it, or [they would] destroy their usefulness as public officials thereafter."[58] However, Brownell and Powell indicated that the adoption of a time provision would do no harm to the ABA consensus. Said Katzenbach, "It is almost impossible for me to envision circumstances where there would, in fact, be delay. For a Vice President to take those steps, [he] would really have to be assured of quick and overwhelming support in the Congress."[59] Bayh noted that "[i]t might well take longer for Congress [to] make a determination in one type of illness than another type of illness. The type of testimony that would be involved to fully disclose to the Members of Congress the condition of the President might take longer in one type of illness than another . . . ."[60] Representative Poff added later in the hearings that he and other proponents of the time provision were "concerned primarily that a filibuster might develop in the other body which might not be altogether pure in its motivation."[61]

In addition to their focus on the recovery procedures of Section 5, the hearings before the House Judiciary Committee are particularly significant for the record made on the meaning and intent of the amendment.* At the hearings Katzenbach again urged that there be "a provision which would clearly enable the President to terminate immediately any period of inability he has voluntarily declared."[62] He said that a President might be hesitant to declare his own inability if the procedures of Section 5 applied to a voluntary declaration. Bayh initially opposed such a provision, stating:

> Suppose, if you will, that such language were added. A President voluntarily divests himself of his powers and duties. Then, when he believes he is fit, he immediately resumes them. Then, pursuant to section 4 of the proposal, the Vice President and majority of the Cabinet declare the President really isn't fit at all. The Vice President immediately resumes the powers and duties of the Presidency. Then, under section 5, the President again declares no inability exists. The Vice President and Cabinet, under section 5, challenge the President's declaration again. Then Congress decides in favor of the President, who immediately resumes the powers and duties again. Here, in the space of a few days, the Nation would have the powers and duties of the Presidency change hands three times. The turmoil this would create is almost unimaginable. As now written, Senate Joint Resolution 1 and House Joint Resolution 1 would keep the transfer of these awesome

---

* In that connection, the testimony of Bayh and Brownell sheds significant light on the legislative history.

powers and duties to an irreducible minimum, thereby enabling as smooth a transition of executive power as possible in difficult circumstances.[63]

A number of witnesses suggested that the amendment also deal with such cases as the simultaneous inabilities of the President and Vice President, the inability of a President when there is no Vice President, the inability of an Acting President, and dual vacancies.[64] With respect to these suggestions, Brownell expressed the dominant view when he said of the amendment, "I believe it covers, in consonance with the basic constitutional principles, at least 90 percent of the cases we could reasonably foresee."[65]

Representative Charles McC. Mathias Jr. of Maryland was particularly strong in his opposition to granting the President power to nominate a Vice President. He felt such a power was undemocratic and autocratic in nature and would be used to select men of weak caliber for the office. Contrasting the presidential candidate's role at the nominating convention, Mathias said, "The man he chooses to run with him will be chosen from motives which may be substantially different from those of the incumbent President who is picking his official heir and successor."[66] "A man who sat in the White House," said Mathias, "might well feel he would appear greater on the pages of history if his Vice President were a weak and pallid kind of an individual . . . ."[67] The presidential candidate, on the other hand, has to be concerned about the prospect of his ticket's winning in the election. Mathias also questioned whether Congress would be even reasonably critical of a President's choice that followed in the shadow of a tragedy.[68]

In response to Mathias's position, Bayh argued that a President acting in the spotlight of public opinion would be motivated by the desire "to get the very best possible man he could get for the job . . . ." If a "namby-pamby person" were sent to Congress, he said, "Congress wouldn't go along."[69] On the question of time limits for congressional action on the nominee, Bayh said that it would be better to omit them and "trust the President and Congress to use their good judgment as to what would be reasonable." He added, "There would be some times . . . when a name would be submitted for which there would be patent reasons for a tremendous amount of debate. Other times a name might be submitted and would be readily acceptable and there would be little reason for a prolonged debate and everyone would recognize this."[70]

With respect to Mathias's preference for congressional selection of the Vice President, Bayh remarked that "we [are] going to proliferate further the executive branch and try to set up someone who would be competing with the President unless we gave the President primary responsibility of picking the man with whom he could work."[71] Poff suggested that, under a system of congressional selection, the leadership of the majority party would actually decide in caucus, so that this approach would not be more democratic.[72]

Following the conclusion of these hearings, H. R. J. Res. 1 was approved on March 24, 1965,* with the following changes.[73] Omitted language is enclosed in brackets and new matter is italicized.

SECTION 1. In case of the removal of the President from office or of his death or resignation, the Vice President shall become President.

SECTION 2. Whenever there is a vacancy in the office of the Vice President, the President shall nominate a Vice President who shall take office upon confirmation by a majority vote of both Houses of Congress.

SECTION 3. [If the President declares in writing] *Whenever the President transmits to the President pro tempore of the Senate and the Speaker of the House of Representatives his written declaration* that he is unable to discharge the powers and duties of his office, *and until he transmits a written declaration to the contrary,* such powers and duties shall be discharged by the Vice President as Acting President.

SEC. 4. [If the President does not so declare, and the Vice President with the written concurrence of a majority of the heads of the executive departments or such other body as Congress may by law provide, transmits to the Congress his] *Whenever the Vice President and a majority of the principal officers of the executive departments, or such other body as Congress may by law provide, transmit to the President pro tempore of the Senate and the Speaker of the House of Representatives their* written declaration that the President is unable to discharge the powers and duties of his office, the Vice President shall immediately assume the powers and duties of the office as Acting President.

[SEC. 5.] *Thereafter,* when[ever] the President transmits to the [Congress] *President pro tempore of the Senate and the Speaker of the House of Representatives* his written declaration that no inability exists, he shall resume the powers and duties of his office unless the Vice President, [with the written concurrence of a majority of the heads of the executive departments or such other body as Congress may by law provide, transmits within two days to the Congress his] *and a majority of the principal officers of the executive departments, or such other body as Congress may by law provide, transmit within two days to the President pro tempore of the Senate and the Speaker of the House of Representatives their* written declaration that the President is unable to discharge the powers and duties of his office. Thereupon Congress shall [immediately] decide the issue, *immediately assembling for that purpose if not in session.* If the Congress, *within ten days*

---

* Dissenting views were expressed by Representatives J. Edward Hutchinson of Michigan and Charles McC. Mathias of Maryland. House Comm. on the Judiciary, Report on Presidential Inability and Vacancies in the Office of Vice President, H. R. Rep. No. 203, 89th Cong., 1st Sess. 17–23 (1965).

> *after the receipt of the written declaration of the Vice President and a majority*
> *of the principal officers of the executive departments, or such other body as*
> *Congress may by law provide,* determines by two-thirds vote of both Houses
> that the President is unable to discharge the powers and duties of the office,
> the Vice President shall continue to discharge the same as Acting President;
> otherwise the President shall resume the powers and duties of his office.

Thus, the ten-day time limitation advocated by Poff and McCulloch was adopted, and language was added requiring Congress to assemble immediately, if not already in session, to pass on a disagreement issue. The committee refused to change the two-day provision of Section 5 relating to the President's resumption of his powers and duties after a declaration of recovery. Section 3 was clarified, as Katzenbach had suggested, to permit the President, in a case when he had voluntarily declared his own inability, to resume his powers and duties upon his declaration of recovery without having that declaration subject to the challenge procedures of Section 5. In order to emphasize this intent, the substance of Section 5 was placed in Section 4, which related solely to cases in which presidential inability had been declared by the Vice President and Cabinet (or such other body established by law). Certain other changes made earlier by the Senate Judiciary Committee also were adopted.[74]

Despite its approval by the House Judiciary Committee, H. R. J. Res. 1 faced criticism in the House Rules Committee.[75] Among the critics were Representative William Colmer of Mississippi, who expressed his dislike of the method of declaring a President disabled because it might encourage a coup headed by the Vice President; and Representative James J. Delaney of New York, who preferred the elective process to fill a vacancy in the vice presidency. Supporters of the amendment prevailed, however, and on March 31, by a vote of 6 to 4, the Rules Committee cleared the proposal for consideration by the full House.

That consideration came on April 13, 1965. In his opening remarks, Representative Emanuel Celler of New York, chairman of the House Judiciary Committee, observed that "[e]veryone will agree that amending . . . the charter . . . of our Nation is not a task to be undertaken lightly. Today, however, we are faced with filling a gap which has existed since our beginnings [i.e., presidential inability], and this gap becomes more threatening as the complexity of the domestic and foreign policy grows."[76] Celler noted that the proposal did not meet every conceivable contingency but rather "[f]oreseen contingencies," especially the "practical human problems with reference to Presidential inability."[77]

During the House debates Representatives Celler, McCulloch, Poff, and others forcefully urged the adoption of H. R. J. Res. 1, as amended. They repeatedly underscored the need for the constitutional amendment and argued that the proposal represented as good a solution as could be found to the problems of presidential inability and vice-presidential vacancy. Said Celler:

This is by no means . . . a perfect bill. No bill can be perfect . . . The world
of actuality permits us to attain no perfection . . . But nonetheless, this bill
has a minimum of drawbacks. It is [a] well-rounded, sensible, and efficient
approach toward a solution of a perplexing problem—a problem that has
baffled us for over 100 years.[78]

Quoting Walter Lippmann, Celler added, " 'It is a great deal better than an endless
search for the absolutely perfect solution, which will never be found and, indeed,
is not necessary.' "[79]

Representative McCulloch stated:

We must provide the means for an orderly transition of Executive power in
a manner that respects the separation of powers doctrine, and maintains
the safeguards of our traditional checks and balances. I believe that House
Joint Resolution 1, as amended . . . answers these needs, and will undoubtedly correct the shortcomings of the Constitution with respect to presidential inability and succession.[80]

Poff observed that to proceed by way of statute rather than constitutional amendment would invite a court test of the constitutionality of the legislation at the worst
possible time—namely, when the President became disabled or asserted his recovery from an inability.[81]

House Minority Leader Gerald R. Ford of Michigan also gave his support for
the proposal, noting that the nation had been without a Vice President sixteen
times and that the proposal would assure "a clear-cut method of action to result in
proper succession."[82] Also supporting the proposal was Representative Peter W.
Rodino of New Jersey, who observed that it assures an orderly presidential succession and that the "requirement of congressional confirmation [in Section 2] is
an added safeguard that only fully qualified persons of the highest character and
national stature would ever be nominated by the President."[83]

As for the specific provisions of H. R. J. Res. 1, Celler, McCulloch, and Poff
asserted that, throughout it, all doubts were resolved in favor of the President.[84]
Thus, in a case of disagreement, "[t]he burden . . . is placed upon the Vice President
and the Cabinet to prove the continuance of the disability and not on the President
who has the primary claim to the office."[85] The Vice President and the Cabinet,
reasoned Poff, were the proper people to be entrusted with the power of decision:

The Vice President, a man of the same political party, a man originally
chosen by the President, a man familiar with the President's health, a man
who knows what great decisions of state are waiting to be made, and a man
intended by the authors of the Constitution to be the President's heir at
death or upon disability, surely should participate in a decision involving
the transfer of presidential powers. The same is true of the Cabinet whose

members were appointed by the President and are closest to him physically and most loyal to him politically.[86]

If future experience should dictate the naming of another body, Poff said, Section 4 would authorize Congress to designate another body "to act with the Vice President."

Poff also noted that the so-called involuntary inability procedures of Section 4 covered such cases as when "the President by reason of some physical ailment or some sudden accident is unconscious or paralyzed and therefore unable to make or to communicate the decision to relinquish the powers of his Office," or when "the President, by reason of mental debility, is unable or unwilling to make any rational decision, including particularly the decision to stand aside."[87]

There was opposition, however, to H. R. J. Res. 1. Representatives J. Edward Hutchinson of Michigan and Basil Lee Whitener of North Carolina argued that Article II, Section 1, clause 6 of the Constitution gave Congress the power to legislate on inability, so a constitutional amendment was unnecessary.[88] Representatives Clarence J. Brown of Ohio, John D. Dingell of Michigan, James G. O'Hara of Michigan, and others felt that Section 2 was demeaning to the House of Representatives because it minimized the chances of the Speaker's succeeding to the presidency. Said Dingell:

> [T]he legislation . . . is in real effect a slap at the Members of the House of Representatives, a slap at our elected leadership, and it in effect says that the Membership of the House of Representatives and our elected leadership are not capable to succeed to the high Office of Presidency.[89]

Brown contended that the amendment would take away "from the House a constitutional right it now has to select a President" by virtue of selecting the Speaker who would be the heir apparent when there was no Vice President, and that "the man named Vice President could be an individual who was never elected to any public office."[90] He conjectured that:

> Under certain conditions and certain circumstances, a vacancy could exist in the Vice-Presidency and a President could name a billy goat as Vice President and some Congresses would approve of that nomination and that selection.[91]

Following Lyndon Johnson's succession, he said, it would have been difficult for Congress to reject anyone he chose for Vice President.

Representative Roman C. Pucinski of Illinois shared Brown's misgivings about the vice-presidential vacancy provision of Section 2, stating that it opened "the door at some future time . . . to a phenomenon which has not bothered or plagued our country heretofore; namely, the problem of palace intrigue."[92] "[I]f we permit a President to name his own Vice President," said Pucinski, "you are in effect setting up a form of dynasty where your Vice President will run for President."[93] Representative Dingell stated that Section 2 was bad legislation, since it would "permit a President to begin an orderly chain of successors through an appointive device, and to effectively deny the citizens of the Nation [the power] to decide who will serve in the highest office in the land."[94] Representative Hutchinson urged that a vice-presidential vacancy be filled automatically by some other officer of the government, such as the Speaker of the House.[95]

Despite these opposing views, a motion by Pucinski to strike Section 2 was defeated by a vote of 140 to 44,[96] and a related motion by Representative Mathias was rejected by voice vote. He had moved to substitute a new Section 2, as follows:

SEC. 2. The Congress may by law provide for the case of a vacancy in the office of Vice President and for the case of removal, death, resignation or inability both of the President and the Vice President, declare what official would then act as President and such official would act accordingly until disability be removed or a President would be elected.[97]

Repeating his criticisms from the committee hearings, Mathias said that if Section 2 remained "we shall have changed the nature of the presidency for the first time in the history of the Republic, and it will be no longer a purely elective office."[98] He asserted:

[I] am opposed to an appointive Vice President. The Presidency since the history of this Republic began has been an elective office and I think it should continue to be an elective office. I believe that we should not have an appointive Vice President who would become the heir apparent of the Presidency and potentially the President.[99]

Mathias also suggested that the analogy to the nominating conventions was inapposite, because "a presidential nominee choosing his running mate is merely presenting a running mate to the people[,] and the electability of the vice presidential candidate is a measure of the accountability of the presidential candidate."[100] He added that the presidential candidate, unlike an occupant of the White House, "will choose a man who has the strength to complement his own candidacy."[101]

Following the rejection of the Mathias proposal, Representative Arch A. Moore Jr. of West Virginia sought to amend that part of Section 4 under which the Vice President would continue to act as President during the period Congress considered a challenge to a presidential declaration of recovery.[102] Moore, John V. Lindsay of New York, and several other representatives argued that the President should resume the discharge of his powers and duties during that period. "[A]ll presumptions," Moore said, "should be in favor of the President of the United States." If the Vice President is permitted to act during this period, declared Moore, "he could resort to many manipulations that would never permit the President of the United

States . . . to present his case to the Congress of the United States."[103] He added that "[t]his could be a very indirect way to impeach a President . . . if you did not want to try him here in the Congress of the United States."[104] Moore pointed out that the President would be placed in the "position of coming here to the Congress and trying to lobby himself back into the job to which the people have elected him."[105] Representative Richard C. White of Texas agreed, stating:

> I do not believe the scepter of power should ever be removed from the President until the Congress itself . . . should so remove this power. This is consistent with our present Constitution and the proper separation of officers.[106]

In reply, Celler, McCulloch, Poff, and others argued that since the capacity of the President would have been seriously challenged by the Vice President and a majority of the Cabinet, it was the wiser and a less hazardous course to have the Vice President act during that ten-day period. "The President," said Celler, "may be as nutty as a fruitcake. He may be utterly insane."[107] Unless the Vice President served, said Rep. Rodino, the issue might never get to Congress since if the President immediately resumed his powers and duties he might immediately discharge his Cabinet before a declaration of challenge could be filed with Congress.[108] Celler said that the impeachment power could be used if the Vice President acted irresponsibly under the circumstances. "We can impeach for high crimes and misdemeanors," he said, "and these high crimes and misdemeanors can mean anything that this Congress wants it to mean."[109] Thereupon, Moore's amendment was rejected by a vote of 122 to 58.[110]

Representative H. R. Gross of Iowa then proposed an amendment requiring a roll call vote whenever Congress voted on a President's nominee for Vice President, indicating that he also would make the same proposal regarding a vote on a disagreement in the case of inability.[111] The amendment was opposed by Celler, who argued that the House and Senate could demand such a vote under their rules and that therefore the amendment was unnecessary. Gross's amendment was defeated on two votes, 102 to 92 and 130 to 115.[112]

One change successfully made on the floor of the House was an amendment offered by Representative Poff but actually suggested by Speaker John W. McCormack of Massachusetts that required Congress, if not in session, to assemble automatically within forty-eight hours after receiving a challenge from the Vice President and Cabinet to a presidential declaration of recovery.[113]

The debate concluded with Speaker McCormack's giving his full support to the measure, stating:

> I have lived for 14 months in the position of the man who, in the event of an unfortunate event happening to the occupant of the White House, under the law then would have assumed the Office of Chief Executive of our country. I can assure you, my friends and colleagues, that a matter of great concern to

me was the vacuum which existed in the subject of determining inability of the occupant of the White House, if and when that should arise. I have in my safe in my office a written agreement.* As has been well said, it is outside the law. It is an agreement between individuals. But it was the only thing that could be done under the circumstances, when we do not have a disability law in relation to the President in existence. We have made a marked contribution by this resolution, and particularly by section 3 and section 4.[114]

He added:

We cannot legislate for every human consideration that might occur in the future. All we can do is the best that we can under the circumstances. The considerations of the committee and the deliberations of the members of both parties have resolved the problem confronting us in the best manner possible, having in mind the fact that with all our strengths we have weaknesses as human beings.[115]

A vote was then taken and H. R. J. Res. 1, as amended, was approved 368 to 29.[116]

CONFERENCE COMMITTEE

In order to resolve the differences between the House and Senate versions of the amendment, a Conference Committee was appointed.† It met several times during the following weeks and was divided along House and Senate lines on whether a time limitation should be placed upon Congress in deciding a disagreement issue. The House conferees insisted on a ten-day limitation, while the Senate conferees preferred no limitation at all.

On June 23, 1965, after a two-month deadlock,‡ agreement was reached on a twenty-one-day limitation.[117] The committee accepted the language of the House version that the recipients of all inability notifications be the Speaker and President pro tempore, instead of the Speaker and "President of the Senate" who, at the time of the notice, would be the Vice President himself. In addition, the committee accepted the House version of Section 3 permitting the President, in the event of a voluntary declaration of inability, to resume his powers and duties immediately upon transmittal of his declaration of recovery to the President pro tempore and the Speaker. The committee compromised on four days as the period within

---

* See supra pp. 55–56.
† The conferees on behalf of the House were Celler, McCulloch, Poff, Byron G. Rogers of Colorado, and James C. Corman of California; and on behalf of the Senate, Bayh, Eastland, Ervin, Dirksen, and Hruska. Bayh chaired the committee.
‡ Bayh's One Heartbeat Away 279–304 presents a fascinating account of the attempts at a resolution during that period and the key role played by Lewis F. Powell Jr.

which the Vice President and Cabinet could challenge a President's declaration of recovery, when they had made the original inability determination. It also agreed to accept the provision in the House version requiring Congress to convene within forty-eight hours, if not then in session, to settle a disagreement.

The expression "the Vice President and a majority of the principal officers of the executive departments, or such other body as Congress may by law provide" was changed to "the Vice President and a majority of either the principal officers of the executive departments or of such other body as Congress may by law provide." This change was made at the suggestion of Senator Hruska to ensure that if Congress in the future designated another body to replace the Cabinet, that body would be required to act with the Vice President.[118]

The conference report was passed by voice vote in the House of Representatives on June 30, 1965, after Poff explained its principal recommendations. He gave this explanation for the time limitation insisted upon by the House of Representatives:

> No one should assume that House insistence upon a time limit was a criticism of the Senate. It is true that the rules of the other body permit unlimited debate and a small minority of Senators hostile to the President and loyal to the Vice President as Acting President could, in the absence of a time limit, make a great deal of public mischief at a most critical time in the life of the Nation. It is no less true that such mischief could be wrought by a small dedicated band of enemies of the President in the House. By tedious invocation of the technical rules of procedure, that little band could frustrate action on the Vice President's challenge for a protracted period of time, during which the Vice President would continue to serve as Acting President and the President, knocking on his own door for readmission, would be kept standing outside. If this little band happened to be one more than half the membership of the House, their task would be much easier, because they could simply meet and adjourn every third day without any action at all. Thus, more than half but less than two-thirds could effectively accomplish by inaction the same thing it would take two-thirds to accomplish by vote if there is no time limit in the Constitution. The conference committee understood this danger, and that is why the 21-day provision is in the conference report.[119]

The report was considered in the Senate later that same day. Senators Robert F. Kennedy of New York and Eugene J. McCarthy of Minnesota expressed reservations about the method prescribed for determining inability. Senator Kennedy said a President might discharge his Cabinet. A conflict could arise, he said, on

> whether the President had, in fact, fired the Cabinet at the time they had met and decided to put in a new President. What we could end up with, in effect, would be the spectacle of having two Presidents both claiming the

right to exercise the powers and duties of the Presidency, and perhaps two sets of Cabinet officers both claiming the right to act.[120]

Kennedy elaborated:

> A Cabinet decides that a President was disabled. The President fires the Cabinet. The members of the Cabinet say they did not receive notice that they were fired until after they had declared the President disabled. The President says he fired them first. If the Congress is in recess, the President appoints another Cabinet, or else he says the Deputies and Under Secretaries are now the Cabinet. There would be two Presidents and two Cabinets. There would be a conflict as to which ones were the members of the Cabinet and as to whether the members of the first Cabinet had made the decision before or after they were fired by the President.[121]

Senator McCarthy added that the amendment was unclear on whether the members of the Cabinet had to be confirmed by the Senate before they could pass on a question of inability. He said that, if it were not for the fact that under Section 4 Congress could designate a body other than the Cabinet, he could not support the amendment.[122] This grant of power to Congress also lessened Kennedy's concern about a coup, which he felt to be a distinct possibility with the Cabinet in the picture.

Senator Albert Gore of Tennessee, however, objected to the wording of Section 4, arguing that it would permit the Vice President to choose between the Cabinet and the other body created by Congress. He said that the use of the expression "either/or" put the two groups on a par.*[123] Senator Bayh, alluding to the abundance of legislative history on the point, said that, under the proposed amendment, the Cabinet would have the responsibility unless Congress passed a law appointing another body. In that event, the "newly created body and not the Cabinet would act with the Vice President."[124] Bayh noted that if a Vice President believed that the President was disabled but the Cabinet refused to concur in that judgment, Congress could, if it agreed with the Vice President, establish another body to function with the Vice President. Senator Jacob Javits remarked that if the power to establish another body were exercised, he would interpret it "to give exclusivity to the other body," since it would be "completely contrary to the purpose of Congress to create two bodies which could compete with one another."[125] Senator John Sherman Cooper of Kentucky said "it would be unreasonable to follow any other position."[126] "[T]he intent of the amendment," said Gore, "is not supported by the

---

* The author called this unintended, possible construction to the attention of staff members of the House and Senate Judiciary Committees shortly after the conference report was issued, but it was too late then for any additional language changes to be made.

language of the amendment."[127] Gore then sought and obtained postponement of further discussion in order to study the question in greater detail.

On Tuesday, July 6, 1965, the measure again came up for consideration in the Senate. Senator Gore reiterated his objection to the proposed amendment because of the "either/or" expression and urged that the proposal be returned to committee. By virtue of this wording in Section 4, argued Gore, "a Vice President would be in a position to 'shop around' for support of his view that the President is not able to discharge the duties of his office." He added that

> if the identity of the determining authority should be subject to conflicting interpretations, this Nation could undergo the potentially disastrous spectacle of competing claims to the power of the Presidency of the United States.[128]

As for Javits's point about exclusivity, Gore stated that he knew of no rule "which provides or could provide that a legislative enactment would take precedence over an express provision of the U. S. Constitution . . . ."[129] Senator McCarthy remarked that

> the word "either" appears to have been dropped into the amendment almost by inadvertence. It was not used as a result of carefully considered judgment. It is not a word that was weighed or was subject to any prolonged discussion in conference.[130]

Senator Bayh observed that

> [a]s a result of the insight and the perseverance of the Senator from Tennessee, we have now written a record of legislative intent, as long as our arms, to the effect that we desire only one body to act on the subject.[131]

Senator Bayh said the language was clear that if Congress designated another body, that body would supersede the Cabinet. Senator Dirksen agreed and said that although he could not imagine a Vice President shopping around, if a Vice President did so, the people would not tolerate it and his political future would be ruined.[132] Dirksen noted:

> [L]anguage is not absolute. . . . [I]nterpretations of all kinds can be placed upon language. . . . Fashioning language to do what we have in mind, particularly when we are subject to the requirement of compression for constitutional amendment purposes, is certainly not an easy undertaking.[133]

He added, "I believe we have done a reasonably worthwhile job insofar as the feeble attributes of the language can accomplish it."[134] Senator Ervin expressed the view that, even if Senator Gore's interpretation were correct, it "would improve, instead of hurt, the amendment by making it more flexible,"[135] and he observed that "the

1965. West Virginia initially sought to ratify the Amendment without the provisions on presidential inability. In Colorado, a snarl developed in July 1965 over whether the Amendment was properly before a special session of the legislature. It nonetheless was voted on, receiving slightly less than the two-thirds vote required by the state's constitution.* The following February, the Colorado legislature ratified by more than a two-thirds vote, but only after an effective campaign in response to an attack against the Amendment by the *Denver Post* and a few members of the Colorado legislature. Senator L. T. Skiffington objected to Section 2 of the Amendment on the ground that it failed to include some qualification, such as a specified number of years of congressional service, as a requirement for appointment as a replacement Vice President. With respect to the inability provisions, he contended that the President could have an unnecessarily difficult time resuming his powers and duties after his recovery. In the Colorado General Assembly, Representative John Carroll led an attack on the Amendment, arguing that it left unclear exactly who would participate with the Vice President in an inability decision and that it set the stage for a constitutional *coup d'état*. He also criticized the twenty-one-day provision of Section 4, stating, "During this time, no one would know who is president, and one president could be countermanding orders given by the other." He added: ". . . Who would order the armed forces into combat? Which president would the armed forces obey?"†

In Alabama the Amendment's proponents did not attempt a vote in 1965, fearing that it might not be ratified and that such a failure could become a states' rights issue and hurt legislative efforts elsewhere.‡ Alabama later ratified the Amendment— on March 14, 1967, a few weeks after it had been added to the Constitution.

---

* Whether such an extraordinary vote requirement is constitutional is a point of contention. Since the Constitution prescribes no vote for ratification, it has been argued that a simple majority is all that is required. See *Hawke v. Smith*, 253 U. S. 221 (1920), and *Leser v. Garnett*, 258 U. S. 130 (1922).

† *Denver Post*, Jan. 23, 1966, at 26.

‡ At the time, George Wallace served as the state's governor and was a strong opponent to the expansion of federal power and a future candidate for President of the United States. The author's files indicate that the bar of the state decided not to push for ratification of the Amendment in July 1966, in connection with a special session of the state's legislature then being called by Wallace, out of fear that the governor and the Speaker of its House of Representatives would use the Amendment as some kind of "whipping boy." The bar of the state, on the other hand, strongly supported the ratification as a result of a unanimous vote of its bar commissioners. As of that point in the ratification cycle, no state had rejected the Amendment and thirty-one states had given their approval (Louisiana on July 5, 1966), and John F. Satterfield, a past president of the American Bar Association from Mississippi, had written to Southern leaders urging ratification, stating: "In all of my years of experience, I do not recall a more non-controversial matter of such tremendous importance to the safety and well being of our great nation." Letter of Bert S. Nettles, Esq. (a young lawyer and rising bar leader) to the editor of the *Birmingham Post Herald*, dated July 18, 1966. The author's article in the *South Carolina Law Review*, in response to Professor Haimburgh's attack on the Amendment's method of filling a vacancy in the vice presidency, was used by the ABA and state bar in Alabama to advance the Amendment, nevertheless wiser state bar officials concluded that the Amendment would be better off without a rejection by the state's legislature.

It is unclear which state became the first, and which the thirty-eighth, to ratify. Nebraska's unicameral legislature ratified the Amendment on July 12, 1965, but because of a question concerning the need for the governor's signature, the ratifying resolution was not signed by the acting governor until the next day. On July 13, the Wisconsin legislature also ratified the Amendment. As a consequence, both states claim to be the first to have ratified. The claim of Nebraska would seem to be the better one, as there is substantial authority for the principle that Article V contemplates ratification by the state legislatures only.[3] On February 9, 1967, North Dakota ratified the amendment, believing that it was the thirty-eighth state to do so. When it learned that it was the thirty-seventh state, the state's legislative leaders declared the ratification illegal on the ground that there was a voice vote in one House. They hoped that once another state ratified, North Dakota would ratify again, making it the thirty-eighth state. However, before North Dakota could act, Minnesota and Nevada ratified the Amendment on February 10. It is interesting that North Dakota never took any further steps toward ratification. Since that time, nine other states have ratified the Amendment. The only states not to ratify are Georgia, South Carolina, and North Dakota.*[4]

The relatively smooth and rapid ratification accorded the Amendment was the result in large measure of the efforts of lawyer groups throughout the country, working in conjunction with the American Bar Association. Young lawyers, in particular, made substantial contributions to the Amendment's success in their states.†

---

* In a letter dated March 20, 1967, to the Archivist of the United States, Robert Bahmer, North Dakota Secretary of State Ben Meier wrote that North Dakota did not ratify the Twenty-Fifth Amendment.
† In a personal book in preparation, I discuss their work in greater detail.

8

An Analysis of Sections 1, 2, 3, and 4 of the Amendment

We had more cooks with more zeal concerned with preparing this "broth" than any piece of proposed legislation I have ever seen in the time I have been in the Senate.

SAM J. ERVIN, July 6, 1965[1]

SECTION 1

In case of the removal of the President from office or of his death or resignation, the Vice President shall become President.

This Section specifically confirms the Tyler precedent whereby a Vice President becomes President when there is a vacancy in the presidential office because of the President's death.[2] It also extends the precedent to cover vacancies in the presidency caused by resignation and removal after an impeachment.[3] In any of these cases, the Vice President takes the presidential oath[4] and serves as President for the remainder of the unexpired term.[5] The contingency of "inability" is removed entirely from this Section.[6]

SECTION 2

Whenever there is a vacancy in the office of the Vice President, the President shall nominate a Vice President who shall take office upon confirmation by a majority vote of both Houses of Congress.

The congressional debates and hearings in 1964 and 1965 established a number of underlying principles with respect to the meaning and intent of Section 2.[7]

First, the "vacancy" terminology is intended as an abbreviated way of covering situations involving the death, resignation, or removal of the President or Vice President.[8] When the Vice President succeeds to the presidency, he is empowered to nominate a successor.[9] The legislative history is clear that an "inability" of the President resulting in the Vice President's having to act as President is not a situation involving a vacancy in the vice presidency.[10] Nor is there a vice-presidential vacancy when the Vice President becomes disabled.[11] Even the inability of both the President and the Vice President does not bring Section 2 into play.[12] Moreover, the legislative history is unclear whether a Speaker acting as President upon a President's inability should nominate a new Vice President when there is no Vice President.[13]

Second, the use of "whenever" and "shall" is intended to make clear that the President is required to nominate a person for Vice President in the event of a vacancy.[14] It is not left to his discretion whether or not to nominate, although mention was made in the 1965 House hearings of the possibility of the President's not having to make a nomination when a vacancy occurs just prior to the end of his term.[15]

Third, the terminology "the President shall nominate a Vice President" contemplates that the President submit one name, not several, to Congress.[16] A proposal made in 1964 for the submission of several names was not accepted for the reason, among others, that it was felt the President should have a free hand in nominating the person he believed best qualified for the office and with whom he could work most closely.[17] Were the President to submit several names, it is questionable whether he would be discharging his obligation under Section 2 of nominating "a Vice President." It is arguable that the submission of several names would in effect transfer to Congress a portion of the nominating function, which function should be exercised exclusively by the President.

In giving the President the role of initiation in filling a vice-presidential vacancy, the Amendment follows the historical practice whereby a presidential candidate has a decisive voice in the selection of his running mate.[18] The Amendment's history is replete with statements to the effect that the President should initiate the nomination to ensure a Vice President of the same party for purposes of continuity[19] and of compatible temperament and views for an effective working relationship.[20] The history also reflects the intent that, before making a nomination, the President seek the advice and views of congressional leaders.[21]

Fourth, should a President's nomination be rejected, the legislative history is plain that the President would be obliged to nominate another person.[22] No limit is placed on the number of nominations that can be made.

Fifth, frequent references are made in the history concerning the "confirmation" role of Congress, bringing into play the "advise and consent" check currently in the Constitution with respect to other appointments.[23] It was contemplated that there might be occasions on which a nominee's qualifications are so well known and readily acceptable that little debate might be required, and other occasions on which his qualifications might have to be closely scrutinized, which would involve congressional hearings and extensive debate.[24] The wording of Section 2 gives to the President and Congress the power each currently has in the process of selecting officials such as federal judges, ambassadors, and Cabinet members.*[25] That Congress was to be the "voice of the people" is a concept which appears throughout the legislative history[26] and was a reason for giving the House of Representatives a confirmatory role.

Sixth, the coupling of "nomination" with "confirmation" instead of the "advise and consent" language of Article II was designed to ensure that a nominee cannot act as Vice President pending congressional confirmation.[27] Consequently, if a vacancy should occur when Congress is out of session, it could not be filled until the next regular session or at a special session called for that purpose by the President. Until a vacancy is filled, whoever is first in the statutory line of succession would be the heir apparent, since the Amendment leaves intact the power of Congress to establish a line of succession beyond the vice presidency.[28] The statutory successor, however, would have no right to act as Vice President because under Article II, Section 1 she is limited to acting as President only.[29] Thus, if at a time a vacancy in the vice presidency exists, the President should die, resign, or be removed, the Speaker, upon his resignation from Congress, would fill out the presidential term by reason of the 1947 succession statute.[30] He also would have the power to nominate a Vice President, since, upon succession, he would assume the discharge of all the powers and duties of President.† The Speaker's succession to the presidency would not be affected by a pending vice-presidential nomination at the time of the presidential vacancy, as confirmation is essential to filling a vice-presidential vacancy.[31] It is not entirely clear whether the intervening events would operate to render the nomination of no further effect, but since nominations made by a President who has died or resigned are treated as still valid when a Vice President succeeds, the result should be no different in the case of a vice-presidential nomination, since Section 2 was

---

* However, not all aspects of the "advise and consent" process were intended to be applicable to the nomination of a new Vice President. The involvement of both Houses of Congress was intended to give Congress a more active role in the selection of a Vice President than the Senate's role in confirming or rejecting other presidential nominations. Second, the use of the term "confirmation" in Section 2 was intended to achieve another distinction between the "advise and consent" process and that of selecting a new Vice President. See text accompanying note 27, *infra*. Third, the rule that the President is under no duty to appoint an officer approved by the Senate would not be applicable, since the selection of a Vice President under the Twenty-Fifth Amendment involves only the steps of nomination and confirmation. Presidential nominations made under Article II involve the steps of nomination, senatorial advice and consent, appointment by the President, and commissioning by the President. See *Marbury v. Madison*, 1 Cranch 137, 155–57 (1803); see Can the President appoint and sign commissions of persons who have been nominated and confirmed during the administration of his predecessor, Department of Justice, Nov. 26, 1963 (informal staff memorandum).

† See 1975 Review hearings, *infra*, and note. In her treatise, Ruth Silva takes the position that the law of 1947 "is based on two irreconcilable premises. It recognizes a designated officer as becoming President by providing for his resignation from his legislative or Cabinet post. At the same time it denies that he becomes President by failing to give him the tenure [i.e., four years] which the Constitution guarantees to a President. It is submitted that this contradiction is rather blatant." Silva, *Presidential Succession* 142.

referred to throughout its legislative history as being analogous to the present "advise and consent" process.[32] It therefore would seem that upon the Speaker's succession he could, and should, either withdraw the nomination and nominate someone else or continue the nomination.* If he continued the nomination and the nominee were confirmed, that nominee would not replace the Speaker but rather would be the former Speaker's Vice President, since in the event of a dual vacancy, the 1947 law provides for the Speaker to act as President for the rest of the established term. One interesting example given in the legislative history involves a situation in which the Speaker is nominated to fill a vice-presidential vacancy and the President dies while confirmation hearings are in progress. Under such circumstances, it was noted, the Speaker would take over the powers and duties of President for the rest of the term by virtue of the 1947 law.[33]

Seventh, the history of Section 2 manifests the intention that there be both a President and a Vice President at all times[34] and that whenever a vacancy occurs in the latter office, both the President and Congress act with reasonable dispatch to fill it,[35] putting aside partisan politics[36] and seeking, as Representative Peter W. Rodino stated in the House debates of 1965, the selection of a person of the "highest character and national stature."[37] Originally, Senate Joint Res. 139 had required the President to make a nomination within thirty days of a vacancy, but the time limit was eliminated because, among other reasons, unforeseeable circumstances might prevent the President from adhering to the limit, thereby causing him to violate the Constitution.[38] A proposal made during the Senate debates to add the word "immediately" to Section 2 was defeated largely because of the concern that it might prevent Congress from conducting a proper investigation of a nominee's background.[39]

Eighth, the phrase "by a majority vote of both Houses of Congress" is similar to that used elsewhere in the Constitution[40] and is designed to make clear that each House votes separately on a nomination and that the required vote in each is a majority of those members present and voting, provided there is a quorum.[41] A proposal for a two-thirds vote was rejected because it was thought to give too much control to those who might oppose a President.[42]

Ninth, the legislative history also is clear that a nominee for Vice President must meet the constitutional qualifications of being a natural-born citizen of the United

---

* Under Rule 38.6 of the Standing Rules of the Senate, a presidential nomination under Art. II continues until it is returned to the President as rejected by the Senate, not acted upon when the Congress adjourns for thirty days or more, or withdrawn by the President. There is no similar House rule since, until the Twenty-Fifth Amendment, it had no role in the nomination process. If a vacancy should occur in the Office of the President while a vice-presidential nomination is pending, it can reasonably be argued that the nomination should subsist in accordance with the general practice of the Senate with respect to other presidential nominations. For a contrary view, see the testimony of Assistant Attorney General Antonin Scalia. Hearing on the First Implementation of Section Two of the Twenty-Fifth Amendment Before the Subcomm. on Constitutional Amendments of the Senate Comm. on the Judiciary, 94th Cong, 1st Sess. 51–55 (1975): but see the 1975 Report of the subcommittee at 5.

States, at least thirty-five years of age, and a resident within the United States for a minimum of fourteen years.[43] Although under the Twelfth Amendment the presidential electors of a state must cast one of their two votes for an inhabitant of another state, a President is not prevented under the Twenty-Fifth Amendment from nominating an inhabitant of his own state.[44]

Tenth, a Vice President selected under the Twenty-Fifth Amendment occupies the same status as an elected Vice President.[45] Thus, when an appointed Vice President succeeds to the presidency, as Gerald R. Ford did in 1974, he may also use the procedures of Section 2.

SECTION 3

Whenever the President transmits to the President pro tempore of the Senate and the Speaker of the House of Representatives his written declaration that he is unable to discharge the powers and duties of his office, and until he transmits to them a written declaration to the contrary, such powers and duties shall be discharged by the Vice President as Acting President.

This Section is designed to make clear that in a case of presidential inability the Vice President simply discharges the powers and duties of the presidency; he assumes neither the office nor the title of President. Rather, he remains the Vice President, exercising presidential power, under the title of Acting President.[46] Accordingly, this Section solves the problem first raised by John Tyler's succession to the presidency.

Although the terms "unable" and "inability" are nowhere defined in either Section 3 or 4 of the Amendment (or in Article II), this was not the result of an oversight. Rather, it reflected a judgment that a rigid constitutional definition was undesirable, since cases of inability could take various forms not neatly fitting into such a definition.[47] The presence of a definition would only give rise to difficult questions of interpretation at a time when the country was confronted with a case of inability. The debates surrounding the Twenty-Fifth Amendment indicate that the terms "unable" and "inability" are intended to cover all cases in which some condition or circumstance prevents the President from discharging his powers and duties and the public business requires that the Vice President discharge them.[48] Situations involving physical and mental illness, temporary or permanent, were the most frequently mentioned cases covered by the expression.[49]

Section 3 deals with a case in which the President recognizes his own inability and wishes to suspend temporarily his exercise of the powers and duties of President.[50] It involves a personal judgment on the part of the President.[51] As Representative Richard C. White of Texas noted in the House debates of April 13, 1965, "There is no requirement that a reason be given other than that the President is 'unable' to act. . . ."[52]

The legislative history of Section 3, however, leaves no dispute about the specific types of cases contemplated. It was intended to cover situations such as the President's entering a hospital for an operation or other medical attention, or going abroad where he might be out of effective communication with the White House.[53] Said former Attorney General Herbert Brownell during the House hearings:

> A typical situation that is covered by this section is one in which the President is physically ill and his doctors recommend temporary suspension of his normal governmental activities, to facilitate his recovery. Other situations that have been visualized are those where the President might be going to have an operation, or where he was going abroad and might be out of reliable communication with the White House for a short period.[54]

Under Section 3 a President is permitted to declare himself disabled either for an indefinite or a specified period of time and to name the hour when the Vice President is to begin as Acting President.[55] The declaration could even be conditional and prospective in nature, stating, for example: "[I]f in the event I am under anesthesia or similarly unable, I wish you to assume those duties. . . ."[56] Once the Vice President commences his role as Acting President, the Amendment contemplates that he would continue in such capacity until the President terminates it by a subsequent declaration of recovery.

Whether Section 3 is broad enough to cover the case of a President's deciding to step aside temporarily—as was suggested during President Richard M. Nixon's last year in office[57]—in order to devote his full time to his defense against impeachment and removal is a debatable question. Although such a use of the Amendment was never mentioned by the Congress that proposed it, it probably would not be beyond the scope of Section 3, since the Section was intended to be broadly interpreted. However, Section 3 does not provide a mechanism for a President to step aside temporarily without justification, thereby neglecting his duties.

Section 3 encourages a President to declare his own inability since, if he does, his declaration of restoration to capacity is not subject to the challenge procedures of Section 4.[58] "A President would always hesitate to utilize the voluntary mechanism if he knew that a challenge could be lodged when he sought to recapture his office [i.e., its powers and duties]."[59]

The Vice President becomes Acting President as soon as the President transmits a written declaration of inability to the President pro tempore and to the Speaker, or, as the case may be, at the time or under the circumstances specified in the declaration. He ceases to be Acting President as soon as the President transmits his written declaration of recovery to these two officials.[60] Whenever the Vice President is called upon to act as President, he loses his title as President of the Senate.*[61] Whether the Vice President would be required to take the presidential oath before serving as Acting President is not entirely clear. The limited legislative history on this point suggests that the President's oath need not be taken.[62] It would seem that it should not, since the Vice President does not become President and the duty of acting as President is encompassed by his vice-presidential oath to perform his duties faithfully.

The legislative history also is not clear on whether the Vice President would be entitled to a presidential salary during the period he serves as Acting President. Given that he does not become President, it would seem that he should not be so paid, although there is legislative history to the contrary.[63] The succession statute of 1947 specifically provides for a statutory successor to be paid at the presidential salary rate in all cases (i.e., death, resignation, removal, and inability), and Congress could, of course, legislate a similar provision with respect to a Vice President who acts as President in a case of inability.

Because of its flexibility, Section 3 is likely to be used in most cases of presidential inability.[†]

SECTION 4

Whenever the Vice President and a majority of either the principal officers of the executive departments or of such other body as Congress may by law provide, transmit to the President pro tempore of the Senate and the Speaker of the House of Representatives their written declaration that the President is unable to discharge the powers and duties of his office, the Vice President shall immediately assume the powers and duties of the office as Acting President.

Thereafter, when the President transmits to the President pro tempore of the Senate and the Speaker of the House of Representatives his written declaration that no inability exists, he shall resume the powers and duties of his office unless the Vice President and a majority of either the principal officers of the executive department or of such other body as Congress may by law provide, transmit within four days to the President pro tempore of the Senate and the Speaker of the House of Representatives their written declaration that the President is unable to discharge the powers and duties of his office. Thereupon Congress shall decide the issue, assembling within forty-eight hours for that purpose if not in session. If the Congress, within twenty-one days after receipt of the latter written declaration, or, if Congress

---

* The President pro tempore serves in that capacity in the interim, because of U.S. Const. art. I, § 3, cl. 5, which provides: "The Senate shall chuse their other Officers, and also a President pro tempore, in the Absence of the Vice President, or when he shall exercise the Office of President of the United States."

† See pages 196–203, *infra*.

is not in session, within twenty-one days after Congress is required to assemble, determines by two-thirds vote of both Houses that the President is unable to discharge the powers and duties of his office, the Vice President shall continue to discharge the same as Acting President; otherwise, the President shall resume the powers and duties of his office.

This Section, like Section 3, provides for an Acting President in a case of inability. It should be noted, however, that the inability procedures of these sections do not apply to the inability of a Vice President, or of a Vice President as Acting President, or to a case of simultaneous inabilities of the President and Vice President when the Speaker is designated to serve as President.*[64]

Section 4 covers the most difficult cases of inability—when the President cannot or does not declare his own inability.[65] Cases involving a mental inability were commonly referred to as falling within this section,[66] as were situations in which the President is kidnapped or captured, under an oxygen tent at a time of an enemy attack, or bereft of speech or sight.[67]

As for the cases falling within this Section, Senator Bayh said in the Senate debates of February 19, 1965:

[T]he word "inability" and the word "unable" as used in [Section 4] . . . , which refer to an impairment of the President's faculties, mean that he is unable either to make or communicate his decisions as to his own competency to execute the powers and duties of his office. I should like for the RECORD to include that as my definition of the words "inability" and "unable."[68]

In the Senate debates of June 30, 1965, Senators Bayh and Robert F. Kennedy referred to cases involving physical or mental inability to make or communicate a decision regarding incapacity and physical or mental inability to exercise the powers and duties of office. The following important exchange took place between Kennedy and Bayh:

MR. KENNEDY of New York. Is it not true that the inability to which we are referring in the proposed amendment is total inability to exercise the powers and duties of the office?

MR. BAYH. The inability that we deal with here is described several times in the amendment itself as the inability of the President to perform the powers and duties of office.

It is conceivable that a President might be able to walk, for example, and thus, by the definition of some people, might be physically able, but at

---

* Language to deal with these contingencies was placed in the record by Representative Poff. Hearings on Presidential Inability and Vice Presidential Vacancy Before the House Comm. on the Judiciary, 89th Cong., 1st Sess. 86 (1965).

the same time he might not possess the mental capacity to make a decision and perform the powers and duties of his office. We are talking about inability to perform the constitutional duties of the office of President.

Mr. KENNEDY of New York. And that has to be total disability to perform the powers and duties of the office.

Mr. BAYH. The Senator is correct. We are not getting into a position, through the pending measure, in which when a President makes an unpopular decision, he would immediately be rendered unable to perform the duties of his office.

Mr. KENNEDY of New York. Is it limited to mental inability to make or communicate his decision regarding his capacity and mental inability to perform the powers and duties prescribed by law?

Mr. BAYH. I do not believe that we should limit it to mental disability. It is conceivable that the President might fall into the hands of the enemy, for example.

Mr. KENNEDY of New York. It involves physical or mental inability to make or communicate his decision regarding his capacity and physical or mental inability to exercise the powers and duties of his office.

Mr. BAYH. The Senator is correct. That is very important. I would refer the Senator back to the definition which I read into the RECORD at the time the Senate passed this measure earlier this year.

Mr. KENNEDY of New York. It was that definition which I was seeking to reemphasize. May I ask one other question? Is it not true that the inability referred to must be expected to be of long duration or at least one whose duration is uncertain and might persist?

Mr. BAYH. Here again I think one of the advantages of this particular amendment is the leeway it gives us. We are not talking about the kind of inability in which the President went to the dentist and was under anesthesia. It is not that type of inability we are talking about, but the Cabinet, as well as the Vice President and Congress, are going to have to judge the severity of the disability and the problems that face our country.

Mr. KENNEDY of New York. Is it not true that what we are talking about here as far as inability is concerned, is not a brief or temporary inability?

Mr. BAYH. We are talking about one that would seriously impair the President's ability to perform the powers and duties of his office.

Mr. KENNEDY of New York. Could a President have such inability for a short period of time?

Mr. BAYH. A President who was unconscious for 30 minutes when missiles were flying toward this country might only be disabled temporarily, but it would be of severe consequence when viewed in the light of the problems facing the country.

So at that time, even for that short duration, someone would have to make a decision. But a disability which has persisted for only a short time would ordinarily be excluded. If a President were unable to make an Executive decision which might have severe consequences for the county, I think we would be better under the conditions of the amendment.[69]

In the House debates of April 13, 1965, Representative Richard Poff said that Section 4 provides for two categories of cases: (1) when the President "by reason of some physical ailment or some sudden accident is unconscious or paralyzed and therefore unable to make or to communicate" a decision; and (2) "when the President, by reason of mental debility[,] is unable or unwilling to make any rational decision, including particularly the decision to stand aside."[70]

At various times in the debates and hearings of 1964 and 1965, it was made clear that unpopularity, incompetence, impeachable conduct, poor judgment, and laziness do not constitute an "inability" within the meaning of the Amendment.[71] As Senator Bayh stated in the Senate debates of February 19, 1965:

> The Senator from Indiana agrees with the Senator from Michigan [Philip A. Hart] that we are not dealing with an unpopular decision that must be made in time of trial and which might render the President unpopular. We are talking about a President who is unable to perform the powers and duties of his office.[72]

Under Section 4, the Vice President and a majority* of the "principal officers of the executive departments" (popularly known as the Cabinet) are empowered to declare the President disabled by transmitting a written declaration of this fact to the President pro tempore and to the Speaker.[73] Few subjects received as much attention as that of the composition of the Cabinet. The debates make clear that the following ten officials were intended, plus the head of any executive department established after July 1965: Secretaries of State; Treasury; Defense; Interior; Agriculture; Commerce; Labor; and Health, Education and Welfare; the Attorney General, and the Postmaster General.[74] The following were not intended: the U.S. Representative to the United Nations; the Secretaries of the Army, Navy, and the Air Force; the Director of the Poverty Program; and the head of the Atomic Energy Commission.[75] Whether an Under Secretary can participate as a member of the Cabinet when there is a Cabinet vacancy was dealt with by the House Judiciary Committee in its report:

---

* A "Majority" and not unanimous action was decided upon in order to take care of a situation in which one member "might be entirely out of sympathy with the national administration." 1965 House Hearings 248.

In case of the death, resignation, absence, or sickness of the head of any executive department, the acting head of the department would be authorized to participate in a presidential inability determination.*[76]

A different view was expressed in the Senate debates of February 19, 1965;[77] but the view of the House Judiciary Committee, which the author believes to be the correct one, was articulated by Senator Robert Kennedy in the Senate debates of June 30, 1965,[78] and was assumed by a number of senators on both June 30 and July 6, 1965, when the discussion centered on the firing and replacement of Cabinet members.[79] These later debates, as well as the earlier Senate debate, also indicate that a recess appointee to the Cabinet would be able to participate in the determination of inability.[80] With respect to the Senate debate of February 19 and the statement that an Under Secretary would not participate when there is a vacancy, it should be noted that the principal subject of discussion concerned not vacancies but whether the expression "heads of the executive departments" included subdivision and bureau heads. Indeed, a memorandum from the Library of Congress was placed in the record to indicate that the latter were not intended to be included.[81]

Under Section 4 the declaration of inability probably would be a joint one, although the Vice President and Cabinet might choose to send separate declarations.[82] In answer to the question concerning the way in which a written declaration might be prepared under Section 4, Brownell stated:

> Undoubtedly the Justice Department would prepare the papers, and the action would be taken at a joint meeting of the Vice President and the Cabinet members. It might not even be a matter of public knowledge as to who signed first. That particular point would fade into insignificance in getting the group action.[83]

The question of whether an inability had occurred could be initiated for discussion purposes by the Vice President or by any member of the Cabinet.[84]

Upon the transmittal of a declaration of inability to the Speaker and the President pro tempore, the Vice President immediately takes over as Acting President and is entitled to discharge all the powers and duties of President.[85] It makes no difference if Congress is not in session at the time of such transmittal.[86] During the period in which the Vice President serves as Acting President, the President is prevented from exercising his powers and duties.[87]

Once the President announces his recovery by transmitting an appropriate written declaration to the Speaker and the President pro tempore, he then must wait four days before resuming his powers and duties.[88] In the meantime, the Vice

---

* It also should be pointed out that 5 U.S.C. § 4 (1964) specifically provides that, in the case of the death, resignation, absence, or sickness of a department head, the first assistant of the department shall, unless otherwise directed by the President, perform the duties of the head.

President continues to act as President,[89] and he and the Cabinet have an opportunity to review the situation. Either the Vice President alone or the Cabinet and Vice President can agree to the President's taking over immediately or at any time short of four days.[90] If they disagree with the President's declaration of recovery, they are required to send, within four days, a written declaration of that fact to the President pro tempore and the Speaker, and Congress then is required to decide the issue, with each House meeting separately.[91] If there is a disagreement between the Vice President and the Cabinet about the President's recovery, the issue is not appropriate for Congress to decide and the President then resumes his powers and duties. Agreement between the Vice President and the Cabinet that the President has not recovered is a condition which must precede congressional consideration.[92] If Congress is not in session at the time an issue of disagreement is raised, it is obliged to assemble within forty-eight hours from the time the Vice President and the Cabinet transmit their declaration to the President pro tempore and the Speaker. It is incumbent upon the Vice President as Acting President to fix a certain time within forty-eight hours when Congress must assemble.[93] If he fails to do so, the President pro tempore and the Speaker are obliged to call their respective House into session within the forty-eight-hour period.[94] Upon their failure to do so, Congress must come into session within forty-eight hours on its own initiative.[95]

Congress has twenty-one days from the date of receipt of the transmittal, if it is in session, or from the time it is required to assemble, if not in session, in which to decide a disagreement issue.[96] Pending the decision of Congress, the Vice President continues to act as President, so that the powers and duties of President will not be in the hands of a person whose capacity has been seriously challenged.*[97] Furthermore, by allowing the Vice President to continue as Acting President during this period, there would be fewer transfers of power and more continuity. Otherwise, there would/could be a ping-pong sort of situation wherein the Vice President takes over as a result of an inability declaration, the President returns immediately by making a recovery declaration, and the Vice President returns by virtue of Congress's decision in his favor on the disagreement issue.[98]

Congress has three choices under the twenty-one-day limitation: to decide in favor of the President; to decide in favor of the Vice President; or to reach no decision at all.[99] Said Poff of the last decision:

---

* During the hearings Attorney General Katzenbach observed: "Now, I suppose the two problems that one is dealing with are the risk to the country of a period, however short, where a President who really is unable nonetheless declares ability, and the problem, how quick the congressional action could be gotten in that situation and the risk to the country in that period of time, as against the problem that you raised, Mr. Chairman, of the usurper, which is the traditional fear of Vice Presidents in exercising their power, that they would be so regarded." Hearings on Presidential Inability and Vacancies in the Office of Vice President Before the Subcomm. on Constitutional Amendments of the Senate Comm. on the Judiciary, 89th Cong., 1st Sess. 17 (1965).

Circumstances may be such that the Congress by tacit agreement may want to uphold the President in some manner which will not amount to a public rebuke of the Vice President who is then Acting President. . . . [This] option furnishes the graceful vehicle.[100]

If Congress fails to reach a decision within this time, or if more than one-third of either House sides with the President, the President automatically reassumes his powers and duties.[101] "[I]f one House voted but failed to get the necessary two-thirds majority, the other House would be precluded from using the 21 days and the President would immediately resume the powers and duties of his office."[102] The twenty-one-day limit is an outside limitation, it being the Amendment's intent that Congress act as speedily as possible under the circumstances presented. If Congress fails to act until the twenty-second day, its decision will be of no effect, since the President automatically would have resumed the discharge of his powers and duties at the end of the twenty-first day. Of course, the Vice President and the Cabinet would have the power to reactivate the procedures of Section 4, since there is no limit on the number of times those procedures can be used. The two-thirds vote is of those present and voting, provided there is a quorum.[103] In deciding the issue, Congress can proceed as it thinks best. It can prescribe rules governing the process.[104] Thus, it may request that the President undergo medical tests and examinations or submit to questioning at hearings.[105] As Senator Roman Hruska said:

Obviously, such a decision must rest on the relevant and reliable facts regarding the President's physical or mental faculties. It must be divorced from any thoughts of political advantage, personal prejudice, or other extraneous factors.[106]

If a challenge is resolved in favor of a Vice President by a two-thirds vote of both Houses,* he continues as the Acting President until the President recovers from his inability. Since an inability decision does not result in the President's removal from office, there is nothing to prevent him, after an adverse congressional decision, from issuing another recovery declaration, thereby activating the process again.[107] The debates indicate that a congressional decision supporting either the President or Vice President is not subject to judicial review.[108]

If future circumstances indicate that the Cabinet is not a workable body, Congress has the power under Section 4 to entrust to another body the responsibility of deciding, with the Vice President, a question of presidential inability.[109] This power can be exercised even in the midst of a case of presidential inability as, for example, when a Cabinet refuses to declare an obviously sick President unable.[110] But any

---

* This requirement is even more strict than that in the case of impeachment since only a simple majority vote to impeach is required of the House of Representatives.

legislation adopted by Congress is subject to the President's veto power.[111] The debates make clear that Congress's power with respect to the creation of "another body" is vast. It can designate itself,[112] expand or restrict the membership of the Cabinet,[113] combine the Cabinet with other officials,[114] require a unanimous vote of the body established by law,[115] and prescribe the rules and procedures to be followed by that body.[116] As Senator Jacob Javits stated:

> Congress has the right to provide for the exclusivity of that body in exercising this authority, as well as the way in which the body shall exercise that authority, and other pertinent details necessary to the creation of such a body, its continuance, its way of meeting, the rules of the procedure, and the way in which it shall exercise its power.[117]

This power, however, cannot be exercised to replace the Vice President.[118] The legislative history of the "other body" provision clearly shows that, when Congress designates such a body, it replaces the Cabinet as the group that must act in conjunction with the Vice President.[119] In this connection, it must be emphasized that the provisions of Sections 3 and 4 cannot operate without a Vice President. He is the key to the effectiveness of the procedures prescribed in the Amendment.[120]

During the hearings and debates, criticism was voiced that the President could discharge Cabinet members before they had a chance to declare him disabled, thus nullifying that prescribed method.[121] While the possibility of removal is there, if a President were to act in such a manner, Congress could cope with the situation by exercising its power under Section 4 to establish another body. Another observation was that a Vice President acting as President would have the presidential powers of appointing and removing Cabinet members during his tenure as Acting President.[122] Should he use these powers for the purpose of stacking the Cabinet in his favor, the President, having declared himself disabled under Section 3, could regain his powers and duties immediately by a declaration of recovery. If the President were declared disabled under Section 4, he could issue a recovery declaration and, assuming a challenge by the Vice President and the Cabinet within four days, could get Congress to pass on the issue. Congress certainly would not look favorably on a Vice President who had acted in an irresponsible manner.

The record is replete with suggestions that irresponsible behavior also might subject a Vice President to impeachment.[123]

This chapter is taken essentially from my article "The Proposed Twenty-Fifth Amendment to the Constitution," 34 Fordham Law Review 173, 196–202 (1965), which was reprinted and made part of the "Selected Materials on the Twenty-Fifth Amendment" in the October 1973 Report of the Senate Constitutional Amendments Subcommittee.

Implementations of the Solution

The Resignation of Spiro T. Agnew

It is unthinkable that this nation should have been required to endure the anguish and uncertainty of a prolonged period in which the man next in line of succession to the Presidency was fighting the charges brought against him by his own government.

ELLIOT RICHARDSON, October 10, 1973[1]

On November 7, 1972, Richard M. Nixon and Spiro T. Agnew received more popular votes for President and Vice President than any other candidates in American history. Less than two years later, both had resigned their offices, and Gerald R. Ford and Nelson A. Rockefeller had become President and Vice President by virtue of the Twenty-Fifth Amendment. Although it is beyond the scope of this book to detail the unique events leading to the fall of Nixon and Agnew,* a summary of certain of these events is necessarily set forth in order to place in context the accessions of Ford and Rockefeller.

On June 17, 1972, five men equipped with illegal bugging devices were arrested for breaking and entering the Democratic National Committee Headquarters in the Watergate complex in Washington, D.C. These five men were later revealed to be a part of a conspiracy and cover-up involving more than seventy people, including Nixon Cabinet members and White House assistants. The president himself, it was eventually revealed, was also a participant in the cover-up.[2]

---

* *See generally,* C. Bernstein & B. Woodward, *All the President's Men* (1974); T. White *Breach of Faith: The Fall of Richard Nixon* (1975); and R. Cohen & J. Witcover, *A Heartbeat Away: The Investigation and Resignation of Vice President Spiro T. Agnew* (1974). *See also* Spiro T. Agnew, *Go Quietly . . . or Else* (1980).

In January 1973, shortly before the second inauguration of Nixon and Agnew, the U.S. District Court for the District of Columbia began hearing the first Watergate break-in case, which was to become a two-year process. The criminal trial of the Watergate burglars resulted in guilty verdicts for G. Gordon Liddy and James McCord of the Committee for the Re-election of the President and in guilty pleas by E. Howard Hunt and four others. That month the Pentagon Papers trial also began, and in February the U.S. Senate created a select committee of four Democrats and three Republicans, chaired by Senator Sam Ervin, to investigate 1972 campaign abuses.

An indication that high-level Republicans had been involved in the Watergate break-in came on March 19, 1973, when McCord wrote to federal judge John J. Sirica that he was under political pressure to plead guilty and remain silent and that perjury had been committed at the trial. Sirica disclosed the letter in open court and deferred final sentencing of the defendants, urging their cooperation with the ongoing Watergate investigation. McCord met with the investigators and appeared before the Ervin committee in closed session. By late April 1973 allegations had been made to government prosecutors that implicated a number of close aides to the President in prior knowledge and the cover-up of the Watergate break-in. On April 30 the White House announced the resignations of Attorney General Richard Kleindienst and presidential aides John Ehrlichman, H. R. Haldeman, and John Dean. In a televised address the President accepted responsibility for the Watergate incident but denied any personal involvement in the break-in or the cover-up. In May federal judge W. Matthew Byrne Jr. dismissed the Pentagon Papers case because of government misconduct and revealed that Ehrlichman had offered him the directorship of the FBI during the course of the trial. At about the same time, the Ervin committee began its televised hearings, and Elliot Richardson and Archibald Cox were sworn in as Attorney General and Special Prosecutor, respectively.

As criticism of the Nixon administration increased, former Secretary of Defense Clark Clifford wrote a provocative article for the *New York Times* in which he expressed the opinion that the public loss of confidence in Nixon was so widespread that the executive branch could no longer function effectively.[3] He suggested that the President employ the provisions of the Twenty-Fifth Amendment and announce that both he and Vice President Agnew would resign, the Vice President resigning first. Then Nixon could nominate a Vice President whom Congress would approve and, after his confirmation, Nixon could resign, leaving a new successor as President. President Nixon, seemingly determined to remain in office, never commented on this proposal.

Throughout June and July 1973 the Ervin committee and Special Prosecutor Cox requested White House files for their investigations, but Nixon rejected these requests on grounds of executive privilege. On July 16 a bombshell struck when Alexander Butterfield, Nixon's former appointments secretary, revealed to the Ervin committee that tape recordings had been made of all conversations and telephone calls in the President's office since 1970. With this revelation, the historic legal battles for the tapes began, which one year later would culminate in Nixon's resignation. Nixon, who had been hospitalized with viral pneumonia for a week, labeled rumors that he would resign as "poppycock." Both the Ervin committee and Cox issued subpoenas for certain tapes and filed suit in federal court to obtain them. By August 1973 the stage had been set for the ultimate legal confrontation.

As these events unfolded, other events unknown to the public were occurring that eventually would cause Agnew to resign as Vice President.[4] In December 1972, the U.S. Attorney's office in Maryland had begun an investigation of political corruption in Baltimore County. In early February 1973, rumors swept Baltimore that Agnew had been implicated in the investigation. George White, the Vice President's personal attorney, visited U.S. Attorney George Beall to inquire whether Agnew was under investigation. Beall assured White that only the current Baltimore County leadership was under investigation and that the prosecutors would do everything possible to protect Agnew's name.[5]

On February 6, 1973, Beall visited Attorney General Richard Kleindienst to inform him that the rumors about Agnew's involvement in the investigation were false. In April, Agnew retained as his counsel Washington attorney Judah Best, a law partner of former White House special counsel Charles W. Colson. On April 19 Best met with Beall and described Agnew's willingness to cooperate with the investigation and his concern about adverse publicity. Beall reaffirmed that the investigation did not involve Agnew. By June, however, the U.S. Attorney's office had uncovered information that Agnew allegedly had received bribes for awards of public works contracts during the period of his service as County Executive of Baltimore County and as governor of Maryland. On July 3, this information was brought to the attention of Attorney General Elliot Richardson. Richardson is said to have remarked that "the continuing capacity of the nation to govern itself" was at stake and referred to the fact that Agnew was a heartbeat away from the presidency. "The President's plane could go down tomorrow," he said. "There could be an assassin's bullet. He could die tomorrow."[6]

The President's possible impeachment for participating in the Watergate cover-up might have been in Richardson's mind as well. Richardson wanted to confront Agnew immediately with the evidence of corruption in the hope that he would resign, but he was persuaded by the prosecutors to wait until the investigation had progressed further. Richardson also decided not to inform the President about the allegations at that time.[7] For the rest of the month, the U.S. Attorney's office in Baltimore developed the evidence against Agnew. On July 27 Richardson and the prosecutors agreed that President Nixon should be informed about the case and that Agnew should be sent a formal letter advising him that he was under investigation for possible violations of federal criminal statutes. Richardson then visited White House Chief of Staff Alexander Haig to schedule an appointment with the

President and learned that Agnew already had spoken with Haig and the President about the investigation and had asserted his innocence.[8]

On August 1, Agnew's attorney was given a letter from George Beall stating that Agnew was under investigation for conspiracy, extortion, bribery, and tax fraud and requesting certain documents. On August 6, Richardson met in the White House with the President, Haig, and special presidential counsel J. Fred Buzhardt and detailed the case against the Vice President. According to Richardson, Nixon's "reaction was remarkably objective and deliberate."[9] It was agreed that Henry E. Petersen, an assistant attorney general, should make an independent evaluation of the evidence against Agnew and report to Richardson and Nixon. While it seemed to Richardson that the White House favored Agnew's resignation, Nixon did not wish to alienate Agnew's constituency, whose support he clearly needed in the unfolding impeachment drama.

At Haig's suggestion, Richardson met that afternoon with Agnew and his attorneys and summarized the status of the Baltimore investigation. Agnew denied the charges, attacked the integrity of the prosecution and its witnesses, and agreed that Henry Petersen should review the case. Late that night, as the *Wall Street Journal* and *Washington Post* published the first accounts of the investigation, Agnew publicly announced that he had been informed about the investigation and that he was innocent of any wrongdoing. For the next sixty-five days, as evidence of President Nixon's involvement in the Watergate scandals developed, the nation simultaneously watched the demise of the Vice President's public career.

On August 7, Agnew conferred privately with Nixon and was told by the President that he had complete confidence in him. But when Agnew returned to his office, he was visited by Haig, who suggested that if the allegations against him were sustainable, Agnew should consider taking some action prior to indictment.[10] On the following day Agnew held a press conference, labeled the rumors about his conduct in Maryland politics "damned lies," and stated unequivocally that he would not resign. He said that he would cooperate with the prosecutors and had "absolutely nothing to hide."

Almost daily thereafter the press printed new stories about the investigation. Some of the articles cited Justice Department or government sources, leading Agnew's staff to conclude that the administration intended to destroy the Vice President through the device of news leaks.[11] On August 15 Agnew released to the prosecutors his personal financial records and in a public relations counterattack published the covering letter, which promised his full cooperation in the investigation. As the news leaks continued, Agnew called his second news conference to charge that officials of the Justice Department "have decided to indict me in the press," and to demand an inquiry into the source of the leaks. Nixon telephoned Agnew to tell him that he would support his call for an inquiry, and in a televised news conference on August 22 the President directed Richardson to conduct a full investigation.[12] Nixon carefully praised Agnew's performance and integrity as

Vice President while refusing to comment on his prior activities. The following day the White House revealed to reporters that the President's lawyers refused to formulate a joint strategy on the issues of executive privilege and indictability because they saw no common interest with the Vice President.[13]

On September 1, Nixon and Agnew met privately for two hours, prompting rumors that Agnew's resignation was being planned. Speculation was increased because Nixon had cut short a Labor Day weekend holiday at the Western White House in San Clemente, California, to return to Washington for the meeting. It is reported that Nixon wanted Agnew to resign but could not bring himself to make a direct request for his resignation.[14] After the meeting, it was reported that they had held a thorough discussion of the investigation and that the subject of resignation was not even mentioned. At some point during the next few days Bryce N. Harlow, a confidant of Nixon's and a good friend of Agnew's, visited the Vice President on behalf of the President and suggested that a resignation would be in the best interests of the country. While Agnew appeared to entertain the suggestion, he demanded assurances that he would not go to prison.[15]

On September 3, Richardson authorized the prosecutors to proceed with the grand jury investigation of the charges against Agnew. As the prosecutors readied their case for presentation to the grand jury, Agnew threatened to ask the House of Representatives to begin impeachment proceedings. Perhaps because of the ominous parallel to the President himself, the White House opposed such a move, fearing that it would resolve the question of whether a President or Vice President must be impeached before he can be indicted.[16] Thereupon, the White House asked Richardson to postpone submitting evidence to the grand jury in the hope of persuading Agnew to abandon the impeachment plan.

On September 10, Haig and Buzhardt met with Agnew and Best. Buzhardt reviewed the case against Agnew, and Haig demanded that he resign. Best protested, and Agnew left the room without replying to the demand. The next day the White House informed Richardson that Agnew's attorneys wanted to discuss the procedural options available to the Vice President. On September 12, Richardson, Petersen, and Beall met with Agnew's attorneys and told them that the Justice Department was prepared to press for an indictment. The next day Best met with Richardson and Petersen and, in effect, opened plea-bargaining negotiations. At this meeting it was indicated that Agnew would resign as Vice President and plead no contest to a single charge of tax evasion in return for the government's recommendation that no jail sentence be imposed.[17] The government subsequently insisted on a settlement provision that all the evidence collected against Agnew be disclosed to the public.

Meanwhile, on September 14 Agnew met with Senator Barry Goldwater of Arizona to discuss the situation, and Goldwater subsequently complained to Harlow about the pressure being exerted on Agnew to resign. On September 18 the *Washington Post* printed an article by David Broder which quoted an unnamed senior

Republican as stating that Agnew would resign within the week. The White House refusal to comment on the report or even to affirm the President's support of Agnew added further momentum to the rumors about his future.

The plea bargaining continued with disagreements over an admission of guilt by Agnew and the plea to a felony charge. It is reported that throughout these discussions Richardson expressed his worry that Nixon "might be impeached, assassinated, he was not in the best psychological condition."[18] On September 20, Agnew met secretly with Nixon and complained that the Justice Department was making it too difficult for him to make a deal.[19] That evening Richardson was summoned to the White House to meet with Haig and Buzhardt. They insisted that Agnew's resignation was the primary goal and that Richardson must not frustrate this result by demanding too much. Richardson, however, refused to alter his conditions.[20]

On September 22, the *Washington Post* printed a story describing the negotiations and Agnew's possible resignation. Convinced that the Justice Department had leaked the story to embarrass him and weaken his bargaining position, Agnew broke off negotiations and disclosed that he was establishing a legal defense fund. The Columbia Broadcasting System that day also quoted Henry Petersen as saying, "We've got the evidence. We've got it cold."

On September 25 Richardson and Petersen spent two hours with the President and told him that, because the plea bargaining had failed, an indictment of the Vice President should be sought. Nixon appears to have been concerned that such a course would weaken his current argument that an incumbent President must be impeached before indictment, and therefore he favored resort to the House of Representatives for an impeachment proceeding.[21] Shortly after Richardson and Petersen left the White House, Agnew arrived and stated that he would seek a House investigation. Nixon then released a statement to the press reporting on his meeting with Agnew. Nixon said that the Vice President had denied the charges made against him and that he was entitled to the presumption of innocence. Richardson also issued a statement in which he said that evidence regarding the Vice President would be presented to the grand jury when it reconvened on September 27.

On the morning of September 25, House Minority Leader Gerald R. Ford and Leslie C. Arends of Illinois, the House Republican Whip, relayed to House Speaker Carl Albert of Oklahoma a request from Agnew for a meeting prior to Albert's taking a call from Richardson. It appears that Ford and Arends had been to the White House earlier in the morning and had seen both Nixon and Agnew.[22] That afternoon, about 3:30, Agnew met personally with Albert and gave him a letter which formally requested that the House of Representatives investigate the charges against him. During this meeting Agnew criticized the Justice Department and expressed his feeling that the White House was going to let him down.

The meeting with Albert, to which the legislative leaders of both parties were called in, lasted about an hour. Following it, Agnew's letter was read to the approximately fifty members present on the floor of the House of Representatives. In his letter Agnew cited a precedent involving Vice President John C. Calhoun and declared that the leaks and newspaper reports had made it impossible for a grand jury to consider the charges against him on the merits. House Minority Leader Ford, Senate Minority Leader Hugh Scott of Pennsylvania, and other Republican leaders urged that Agnew be granted an impeachment hearing.[23] On September 26, Albert, who, like Ford, had been alerted by Richardson to Agnew's impending indictment, refused Agnew's request on the ground that the House should not interfere with a matter before the courts.* Ford called the decision unfortunate and political, stating, "They made a Democratic decision. I don't think there's anything we can do since we are in the minority."[24] Another Republican leader remarked that the Democrats "won't bail the Vice President out of his predicament."[25] Supporting the decision, Democratic Representative John Conyers Jr. of Michigan reportedly said, "We should not interrupt the legal process. I would trust 12 honest citizens of Maryland rather than 435 members of Congress."[26]

On September 27, the grand jury began to hear evidence against Agnew, causing him to institute court proceedings the next day in an effort to stop the grand jury. Agnew maintained that the Constitution prohibits criminal proceedings against an incumbent Vice President and, further, that leaks had deprived him of the possibility of a fair trial on the merits. Agnew then began a public relations offensive.

A *New York Times* article on September 28 by James Reston quoted Agnew as saying that he would not resign but would fight through the courts and keep appealing to the House of Representatives. In the article, Agnew also criticized Henry Petersen and certain members of the President's staff. On September 29, in a Los Angeles speech before more than 2,000 women, Agnew emotionally stated, "I will not resign if indicted." He again criticized the Justice Department, saying that its members were "severely stunned by their ineptness in the Watergate case. . . . They are trying to recoup their reputations at my expense. I am a big trophy."[27] On October 2, Agnew's press secretary predicted that the Vice President's next speech would contain additional attacks. Haig almost immediately telephoned Agnew's top assistant, stating that the President wanted no more attacks on Petersen, the Justice Department, or the administration and indicating that unless such attacks ceased there would be no plea bargaining and Agnew could end up behind bars. Haig demanded that Agnew's press secretary be dismissed, and he was subsequently relieved of duty.[28]

---

* For an interesting account of Democratic Majority Leader Thomas P. ("Tip") O'Neill's efforts to persuade Speaker Albert and Chairman Rodino of the Judiciary Committee to decline Agnew's request, see J. Breslin, *How the Good Guys Finally Won* 57–65 (1975). According to Breslin, O'Neill feared that if Agnew's request was granted, the House would be left with insufficient time and resources to deal with the question of Nixon's impeachment. Of Agnew's request for a House investigation, Albert has stated, "I don't know to this date whether the White House contrived this situation to get this matter before the House of Representatives, or whether the Vice President and the President were really at odds." Albert, *The Most Dramatic Events of My Life*, Oklahoma State University Outreach 5 (March 1974).

Agnew's repeated protestations of innocence and his criticisms of the press for leaking confidential grand jury information won him public sympathy . On October 3, federal district judge Walter E. Hoffman granted Agnew's request to conduct an investigation of Justice Department leaks, including the right to serve subpoenas and to begin taking depositions as soon as possible. That same day Nixon held an informal press conference. While calling Agnew's decision not to resign "an altogether proper one," he characterized the charges against Agnew as "serious and not frivolous" and defended Henry Petersen.[29] The President also stated that he had not asked Agnew to resign or developed a list of possible vice-presidential replacements. On the following night at a speech in Chicago, Agnew stated, "A candle is only so long, and eventually it burns out."

One day later, on October 5, the Justice Department expressed the view that Agnew could be indicted without first being impeached and that, upon an indict-ment, the Congress had the power to proceed by way of impeachment.[30] This report further isolated Agnew from the President. Then, the same day, Agnew abruptly indicated his interest in working out a settlement, which was secretly concluded in the following days. Present at some of the critical negotiations was Judge Hoffman. The settlement embodied the terms discussed at the first meeting, as well as a full disclosure by the government of the evidence developed against him. At a meeting in the White House on the evening of October 9, Agnew informed Nixon of his decision to resign.[31]

Shortly after 2:00 P.M. on Wednesday, October 10, Agnew, his attorneys, Rich-ardson, and other representatives of the Justice Department appeared before Judge Hoffman in Baltimore's federal district court and implemented the terms of the settlement, to wit: Agnew pleaded *nolo contendere* (no contest) to the felony of tax evasion for the year 1967, the Attorney General announced the dismissal of all further prosecution of Agnew and the release of a forty-page summary of the evi-dence against him, and Agnew announced his decision to resign. Said Hoffman: "You are submitting your resignation as Vice President of the United States. I want you to know that no Federal Court could require you to take this action."[32]

In explaining the settlement, Richardson told the court that a prosecution or impeachment of Agnew would have consumed years, "with potentially disastrous consequences to vital interests of the United States." He concluded by urging that the court not confine Agnew, basing his request on compassion, respect for the office of Vice President, and the fact that Agnew had spared the nation protracted agony by his resignation.

Agnew admitted that he had received certain unreported taxable income in 1967 but denied any other wrongdoing, stating:

In all the circumstances, I have concluded that protracted proceedings before the Grand Jury, the Congress and the courts, with the speculation and controversy surrounding them, would seriously prejudice the national interest.

His plea was accepted, and he was fined $10,000 and placed on three years' probation.

Concurrently with the court proceedings, Agnew's staff in Washington was informed of the resignation and a formal letter of resignation was delivered to the Secretary of State. In an exchange of letters with the President that day, Agnew stated that "it is in the best interest of the Nation that I relinquish the Vice Presidency." Nixon replied:

> The most difficult decisions are often those that are the most personal, and I know your decision to resign as Vice President has been as difficult as any facing a man in public life could be. Your departure from the Administration leaves me with a great sense of personal loss. You have been a valued associate throughout these nearly five years that we have served together. However, I respect your decision, and I also respect the concern for the national interest that led you to conclude that a resolution of the matter in this way, rather than through an extended battle in the courts and the Congress, was advisable in order to prevent a protracted period of national division and uncertainty.
>
> As Vice President, you have addressed the great issues of our times with courage and candor. Your strong patriotism, and your profound dedication to the welfare of the nation, have been an inspiration to all who have served with you as well as to millions of others throughout the country.
>
> I have been deeply saddened by this whole course of events, and I hope that you and your family will be sustained in the days ahead by a well-justified pride in all that you have contributed to the nation by your years of service as Vice President.[33]

Gerald Ford was listening to a debate in the House of Representatives on home rule for the District of Columbia when he was informed by a colleague of Agnew's resignation. Upon hearing the news, Ford replied, "You're kidding." Ford, who said that he had had no prior knowledge of Agnew's decision to resign, described his first reaction as "one of disbelief, his second . . . one of great sadness."[34] It was reported that Ford was relieved that Agnew had resigned, since the Republican Party was having enough trouble defending Nixon. "How much could the country take?" Ford reportedly said to a friend on the day Agnew resigned. "It's the best thing that he's now out."[35]

According to White House press secretary Ronald L. Ziegler, President Nixon "played no direct role in the arrangement that was worked out or the decision which has been announced today." He added that "[t]he President and the White House and the Vice President have made the point that this is a . . . personal decision which only the Vice President could make. The President, of course, respected that."[36]

Obviously, President Nixon had played an important part in the resignation drama. According to Richardson, "[t]he President was kept . . . fully informed at all times. He fully approved each of the major steps that were taken in the course of these negotiations."[37] Once the White House recognized the gravity of the charges against Agnew, it sought to compel his resignation. For, of the three solutions available to Agnew—resignation, indictment, or impeachment—either indictment or impeachment would have set a potentially dangerous precedent for a President facing a similar situation. It was to Nixon's advantage to avoid a legal confrontation that might impair his own ability to defend himself against the inevitable Watergate attacks, and to re-establish credibility for his administration by the selection of a new Vice President. Attorney General Richardson seems to have realized that the nation could not bear possible simultaneous criminal prosecutions of both the President and the Vice President, and, therefore, he sought Agnew's resignation in the national interest, knowing that a procedure existed for selecting a new and untarnished Vice President.

Ford's nomination was received favorably throughout the country, especially by members of both parties in Congress. Democratic Senator Kennedy summed up the general reaction when he said that Ford had had "an outstanding career and I foresee no difficulty whatever in his confirmation by the Senate."[22] Said House Democratic Majority Whip McFall, "He should have no trouble at all."[23]

CONFIRMATION

The Assignment to Committee

With the imminence of a vice-presidential nomination under the Twenty-Fifth Amendment, questions immediately were raised about the appropriate congressional committees to consider the nomination. Since the nomination and confirmation process constituted the first application of Section 2 of the Twenty-Fifth Amendment, involved government officials had no precedents on which to draw.[24] At an informal meeting of the joint leadership of the Senate held on the afternoon of October 10 that was attended by representatives of the Senate Rules and Judiciary committees and other interested senators, a number of suggestions were advanced and debated,[25] but no agreement was reached that afternoon or at another informal meeting held the next day. Some senators, including Bayh, advocated the creation of a select Senate committee. Other suggestions were to use a joint committee of both Houses, the Rules and Administration Committee, the Senate Committee on the Judiciary, the Government Operations Committee, or a Committee of the Whole Senate.* The claim of the Rules Committee was based on a rule that brought within its jurisdiction matters relating to presidential succession and the election of a President and Vice President. The Judiciary Committee based its claim on a rule giving it jurisdiction over constitutional amendments as well as its expertise in passing on presidential nominations generally. The claim of the Government Operations Committee derived from its general supervisory responsibilities of government departments.

The two alternatives mentioned most prominently at the October 11 meeting were a referral to the Rules Committee and the creation of a special committee consisting of representatives of the Senate Rules and Judiciary Committees and from the Senate at large. However, "the prevailing view," said Mansfield, was "that to avoid duplication and accommodate expedition, the idea of conducting joint hearings with the House on the nomination be explored with the Speaker."[26] Both Albert and Mansfield seemed to favor joint hearings. Albert, however, yielded to

---

* Underlying the question of which committee should consider the nomination was the ideological complexion of the committees—the Senate Rules and Administration Committee was of a conservative orientation whereas the Judiciary Committee had a significant number of senators of a liberal persuasion.

the feelings of a number of representatives who wanted the House to hold its own hearings. Some House members reportedly were of the view that its members are upstaged when they participate in joint activities with the Senate.[27] There was no question that the House Judiciary Committee was the appropriate House committee for any separate hearing.

On October 11, Democratic Senator Lawton Chiles of Florida asked for immediate consideration of a resolution that any nomination bypass committee action and be considered directly by the entire Senate. He said that senators with whom he had spoken wanted to participate in the selection process in order to find the best-qualified person for the position of Vice President. Nothing could be more representative, said Chiles, than one hundred senators sitting as the committee, especially at a time when public opinion of government was low.[28] His request for unanimous consent was denied, with the result that the resolution automatically was continued to the following day.[29] During the Senate discussion of October 11, Senator Hubert Humphrey suggested that a joint committee of both Houses be established, stating that it would lift the nomination "out of normal legislative procedures" and put "it on a higher plane of constitutional prerogative." He asserted that the nation would be better served by "one set of hearings, one inquiry, one investigation so to speak, in the sense of the qualifications and credentials of the nominee."[30]

On the morning of October 12 the subject was discussed at a Democratic Policy Committee meeting and then at a meeting of the Democratic Conference, which, by a vote of 24 to 20, decided that the nomination should be referred to the Senate Rules Committee and that the committee should be expanded by six members—three appointed by the majority leader and three by the minority leader, with the majority leader being one of the six.[31] At a meeting of the Republican Conference that day it was decided unanimously that the nomination should be referred to the existing Rules Committee without additional members.

That afternoon the question was debated extensively in the Senate, the House already having decided to send the nomination to its Judiciary Committee.[32] Senator Chiles objected to a unanimous consent request by Majority Leader Mansfield for immediate consideration of a resolution embodying the action taken at the Democratic Conference. His objection was interpreted as a ploy to delay a decision on the committee question until after the President had announced his choice for Vice President, which was scheduled for 9:00 P.M. Senators John O. Pastore, Scott, Mansfield, Edward W. Brooke of Massachusetts, and others urged Chiles to let the matter come to a decision before the nominee was named. Said Brooke, "[Chiles] wants to get into the politics of the nominee. But it is not important for us to consider who the nominee is when we are considering the procedural question. We should resolve the procedural question first . . . ."[33]

Pastore said that it would be "next to folly" to delay the matter to the next day. Chiles strongly disagreed, stating, "This is the appointment of a man who will be a heartbeat away from the Presidency at a time when the country is wondering whether there is an honest man to hold office. Is there someone we can put our trust and confidence in?"[34] He added: "[M]y feeling is that if we can sit to impeach a Vice President, we ought to have sense enough to act on the name of one who has been nominated and determine his qualifications." Toward the end of the debate Senator Kennedy argued that "the unique and unprecedented nature of the question before us is ample warrant for action by the Senate to name a select ad hoc committee."[35] He said that the Committees on the Judiciary and Government Operations had as much claim to jurisdiction as the Rules Committee, adding, "There has never been an instance in the history of this country in which the Rules Committee has considered a nomination."[36]

Senator Joseph R. Biden Jr. of Delaware added, "[T]he one thing I think we must impress upon the American people is that we do not think this is business as usual, that the man whom we are going to confirm as the Vice President of the United States may very well be the next President within the next 3 years."[37] Senator Marlow W. Cook of Kentucky noted:

> So I can only say that I have a notion and a terrible suspicion that the House . . . will send the nomination to . . . committee, . . . have its hearings, . . . move that nomination to the floor, . . . have its up and down vote, and this distinguished body will still be sitting here making a determination of how it is even going to consider the nomination in the first place.[38]

"[I]f we find ourselves in that position," Cook continued, "then we have proven to the country that we are the kind of body that, in many of their minds, they think we are." The eloquence notwithstanding, the resolutions offered by Chiles and Mansfield were put over to October 13, with Chiles's the first to be considered.

On October 13, with Ford's nomination now known, Chiles withdrew his resolution and the nomination was referred smoothly to the nine-member Rules Committee.[39] Since Gerald Ford did not fall in the category of a potential 1976 presidential candidate and since his confirmation seemed certain, the opportunity for members of the Senate to participate in the hearing process no longer appeared as politically significant as it had before the name of the nominee was known. Had the nominee then been considered a potential Republican presidential candidate for 1976, it is likely that considerable additional debate on the committee question would have ensued in the Senate.

Action by the Senate

Following his nomination, Ford became the subject of the most extensive investigation accorded any candidate for national office.[40] In fact, Ford had "twice the scrutiny" Teamster boss Jimmy Hoffa had during the latter's hearings before Congress. The FBI dispatched more than 350 agents from 33 field offices to inquire into every aspect of his life. The Library of Congress concurrently undertook to make available to the committees of Congress all the information it could assemble on his life and public career. Staff personnel from the General Accounting Office and the Government Operations Permanent Investigations Subcommittee were made available to assist in the investigation. Ford's tax returns for the past seven years were examined, and those for the previous five were audited by the Internal Revenue Service and by the staffs of the House Judiciary Committee, the Senate Rules Committee, and the Joint Congressional Committee on Taxation. Ford's medical records were examined, and persons who might have treated him questioned. Campaign reports, records, and statements on file with the House of Representatives and in Michigan were studied. His bank accounts, correspondence with government agencies, speeches, and office printing and payroll records were scrutinized; bar association and police records were examined for references to him. To illustrate the exacting detail into which the investigation delved, a player on a college football team against whom Ford had an unnecessary-roughness penalty was interviewed about the reason for the penalty.[41] Ironically, Ford's popularity in Congress, especially in the House, provided reason to proceed deliberately. Speaker Carl Albert worried that too speedy a confirmation might appear to reflect cronyism that would undermine Ford's legitimacy and that of the Section 2 process.[42]

As a result of this investigation, which included interviews with more than 1,000 persons, the FBI collected more than 1,700 pages of raw data that were inspected by the chairman and the ranking minority member of the Senate Rules Committee and the chairman and seven other members of the House Judiciary Committee.

Ford's confirmation hearings took place under the most ominous of circumstances. Less than two weeks before the start of the hearings, over the weekend of October 20, President Nixon had dismissed Special Prosecutor Archibald Cox and abolished his office—an action that led to the immediate resignations of Attorney General Richardson and Deputy Attorney General Ruckelshaus. These events prompted demands throughout the nation for the President's resignation or impeachment.* Western Union reported that more than 150,000 telegrams flooded Washington in the following three days, "the heaviest concentrated volume on record." More than twenty proposals were introduced in the House of Representatives calling for either Nixon's impeachment or an impeachment investigation. A number of these resolutions were referred to the House Judiciary Committee, which was instructed to begin an impeachment inquiry. Chairman Peter Rodino declared on October 24 that his committee would "proceed full steam ahead," despite the President's decision earlier that week to turn certain Watergate tapes over to

---

* In mid-November 1973, as demands for Nixon's impeachment increased, White House counsels Leonard Garment and Fred Buzhardt concluded that the President should resign. In weekend discussions with Alexander Haig and Ronald Ziegler they urged his resignation, but since Ford had not yet been confirmed as Vice President, they did not act further. The President himself seemed determined not to resign. Theodore H. White, *Breach of Faith: The Fall of Richard Nixon* 271–72 (1975).

the federal district court. On October 25 Ford said that the House should "carry on" its impeachment inquiry. Several days later the nation again was startled, this time by the disclosure that certain of the subpoenaed tapes did not in fact exist. On November 1, the day Ford's confirmation hearings opened before the Senate Rules and Administration Committee, the office of Special Prosecutor was reestablished, the appointment of Leon Jaworski as Special Prosecutor was announced, and the President indicated that he would cooperate with the ongoing investigation.

To highlight the immediate need for action, Speaker Albert, next in line of succession should Nixon be impeached and convicted before a new Vice President was confirmed, prepared, at the advice of Theodore Sorensen, special counsel to and speech writer for President John F. Kennedy, a contingency plan. This contingency plan was to be locked in a safe and kept in secrecy unless it was needed. The contingency plan was important because as Speaker Albert wrote to Sorensen, "[T]he consequences of not acting swiftly and correctly, should catastrophe ever strike, are too great for one not to have some advance knowledge of what he should do." The memorandum prepared by Sorensen was locked in Albert's safe for nine years untouched.[43]

At the outset of the televised Senate hearings, Chairman Howard Cannon of Nevada stated that the committee "should view its obligations as no less important than the selection of a potential President of the United States."[44] He expressed his view that under the Twenty-Fifth Amendment the President has the right to choose a person "whose philosophy and politics are virtually identical to his own" and that it is not proper to withhold confirmation based on a nominee's voting record in Congress. Rather, said Cannon, the committee's function was to examine a nominee's qualifications for Vice President—his morals, integrity, financial history, and the like. He concluded:

> It is for the members of this committee to establish a precedent—a solid, constitutional precedent—by pursuing an orderly, logical, thorough, and honest inquiry into the nominee's qualifications. This is being done in the public interest, because the citizens of the United States who normally choose the President and Vice President are participating only vicariously in this confirmation proceeding by following each action taken by the respective branches of the Congress.[45]

Ford was the first witness to testify before the committee. In his opening remarks he made clear his intention not to be a candidate for public office in 1976, stating, "I have no intention to run, and I can foresee no circumstances where I would change my mind."[46] He acknowledged the committee's responsibilities under the Twenty-Fifth Amendment and said that it would receive his full cooperation. During the course of his two days of testimony Ford was interrogated on his personal and campaign finances, real estate holdings, directorships, and stock holdings; his role in the award of certain government contracts; and his role in the attempted impeachment investigation of Supreme Court Associate Justice William O. Douglas.

A great deal of the committee's attention in its questioning of Ford focused on charges made against him by a Washington lobbyist that he had received money for political favors, that his staff had received gifts from the lobbyist,* and that he had been a patient of a New York psychiatrist. Ford's views on such issues as inflation, education, NATO, foreign relations, busing, and tax reform were elicited. His views on Watergate-related issues were also explored, including the subject of presidential immunity, impoundment of funds by the President, executive privilege, the independence of the special prosecutor, the missing Watergate tapes, the role of the FBI, and ways to improve President Nixon's credibility. It is interesting that, when Cannon asked Ford whether a successor President would have the power to prevent or terminate a criminal prosecution against his predecessor, Ford responded, "I do not think the public would stand for it. I think—and whether he has the technical authority or not, I cannot give you a categorical answer. The Attorney General, in my opinion, with the help and support of the American people, would be the controlling factor."[47]

In his answers to Watergate-related questions, Ford was careful not to undermine the positions taken by Nixon. For example, Ford indicated his support for a special prosecutor appointed by the executive branch rather than by the Judiciary or by Congress.[48] On executive privilege, he expressed the view that documents and tapes bearing upon the possible commission of crimes should not be withheld, but those bearing on national security and foreign relations were within the umbrella of the privilege.[49]

Ford's role in halting an early Watergate investigation by the House Banking and Currency Committee was also examined by the Rules Committee. His political philosophy was probed, as were his views on impeachment and the nature of impeachable offenses, the public financing of elections, the role of the Vice President, the relationship between the executive branch and Congress, and the role of the Attorney General.

In the course of his testimony, Ford said of his qualifications to be Vice President:

> I believe I can be a ready conciliator and calm communicator between the White House and Capitol Hill, between the reelection mandate of the Republican President and the equally emphatic mandate of the Democratic 93d Congress.[50]

---

* A lobbyist named Robert Winter-Berger wrote a book in which he stated that members of the House had given him funds. The reference in the book to the date he met with then-Representative Ford was later found to be erroneous because Ford was out of the country at the time. Benton Becker, *Adequacy of Current Succession Law in Light of the Constitution and Policy Considerations*, 79 FORDHAM L. REV. 897, 899 (2010).

He said that, if confirmed, he would adopt President Eisenhower's precept of doing "what I believe is best for America," and Lincoln's of doing it "with firmness in the right, as God gives us to see the right." He observed that "[t]ruth is the glue or the bond that holds government together, and not only government, but civilization itself."[51]

Upon the conclusion of Ford's testimony, Senator Bayh testified on the meaning and intent of the Twenty-Fifth Amendment, stating that the fundamental question was whether Ford could "serve our country as President." Bayh said that the intent of the Twenty-Fifth Amendment "was to get a Vice President who would be compatible and could work harmoniously with the President." Bayh suggested that the following criteria be considered: "Honesty, integrity, no skeletons in the closet that do not exacerbate the confidence problem as we have it right now, and appropriate respect for and dedication to reasonable interpretation of the Constitution."[52] He indicated that on the basis of such criteria he would support Ford, even though he and Ford had voted differently on a number of issues.

Ten members of the House of Representatives, representing both parties and different points of view and parts of the country, then testified in support of Ford's nomination. One of the ten presented a poll of his constituents which showed that 79.1 percent favored Ford's confirmation.[53] Underscored throughout the testimony of these members of Congress was the respect and the esteem Ford had earned as a result of his twenty-five years in Congress. They described Ford as "honest," "reasonable," "absolutely fair," a person of "calm judgment," "straight-forward," and "humble." They said he possessed "integrity" and "an ability to draw people together," to "rise above partisanship," and to inspire "mutual respect and good will." Said Representative Martha W. Griffiths of Michigan, a Democrat:

> Some people appear to believe that the Congress should not confirm as a Vice President a person who is not committed to the philosophy of the person writing or speaking. In my judgment, Congress cannot take such an attitude. We are not here to say that unless the choice of the President agrees with us on ecology or defense or some other popular issue, that Congress should not vote to confirm him. This is not the purpose of the 25th amendment, and it is not within the province of this body to say, because we do not agree with him on the issues, we will not support him. We are here to check Jerry Ford's integrity, his ability, his leadership ability, and with any confirmation, to give the stamp of approval upon those items.[54]

Testimony was also received against the nomination. Representative Bella S. Abzug of New York, also a Democrat, testified that the Twenty-Fifth Amendment did not envision a situation in which the elected President and Vice President both left office, and she urged that a special election be held under such circumstances.[55] She suggested that action on the Ford nomination be deferred until the House decided whether to impeach Nixon and hold a special election. Abzug added that she would vote against Ford's confirmation since she disagreed with his policies. Clarence Mitchell of the NAACP* testified that Ford had shown a narrow approach to civil rights, but he hoped that if Ford became Vice President he would improve in this area, as Lyndon Johnson had after he succeeded to the presidency. Another black witness, Maurice Dawkins of Opportunities Industrialization Centers, however, praised Ford for his work for and support of minority enterprise programs throughout the nation.

Joseph L. Rauh Jr., national vice-chairman of Americans for Democratic Action, argued that the Twenty-Fifth Amendment contemplated an active role for Congress, and that it reflected no presumption in favor of confirmation. He said that Congress was to be a surrogate for the voters, obligated to use the tests applied by the voters, such as stature, competence, experience, and philosophy. "[T]he appropriate standard," said Rauh, "is whether Mr. Ford is qualified to be President of the United States, and whether he is among the group of persons that a majority of the Members of both Houses of Congress want to see as President of the United States."[56] Basing his position on, among other things, Ford's voting record and his lack of experience in foreign affairs, Rauh urged that he not be confirmed. Rauh noted that many in the liberal community favored Ford's confirmation on the ground that it was a necessary precondition for impeachment of Nixon. Such a view, he said, was short because once people realized "more and more that Mr. Ford is not qualified for the job . . . he is going to give President Nixon job insurance."[57]

Another witness, John F. Banzhaf III, a George Washington University law professor, stated that the Twenty-Fifth Amendment did not allow a President to force a Vice President out of office and then nominate his successor. Banzhaf requested that Congress determine whether Agnew had been driven from office before it consider the Ford nomination.

Besides holding public hearings on November 1, 5, and 14, the committee met in executive session on November 7 to receive testimony regarding the charges made against Ford. At this session the lobbyist, Robert N. Winter-Berger, was unable to document his charges,† and the psychiatrist, Dr. Arnold Hutschnecker, labeled the reports that Ford had been his patient as "lies" and "fantasies." At the end of the hearing the committee decided to make public the transcript of its proceedings. On November 15 the committee made a number of other decisions, including one not to disclose Ford's tax returns, since no other official was required to do so. A statement of Ford's net worth as of September 30, 1973, was placed in the record, together with a statement from his accountant of his earnings and taxes over the

---

* National Association for Advancement of Colored People.

† After Winter-Berger appeared and testified, the House sent the testimony to the FBI to review and determine if perjury had been committed. Becker, *supra*, at 899.

past five years. The committee also decided to have the transcript of its November 7 executive session reviewed by the Department of Justice for possible violations of law by the lobbyist, including perjury.

On November 20, thirty-eight days after beginning its inquiry, the Senate Rules and Administration Committee approved Ford's nomination, 9 to 0. In its report the committee said that not every member agreed with Ford's voting record, philosophy of government, personal and political views, and public actions during his twenty-five years in Congress, but judging him on his total record it saw no impediment that would disqualify him. The report stated that under the Twenty-Fifth Amendment a President would be expected to nominate a person of his own party and perhaps his own political philosophy, and it added that some members of the committee and electorate might not agree that Ford was the best choice the President could have made from available Republicans. In conclusion, the committee stated that in the critical areas of philosophy, character, and integrity, Ford "fully met reasonable tests."[58]

Ford's nomination came to the floor of the Senate on November 27. The debate that followed was not extensive and reflected widespread support for Ford and little opposition. Democratic and Republican senators alike praised Ford's openness, candor, and integrity. A number of senators indicated that they would vote for confirmation despite their disagreement with his political philosophy. Democratic Senator Ted Kennedy's remarks were typical:

> [T]he nature of the 25th amendment is such that it intends not for the Senate to choose on its own a candidate for the Vice-Presidency who reflects the political beliefs of each Senator or of the body as a whole, but to "advise and consent" to the nomination of an individual.[59]

Democratic Senator Frank Church said:

> Mr. President, some have argued that Gerald Ford is not the man of their choice for Vice President. Neither is he mine. But the Constitution leaves it with the President—not with Congress—to do the choosing. Our duty is either to ratify or reject the President's choice. If the hearings had revealed any basis on which to conclude that Mr. Ford were ineligible to serve as Vice President, I would, without hesitation, vote against him. The record, however, reveals nothing in Mr. Ford's background that would disqualify him from holding this office.[60]

Democratic Senator John V. Tunney of California added:

> I do not always share his political views, but I believe that while Congress may impeach a President, it should not repeal the platform that elected him.[61]

Senator Philip Hart declared that Ford met the Twenty-Fifth Amendment tests articulated by Bayh during the confirmation hearings and that, "should he be called to the Presidency, he would be a steady, decent, and believable Chief Executive. And those attributes, I believe, are what this Nation needs most at this particular moment in history."[62] One Democratic senator, Gaylord Nelson of Wisconsin, said that his philosophical differences with Ford were so fundamental that he could not compromise his principles by voting for him. Another Democratic senator, William D. Hathaway of Maine, inquired whether the emoluments of the vice presidency had been increased recently and thereby raised a question about the applicability of Article 1, section 6 of the Constitution.* Cannon replied that they had not been increased during the period of Ford's current term and added that he had been advised that a Vice President was not a "civil officer" within the meaning of that provision.[63]

Throughout the debate senators acknowledged the possibility that Ford might become President. Thus, immediately after his nomination was approved, by a vote of 92 to 3,† Senator Tunney stated:

Mr. Ford, within the next year, may, indeed, be President. So today's action not only initiates the 25th amendment of our Constitution, but may, in fact, ordain the 38th President of our Nation.[64]

Action by the House

On November 15, the day after the Senate Rules Committee closed its public hearings, the thirty-eight-member House Judiciary Committee opened its televised hearings, with Gerald Ford as the first witness. Almost half the witnesses who testified before the Senate Rules Committee also testified before or submitted statements to the House Judiciary Committee. Prior to the commencement of the hearings, the House leadership made clear its determination that Ford's confirmation should not be delayed, as advocated by several members of the House, pending the outcome of the Nixon impeachment investigation, and that the confirmation hearings should be thorough so as to avoid charges of cronyism being leveled against the House.[65]

In opening the House hearings, Chairman Rodino emphasized the need for both expeditious action and a thorough examination of Ford's qualifications and

---

* Which provides, in part: "No Senator or Representative shall, during the Time for which he was elected, be appointed to any civil Office under the Authority of the United States which shall have been created, or the Emoluments whereof shall have been increased during such time. . . ." The focus of attention was on an act passed by Congress on October 24, 1973, which increased the retirement annuities of certain federal employees, including possibly the Vice President.

† Voting against were Democratic Senators Hathaway, Nelson, and Thomas Eagleton of Missouri. Absent on official business was, among others, former Democratic presidential candidate George McGovern of South Dakota.

fitness for the vice presidency. He stated that under the Twenty-Fifth Amendment Congress "must act as the surrogate for the electorate in evaluating this nomination" and recognize that "the President has the right to nominate a man with whom he can work in concert, ideologically, and politically." "I am hopeful," said Rodino, "that these hearings can produce a new sense of trust in the essential decency of our Nation and in its ability to meet the challenges to its Government's integrity."[66]

Throughout the hearings the prediction was repeated that Ford might soon be President. Said Representative George E. Danielson, Democrat of California, on the second day of the hearings, "I am thinking you are going to be President within a year . . . ."[67] Another Democratic committee member, Representative Edward Mezvinsky of Iowa, observed that "[w]e could face it again [i.e., another nomination under the Amendment], as some said, within a year."[68] In his testimony before the committee, Democratic Representative Edward P. Boland of Massachusetts remarked that "[t]his is the first time in the history of this Nation that a Vice-Presidential nominee has sought confirmation under the provisions of the 25th Amendment. It is also one of the few times when it seems possible that a Vice-Presidential nominee has a more than average chance of succeeding as President."[69] Toward the end of the hearings Representative Jerome R. Waldie, Democrat of California, said, "I am quite convinced you will, despite my own personal opposition and reservations, become President of the United States . . . ."[70]

Perhaps with this possible succession in mind, Chairman Rodino made plain at the outset that Ford would be accorded no special privileges as a member of Congress. Accordingly, Ford was intensively interrogated by the committee for four of its six days of hearings. Of the thirty-six hours of testimony heard by the committee, nineteen were devoted to questioning Ford on many of the matters covered in his Senate testimony as well as on new issues.

Ford's role in the attempted impeachment of Justice Douglas came under closer scrutiny than it had in the Senate, and new information was developed about the political nature of that effort. Representative Waldie, in particular, closely questioned Ford about his relationship with the Justice Department at the time of the Douglas impeachment inquiry. At one point during Waldie's interrogation, Ford exhibited an issue of *Evergreen* magazine containing photographs of nudes near excerpts from a book written by Douglas. This prompted some members of the committee to criticize Ford, one member characterizing the display as "incredibly insensitive."[71]

Ford's testimony on the 1970 invasion of Cambodia and his justification for a President's withholding information from Congress also brought critical responses from several members of the committee.[72] As in his Senate testimony, Ford was careful not to undermine President Nixon's positions. Although he testified that the impeachment inquiry should go forward expeditiously, he also expressed the view that on the information available, there were no grounds for impeachment.[73] He testified about the approach Nixon should take to restore confidence in his administration but at the same time defended Nixon's firing of Cox, the invasion of Cambodia, and the impoundment of funds.[74]

One area of controversy that arose during the hearings was the denial to most committee members of access to the raw data assembled by the FBI. Representatives Danielson, Mezvinsky, John Conyers Jr., William S. Cohen of Maine, Elizabeth Holtzman of New York, Charles B. Rangel of New York, and John F. Seiberling of Ohio—all Democrats except for the Republican Cohen—criticized the Department of Justice's limitation of such access to the committee's chairman and its seven senior members.*[75] Rangel argued that the committee could not discharge its responsibilities properly without such information and suggested that Ford's nomination be delayed pending its availability.[76] In response, Republican Representatives Thomas F. Railsback of Illinois, Robert McClory of Illinois, David W. Dennis of Indiana, and others contended that the hearings had already been delayed and that it was important to bring them to a close. The latter point of view prevailed with the close of the hearings on November 26, eleven days after their opening.

Furthermore, Ford's own aides and advisors were not allowed to view the reports the FBI had compiled about Ford's background.† A list of witnesses was also not provided to Ford's staff. However, Ford's staff was able to informally obtain information generally through Senator Bob Griffin of Michigan.[77] Another area of disagreement involved the role of Congress under the Twenty-Fifth Amendment. Many accepted the view that the Amendment gave the President the right to choose a person who would be ideologically compatible with him. According to Republican Representative J. Edward Hutchinson of Michigan:

> [T]he role of this committee is not to determine whether Gerald R. Ford's views on domestic and foreign policy are consonant with those of its members, but rather to determine whether he is qualified to assume the tensions and troubles of the Presidency if that office should for any reason devolve upon him, as well as to determine whether he is the kind of person in whom the people can place their trust.[78]

Gerald Ford testified that:

---

* This criticism undoubtedly prompted the Department of Justice a year later to turn over to the entire committee the raw data assembled in connection with Nelson Rockefeller's nomination for Vice President.

† Alexander Haig, Nixon's chief of staff, attempted to feed Ford's staff information prepared in the FBI reports. Once Ford's staffers heard that Ford had had at least one phone conversation with Haig wherein Haig shared some information, Ford's staff contacted Haig and told him "in a very forceful way" not to contact Ford and that no assistance from the White House was desired. Becker, *supra*, at 900.

the person so nominated must have a record that has been thoroughly investigated, that would justify the Congress and the American people in having faith and trust in his honesty, his experience, and his judgment. I think that is the criteria.

The 25th amendment says nothing about the qualifications on a partisan basis or philosophical basis.[79]

Others disagreed, suggesting that Congress should take into account changes in public opinion since the most recent presidential election. The following exchange between Ford and Representative Robert F. Drinan, Democrat of Massachusetts, is illustrative:

> MR. DRINAN: But what are the rights of the people under the 25th amendment and, if I may, let me tell you a little bit about my district, and I am their surrogate or their Representative here.
>
> Senator [George] McGovern got more votes [in the 1972 presidential election] in my district than I did. They believe in new priorities and they were overwhelmingly against the war. There is almost a majority so far as we know who want the impeachment of the President[,] and both Elliot Richardson and Mr. Cox are my constituents. . . .
>
> MR. FORD: Mr. Drinan, obviously I couldn't get elected in that district.
>
> MR. DRINAN: I don't know. After the last 2 days, I think you could.
>
> But the people who are disillusioned with this administration, and I am just asking your assistance, what are their rights in this matter? What is the role of the voters, in other words.
>
> If a reliable poll were taken should I, as Congressman, should I follow that? . . . To what extent am I the surrogate, so to speak, under the 25th Amendment.
>
> MR. FORD: Under these most unusual circumstances where we have never had any experience, where the Constitution is being newly tried, we almost have to play it by ear. But my feeling would be, if I were in your position, that they sent you here to exercise your good judgment, and that if you don't use judgment that coincides with theirs you may find some political difficulties a year from November or next November . . . .
>
> MR. DRINAN: Well, would you say, Mr. Ford, that this is really an election by the House, that it doesn't really compare with the "advice and consent"? It is not an approval, it is really an election similar to what the House has under the 12th amendment in unusual cases. Assuming that is so, and I think the legislative history demonstrates that it is at least a mini-election, then political ideology is relevant and to some extent partisan concepts may be employed, and compatibility is not the sole consideration. But I suppose you have to come to priorities and your

voting record, and the priorities that you have chosen from your convictions and your conscience are not the priorities of the vast majority of the
people that I represent . . . .

Now, to what extent do all those priorities enter in. I am asking the
question I think in a more difficult way, to what extent should I say that
I am simply the surrogate, the representative, and I follow a Gallup poll?

MR. FORD: I would try to put myself in your position if I were in that
position, and in the last election, the voters had chosen, we will say, a liberal
Democrat, and as President, and Vice President, and the Vice Presidency
was vacant and it then—and the then President recommended somebody
with political philosophy compatible with his own, which would mean a
nominated Vice President who was likewise liberal philosophically, I think
I would act in those circumstances to confirm that individual, providing
he passed the other tests of forthrightness, honesty, truth, et cetera.[80]

Witness James Larson of the National Lawyers Guild asserted that the most
recent election was void and that Nixon consequently did not have the right to
nominate anyone under the Twenty-Fifth Amendment.[81] Representatives Conyers, Robert W. Kastenmeier of Wisconsin, and others thought it inappropriate
for confirmation hearings to take place until the question of impeachment had
been settled.[82] This led Representative McClory to declare, "To suggest that we
must await with the expectation or hope on the part of some that perhaps the
President might be removed from office before acting to fill the office . . . seems
to me entirely erroneous and quite inappropriate . . . ."[83] The Amendment, said
McClory, calls for an expeditious filling of the office of Vice President whenever
it becomes vacant.

Ford's reputation in Congress and his conduct during the hearings provided a
solid base for confirmation. As in the Senate hearings, members of both parties and
witnesses constantly referred to his qualities of openness and honesty. While
expressing his disapproval of Ford's civil rights record, Clarence Mitchell of the
NAACP nevertheless stated that Ford was the "kind of person I would be glad to
go on a hunting trip with; I know I would not get shot in the back."[84] But, said
Democratic Representative Michael J. Harrington of Massachusetts, "honesty and
decency are not enough. We also must look for proven qualities of leadership and an
ability to serve as a focal point around which a country, a troubled country as I view
it, can rally."[85] For Harrington, Rauh, and Mitchell, Ford did not possess these
qualities. However, the image Ford presented at these televised hearings earned him
accolades across the nation. Said Rodino to the nominee, "With the question of
candor before the public and so absolutely important and so much talked about, you
certainly have displayed that kind of candor that has to be commended."[86]

On November 29, 1973, two days after the Senate had voted on Ford's confirmation, the House Judiciary Committee recommended Ford's confirmation

by a vote of 29 to 8, with one member voting present.* In its report the committee said:

> Finally, not every member of the Committee subscribing to this Report finds himself in complete agreement with the totality of Mr. Ford's voting record, or even with all aspects of his general philosophy of government. Some, though by no means all, are disturbed with elements of his voting record in the area of civil rights and human rights.
>
> But looking at the total record, the Committee finds Mr. Ford fit and qualified to hold the high office for which he has been nominated pursuant to the Twenty-fifth Amendment.[87]

The eight dissenting members generally expressed the view that Ford had not demonstrated the ability to be a capable and effective President. His lack of executive experience and of background in international affairs, his role in the attempted Douglas impeachment, and his voting record in the areas of civil and human rights were all cited as reasons why he should not be confirmed. Thus, Representative Edwards declared that Nixon should have provided a nominee who "would inspire and motivate the Nation"; Kastenmeier, that Ford was too close to Nixon and that under existing circumstances the nominee should "harmonize more with the Congress and the public at large"; and Holtzman, that his twenty-five years in Congress "are barren of creative and independent legislative initiatives on matters of substantive policy." Exclaimed Waldie:

> When succession to the Nixon Presidency occurs, the person succeeding will confront a shambles that has never been equaled in any previous Presidential succession. Nixon will have left the Executive Branch machinery in complete chaos and disarray; the confidence of the people that normally is willingly and earnestly extended to a Presidential successor will be absent and not transferable with ease to Nixon's successor.[88]

Ford did not measure up to such "enormous" and "unique" responsibilities, Waldie said.

On December 6, 1973, the full House of Representatives took up Ford's nomination. During the almost six hours of debate, views were expressed similar to those aired at the hearings. A number of representatives said that they were voting

---

* The eight dissenters were all Democrats: Representatives Kastenmeier, Conyers, Waldie, Drinan, Rangel, Holtzman, Don Edwards of California, and Barbara Jordan of Texas. Representative Seiberling, also a Democrat, voted present. Although he did not support the nomination, Seiberling believed that the House should consider it. Consequently, he also refused to vote against approval, fearing such a vote could be construed as an effort to prevent the House from voting on the nomination. H.R. REP. No. 93-695, at 27–68 (1973).

in favor of confirmation on the basis of their understanding of the Twenty-Fifth Amendment even though they differed with Ford's philosophy and voting record. Representative James G. O'Hara, Democrat of Michigan, said:

> I fail to see, in my reading of the 25th amendment, any requirement that the Congress withhold its consent to the nomination of a Vice President because his views are at variance with those of the majority of the Congress. I submit that to allow ourselves to be caught up in measuring Mr. Ford's qualifications for office against the subjective yardstick of our own philosophies would be to disserve the American people who expect Congress, at this critical moment in history, to rise above partisanship.[89]

Numerous representatives expressed their admiration for Ford's candor, openness, integrity, and ability and for his conduct during the most exhaustive and thorough investigation ever accorded a candidate or nominee for national office in American history. Experiences that members of Congress had shared with Ford during his twenty-five years as a member of the House were recited to show his qualifications for the vice presidency. "[A]t a time when many Americans are questioning the honesty of public officials and . . . have lost faith in those who serve in public office," said Robert E. Bauman of Maryland, a Republican, "Gerald Ford's greatest attribute is his integrity."[90]

In supporting his confirmation, members of the House emphasized that Ford had the ability to work effectively with both parties in Congress, had a compassionate nature, kept his word, and respected opposing points of view. The results of Gallup and various congressional district polls were introduced to show that the people of the country supported his confirmation.[91] Said Republican Representative Samuel L. Devine of Ohio, "If I have any ability to read the pulse of the folks back home, they desperately crave an era of peace, tranquility, calm and serenity. Jerry Ford is just the man to lead us in that direction."[92] In urging Ford's confirmation, Democratic Representative Bo Ginn of Georgia stated:

> These are troubled times in our Nation. We are faced with the recurring problems of the Watergate affair, we are confronted with a critical energy shortage, and with the problems of crime, drug abuse, and many other areas of grave concern to us all. This is a time, then, when we here in Washington must put aside political bickering and pull together to solve these great problems that face us all.[93]

Other representatives argued that Ford's confirmation satisfied the intent of the Twenty-Fifth Amendment. Since he held the same philosophy as President Nixon, his confirmation would continue the election mandate of 1972 in the event that anything should happen to the President.[94] Representative Andrew Young, Democrat of Georgia, said that he was voting for Ford's confirmation because "his accession to the Vice-Presidency will facilitate either the resignation or impeachment of the present occupant of the White House."[95]

But the nomination was opposed by some representatives. Representative Rodino, although praising Ford's integrity and ability and stating that the election mandate of 1972 must be maintained, registered his dissent to the nomination on the grounds that the Nixon administration had been indifferent in the area of human rights and the cause of working people.[96] Other representatives expressed their disapproval on the grounds that Ford had a poor record in civil rights, lacked executive experience, was too partisan, and did not in their view possess the ability to move the country in the right direction. Some pointed to Ford's role in the attempted impeachment of Justice Douglas. Representative Abzug argued that there was a strong possibility that Ford was ineligible because of the emoluments clause of the Constitution. Consequently, she urged that the nomination be deferred pending congressional hearings on the subject.[97]

Some representatives registered their disapproval of Ford on the grounds that the people of the country or of their districts would not select him in an open election.[98] Democratic Representative Jonathan B. Bingham of New York, on the other hand, despite a poll that showed his constituents favoring Ford, voted against confirmation because of his opposition to Ford's voting record and his view that Nixon should have nominated a person with views halfway between the President's and those of a majority of Congress.[99] Other representatives said that under existing circumstances Congress actually was selecting a President, and that Ford did not qualify for that position. "[I]t is my firm opinion," said Representative Danielson, "that he will soon become the President of the United States."[100] Representative Boland stated that there was a better than even chance of Ford's succeeding to the presidency.[101] Democratic Representative Edward R. Roybal of California stated that Ford was highly qualified for the office of Vice President, but since the surrounding circumstances indicated he might become President, he felt obliged to determine whether Ford would be acceptable to a majority of his constituency. After reviewing Ford's voting record, Roybal concluded that it did not represent the views of his district and that his constituents would not have elected Ford as Vice President.[102]

In opposing Ford's nomination, Representative Waldie stated that in reality Congress was electing a President, adding:

> But I suggest to the Members that we do not fulfill our responsibility if we are just voting for Gerald Ford because it will make it easier, under whatever theory we approach it, to obtain the removal of the incumbent President of the United States.

We know we hear that. We hear that all over the floor, and we see it on the wire services, and prominent members of the Republican Party and of the other House are suggesting that the moment Gerald Ford is confirmed, the requirement that confronts the country of removing the President will be more easily and readily obtainable.[103]

Throughout the House debates on Ford's nomination, unlike the Senate debates, differences of opinion were expressed concerning the intent of the Twenty-Fifth Amendment. Some said it embodied a presumption in favor of the President's choice and that it was improper to reject a nominee because his political philosophy was the same as the President's.[104] Representative Conyers argued that "a Member of Congress should vote against . . . any nominee if in his judgment that nominee holds views or has a philosophy which when brought to that high office would in the judgment of the Congressman be unsatisfactory or harmful to Nation as a whole."[105] In response, Republican Representative Charles E. Wiggins of California stated that such a standard would permit a repudiation of the popular mandate from the previous election. Added Wiggins, "It is my point of view . . . that individual Members of Congress must rise against their personal notions of philosophy in order to maintain a continuity in the administration."[106] Democratic Representative Patricia Schroeder of Colorado asserted that, in voting on the nomination, the Congress, "acting as surrogates for the people, [has] the responsibility to weigh Mr. Ford's judgment, independence, and philosophical outlook, all in the context of whether he is a person we can conscientiously endorse as a potential President of the United States."[107] Said Representative M. Caldwell Butler, Republican of Virginia, "I am not impressed by the suggestion that we are but surrogates of our constituents. We were elected to bring our best judgment to bear on the questions that come before us."[108]

Several representatives argued that the Twenty-Fifth Amendment was never intended for the selection of a President, which they believed was occurring by virtue of the surrounding circumstances. Representative Abzug said that there should be a special presidential election in the event of dual vacancies. Declared Republican Representative Wiley Mayne of Iowa, "[T]hey [i.e., the dissenting members of the House Judiciary Committee] want to substitute some other method of choice than that which is provided in the 25th amendment. The hang-up is that they want to abandon the 25th amendment and substitute a new and different method of choosing a Vice President."[109]

During the debate of December 6, Representative Rangel referred to the arrangements already set for Ford's swearing-in and observed, "I feel somewhat superfluous in my role as a Member of the House debating and voting on this confirmation. It appears as if we do not hurry[,] the ceremony will begin before we have a chance to vote."[110] After six hours of debate, Ford's nomination was favorably acted upon by a vote of 387 to 35. Among those voting against the nomination were the eight dissenting members of the House Judiciary Committee and a number of Democratic representatives of liberal persuasion. No Republican cast a negative vote.

Immediately following his confirmation as the fortieth Vice President, Ford was administered the vice-presidential oath by Chief Justice Warren E. Burger before a joint meeting of the Congress held in the chamber of the House of Representatives. Among those in attendance were the justices of the Supreme Court, the members of the Cabinet, ambassadors and ministers of foreign countries, and President Nixon.*

---

* For more information in President's Ford's own words, see Gerald R. Ford, *A Time to Heal: The Autobiography of Gerald R. Ford* (1979).

11

The Resignation of Richard M. Nixon and Succession of Gerald R. Ford

Fellow citizens: God reigns, and the Government at Washington still lives.

JAMES A. GARFIELD, April 15, 1865[1]

The confirmation of Gerald Ford as Vice President suggested to some the solution to the tangle of Watergate.[2] While Agnew was next in line for the presidency it was difficult for many congressmen to consider removing Nixon. Moreover, during the period when the vice presidency was vacant after Agnew's resignation, Nixon remained secure, since it was unlikely that a Democratic Congress would risk the political consequences of appearing to "steal" the White House by installing Democratic Speaker Carl Albert in the presidency. With Ford's selection as Vice President, however, there now existed an attractive alternative to Nixon. It is not surprising, therefore, that during Ford's vice presidency the momentum for exposing the truth about Nixon's involvement in Watergate increased.

Ford's vice-presidential confirmation under Section 2 of the Twenty-Fifth Amendment, however, was not free of hostility. Benton Becker, who served as Ford's attorney during the confirmation hearings, recalled 1973 as "difficult and trying times."* The investigation of then-Congressman Ford was, as expected, "far beyond the scope of inquiry of any Cabinet member or Article III judge confirmation procedure," because of the uneasy political climate surrounding Nixon's imminent departure from the White House.

---

* Benton Becker, *Adequacy of Current Succession Law in Light of the Constitution and Policy Considerations*, 79 FORDHAM L. REV. 897, 897 (2010).

When the Twenty-Fifth Amendment was implemented in 1973, it was a mere six years old. Consequently, there was no model of application on which to base Ford's confirmation hearings, or by which his team could use to anticipate the upcoming challenges. Becker recalls, "There were no procedures. There were no standards. There were no rules." Without prior instances of implementation, all Becker and his colleagues could look to was the language of the Twenty-Fifth Amendment.

The background check on Ford was extensive. "Some 350 FBI agents spent three weeks investigating Ford and produced 1,700 pages of new data; some fifty agents from the Internal Revenue Service, General Accounting Office, and the Senate Rules Committee staff also participated."[3] Becker recalls one particular example of the high scrutiny to which Ford was subjected:

> This was 1973. In the early 1940s, Gerald Ford played football for the University of Michigan. He played sixty minutes. He was the center and he was a linebacker. Against Ohio State, in his third year, linebacker Gerald Ford was called for a penalty for tackling a halfback from Ohio State and the penalty was unnecessary roughness . . . . Two FBI agents found that halfback and asked him, "What did the linebacker do to you?" . . . They left no stone unturned, none at all.[4]

Such serious examination, however, was necessary under the circumstances.[5]

Ultimately, Ford was confirmed in under two months, an achievement that "was impressive especially when the surrounding circumstances are considered."[6] Section 2 of the Twenty-Fifth Amendment proved successful in "extricating America from the unique circumstances"[7] surrounding Watergate. It also provided a clear procedure that allowed the Republican Party to remain in control of the White House.[8]

As the Watergate drama unfolded, Vice President Ford found himself in a difficult position because both critics and supporters of the Nixon presidency constantly looked to him for comments. Furthermore, when he ascended into office, "there were people . . . in high positions in the Nixon White House who honestly believed, and carried out their beliefs with their behavior, that Gerald Ford, the Vice President of the United States, was nothing more than another middle-level officer, who could be told what to do and punished if he didn't do it."[9] In the months following his confirmation, Ford acquired a reputation for vacillation and inconsistency in dealing with the Watergate battles. Sometimes he spoke as a mediator between the congressional Watergate committees and President Nixon and urged Nixon to compromise with their requests for information.[10] Invariably, the White House failed to endorse these suggestions.[11] At other times, Ford defended Nixon as the victim of "a few extreme partisans" bent on using Watergate to crush his policies.[12] Thus, speaking before the American Farm Bureau in January 1974,

Ford delivered a speech—which he admitted had been written by the White House—in which he charged that the attacks against Nixon were led by radicals, Nixon-haters, the press, and "super-welfare staters" who sought to drive Nixon from office for their own political purposes.[13] Two hours later it was disclosed in federal court that an eighteen-minute gap on a crucial Watergate tape had been caused by five separate erasures.[14] As a consequence, Ford received widespread criticism for acting as a Nixon apologist instead of maintaining his neutrality. A few days later Ford announced that the White House possessed information that would refute the testimony of former presidential counsel John Dean and exonerate the President, but that he had not had time to read the information.[15] President Nixon assured him, Ford said, that the release of key Watergate tapes was "being actively considered."[16] But the White House, citing executive privilege, refused to release those tapes.

In his first three months in office, Ford traveled nearly 30,000 miles, campaigning for Republican candidates and addressing party meetings. His popularity and self-confidence increased as the administration was weakened by daily Watergate revelations. Although he still defended Nixon, by March 1974 Ford was focusing on Republican Party achievements and occasionally criticizing Nixon for not co-operating with the investigations. He was disturbed that the Republicans had lost three out of four special congressional elections, including one for his former House seat in Michigan, and tried to enlist support for Republican candidates by forecasting a grave threat to the two-party system in overwhelming Democratic victories. So Ford walked "the fine line between loyalty to the President and loyalty to his fellow Republicans facing the electorate."[17] At a meeting of Middle Western Republican leaders in late March, he blasted the Committee for the Re-election of the President as an "arrogant, elite guard of political adolescents" that had bypassed the regular organization and had dictated the terms of the national election.[18] Later that day he commented that he was not criticizing the President personally.[19]

Throughout the spring of 1974, Ford vacillated between defense of the President and subtle criticism of Nixon's failure to cooperate with the investigations. On April 14, he admitted that he had tried and failed to reach a compromise to avoid a subpoena by the House for certain Watergate tapes.[20] In California that month Ford advised Republicans to stress the individual merits of congressional candidates and the basic differences between the Republican and Democratic parties so that the fall mid-term elections would not become a referendum on President Nixon.[21] Yet several days later in Oklahoma he linked the fortunes of the Republican Party with Nixon's and urged strong support for the President as a means of aiding Republican candidates for Congress.[22] On April 29, Nixon released to the House Judiciary Committee and made public edited transcripts of the Watergate tapes. When the committee voted to reject the transcripts as a substitute for the tapes, Ford suggested that the White House should be more flexible in permitting verification of the tapes by the committee.[23] He also said that he was "a little disappointed" by the transcripts because they did not reflect the Richard Nixon he had known for twenty-five years.[24]

As the end of Nixon's presidency approached, criticism of Ford's speeches increased. He was variously described as a "rudderless tongue" and a person without firm convictions who was adding to the climate of political confusion.[25] In answer to these criticisms, Ford said that he considered it his duty "to try to head off deadlock and seek a reasonable and prompt resolution of the nagging Watergate issue . . . ."[26] In May 1974, *Newsweek* magazine reported that Nixon was considerably disenchanted with Ford and that, in a private meeting with Nelson Rockefeller, he had asked contemptuously whether Rockefeller could imagine Ford sitting in the presidential chair.*[27] Ford declined to comment on the report.

In June, Nixon traveled abroad, visiting the Middle East, Brussels, and Moscow,[28] as if seeking to quell the domestic turmoil with international successes. At about the same time, it was revealed that Nixon was suffering from a mild case of phlebitis (inflammation of a vein) in his leg and that he was receiving medical treatment but was in "no danger."[29] The President's health had been a topic of discussion throughout the Watergate period, with attention focused on his actions under stress, his physical appearance, and his behavior.[30] There was even speculation that he might use the inability provision of Section 3 of the Twenty-Fifth Amendment to escape impeachment by declaring that he was physically unable to carry out his duties and thereupon turning over his powers and duties to the Vice President as Acting President.[31]

Even apart from the possibility of Nixon's using the Twenty-Fifth Amendment because of a physical inability, the Amendment, it may be argued, offered him an opportunity to step aside temporarily during an impeachment inquiry. In fact, several members of Congress, including Republican Senators Jacob K. Javits of New York[32] and Milton R. Young of North Dakota,[33] suggested that he consider standing aside under the Twenty-Fifth Amendment on the ground that he was unable to discharge the duties of his office because of the constitutional controversies attending Watergate.

Such a move, it was reasoned, would ensure national stability under the leadership of Acting President Ford while freeing Nixon to concentrate on his Watergate defense.[34] However, the President himself continued to assert that he would never resign from office and, in an interview with James J. Kilpatrick, said that he would

---

* According to former presidential counsel Charles Colson, Nixon also supposedly said, "Maybe what this country needs is a nice, clean Jerry Ford. But the trouble with Jerry Ford is, it would take him two years just to get up to speed." Newsweek, February 17, 1975, at 21.

"rule out the rather fatuous suggestion that [he] take the 25th Amendment and just step out and have Vice President Ford step in for a while."[35]

During the month of July 1974, the fate of the Nixon presidency was sealed. On July 24, 1974, the U.S. Supreme Court ruled unanimously that the President must turn over to Judge John J. Sirica sixty-four tapes of conversations that constituted evidence for the Watergate criminal cover-up trial.[36] It has been reported that Nixon considered defying the Court and refusing to release the tapes on the ground that he had a constitutional right to withhold the tapes even from the judiciary. Special presidential counsel James D. St. Clair persuaded Nixon that impeachment by the House and conviction by the Senate would undoubtedly be the congressional reaction to such defiance.[37] Eight hours after the Supreme Court's decision, St. Clair announced that the President would "comply with that decision in all respects."[38]

That evening, the House Judiciary Committee began hearing witnesses in its impeachment inquiry. By July 30, the committee had approved three articles of impeachment, charging, first, that Nixon had engaged in a course of conduct designed to obstruct justice;[39] second, that he had abused his presidential power;[40] and finally that he had unconstitutionally defied the House subpoenas for Watergate tapes and documents.[41] In view of the committee's heavy, mostly bipartisan vote, it seemed likely that the full House of Representatives would vote to impeach the President, but the outcome of a consequent Senate trial, in which a two-thirds vote was needed for removal, was far from clear. On July 31, St. Clair learned why Nixon had tried so zealously to repress the tapes. Among those to be released to Judge Sirica were three tapes of conversations on June 23, 1972, between the President and White House Chief of Staff H. R. Haldeman. These conversations revealed that Nixon had taken part in the cover-up by ordering the FBI not to investigate the burglary.

Against this background, the President's closest advisers began a campaign in early August to persuade him that resignation would serve the nation's and his own best interests. Although Nixon at first argued that the evidence was "inconsequential," he was finally convinced that impeachment and conviction were inevitable.[42]

As the pressure for Nixon to resign increased, Chief of Staff Alexander M. Haig met with Ford on August 1 to inform him of the devastating tape evidence and the likelihood that Nixon would be impeached by the House of Representatives. Haig inquired of Ford whether he was prepared to assume the presidency and whether he had any recommendations as to what course of action Nixon should follow. Haig mentioned that various options were being considered by the White House, including Nixon's temporarily stepping aside under the Twenty-Fifth Amendment and resigning after granting himself a pardon. In response to a question by Ford about the President's pardoning power, Haig expressed the view that a President has the power to grant a pardon even before indictment. Ford concluded the meeting by saying that he needed time to consider what had been said. Early the next morning Ford met with James St. Clair and late that afternoon called Haig to make clear that he would have no recommendations for Nixon on his course of action.*

On Saturday, August 3, Nixon retired to the presidential retreat at Camp David with his family and principal aides to draft a public statement to accompany the release of the tapes. It was reported that he still resisted resignation and thought he could survive the impeachment process.[43]

On August 4 Ford said in a speech, "I believe the President is innocent. I don't want any impression created that I've changed my mind about the President's innocence." On August 5, the tapes were made public along with Nixon's statement acknowledging that the conversations therein were "at variance with certain of my previous statements" and that he had not disclosed the evidence to his lawyers or supporters on the House Judiciary Committee.[44] Public and congressional reaction was devastating. The President's staunchest supporters on the House Judiciary Committee agreed now that he should be impeached and in public and private statements urged that he resign. Vice President Ford issued a statement that "the public interest is no longer served by repetition of my previously expressed belief that . . . the President is not guilty of an impeachable offense."[45]

On August 6, Nixon met with his Cabinet and declared that he would not resign but would let the constitutional process run its course.[46] Ford was present at the meeting and stated that he had no recommendations as to what Nixon should do in light of the new evidence. It is reported that Secretary of State Henry A. Kissinger stayed after that meeting to warn Nixon that the balance of international affairs might be upset if a powerless President continued in the White House.[47] Despite the counsel of his advisers, Nixon appeared determined to remain in office.

The next day Representative Robert McClory, a senior Republican of the House Judiciary Committee, was informed by two key Democrats—Speaker Carl Albert and Judiciary Chairman Peter Rodino—that they were prepared to drop the impeachment proceedings against Nixon if he resigned. When McClory tried to pass the information along to the White House by way of the office of Vice President Ford, he was told by a Ford aide, "The Vice President is not taking part in the events occurring now. He would not want to have anything to do with it."†

Subsequently, the information was delivered by McClory to William E. Timmons, a White House aide, who gave the message to Nixon.

That same day Nixon was visited by Republican Senator Barry Goldwater, Senate Minority Leader Hugh Scott, and House Minority Leader John J. Rhodes of

---

* Ford's version of the events of the first week in August is described in his testimony on Nixon's pardon. Hearings on the Pardon of Richard M. Nixon and Related Matters, Before the Subcomm. on Criminal Justice of the House Comm. on the Judiciary, 93d Congress, 2d Sess. 90–111, 148–58 (1975).
† This incident was disclosed by the *Los Angeles Times* in its issue of December 16, 1975 at 1, 7.

Arizona. Prior to this meeting, Haig had privately told these members of Congress not to make a direct recommendation of resignation because Nixon was considering it and might balk if he felt pressured.[48] At the meeting only Nixon himself mentioned resignation as on option, although the conversation indirectly centered on resignation. Nixon said he understood that only ten members of the House of Representatives would support him and asked about his chances in the Senate. Goldwater and Scott estimated that he might have up to fifteen votes. Then Goldwater listed lifelong Nixon admirers, both Republicans and Southern Democrats, who would vote for conviction. Nixon called the situation "damn gloomy," while Goldwater termed it "hopeless." As the meeting adjourned, Nixon intimated that he understood that resignation was his only choice.[49] That evening his speechwriters were told to prepare a resignation statement, and Nixon informed Kissinger of his decision to resign.[50]

On August 8, at about 11:00 A.M., President Nixon summoned Vice President Ford to the White House and informed him of his decision. They talked for about an hour and discussed the timing of events.[51] At eight that evening Nixon met with about forty of his most loyal congressional supporters and at nine announced to the nation on television that he would resign the next day at noon. He made no mention of his imminent impeachment but rather cited the erosion of his political base in Congress as the reason for his resignation. The speech was a recitation of the accomplishments of the Nixon administration with no reference to the matters that destroyed it.[52]

On Friday morning, August 9, after a brief farewell to his staff, President and Mrs. Nixon boarded *Air Force One* for the Western White House in San Clem-

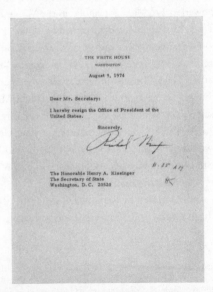

President Richard M. Nixon's letter of resignation. (Courtesy National Archives.)

ente. His letter of resignation was delivered to Secretary Kissinger at 11:30, and at noon Gerald R. Ford was sworn in as the thirty-eighth President of the United States. In an emotion-charged address, he declared, "Our long national nightmare is over." He called upon the nation to "bind up the internal wounds of Watergate," adding, "Our Constitution works. Our great Republic is a government of laws and not of men. Here, the people rule." While noting that he had not been elected President by the ballots of the people, he stated that he had been confirmed by members of "both parties, elected by all the people and acting under the Constitution in their name." In his concluding remarks, Ford said, "May our former President, who brought peace to millions, find it for himself."[53]

What followed was an orderly transfer of power, with Ford acting quickly to open communications with Congress, reduce the White House staff, and shift some authority back to the Cabinet.

The smoothness of the transition was not accidental. Transition planning for a Ford presidency had begun secretly in May 1974.[54] Philip Buchen, former law partner of and close adviser to Ford, apparently concluded at the time that there was a good chance Ford would be suddenly thrust into the presidency. Without informing Ford, Buchen enlisted the help of Clay T. Whitehead, Nixon's adviser on telecommunications. Whitehead served on the staff that guided the transition from the Johnson administration to the Nixon administration, and Buchen considered him a trustworthy ally. They acted in total secrecy so that Ford would not be embarrassed by appearing to lack confidence in the President. It is of interest that when on May 11 reporters asked Ford if anyone on his staff was working on a possible transfer of power, Ford replied, "If they are, they are doing it without my knowledge and without my consent." Whitehead later said that he and Buchen regarded Ford's response as an implicit statement that he actually hoped someone was doing it but did not want to know about it.[55]

During the early summer of 1974 Buchen, Whitehead, and three unidentified acquaintances met several times at Whitehead's home to discuss a possible inauguration ceremony, transition team, and policy statements. As a result of these meetings, they developed a one-page checklist of issues* that would be initially important to Ford. When on August 6, at 10:30 P.M., Buchen told Whitehead that Nixon's resignation was probable, the final planning began. Ford was advised about the planning and gave Buchen the names of five friends whose views he wanted. On the night of August 7 the enlarged team met to discuss the elements of transition. Present in addition to Buchen and Whitehead were former Governor William Scranton of Pennsylvania, Republican Senator Robert Griffin of Michigan,

---

*The checklist included such topics as first principles, themes, objectives, the transition team, the "first week," nationwide address, the press and Congress, background policy papers, the organization of the presidency, and key personnel actions. James M. Naughton, *The Change in Presidents: Plans Began Months Ago*, N.Y. TIMES, Aug. 26, 1974, at 1.

President Gerald R. Ford in the Oval Office on August 11, 1974, with Donald H. Rumsfeld, Representative of the United States to NATO (*left*), and the President's personal attorney, Benton Becker. (Courtesy Gerald R. Ford Presidential Library.)

former Representative John W. Byrnes of Wisconsin, Bryce Harlow, and William Whyte, a vice president of U.S. Steel. Until about midnight they discussed the essential elements of transition. They agreed that Robert Hartmann, the Vice President's chief of staff, would draft a brief speech for Ford to deliver after he became President and that Jerald F. terHorst, then the Washington correspondent for the *Detroit News*, would be suggested for White House press secretary. Throughout the meeting they expected a news bulletin of Nixon's resignation, but the meeting adjourned without any such announcement.[56] After Nixon informed Ford of his plans the next morning, the transition planners met to formalize their recommendations. Draft memoranda were prepared as well as formal notices of Ford's succession to the presidency. The men paused to watch Nixon's resignation address and finally completed their work around 3:00 A.M. on Friday, August 9.[57]

The nation greeted the Ford presidency with a sense of profound relief. During his first week in office Ford addressed a joint session of Congress and met with governors, mayors and county officials, members of the Congressional Black Caucus, and representatives of several women's groups.[58] After ten days in the presidency, he addressed a meeting of the Veterans of Foreign Wars in Chicago and suggested a program of conditional amnesty for Vietnam War draft dodgers and deserters, to the dismay of his audience and conservative followers. On August 20, with his popularity soaring, Ford nominated Nelson A. Rockefeller to be Vice President under the Twenty-Fifth Amendment.[59]

12

The Installation of Nelson A. Rockefeller

This situation is particularly unique . . . in that we have a nominee selected by a president who was himself placed on the presidential succession ladder through the provisions of the 25th Amendment. We have learned through our first experience with the 25th Amendment that vice presidential nominees must be judged as we would judge a prospective president.

ROBERT W. KASTENMEIER, December 17, 1974[1]

NOMINATION

On August 6, three days before Nixon's resignation, Melvin Laird, a close adviser to Ford, predicted flatly that Nelson Rockefeller would be Ford's choice as Vice President.[2] When questioned about Laird's statement on August 7, Ford replied that it was premature to discuss a vice-presidential successor.[3] This did not stop political commentators from speculating, however, and Rockefeller, George H.W. Bush, Elliot Richardson, Melvin Laird, and Senators Howard Baker, Hugh Scott, and Barry Goldwater were all named as front-runners for the post.[4]

Following his swearing-in as President on August 9, Ford told congressional leaders that he would nominate a Vice President within ten days.[5] This would be his first and possibly most important decision, and the nation regarded it as the first test of the new President's judgment. Republican governors, Cabinet members, and political and congressional leaders were asked by Ford to submit preferential lists of their choices for Vice President.[6] Laird was quoted as saying that Nelson Rockefeller "would be the best choice to reassure foreign nations, heal the Republican Party and attract fresh talent to the depleted Federal establishment."[7] Conservative

President.[26] Ford said it was an act of compassion* designed to heal the wounds of Watergate.[27] In accepting the pardon, Nixon made no admission of deliberate wrong-doing but cited only "mistakes and misjudgments."† Ford also released an agreement giving Nixon title to and control of all Watergate tapes and documents.

The pardon provoked an outpouring of public and congressional criticism that signaled the end of Ford's "honeymoon" period in the White House. A flood of critical telegrams and telephone calls inundated the White House. In the three days following the pardon "about 110,000 telegrams, mailgrams, and personal opinion messages poured into Washington, according to Western Union."[28] Instead of marking the end of the Watergate era, the pardon left unanswered many questions relating to the crisis and succeeded in dividing the country. Two days after the Nixon pardon, the President indicated that he was considering pardons for all persons convicted or accused of crimes in the Watergate and related scandals. The suggestion was greeted with outrage by most commentators, and it was predicted that such an act would "perpetuate that scandal with far graver political, legal and moral consequences than those the country has already suffered."[29] A Gallup poll showed that support for Ford declined sharply after the pardon, and that more than 60 percent of those polled disapproved of Ford's action.[30]

In addition to its impact on the popularity of the Ford administration, the pardon provoked suggestions that Ford might have made a deal with Nixon: a promise of a pardon in exchange for Nixon's resignation. Although there was no evidence of a deal, public suspicions remained even after the President made an unprecedented voluntary appearance before a subcommittee of the House Judiciary Committee on October 17 to answer questions about the pardon.[31]

It was against this backdrop that the Rockefeller confirmation proceedings took place.

CONFIRMATION

As the congressional committees began their investigations prior to the formal hearings, Rockefeller submitted his tax returns for the previous seven years as well

---

* In its issue of December 18, 1975, the *Washington Post* reported that Alexander Haig discussed with Ford at some point on August 28, 1974, the subject of a pardon for Nixon. The *Post* also reported that former White House counsel Leonard Garment had given to Haig that day a memorandum urging that Nixon be pardoned. Among the points made in Garment's memorandum was that Nixon's mental and physical condition could not withstand a criminal prosecution and that, possibly, he might take his life unless he was pardoned. These disclosures are in apparent contradiction of Ford's testimony at the October 17, 1974, hearing that nobody had made any recommendation to him for a Nixon pardon or brought up on behalf of Nixon after August 9 the subject of a pardon. Following these disclosures, Rodino announced that the House Judiciary Committee would review the matter to see whether the record of the subcommittee's hearing needed to be supplemented. Upon review, it was decided not to reopen the hearings. *Panel Bars Inquiry into Nixon Pardon*, N.Y. TIMES, Feb. 20, 1976, at 12.

† N.Y. Times, Sept. 9, 1974, at 1.

as a statement of his personal wealth, but he indicated he would limit their public disclosure.[32] Rockefeller said that he would do whatever was appropriate to resolve any conflicts of interest arising from his vast financial holdings and suggested that he might put his personal investments into a blind trust for the term of his vice presidency.[33]

On September 11 the Senate Rules Committee voted to ask Rockefeller to disclose publicly his financial holdings in lieu of any requirement that he divest himself of any investments or establish a blind trust. The committee concluded that a blind trust would be ineffective because of the breadth of his investments and that divestiture could adversely affect the economy. Under these circumstances it felt that full disclosure would best protect against conflicts of interest.[34] Rockefeller agreed to release a detailed disclosure of his assets, liabilities, and net worth at the start of the Senate public hearings on September 23.[35] But, on September 19, to counter what he described as misleading press leaks of information he had turned over to the committee, he reported that his net worth was $62.5 million plus the income from two trusts totaling $120 million.[36]

As the Senate hearings neared and the House hearings remained unscheduled, House Republicans began to complain that the Democrats were delaying the House investigation in an effort to prevent Rockefeller from campaigning in the fall elections.* Representative Thomas F. Railsback sent Chairman Peter W. Rodino a letter urging that the House Judiciary Committee, and the full House if necessary, stay in session through the November election until the confirmation was completed, stating that the nation "can ill afford to be without the services of a Vice President."[37] House Democrats, on the other hand, replied that the slow pace was caused by the need for a detailed financial investigation. Said Speaker Carl Albert, "There is no inclination on the part of the [House] leadership to delay the matter. We want to expedite it, but I don't want to dictate to the Judiciary Committee how much investigation is necessary."[38]

On September 23, the opening day of the Senate hearings, Rockefeller submitted a seventy-two-page autobiographical statement, including summaries of his tax returns for the previous ten years and of his financial position.[39] He said that he hoped the "myth or misconception" about the Rockefeller family fortune and its influence would be "exposed and dissipated." However, the disclosure that his total holdings amounted to $218 million with an average annual income over the previous ten years of $4.6 million before taxes reinforced his image as a man of

---

* The delay also gave rise to a number of legal questions not clearly answered by the legislative history of the Twenty-Fifth Amendment, such as what would happen if Rockefeller's nomination were not acted on until the new Congress met in January 1975. Would the nomination still be valid? Would favorable action by one House of Congress in 1974 have to be repeated by that House in 1975? Concern also was expressed about the status of the nomination in the event of President Ford's death. *See Hearing on the First Implementation of Section Two of the Twenty-Fifth Amendment Before the Subcomm. on Constitutional Amendments of the Senate Comm. on the Judiciary*, 94th Cong. 55 (1975).

substantial wealth. To correct the widespread belief that his family dominated the oil industry, Rockefeller revealed that the total family holdings did not amount to more than 2.06 percent of the stock of any oil company and that no family member was on the board of any Standard Oil Company or had any control over the management of these companies.

Committee members focused their questions on possible conflicts of interest between Rockefeller's economic concerns and the national interest if he were to succeed to the presidency. Rockefeller assured them that the public good would always be his prime consideration and relied on his record as governor of New York to demonstrate that his executive decisions had never been influenced by his private concerns. The committee inquired also about his views on taxation, welfare, abortion, and drug laws. A topic of considerable concern was his handling of the 1971 Attica prison revolt, which resulted in the deaths of forty-three inmates and hostages. Rockefeller detailed the occurrences of the riot and admitted for the first time that the proper way to proceed would have been to stop the riot in the beginning without weapons.[40]

Throughout the questioning, Rockefeller was careful to give clear explanations of his views and policies. He refused to give an opinion on several of President Ford's actions, such as the Nixon pardon of September 8,[41] the Nixon tapes agreement,[42] or Ford's Senate testimony the previous year that the country would not stand for a pardon.[43] He also refused to commit himself on issues of executive privilege,[44] future pardons for Watergate defendants,[45] or pardons for a resigning President prior to criminal investigation or prosecution.[46]

Following Rockefeller's testimony, which lasted for two and one-half days, the committee for a half-day heard testimonials in support of the nomination from ten members of Congress from both parties.[47] On the fourth day, testimony from outside interest groups was heard, including critics and supporters of Rockefeller's abortion stance, critics of the Attica problems, and conservatives who feared his internationalism.[48]

As the second day's hearings recessed, Senate Majority Whip Robert C. Byrd of West Virginia, who had been the most aggressive questioner of Rockefeller, agreed with committee Chairman Howard Cannon that nothing had emerged which would be a barrier to Rockefeller's confirmation,[49] and most commentators agreed that "Congress seems all but certain to approve overwhelmingly"[50] the Rockefeller nomination. The hearings were recessed on September 26, but no vote was taken pending receipt of an audit of Rockefeller's taxes by the staff of the Joint Committee on Internal Revenue Taxation.

On September 28, First Lady Betty Ford underwent surgery for the removal of her cancerous right breast. This sudden development immediately gave rise to reports that Ford would not be a candidate for President in 1976. The President himself indicated that he was rethinking his plans to run in 1976, saying, "[w]e haven't thought beyond next week."[51] Thus, the congressional hearings became even more important.

In the next few weeks a number of political bombshells exploded that reversed the tide flowing toward confirmation, and by the end of October Rockefeller's nomination seemed destined for defeat. The absence of any congressional hearings during that month and a deluge of press leaks played a large part in this reversal. The first bombshell occurred on October 5, when Rockefeller disclosed that he had made gifts of $50,000 to Henry A. Kissinger; $86,000 to L. Judson Morhouse, former New York State Republican Party chairman; and an unspecified sum to Dr. William Ronan, chairman of the Port Authority of New York and New Jersey and a senior adviser to the Rockefeller family. Hugh Morrow, Rockefeller's press secretary, explained the circumstances of each gift and noted that appropriate gift taxes had been paid. The gift to Kissinger was made in 1969 after he had ended a fifteen-year position as a Rockefeller adviser and before he became national security adviser to former President Nixon. The gift, said Morrow, was an expression of Rockefeller's gratitude for Kissinger's long years of service.

The gift to Morhouse, in 1973, was in the form of the cancelation of an outstanding loan made to him in 1960 to invest in commercial real estate on Long Island. At that time the job of Republican State chairman was unsalaried, and the loan was intended to provide Morhouse with income to help him resist "temptation to misuse political influence," according to Morrow. Morhouse resigned his party position in 1962, and in 1966 he was convicted of bribery and other charges arising from a State Liquor Authority scandal and sentenced to prison. In 1970 Governor Rockefeller commuted his sentence because Morhouse was reported to be seriously ill with cancer and Parkinson's disease.[52] In response to these disclosures, Senator Byrd said on October 5 that he saw no need to recall Rockefeller for further questioning and saw "nothing on the surface that appears to be sinister."[53]

On October 7, additional gifts and campaign contributions by Rockefeller were disclosed, including recent contributions to several Republican members of Congress who would be voting on Rockefeller's nomination. Senator Jacob Javits of New York received a $15,000 contribution, and Representative Peter Peyser of New York had received $10,000 from Rockefeller family members, including $5,000 from Nelson. Other politicians who received "nominal contributions" included Senators Peter H. Dominick of Colorado, Charles McC. Mathias of Maryland, and Milton R. Young of North Dakota, and Representative William S. Cohen of Maine. Morrow also disclosed that Rockefeller had made him a gift of $100,000 by paying off a bank loan he had taken for medical and educational expenses for his family. It was also disclosed that in 1972 Nelson Rockefeller, his brothers Laurance and John, and his sister, Mrs. Abby Mauzé, each gave $50,000 to President Nixon's reelection campaign.[54]

Morrow further disclosed that the gift to Ronan consisted of the cancelation of $550,000 in debts owed to Rockefeller. He said that the gift actually cost Rockefeller $880,000, including federal and state gift taxes. It was made during the interval between Ronan's resignation as head of the Metropolitan Transportation Authority

(MTA), a job with a salary of $85,000 per year, and his assumption of the unsalaried chairmanship of the Port Authority. Morrow could not say how many separate loans there were or when they were made or whether they were interest-free or whether Ronan had paid back any money to Rockefeller.[55]

These gifts and contributions raised questions of both a political and a legal nature. Some commentators argued that the disclosure showed that Rockefeller was insensitive to the apparent impropriety of rewarding public figures. It was pointed out, for example, that shortly after the cancelation of his debts, Ronan became head of the Port Authority, which played a crucial role in planning the development of New York City, in which the Rockefellers had vast financial interests. Others challenged the legality of the gifts under New York law. One section of the state penal law bars giving to a public official "unlawful gratuities"—that is, conferring a benefit upon a public servant for a duty he is required or authorized to perform. A second state law, Section 73 of the New York Public Officers Law, which became effective on January 1, 1966, forbids any state employee from accepting gifts or loans of $25 or more "under circumstances in which it could reasonably be inferred that the gift was intended to influence him, or could reasonably be expected to influence him, in the performance of his official duties or was intended as a reward for any official action on his part."

In a statement on the Senate floor on October 15, Senator Helms questioned whether the loans to Ronan occurred after Section 73 had become effective and while he was a state official. If the loans were made during that time, Helms suggested, then the law would apply ifa reasonable inference could be drawn that the loans were intended to influence Ronan. Recognizing that Ronan as head of the MTA could affect the success of the Rockefeller governorship, Helms asked whether "an invidious inference is 'reasonable' under the circumstances."[56]

Senator Cannon responded to these disclosures with a request that Rockefeller supply detailed background information to the Senate Rules Committee. As rumors spread that the gifts disclosed were only the beginning, it appeared certain that the committee would reopen its hearings. Representative Jerome R. Waldie said that he found it "beyond comprehension" that the Senate Rules Committee, with information on the gifts, had not questioned Rockefeller about the subject. Senator Helms called for the committee to reconvene and labeled the gifts as raising "a grave question of propriety."[57] In addressing the Senate, Helms declared that "[u]ntil we, as U.S. Senators, know the full extent of the way in which Governor Rockefeller may have used the power of his fortune in building a network of political dependency, we will not be able to resolve the question of whether he ought to be confirmed as Vice President of the United States."[58]

Helms also observed that in the Rockefeller tax returns already made public was an enumeration of almost $4 million in gift taxes paid during the past ten years. Since it was acknowledged that a number of gifts were made to political figures, Helms called for a complete disclosure of the beneficiaries and demanded that

Rockefeller and Ronan testify before the Rules Committee.[59] Helms also questioned the 1968 merger of the Triborough Bridge and Tunnel Authority and the Metropolitan Transportation Authority, which was negotiated by David Rockefeller—Nelson's brother—of the Chase Manhattan Bank representing the Triborough bondholders and Ronan on behalf of the MTA. The agreement increased the interest payments to the Triborough bondholders and permitted the Triborough profits to be applied to the MTA deficits. Helms called for full disclosure of the agreement.[60] There were news reports of other Rockefeller gifts and favors to aides and associates, including the use of Rockefeller properties, airplanes, and helicopters; appointments to high-salaried positions; and financing of New York Republican campaigns. It also was reported that Rockefeller had assisted his brother David, president of the Chase Manhattan Bank, in numerous ways.[61]

On October 9, Senator Cannon announced that he would make public Rockefeller's response to the questions about his financial gifts. He also stated that no decision on reconvening the Senate hearings would be made until after the November 5 mid-term elections, when the tax report would be completed.[62] In a press conference that afternoon, President Ford asserted that he had investigated the gift to Kissinger and found no impropriety.[63] But congressmen and political commentators began to question whether, in the words of a *New York Times* editorial, Rockefeller "may be insufficiently aware of the dangers to the democratic process that lie in even the most benevolent application of enormous concentrations of wealth and economic power."[64]

Meanwhile, Governor Brendan T. Byrne of New Jersey said that he would wait for more details about the gift to Ronan so that he could evaluate whether Ronan could serve the interests of New York and New Jersey impartially.[65] Later, on October 21, the New Jersey legislature ordered an investigation of the Rockefeller gift to Ronan, which was said to have "raised serious questions" about Ronan's capacity to serve as Chairman of the Port Authority.[66] New York Attorney General Louis J. Lefkowitz also said that he planned to investigate whether any state laws or ethical standards had been violated by the Ronan–Rockefeller arrangement[67] and subsequently requested that his advisory committee on ethical standards explore the gifts and loans for possible violations.*[68]

In response to such criticisms, Ronan held a news conference on October 10. To counter charges of violations of the New York Public Officers Law, he stressed that the gift had been made during a two-week period when he was not on the state payroll. He stated that in his capacity as senior adviser to the Rockefellers, he had never given advice about Port Authority plans, and that the Chase Manhattan

---

* The committee later concluded that the Rockefeller gifts did not violate the State Code of Ethics but were "not in the public interest." Frank Lynn, *Rockefeller Gifts in State Criticized but Found Legal,* N.Y. Times, Jan. 28, 1975, at 1.

Bank had not received any special favors from the Port Authority. Several times during the news conference Ronan said that he saw no conflicts of interest in his roles as state official, Rockefeller adviser, corporate board member, and trustee of two small banks.[69] It was rumored that Rockefeller was unhappy that his motives were being questioned, since his lawyers had approved the gifts and reported them on his tax returns.[70]

On October 10 a second political bombshell exploded that further clouded Rockefeller's prospects for confirmation. It was reported that the House Judiciary Committee had begun an investigation into the subject of an FBI report that Rockefeller, through intermediaries, might have been involved in underwriting a critical biography of Arthur Goldberg, his Democratic opponent during the 1970 gubernatorial campaign. The book, *Arthur J. Goldberg: The Old and the New*, by Victor Lasky, claimed that Goldberg did not have the background and experience to be a successful governor.

When first asked about the book, press secretary Morrow replied that Nelson Rockefeller had had nothing to do with it in any way. An hour later he released a statement by Rockefeller revealing that a New York lawyer, John A. Wells, a close Rockefeller associate, had told the governor early in the 1970 campaign that Victor Lasky was working on a Goldberg biography and some time after the book was published Rockefeller was shown a copy. The statement also revealed that when the FBI had interviewed Rockefeller in connection with his nomination, he was asked about the rumors that he had financed the Lasky book. Rockefeller replied that he had heard of the book but knew nothing of its preparation or financing. Subsequently, said Rockefeller, he was informed that his brother Laurance had invested $60,000 in a company set up to produce the book and later lost $52,000 when the book proved a failure. Although the investment was said to be a business venture, Laurance Rockefeller did not take a tax deduction for a business loss. Nelson Rockefeller added, "Had he only told me about it at the time, I would have been totally opposed to it and would have strongly advised against his participation in any form."[71] Upon being informed of Rockefeller's statement, Goldberg commented that he was shocked by the disclosure and demanded an apology for the financing of a "scandalous and libelous book."[72]

On October 11, the publishers of the book said that Wells had arranged for its publication and offered to purchase 100,000 copies for distribution in the 1970 campaign. It also was disclosed that the $60,000 from Laurance Rockefeller had paid for the entire publishing project and that a total of 116,000 copies were published, of which 100,000 were given to the Rockefeller reelection campaign. Victor Lasky revealed that Wells had approached him about writing a campaign biography of Goldberg. It was also reported that the financing of the book was arranged through Literary Properties, Inc., a Delaware corporation organized to produce the book, and that funds were channeled to the corporation through Philadelphia. In light of these disclosures, Goldberg asked the House Judiciary Committee and the Senate Rules Committee to hold formal hearings into the circumstances surrounding the publication of the book.[73] Of Nelson Rockefeller, Goldberg stated, "[H]e is not fit to be Vice President, based upon what occurred and the cover-up story."[74]

In response to the request of the Senate Rules Committee for detailed information about his gifts, Rockefeller released on October 11 a list of twenty present and former public officials and staff assistants to whom he had given a total of $1.97 million over the previous seventeen years. The largest gift was to Ronan and was listed as $625,000. Other substantial gifts were made to Emmett J. Hughes, a former Rockefeller speechwriter, and to Edward J. Logue, Chairman of the New York Urban Development Corporation. Rockefeller explained that he had given money to help friends with such problems as medical expenses, marital difficulties, educational expenses, and relocation costs. He also complained that leaks from congressional committees checking his tax returns were creating an atmosphere of uncertainty and suspicion.[75] The House Judiciary Committee requested more gift tax information and was said to be interested in gifts of less than $3,000, which were not required to be reported to the IRS.[76]

The disclosure of the list of Rockefeller gifts generated widespread discussion in the press about the relationship of personal wealth and political power. Rockefeller argued that his loans and gifts had enabled some of the recipients to remain in public service when they might have been tempted to return to more lucrative positions in the private sector. On the other side, it was urged that when a person will engage in public service only if compensated by a third person, his loyalties necessarily become suspect. William Safire observed in the *New York Times* that in 1973 an elected Vice President was forced from office because he was "on the take," while in 1974 the vice-presidential nominee was under fire for being "on the give."[77] Safire noted that although the gifts were well intentioned, they created an obvious conflict of interest, and that to assure his confirmation Rockefeller must admit that the practice is wrong and promise not to engage in it again.[78]

On October 12, Rockefeller sent a telegram to Goldberg offering his "sincere and unqualified apology." Rockefeller said that "[i]t is quite clear that when the project was brought to my attention, I should have immediately taken steps to see to it that it was stopped as utterly alien to and incompatible with the standards I have always tried to observe in my political life. I take full responsibility for the whole regrettable episode."[79] Rockefeller also telephoned President Ford to read his apology and to discuss the congressional confirmation proceedings. An aide said that President Ford assured Rockefeller that "there is no problem."[80]

With the release of the Rockefeller gift list and the "dirty trick" charge about the Goldberg book, congressional support for Rockefeller waned. Senator Cannon said that in all probability he would recall Rockefeller to testify before the Senate Rules Committee and suggested that as a result of the developments a vote on the nomination might be delayed until late December.[81] Meanwhile, the House Judiciary

Committee was reported to be investigating whether there was any connection between the Rockefeller family contributions to President Nixon's 1972 campaign and the President's subsequent approval of the acquisition of Caribair, a Puerto Rico–based airline, by Eastern Airlines, in which the Rockefellers had large interests. The Rockefellers had contributed $200,000 to Nixon's campaign, and, less than a year later, Nixon, citing foreign policy reasons, had reversed two Civil Aeronautics Board rulings that had denied the acquisition. The matter was included in the expansion of the House inquiry into the Rockefeller nomination to members of the Rockefeller family and their influence on governmental agencies and policy.[82]

On October 15, Rockefeller requested that both the Senate and the House conduct immediate hearings because of continuing leaks of financial information that, he said, were trying him in the press. Both committees refused the request because their investigations and the tax audit were not completed. Most Republicans on the committees supported Rockefeller's position, however, since the delays were weakening his chances of confirmation.[83]

On October 18 a third damaging blow struck. As a result of the IRS audit of Rockefeller's federal income and gift taxes, additional assessments were made of a total amount of $903,718: $820,718 in income taxes and $83,000 in gift taxes. In a letter to the Senate and House committees, Rockefeller disclosed that adjustments were made in his deductions for office and investment expenses and charitable contributions. No penalty charges were assessed, which suggested that no fraud or improper intent had been found. For the five-year period, the underpayment amounted to one-fifth of the taxes that had been paid.[84] President Ford, through his press secretary, reaffirmed his complete faith in Rockefeller's integrity and his belief that he would ultimately be confirmed.[85]

The day after this disclosure, Rockefeller released a list of his charitable donations over the previous seventeen years, which showed gifts totaling $24.7 million to 193 organizations. Political commentators pointed out, however, that since Rockefeller paid about two-thirds of his total income to the federal government, the cost to him of the contributions was closer to $8 million.[86] The press continued to request more detailed financial information until October 22, when Rockefeller announced that it had become impossible for him to fulfill the requests of the congressional committees while responding to press demands as well. Consequently, he determined to postpone answering further questions.[87]

On October 19, President Ford told newsmen that while some conservative Republicans had urged him to drop the Rockefeller nomination, he did not take the advice seriously. "I'm still convinced he would make a good Vice President," said Ford.[88] There was speculation that Rockefeller might withdraw, and many observers questioned whether any rich man could be confirmed, or even whether anyone at all could be confirmed when subjected to such intense scrutiny.[89] Senator Goldwater backed away from his initial support of Rockefeller and was reported to be undecided. In a radio interview he said that there was a good chance that

Rockefeller's name would be withdrawn to spare him additional questioning. Goldwater's views were considered significant to other congressional conservatives and were a bad sign to Rockefeller supporters.[90]

On October 28 Rockefeller released a list of loans, revealing that he had advanced a total of $507,800 over the previous seventeen years to friends, associates, and family members. The new loan list supplemented the previously released list of gifts, which were often in the form of forgiven loans. The largest loan ($84,000) had been made in 1957 to Robert B. Anderson, former Secretary of the Navy and subsequently Secretary of the Treasury. The loan was made before President Eisenhower appointed Anderson to the Treasury position and was repaid after his appointment. Anderson said that he used the loan to purchase stock in a Rockefeller-controlled corporation with extensive Latin American holdings but that after his appointment as Treasury Secretary he sold the stock back to Rockefeller because of the possibility of his participating in decisions that might affect the corporation.[91]

It is not surprising, then, that, while all these disclosures were being made, Rockefeller's nomination became an issue of discussion in congressional and state elections throughout the country. After the November elections, the timing of the hearings presented more potential troubles for the nominee. If the hearings were completed and Rockefeller were confirmed by a close vote in the "lame duck" Congress, in which many defeated or retiring Republicans would vote, his legitimacy as Vice President could be clouded. On the other hand, if the confirmation vote were delayed until the next Congress, it was possible that new hearings would be required, and the anticipated enlarged Democratic majorities might be less willing to confirm such a powerful political figure.*[92]

On November 12 Rockefeller arrived in Washington to appear for a second time before the Senate Rules Committee. He told reporters that he was "hopeful, not confident," that Congress would confirm him and later met with President Ford to review his prepared testimony. As one indication of the change in the status of the nomination from certain to controversial, the major television networks agreed to broadcast the hearings live on a rotating basis.[93] House Speaker Albert told President Ford that he hoped to complete action on the nomination before Christmas.[94]

The Senate Rules Committee reopened the Rockefeller hearings on November 13. Rockefeller read from an opening statement that explained his political gifts and loans and his involvement in the publication of the Goldberg book. Regarding

---

* Decried Senator Hugh Scott on October 17: "Mr. President, as a member of the Senate Committee on Rules and Administration, I have personally urged that further hearings on the nomination of Nelson Rockefeller be held promptly in the cause of fairness to Governor Rockefeller and to the country. My urging has been for naught. The chairman (Mr. Cannon) and the majority members of the committee have decided to postpone further hearings until after the election. This is a great disservice to the Nation." 120 CONG. REC. S19,382 (daily ed. Oct. 17, 1974). *See* 120 CONG. REC. S20,148 (daily ed. Nov. 26, 1974).

the Goldberg book, he described for the first time what he said was the full story "pieced together" from his memory and the recollections of others involved in the incident. He said that during the 1970 campaign John Wells had dropped by his office to discuss a Goldberg biography to be written by Victor Lasky. Rockefeller said that he referred Wells to Donal O'Brien, one of his attorneys, and "sent a message to my brother, Laurance, asking if he could help Jack Wells find some investors. That was the extent of my involvement with the project."[95] The complicated arrangement for financing the book through a dummy corporation was not an effort to launder the money, said Rockefeller, but an attempt to conceal the Rockefeller name from other potential investors.[96] He attributed to an "extremely sketchy" memory his failure to inform the FBI about his relationship to the biography and his conflicting reports to the press.[97]

Senator Byrd questioned Rockefeller closely about the Goldberg book and complained about the "devious" way in which the book was financed and published and the slow revelation of Rockefeller's involvement with it.[98] Rockefeller replied that it was common for members of his family to make investments through a third party to conceal their identities so that other investors would not be influenced.[99] He also defended his delay in making a full disclosure by reminding Senator Byrd that he had requested an opportunity to testify before the committee in October but had been denied that chance.[100] Senator Claiborne Pell of Rhode Island asked why Laurance Rockefeller had not claimed a capital loss on the publication of the book if it were truly a business investment.[101] Rockefeller answered that his brother's tax lawyers thought the IRS would question such a deduction and accordingly did not claim it in order to avoid controversy.[102]

Of the loans and gifts to his aides and political associates, Rockefeller stated that not one had been designed to corrupt or did in fact corrupt either the recipient or the giver, and that all had been motivated by affection, respect, and compelling need. He stressed that all the public officials or staff members who were listed as recipients of gifts had been appointed by him and were administratively responsible to him, so that they could not be of special use to him even if they could have been influenced by his gifts.[103]

The loans to Ronan, he said, were made between 1962 and 1969 to help him meet family responsibilities and assist him in meeting continuing financial burdens after his retirement. In 1974, he said, he forgave the loans and gave Ronan an additional $40,000 in appreciation of his friendship and eighteen-year association.[104]

Defending the merger of the Triborough Bridge and Tunnel Authority with the Metropolitan Transportation Authority, Rockefeller quoted a *New York Times* statement that the consolidation was "the greatest advance in the metropolitan transportation system in at least half a century."[105] Rockefeller explained his gifts to James W. Gaynor and Edward Logue as attempts to facilitate their moving to New York state from Colorado and Massachusetts, respectively, and joining the public housing effort in New York.[106] To assist the unsalaried Republican State Chairman, L. Judson Morhouse, Rockefeller lent him $100,000 to enter a real estate business and requested further assistance from Laurance Rockefeller. Through Laurance a loan of $49,000 was arranged to purchase stock in two venture capital companies that Laurance had helped to finance. A year and a half later, Morhouse sold some of the stock, which had appreciated in value, and repaid the loan.[107]

Along with his statement Rockefeller released a summary of his political contributions since 1957, which totaled $3,265,374 (including $1,000,228 to his own presidential campaigns and $80,599 to his New York gubernatorial campaigns). He also revealed that his brothers and sister had contributed $2,850,000 to his campaigns and that his stepmother, Martha Baird Rockefeller, had contributed a total of around $11 million to his campaigns.[108]

The basic question presented by these disclosures of gifts, loans, political contributions, and involvement in financing the Goldberg biography was whether Rockefeller had used his money to buy political power. For the members of the Senate Rules Committee, the confirmation of Rockefeller would depend on their judgment as to whether Rockefeller would use his wealth improperly as Vice President, or possibly as President, and whether his background would impair his ability to determine and promote the best interests of the American people. Many commentators argued that sizable gifts would necessarily place the recipients in positions of "psychological servitude," regardless of the donor's intent. Tom Wicker of the *New York Times* observed that Rockefeller's attitude toward use of his private wealth in public office gave the public no protection except his own promise to act for good purposes. And "in the long run it is the practice, not the purpose, of using private resources to supplement public office that is at issue."[109]

When the hearings continued on November 14, Rockefeller submitted a statement regarding gifts and loans to public officials. To avoid the misunderstandings that had arisen from the loans and gifts he made while governor of New York, Rockefeller proposed that if confirmed as Vice President he would make no gifts or loans to any public official with the following exceptions: gifts of nominal amounts to friends for Christmas, weddings, and birthdays, and, under exceptional circumstances, assistance to friends in the event of special hardship of a compelling human nature.[110]

Senator Byrd quoted the two sections of the New York statutes that prohibit gifts to public officials under certain circumstances and intensely questioned Rockefeller about their applicability to his loans to Ronan.[111] Rockefeller responded that his lawyers had approved the transactions, and that he, as governor, had signed the statutes and was fully familiar with their intent.[112]

The second witness of the day, Arthur J. Goldberg, testified that Rockefeller's explanation of the financing of the Lasky book was "inherently noncredible."[113] Goldberg said that the public was entitled to candor and openness from those who hold or seek public office, and that "[c]arefully crafted public relations efforts, designed to forestall pursuit of relevant information and the entire truth, are simply unacceptable."[114]

That night at a news conference in Phoenix President Ford affirmed his support for Rockefeller, saying that he could imagine no circumstances under which he would withdraw Rockefeller's name. Ford complained that it was time for Congress to complete action on the Rockefeller nomination and "fish or cut bait." The President also suggested that the next Congress should consider changing the Twenty-Fifth Amendment to provide a specific deadline for the President to nominate and for the Congress to confirm a Vice President. The nation "need[s] a Vice President at all times" and the delay in confirmation leaves no one prepared to assume the presidency on a moment's notice, explained Ford. However, he reaffirmed his intention to travel to Japan and the Soviet Union even though Rockefeller had not been confirmed.[115] The next day Ford said through his press secretary that he would definitely run for election in 1976.[116]

The third day of the resumed Senate hearings centered on the financing of the Goldberg biography, with witnesses who were involved in the 1970 campaign promotion. John Wells testified that he convinced Victor Lasky that a critical biography of Arthur Goldberg was needed and might be profitable. He later met with Nelson Rockefeller to explain the concept to him and seek suggestions from him of persons who might invest in the book. Rockefeller arranged for Wells to meet with several family lawyers and financial advisers, who agreed to name a nominee to hold stock in a corporation organized to finance the book.[117] Donal O'Brien, chief Rockefeller family counsel, recalled that after meeting with Wells he reported back to Nelson Rockefeller. He was told that Rockefeller would not participate in the venture but would contact his brother Laurance to see if he could locate investors.[118]

From the testimony of Donal O'Brien[119] and Laurance Rockefeller, it appeared that Mrs. Louise Boyer, an executive assistant and trusted adviser to both Rockefellers, described the idea to Laurance Rockefeller as a commercial venture and asked him to help organize a group of investors to finance the book.[120] Laurance Rockefeller replied that he did not have time to contact other investors but would agree to underwrite the venture himself, adding that he had had no further conversation with anyone, including his brother Nelson, concerning the book, until a few months prior to his testimony, when the FBI questioned his financial adviser about it.[121] When examined by the committee, Laurance Rockefeller agreed that he had acted more quickly and with less information on this investment than on most other venture capital proposals but stated that he acted out of confidence in Mrs. Boyer's judgment and integrity.[122]

Nelson Rockefeller also provided details about his loan to L. Judson Morhouse and the Eastern Airlines acquisition of Caribair.[123] Following his testimony, Senator Byrd predicted that the Senate would probably confirm Nelson Rockefeller as Vice President, barring any unexpected development. Explaining that while it was his duty to ask difficult questions, Byrd said he intended to vote for confirmation.[124] The fact that Byrd had become the most persistent interrogator of Nelson Rockefeller was in sharp contrast to his early support for the nominee. It was reported that President Ford telephoned Byrd in August 1974 to solicit his advice on a choice for Vice President and that Byrd had told the President that he favored Nelson Rockefeller because of his experience and ability. In the hindsight of November, Byrd reflected, "[had] I known then what I know now, I'm not sure I would have reacted exactly as I did to Mr. Ford's question."[125]

The Senate Rules Committee completed its hearings on November 18 with testimony from four of the recipients of Rockefeller gifts and the vice-chairman of Americans for Democratic Action. The principal witness was Ronan, who testified that to make adequate provision for his family in the future and for his retirement, he borrowed funds from Rockefeller for investment purposes. He said that "[t]he initiative, in this, was really mine"[126] and that "at no time did I consider the Governor was under any continuing obligation to loan me money."[127] Ronan also stated that the loans did not affect his willingness to stay in state service and did not alter his outlook on any matter of public policy.[128] Senator Byrd questioned Ronan about whether prior to his resignation from the MTA he had discussed with Rockefeller the possibility that the outstanding loans might be forgiven. Ronan denied any such understanding. Senator Byrd again expressed concern that the two New York statutes prohibiting gifts to state employees might have been violated but concluded that Rockefeller should be given the benefit of the doubt.[129]

Later in the day, the committee questioned Edward Logue, president of the New York State Urban Development Corporation (UDC), about the gifts and loans he had received from Rockefeller. When in 1968 Rockefeller asked Logue to become the first president of the UDC, Logue said he told Rockefeller that it would be difficult for him to move from Boston to New York because of a debt of $30,000 incurred during his unsuccessful campaign for mayor of Boston in 1967, and because of the problem of locating comparable housing for his family in New York City without substantial financial sacrifice.[130] Rockefeller made a gift to Logue of an amount sufficient to liquidate his campaign debt and in 1969 lent him $145,000 for the purchase of a cooperative apartment. Logue testified that without Rockefeller's assistance he "would not have been able to leave my private life in Boston to accept the appointment he offered."[131] Another former New York housing official, James W. Gaynor, testified that Rockefeller's gift had helped him move to New York from Denver.[132]

The final committee witness was Joseph L. Rauh Jr. of Americans for Democratic Action. Rauh urged, as he had done during the Ford confirmation hearings, that the committee establish as the standard for confirmation of a vice-presidential nominee that he be among the group of persons whom a majority of the Congress would want as President of the United States.[133] The breadth of Rockefeller economic interests, Rauh asserted, should disqualify him from the presidency because of the inevitable conflicts of interest that would arise. As President, he would have to make decisions affecting business and financial interests and would be unable to act without provoking suspicion that he was influenced by his own interests.[134]

On November 22 the Senate Rules Committee voted unanimously to recommend the confirmation of Nelson Rockefeller to the full Senate. But Senators Byrd and James B. Allen of Alabama said that they had not decided whether they would defend the nomination on the Senate floor. Committee Chairman Cannon said that it was undecided whether the Senate would vote before the conclusion of the House Judiciary Committee hearings.[135]

The House hearings had begun the day before with the suggestion by Chairman Rodino that the committee must measure "the network of Rockefeller wealth, family wealth, and place it into the perspective of both the American economy and the American political system."*[136] There were indications that other committee members would inquire about the family wealth, especially in light of its huge contributions to Rockefeller's political campaigns.

Representatives Mezvinsky and Kastenmeier requested that Rockefeller ask his brothers to disclose their holdings, securities, and trusts in order to dispel the suspicions that there was a pattern of economic control by the family.[137] Rockefeller agreed to discuss the request with members of his family.

In his opening statement, Rockefeller promised that if confirmed he would place his financial holdings in a blind trust and arrange to have the family trusts of which he was lifetime beneficiary administered in a "blind manner."[138] Many of the committee Democrats indicated that they regarded the use of a blind trust as an empty gesture that would not resolve their worries about conflicts of interest.[139] The committee focused other questions on the 1971 Attica prison revolt, the pardon of L. Judson Morhouse, and Rockefeller's loans to public officials that were forgiven when the officials retired from public service. Rockefeller admitted that he had made a "serious mistake" in handling the Attica uprising when he failed to order state police to retake the prison in the early stages of the rebellion.[140]

At the conclusion of Rockefeller's testimony, the committee heard two days of testimony from outside witnesses. The same groups that had appeared before the Senate committee gave testimony again, and in several instances the same individuals merely reread their Senate testimony. Abortion, Attica, and internationalism were the main issues addressed. Committee members were more critical of these witnesses than the senators had been. Support for Rockefeller's nomination was

---

* Although they had covered the Senate hearings, the major networks decided not to televise these hearings.

voiced by four members of the House of Representatives who had previously testified before the Senate committee. The only congressional critic was Representative Bella Abzug of New York, who stated that the immense economic holdings of the Rockefeller family would create intrinsic conflicts of interest that would further weaken public confidence in the executive.[141] She also suggested that members of the 94th Congress should pass on the nomination, since their recent election would best reflect the present views of the electorate.[142] Following the Thanksgiving recess and after four more days of testimony, the House Judiciary Committee concluded its hearings on December 5. It received testimony from two professors about the collective Rockefeller financial network,[143] following which J. Richardson Dilworth, the Rockefeller family's senior financial adviser, sought to dispel the notion that the family acted in concert. He stressed that the investments of each family member were handled individually, without reference to those of other members. Dilworth released five tables showing the aggregate investments and stock holdings of the Rockefeller family, which totaled more than $1 billion in securities owned outright and in trusts, and stated the tables were the first attempt to aggregate the family holdings in this or any other way. The stock holdings were dispersed among more than two dozen companies, and the percentages of outstanding shares were insignificant except for about 1 percent of the stock of Exxon, 1.7 percent of the Mobil Corporation, and 2 percent of Standard Oil of California.[144] Committee members seemed so staggered by the vast amounts of money involved that it was difficult for them to question Dilworth.

Laurance Rockefeller and Ronan also testified before the House Judiciary Committee and essentially repeated their Senate testimonies. One surprise was the disclosure by Laurance Rockefeller of a loan of $30,000 in 1961 to William E. Miller, then chairman of the Republican National Committee and later the 1964 Republican vice-presidential nominee. Rockefeller had told the Senate Rules Committee that he had made no loans to political figures except for the loan to L. Judson Morhouse in 1959. In reviewing his records since then, he said, he had found the loan to Miller. Rockefeller also testified that he assumed his brother Nelson had requested the loan because he did not know Miller. The loan had been repaid in 1964.[145] The committee members questioned Rockefeller about the loan, about his political contributions, and, to a lesser extent, about the Goldberg biography and the Caribair acquisition. Several committee Democrats were so angry that the Miller loan had not been revealed earlier that they demanded Laurance Rockefeller supply a list of all loans and gifts he had ever made. Chairman Rodino restrained them by declaring that such a request was beyond the committee's authorization.[146]

Nelson Rockefeller returned as the final witness before the committee. He explained that he had asked Laurance to make the loan to Miller for an investment in venture capital and stated that there was nothing "unusual, wrong, immoral or questionable" about the loan.[147] He did not, however, explain his failure to disclose the loan earlier. Nevertheless, as the hearings concluded, confirmation of Rockefeller as Vice President seemed certain.

The formal debate on his confirmation began in the Senate on December 9. In opening the debate, Senator Cannon described the hearings of the Rules Committee and the investigations of the nominee by the FBI, the IRS, and congressional committee staffs. He said that, after judging Rockefeller by his entire record, the committee found no bar or impediment to disqualify him from the vice presidency and therefore unanimously recommended his confirmation.[148] Numerous other senators, while expressing concern about the Goldberg biography and political gifts, added their support for the nominee.

The few critics of the confirmation voiced different reasons for their opposition. Republican Senator William Scott of Virginia based his opposition on the lack of support for the nomination in his constituency and the suspicions engendered by the gifts and loans, the Goldberg book, and the family wealth and influence.[149] For Democratic Senator James Abourezk of South Dakota, Rockefeller's views on the use of nuclear weapons, antitrust policy, and covert CIA operations disqualified him from the vice presidency.[150] Reversing his initial support for Rockefeller, Senator Goldwater concluded that Rockefeller had used his personal wealth "to accomplish the purchase of political power" and that the nation would be better served by the selection of a younger man.[151] Senator Helms repeated many of his earlier criticisms of the nominee in announcing his opposition to confirmation.[152]

On December 10, one additional hour of debate was held before the confirmation vote. Two more senators spoke in opposition to Rockefeller. Gaylord Nelson, a Democrat of Wisconsin, asserted that the nominee was insensitive to the threats to freedom posed by vast concentrations of wealth and power.[153] Senator Bayh viewed the restoration of public confidence in government as the most important consideration and regarded Rockefeller's conflict-of-interest problems as insurmountable.[154] Rockefeller was confirmed by a vote of 90 to 7,[155] his assumption of the vice presidency awaiting only approval by the House.

Later that week the House Judiciary Committee recommended that Rockefeller be confirmed by a vote of 26 to 12.*[156] All the committee Republicans voted in favor of confirmation, while the twelve Democrats who opposed the nominee cited the conflict of interest inherent in the combination of high political office and massive wealth and economic power. Ten of the dissenters agreed that in a direct election the people might approve Rockefeller but that the Congress acting alone should not do so.[157]

---

* Six of the eight members who had voted against Ford's nomination also voted against Rockefeller's. The exceptions were Representatives Rangel and Jordan. *See supra* note 146. The remaining six dissenters were also Democrats: Representatives Danielson, Edwards, Mezvinsky, Joshua Eilberg of Pennsylvania, Paul S. Sarbanes of Maryland, and Wayne Owens of Utah.

The final debate and confirmation vote in the House occurred on December 19. During six hours of debate, sixty-six representatives argued for and against the confirmation.* The House confirmed Rockefeller by a vote of 287 to 128.[158]

The majority agreed with Congressman Rodino, who praised Rockefeller's experience, competence, and dedication to public service.[159] Others cited the intense scrutiny of the investigation and the nation's need for a Vice President.[160] If Rockefeller were defeated, some feared a less qualified nominee whose confirmation would be greatly delayed.[161] The negative votes were cast by conservative Republicans who criticized Rockefeller's "liberal ideology" and "big spender" reputation,[162] and by liberal Democrats who worried about his tremendous wealth and its political ramifications.[163] Many questioned his judgment regarding the Attica incident, political loans and gifts, and the Goldberg biography.[164] Although a sizable number of representatives opposed confirmation, there was never any doubt about the result. As Democratic Representative Otis G. Pike of New York observed, it was obvious that "the TV time has been ordered, the champagne is cooling in the bucket."[165]

Immediately after the House vote, President Ford traveled with Rockefeller to the Senate Chamber, where Rockefeller was sworn in by Chief Justice Warren E. Burger as the forty-first Vice President of the United States. In a short speech, the new Vice President expressed his "gratitude for the privilege of serving the country I love" and pledged himself to work with the President and Congress to solve the problems facing the nation.[166]

Rockefeller's vice presidency was never to realize the expectations that were expressed by many at the time of his confirmation hearings. Despite his capabilities and willingness to undertake assignments for the President, Rockefeller was unable to quiet the conservative critics who had opposed his nomination. Personal tours of the South and the Midwest and other advances toward conservative Republicans notwithstanding, he continued to be seen as a political liability throughout 1975 as Ford contemplated the 1976 election. By summer 1975 former Representative Howard H. Callaway of Georgia, Ford's campaign manager, was publicly stating that Rockefeller would damage Ford's chances for the nomination, and the President himself was giving no assurances that Rockefeller would be his running mate.[167]

As the nation's economic ills continued and the concept of détente with the Soviet Union was increasingly questioned, former Governor Ronald Reagan of California began to mobilize a conservative challenge to Ford. Ford seemed more vulnerable than the usual incumbent President. His frequent use of the veto power

---

* As in the Ford confirmation debates, a number of representatives presented the results of polls they had taken of their constituents. As had not been the case with Ford, the results were adverse to Rockefeller in a number of instances. *See,* e.g., 120 CONG. REC. H12,381 (Stratton), 12,392 (Crane), 12,393 (Ketchum), 12,402 (Ichord), 12,421 (Randall), 12,424 (Carney), 12,432 (Goldwater), 12,442 (Bingham), 12,443 (Bowen). *But see,* e.g., 12,383 (Studds), 12,383 (Jones), 12,423 (Paris) (daily ed. Dec. 19, 1974).

had cast his presidency in a negative light, and since he had never before waged a national campaign, he had no experienced political organization. As a means of diminishing Ford's presidential aura, Reagan emphasized that he had not been elected by a vote of the people.*

In response, Ford adopted a more conservative stance and in the fall of 1975 selected New York City's financial crisis as an issue to solidify his Republican support. Ford not only declared that there would be no federal help for New York but also criticized the city and its past leadership in speeches throughout the country. Such criticisms of New York obviously reflected on the Vice President who had served as that state's governor for fifteen years.

On November 3, 1975, in a letter to President Ford, Rockefeller announced that he would withdraw his name from consideration for the 1976 vice-presidential nomination so that Ford's "range of options" might be "simplified at the earliest time."[168] The letter also stated:

> My acceptancy of the Vice-Presidency, as you know, was based upon my concern to help restore national unity and confidence after the shattering experience of Watergate. Working under your leadership toward this goal has been challenging and rewarding as our basic institutions are surmounting our unprecedented crises and the nation is returning to its regular elective Presidential pattern next year.
>
> Regarding next year and my own situation, I have made it clear to you and to the public that I was not a candidate for the Vice-Presidency, that no one realistically can be such, and that the choice of a Vice-Presidential running mate is, and must be, up to the Presidential candidate to recommend to a national party convention.
>
> I shall, of course, continue to serve as Vice President, to discharge my constitutional obligations and to assist in every way . . . until the installation once again of a President and Vice President duly elected by the people of this great Republic.

At a news conference several days later Rockefeller explained that his possible presence on the ticket was creating "party squabbles" that were distracting the President from the serious problems facing the country. Yet he dismissed the Republican right, which opposed him, as a "minority of a minority." He also expressed lukewarm support for President Ford but did not rule out his own possible candidacy in 1976 if Ford should be defeated in the early primaries and withdraw from the race.[169] It was generally thought that Rockefeller had submitted his with-

---

* Reagan was not alone in calling attention to Ford's "unelected status." Similar comments ware uttered by a few Democratic public figures during 1975 in speeches critical of Ford. *See* Yaeger, *Letter to the Editor*, N.Y. TIMES, Mar. 6, 1975, at 36.

drawal to protect himself from the humiliation of being dumped by Ford at a later time.

While liberal Republicans decried the sacrifice of Rockefeller to their party's right wing, the Rockefeller decision made no great impact on conservatives. Reagan commented, "I'm certainly not appeased."[170] Simultaneous with the Vice President's withdrawal came the announcement of a major reorganization of Ford's Cabinet. Any gains the President had scored by Rockefeller's departure were muted by the removal of Secretary of Defense James R. Schlesinger, who had become an outspoken critic of détente and a supporter of increased defense spending. Ford's replacement of him with Donald H. Rumsfeld and his appointment of George H.W. Bush to succeed William Colby as director of the Central Intelligence Agency incensed many.

Moreover, the reorganization failed to impress a large segment of the nation as a wise exercise of executive leadership.[171] It appeared ill timed and politically motivated. The reorganization stressed political, not policy, attributes and the Rockefeller withdrawal left Ford free to dangle the vice-presidential nomination before other segments of the Republican Party. As 1975 ended, public opinion polls indicated that Ford's road to obtaining his party's presidential nomination and election to a full four-year term was laden with major obstacles.[172]

The Uses and Non-Uses of Section 3

March 30 taught me how fragile it all is, how unanticipated events can change the course of history in an eyeblink.

JAMES A. BAKER III[1]

In the presidential administrations running from Ronald Reagan to George W. Bush, the inability provisions of the Twenty-Fifth Amendment were invoked, considered seriously, and discussed with the public.

PRESIDENT RONALD REAGAN'S DISABILITIES

The Assassination Attempt

On March 30, 1981, just seventy days into his tenure, President Ronald Reagan exited the Washington Hilton Hotel after delivering a speech to the Building and Construction Trades Department of the AFL–CIO. On his way to his limousine, Reagan smiled and waved as he passed a crowd of reporters who were standing behind a security rope. Mike Putzel, an Associated Press reporter standing with the other reporters, shouted, "Mr. President!" in an attempt to ask him a question.[2]

Just then, a shot was fired, followed by a rapid series of five more shots. A look of "stunned disbelief" swept across the President's face. James S. Brady, his press secretary, was critically injured and fell to the ground. Next to him, a wounded District of Columbia plainclothes police officer, Thomas Delahanty, had fallen. A few feet away, Tim McCarthy, a Secret Service agent, agonized in pain on the sidewalk as a result of a bullet wound. By the sixth shot, police and Secret Service agents had jumped on the suspected assailant, a blond-haired man in a raincoat, and wrestled him up against a wall of the hotel. As Putzel would later recall, Reagan "just sort of stood there when the shots rang out. Then the smile just sort of washed off his face."[3]

Eyewitnesses said John W. Hinckley Jr., the assailant, had positioned himself among a crowd of reporters and television crews outside the hotel exit and was only ten feet away when he fired at the presidential entourage. The twenty-five-year-old Colorado native was arrested at the scene of the attack. Later that night, he was formally charged with the attempted assassination of the President and assault on a federal officer.*

Jerry S. Parr, the special agent in charge of the Presidential Protection Division of the Secret Service, was standing directly behind Reagan when the shots rang out. He immediately pushed the President into the open door of the limousine and jumped in behind him. At first, it was not known whether one of the bullets had struck Reagan in his left side, or if he had broken a rib when Parr shoved him out of danger. In fact, a bullet had bounced off the armor-plated limousine and hit the President. Luckily, the bullet, a "devastator" bullet designed to explode on impact, never exploded.[4]

The limousine initially sped toward the White House but was quickly diverted to George Washington University Hospital after a Secret Service agent saw that Reagan was bleeding from the mouth. Reagan was able to walk into the hospital on his own accord, but once inside, he nearly collapsed.[5] In the emergency room, the President's left lung, which had collapsed when the bullet pierced it, was reinflated, and a large volume of blood was drained from his chest cavity.

Reagan's wife, Nancy, rushed to the hospital, along with senior White House advisers. Despite his condition, the seventy-year-old President remained in good spirits. "Honey, I forgot to duck," Reagan told his wife. While he was being pushed down a corridor on a hospital gurney, he told Senator Paul Laxalt of Nevada, a close friend, "Don't worry about me."[6]

At 3:24 P.M., less than an hour after arriving at the hospital, Reagan was wheeled into an operating room for removal of the bullet. The entire procedure lasted about three hours. Dr. Dennis O'Leary, a spokesperson for George Washington University Hospital, said that surgeons made an incision about six inches long just below the left nipple. The bullet was removed, and Reagan received a large volume of blood through transfusions. Dr. O'Leary called this a "relatively simple procedure."[7] In fact, there was nothing relatively simple about it. One newspaper commented:

> Mr. Reagan's medical team found the right [voice to calm the country] in the remarkably fluent Dr. Dennis O'Leary of George Washington University Hospital. "Let the anesthesia wear off," he assured the country, "and the

---

* After an eight-week trial in the summer of 1982, John Hinckley was found not guilty by reason of insanity and has been confined in a District of Columbia federal mental hospital ever since.

President could decide anything." Among all those minding the store, it was the doctor who won authority, with little more than candor, knowledge and charm.[8]

Unlike the medical reports of the injuries to James Brady, the prognosis the doctors gave for the President's recovery was incredibly positive. Dr. O'Leary said that because the bullet had not struck the heart, the President "was never in any serious danger."[9] He speculated that Reagan would be able to go home in about two weeks. He added that the President was "clear of head and should be able to make decisions by tomorrow."[10] Asked if it was "medically extraordinary" for Reagan to have walked into the hospital, Dr. O'Leary said, "Maybe not medically extraordinary, but just short of that."[11]

By 8:50 that evening, the President reportedly joked with his doctors in the recovery room. With tubes in his throat, he wrote a note to his doctors that said, "All in all, I'd rather be in Philadelphia."[12] Indicators of the upbeat mood of the President, despite his grave condition, continued to reach the public via White House briefings and reporters' investigations.

One newspaper claimed that Reagan was "capable of handling the few things that absolutely require his decision" as soon as he had regained consciousness. "[H]is bedside manner has been so amiable and the sympathy of the country for him has been so great that he is likely to get more support for his legislative program than he had before he was wounded."[13]

When Reagan was shot, Vice President George H.W. Bush was flying from Fort Worth to Austin, Texas, where he was to address the Texas legislature. Bush headed for Washington immediately upon hearing the news. As he flew toward the capital, members of the President's Cabinet and staff rushed to the White House Situation Room. Among those who assembled there were Secretary of State Alexander M. Haig Jr., Defense Secretary Caspar Weinberger, Attorney General William French Smith, White House Counsel Fred F. Fielding, Secretary of the Treasury Donald Regan, National Security Advisor Richard B. Allen, and Richard Darman, a presidential aide. From the Situation Room, an open line was established with Deputy Chief of Staff Michael Deaver, White House Political Director Lyn Nofziger, and Edwin Meese, Counsel to the President, all of whom were at the hospital.

By most accounts, as the President underwent surgery, the events at the White House were characterized by a lack of coordination. The seventy-day-old administration had not yet developed any concrete guidelines for dealing with a case of presidential inability. It was not until after the assassination attempt that they completed a book defining the appropriate responses in cases of presidential inability.[14]

As Donald Regan noted in his book:

[T]he men at the heart of the government did not possess much more information than the ordinary citizen about a situation that involved the life of the President and might have involved the safety of the nation. Even less did the men gathered in the Situation Room know what action they were authorized to take or expected to take. Together, they represented a considerable depository of experience, ability, even wisdom . . . but in the absence of a framework of authority and procedure, they could do little besides react to events about which they had only limited information . . . . [15]

Along similar lines, Haig noted in his memoirs that the officials handling the crisis in the Situation Room were "an ad hoc group; no plan existed, we possessed no list of guidelines, no chart that established rank or function. Our work was a matter of calling on experience and exercising judgment."[16]

In a meticulously detailed account of that day, Del Quentin Wilber has written that as Attorney General Smith left the Justice Department for the Situation Room, he asked his chief aide, Theodore Olson, "to find out what procedures are necessary if we have to transfer power to the vice president."[17] Olson's old pocket copy of the Constitution did not contain the Twenty-Fifth Amendment, but that was rectified almost immediately. Wilber added that "there were no precedents, no legal opinions, no briefing materials. They [lawyers in the Justice Department] would have to devise their own directives on the fly." This was not so in the case of White House counsel Fred Fielding, who had studied succession contingencies shortly after Reagan's inauguration and begun to put together a binder, which included draft letters to trigger Sections 3 and 4 of the Amendment. Fielding later said at a program at Fordham University that when he reviewed the provisions of the Amendment in the Situation Room that afternoon, the eyes of the people in the room "glazed over" as "most of them didn't have a sense of that obligation" and the "line of succession was equally opaque to some people."[18] Wilber provides a further gloss on the meeting in the Situation Room, stating that "[presidential adviser] David Gergen approached the table and queried Haig about the president's condition. 'Is he under sedation now?' Gergen asked. 'Is he conscious?' 'He's on the operating table,' Haig replied. . . . 'So the helm is right here,' Haig said. 'And that means right here in this chair for now, constitutionally, until the vice president gets here.' "[19] Fielding has added as to that day, "I have read that during that tense afternoon the draft Sections 3 and 4 letters were pulled from my hands and sealed in a safe. It's not so. But think how silly that sounds. It wasn't a great secret that the Twenty-Fifth Amendment was in play, if you will. To say that suddenly things were pulled and put in a safe sounds very silly."[20]

To calm the nation, Deputy Press Secretary Larry Speakes conducted a press briefing less than two hours after the shooting, during which he was unable to answer a number of questions about the President's health and about the administration's crisis management plan.* Haig, believing Speakes to be foundering with his answers, dashed from the Situation Room up to the White House press room. Out of breath and sweating, he made a statement that included this exchange:

> Q: Who is making the decisions for the government right now? . . .
>
> HAIG: Constitutionally, gentlemen, you have the President, the Vice President, and the Secretary of State in that order and should the President decide he wants to transfer the helm to the Vice President, he will do so. He has not done that. As of now, I am in control here, in the White House, pending return of the Vice President and in close touch with him. If something came up, I would check with him, of course.[21]

In addition, Haig stated that, "there are absolutely no alert measures that are necessary at this time or contemplated."[22] Regrettably, his effort to reassure the country and the world had the opposite effect. As Michael Deaver noted later, "What undid Haig was his failure to collect himself before he went on national television. His instincts were right. He wanted the world to know that our guard was up, that the government was working. But he looked like a man about to crack."[23]

When Haig returned to the Situation Room after his appearance, Weinberger informed him that he had misstated the alert condition of the U.S. military forces during the briefing. Haig argued that it would not have been a good idea to tell the public that the alert status had been raised.[24] In his memoirs, Weinberger stated:

> [I]t was my understanding that I had to make decisions in that field, and that the decisions I had made represented my best judgment. [Haig] said that I should read the Constitution. Haig seemed to be referring to the old statute, under now superseded constitutional provisions, that established the Secretary of State as the next to take over in the event of the death or disability of the President and the Vice President. That statute has long since been changed by the Congress . . . under the Twenty-fifth Amendment. . . . I repressed an impulse to tell him that if he had read the current version of the Constitution he would find that some of his statements on television were not correct . . . .
>
> At no time was there any "violent quarrel" or any major disagreement between Al Haig and me as reported. . . . The conversations . . . were low key and represented simply different views as to the necessity and desirability

---

* For example, when asked, "Is the President in surgery?" he replied, "I can't say." When asked, "Who's running the government right now?" his reply was, "I cannot answer that question at this time." Finally, when asked, "Who'll be determining the status of the President and whether the Vice President should, in fact, become the acting President?" he replied, "I don't know the details on that." Press Briefing, The White House, Mar. 30, 1981.

of increasing the alert condition of the Strategic Air crews. I never felt I had, or was supposed to have, "command of the Situation Room," nor did I object to Al Haig's actions. . . . At no time did we argue about who had the authority or anything of the kind, other than as recorded above.[25]

Meanwhile, over at the hospital, Deaver; Meese; James Baker, then Chief of the White House Staff; and First Lady Nancy Reagan waited while the President underwent surgery. Baker spoke by phone with Daniel Ruge, the White House physician, and then announced to those around him that the President's condition was stable. According to Deaver, "[t]he three of us [Baker, Meese, and Deaver] looked at each other and nodded. The decision was made right there: not to invoke the Twenty-fifth Amendment . . . ."[26]

Wilber provides this riveting account: "Baker and Meese left the chapel and found . . . an out-of-the-way janitor's closet where . . . they debated whether to temporarily transfer presidential authority to Vice President Bush. . . . It was an option both were loath to take. . . . Taking all these factors into consideration, Baker and Meese decided that it would be wisest not to transfer presidential authority to Bush, at least not yet."[27]

Although versions of the decision not to invoke the Amendment vary, it seems clear that the issue was resolved by a handful of officials without the kind of formal action by the Cabinet and Vice President that the Amendment contemplated. The officials concluded that given the President's stabilized condition and the prospects for his recovery as indicated by his physicians, it would have been unduly alarming if the Amendment had been invoked. For example, Larry Speakes opined, "It was decided that we would not formally invoke the Twenty-fifth Amendment, because it would have alarmed the American people and our allies, giving them reason to believe that the President was much more seriously wounded than he now appeared to be."[28] Haig stated:

If the President was able to sign [a dairy bill the next day as scheduled] . . . , then all doubt as to his capacity would effectively be dispelled. So far, there was little reason to believe that he would not be able to sign the bill and otherwise perform his duties. Weinberger, Regan, and Smith held the same views and expressed them forcefully.[29]

The extent to which Vice President Bush was involved in the consultation process leading to the decision not to invoke the Amendment is unclear. Fielding and Smith did review the Amendment with him on his return to Washington. Bush, however, was particularly wary of taking any action that could even remotely be construed as an attempt to usurp presidential power.[30] In a chapter revealingly entitled "Only the President Lands on the South Lawn," Bush explained that his primary concern was to reassure the nation and the world by avoiding any actions that could be interpreted as a challenge to the President's authority.[31] For example, when he arrived in Washington on the evening of the shooting, he decided to proceed first to the Vice President's residence and then drive to the White House, rather than fly by helicopter directly to the South Lawn of the White House from Andrews Air Force Base.

Fielding said at the Fordham program that the news of the bullet being removed from the President's lung and that the doctors were confident of a full recovery "quelled any further thoughts or discussions of the Amendment's invocation until the Vice President had returned." He described a meeting in the Vice President's office that evening attended by the Attorney General, Chief of Staff, and Secretary of Defense at which the invocation of Section 4 at that point was considered. He said that, "the decision was made that it should not be," adding that the President was alert the next morning, joking, writing notes, and conducting some "minor official tasks."[32]

The next day, Bush performed ceremonial and other daily presidential duties. In deference to the President, Bush continued to use his own office instead of the Oval Office when he met with staff aides, and during a morning Cabinet meeting he sat in his own chair, not the President's.[33] Throughout this period, he stressed that Reagan was still completely in charge of the government.*

From the moment the President was shot until he left the hospital thirteen days later, it seems clear that the general public assumed that Reagan was governing the country "as usual." Though he was under anesthesia during surgery and the influence of mind-altering drugs during recovery, the picture was conveyed of the President's being "in charge."

In fact, Vice President Bush presided over Cabinet meetings in place of Reagan for almost four weeks.[34] Further, it was not until June 3, more than two months after the assassination attempt, that the President worked a full day.[35] He made his first trip after the shooting incident on May 17, when he went to Notre Dame University to receive an honorary degree.[36] After nine weeks of recuperation, President Reagan declared himself recovered.[37] However, according to Dr. Ruge, it was as late as October 1981 when Reagan said, "Now I really feel like I am all the way."[38]

Cancer Surgery

In July 1985, the Twenty-Fifth Amendment was implicated for a second time during the Reagan presidency. On July 12, President Reagan entered Bethesda Naval Hospital for a scheduled procedure to remove a benign polyp from his colon. During the procedure another large polyp, feared to be cancerous, was discovered. That polyp required surgical removal, and it was decided that the President should

---

* At the time of the assassination attempt, a crisis existed in Poland, and the Soviet Union was threatening to intervene. While Reagan was incapacitated, Bush warned against Soviet intervention. The crisis became no worse as a result of Reagan's condition.

undergo surgery the next day.[39] On July 13, before receiving anesthesia, Reagan signed a document prepared by his counsel, Fred Fielding, in consultation with Attorney General Edwin Meese and Chief of Staff Donald Regan.* The document transferred power to Vice President Bush as Acting President but disclaimed any formal use of the Twenty-Fifth Amendment.

> After consultation with my Counsel and the Attorney General, I am mindful of the provisions of Section 3 of the 25th Amendment to the Constitution and of the uncertainties of its application to such brief and temporary periods of incapacity. I do not believe that the drafters of this Amendment intended its application to situations such as the instant one.
>
> Nevertheless, consistent with my long-standing arrangement with Vice President George Bush, and not intending to set a precedent binding anyone privileged to hold this Office in the future, I have determined and it is my intention and direction that Vice President George Bush shall discharge those powers and duties in my stead commencing with the administration of anesthesia to me in this instance.[40]

This document was transmitted to the Speaker of the House of Representatives and the President pro tempore of the Senate.

Several hours after the successful completion of the surgery, Regan and Fielding informally tested Reagan to determine if he was ready to resume his powers and duties. The test consisted of handing him a two-sentence letter addressed to the congressional leaders, notifying them that he was ready to resume his position. "Following up on my letter to you of this date, please be advised I am able to resume the discharge of the Constitutional powers and duties of the Office of the President of the United States. I have informed the Vice President of my determination and my resumption of those powers and duties."[41] Based on Reagan's quick response—"Gimme a pen"—it was determined by Regan and Fielding that he "knew exactly what was going on,"[42] and Reagan proceeded to sign the letter.†

Fielding said they gave him a draft letter regarding the resumption of his powers and duties and offered to come back in a few hours and ask him then to sign the letter, prompting the President to reply, "Oh, heck no. I don't want you to wake me up later. I want to sign it now."[43] Fielding noted that there was no reason to rush the President since Bush was available and ready for the transfer, except that Reagan "has seemingly sufficiently regained his consciousness and his wits about

---

* At the time of the assassination attempt in 1981, Meese was Counsel to the President and Regan was Secretary of the Treasury.
† The author's conversations with Fred Fielding on March 2, 1992, confirmed that this was the procedure used to determine whether Reagan was ready to reassume the powers and duties of the presidency.

him. . . ."[44] He also said that "when we offered him additional time, the President was very convincing in saying no."[45]

During the eight hours that Bush was Acting President, he signed no laws, made no appointments, and authorized no military action. Nor did he go to his White House office. He simply stayed at his residence and waited for Reagan to emerge from the anesthesia.[46]

Reagan spent the next seven days recuperating in the hospital, during which time Regan acted as the main link between Reagan and Bush and the Cabinet. On July 22, Reagan left the hospital, and by Labor Day he was busily involved in the work of the presidency.

Although the document signed by Reagan on July 13 disclaimed any invocation of the Twenty-Fifth Amendment, he nonetheless must have used Section 3 of the Amendment.* He followed all the guidelines and procedures of Section 3, doing everything that was required by the Amendment. Moreover, there was no provision other than the Twenty-Fifth Amendment that would have allowed him to make such a designation of Vice President Bush as Acting President. It is clear enough that Reagan's disclaimer was made for two specific reasons: fear of the reaction of the country and the world to a "President" who admitted to being disabled, and concern that admitting to the Amendment's invocation would set a harmful precedent for the presidency.

It is interesting that Fielding later told a special study commission that the letter transferring power to Vice President Bush "would accomplish the activation of the 25th Amendment."[47] Additional evidence that the Amendment was invoked is to be found in the memoirs of President and Nancy Reagan and in other writings. According to President Reagan's account:

> Before they wheeled me into the operating room, I signed a letter invoking the Twenty-fifth Amendment, making George Bush Acting President during the time I was incapacitated under anesthesia. They gave me a shot of Pentathol and I awoke several hours later feeling groggy and confused. . . . Later, when I was fully alert, I signed a letter reclaiming the presidency from George . . . .[48]

Nancy Reagan's account mirrored the President's assertion that the Twenty-Fifth Amendment had been invoked:

> The operation began at eleven o'clock that Saturday morning. Half an hour earlier, Ronnie had signed the papers authorizing George Bush to be Acting

---

* Section 3 states: "Whenever the President transmits to the President pro tempore of the Senate and the Speaker of the House of Representatives his written declaration that he is unable to discharge the powers and duties of his office, and until he transmits to them a written declaration to the contrary, such powers and duties shall be discharged by the Vice President as Acting President." U.S. Const. amend. XXV, § 3.

Section 3 was once again used by President George W. Bush, in July 2007. On July 21 the President had another colonoscopy, during which he was anesthetized. This time his doctors found five polyps, which were later determined to be benign.[80] The President transferred power to Vice President Cheney for a total of two hours and five minutes, the surgery lasting only thirty-one minutes.[81] While serving as Acting President, Cheney was not actually in Washington, D.C., but instead at his home on the eastern shore of Maryland,[82] where he wrote a letter to his grandchildren.[83]

As provided by Section 3 of the Amendment, the President transmitted letters to House Speaker Nancy Pelosi and President pro tempore Robert Byrd declaring inability[84] and the subsequent resuming of presidential powers.[85] Though the White House did not explicitly specify reasons, it declined to advise the public of the specific times of the procedure and when Cheney would serve as Acting President. During a news conference Press Secretary Tony Snow stated, "We're not telling you. We'll let you know after everything is done."[86] After the surgery, Bush was in good spirits and planned on taking a bike ride.[87]

VICE PRESIDENT RICHARD CHENEY
AND VICE-PRESIDENTIAL INABILITY

Contingency planning appears to have been a subject of great importance to Vice President Cheney. In his autobiography, *In My Time*, he reveals that he asked his general counsel, David Addington, in early 2001 to review the contingency plans in effect for dealing with an enemy attack. He learned from that review that there was no mechanism for dealing with his own incapacity. As he noted, "A Vice President is required in order to carry out the Twenty-Fifth Amendment . . . and if I were incapacitated, I might stand in the way of the removal of a President unable to discharge his duties—or I might become an incapacitated Acting President. Neither of these was a good outcome for the country."[88] Aware of his own long history of coronary artery disease, he decided to write a letter of resignation as Vice President shortly after he was sworn in, to be effective upon its delivery to the Secretary of State. Cheney said to his counsel:

> I won't give specific instructions about when the letter should be triggered. But you need to understand something. This is not your decision to make. This is not [his wife] Lynne's decision to make. The only thing you are to do, if I become incapacitated, is to get this letter out and give it to the President. It's his decision and his decision alone, whether he delivers it to the Secretary of State.

Aside from Cheney's counsel, President Bush was the only other person with whom he discussed the letter. Cheney recounts in his book that his counsel double-wrapped the letter in two manila U.S. government envelopes, took it home, and put it in his dresser drawer. Addington decided not to keep it in a safe at work because he didn't want to be unable to get to it in case the worst did happen and the White House was in crisis mode. Two years later, when Addington's house was destroyed by a fire, he grabbed two things—a folder with his family's financial documents and birth certificates in it and the envelope containing Cheney's letter of resignation.

Continued Interest and Efforts to Change

Congressional Action

As the presidency has increased in importance in American political life, politicians have sought to reshape the office via the amending process. But such attempts to expand, restrict, or restructure Presidential powers have been unavailing.

RICHARD B. BERNSTEIN[1]

The terrorist attack on the World Trade Center on September 11, 2001, was unprecedented in its tragic impact on the lives of innocent Americans. It ushered in an era of threat to the security and well-being of the nation. Following the devastation on American soil, many efforts were designed to anticipate and meet danger before it struck. Within a year a new Cabinet department was established, the Department of Homeland Security, and not long after that Congress commenced hearings on the subjects of "Ensuring the Continuity of the United States Government: The Presidency" and the "Presidential Succession Act of 1947." Proposed constitutional amendments and bills were introduced as well in Congress to address perceived weaknesses in the presidential succession system. A review of the hearings and proposed legislation follows.

REVIEW OF CONGRESSIONAL HEARINGS

Senate Hearings

On September 16, 2003, a joint Senate session was held of the Judiciary Committee's Subcommittee on the Constitution, Civil Rights, and Property Rights, chaired by Republican Senator John Cornyn of Texas, and the Committee on Rules and Administration, chaired by Republican Senator Trent Lott of Mississippi. After briefly recounting that the first hearing ever held by the committee he chaired ultimately led to the 1947 succession statute, Senator Lott detailed the history of succession laws, noting, "[s]ince those 1947 hearings, no substantive legislation has been passed to deal with the gaps in the current Presidential succession system," other than the Twenty-Fifth Amendment.[2] Indeed, during the Ford and Rockefeller implementations of Section 2, Senator Lott had been a member of the House Judiciary Committee, the committee that dealt with the confirmation process of the Vice President under the Amendment.

Turning to the topic of the hearing, the senator distinguished the concerns in 1947 from those of the present day. Then, the primary concern was the atomic bomb. Today, that threat still remains along with "dirty bombs" as well as other potential disasters. Focusing on the particular problems of the 1947 succession law, he pointed to the problems resulting from the bumping provision of the present statute. The remainder of the senator's opening remarks focused primarily on the problems with having legislators in the line of succession, primarily the potential for a change in party in the instance of a legislator acting as President. The post-1994 House of Representatives was used as an example, wherein House Speaker Newt Gingrich of Georgia, a Republican, could have acted as President were President Clinton and Vice President Gore, both Democrats, unable to serve.

Senator Cornyn was next to speak. Describing the present succession system as "intolerable" in that "[w]e must have a system in place so that it is always clear beyond doubt who the President is, especially in times of national crisis."[3] He identified four situations wherein both the President and the Vice President die with a resulting confusion over who would succeed to the Presidency.[4] In the first instance, the Speaker of the House is from another party. Out of party loyalty, the Secretary of State asserts a competing claim to the presidency, maintaining that legislators are not officers and thereby are not constitutionally eligible to succeed to the presidency.

In a second scenario, the Texas senator described the potential situation wherein both the Speaker and the President pro tempore decline to serve as Acting President, allowing the Secretary of State to assume the office. However, weeks later the Speaker decides to assert his or her right under the succession law to become Acting President. In response, the Secretary claims that under the Constitution he is Acting President "until the disability be removed, or a President shall be elected."[5]

Even worse would be a third situation, in which not only the President and the Vice President die but also the Speaker of the House as well as many House members. Here, it is conceivable that the remaining House members, possibly from a small portion of the country or narrow ideological spectrum, claiming a quorum, might elect a new Speaker with both the President pro tempore and the Secretary of State making conflicting claims of being the Acting President.

Finally, Senator Cornyn pointed out that most individuals in the line of succession reside in the general Washington, D.C., area. It is conceivable that an attack would knock out the entire line of succession. In such an instance, who would be the President?

The senator concluded that any one of these horrific possibilities could happen under the current succession law. This is especially evident in the wake of September 11, when the Secret Service for the first time implemented its emergency plan to protect the presidential line of succession.

Both chairs left no ambiguity as to where they stood on issues of reform. Senator Lott said, "I do not want to tell Senator [Ted] Stevens [of Alaska, then President pro tempore] this yet, but I have come to the conclusion that congressional leaders should be taken out of the line of succession. . . . I think it is a real problem, and I have for years." Senator Cornyn stated, "I believe we must fix the Presidential succession law, and fix it now, so that these nightmare scenarios will never come true and will never again be able to haunt the American people or our form of Government."

Senator Lott then introduced the witness panel. Yale Law School professor Akhil Amar spoke first before the committee. Beginning by making reference to his 1994 testimony on the same subject and referring to related material he had published, Amar described 3 U.S.C. section 19 as "a disastrous statute, an accident waiting to happen."* In his view, the statute violates the Succession Clause of the Constitution, as Senate and House leaders are not "officers" within the meaning of the clause. Section 19(d)(2), the bumping provision, is also in violation of the clause, he said. Echoing the problems identified in Senator Cornyn's second hypothetical, Amar said that the bumping provision allowing for the removal of an Acting President is not in accord with the Constitution. In doing so, it "weakens the Presidency itself and increases instability and uncertainty at the very moment when the Nation is most in need of tranquility."[6]

Moving beyond purely constitutional concerns, Amar addressed policy ramifications of the statute. Among these was the requirement that the Acting President resign his previous position, which creates potentially perilous decisions in the event of a temporary disability. Further, its approach runs counter to that of the Twenty-Fifth Amendment, which provides for a smooth relinquishing and regaining of power in instances of short-term disability.

Another policy problem resulting from the Succession Act is, he testified, its creation of potentially untoward motives in Congress's power to impeach and also

---

* The 1994 Hearing (*Presidential Succession between the Popular Election and the Inauguration: Hearing Before the Subcomm. on the Constitution of the S. Comm. on the Judiciary*, 103th Cong. 22–35, 26 (1994)). In addition to Akhil Amar, testimony was received from Senator Birch Bayh, Assistant Attorney General Walter Dellinger, Federal Election Commission Chairman Trevor Potter, and Georgetown Professor Walter Berns and a prepared statement from Lawrence University Professor Lawrence D. Longley. For Professor Amar's most in-depth analysis of the 1947 Presidential Succession Act see Akhil Reed Amar & Vikram David Amar, *Is the Presidential Succession Act Constitutional?*, 48 Stan. L. Rev. 113 (1995).

to delay confirmation of vice-presidential nominees. A third problem is that Section 19 of the 1947 Act could effectively reverse an election by placing a different party's leader in the White House. Pointing to gaps in the succession system, Amar then turned to the fact that the succession statute as is does not provide any way to determine disabilities in the vice presidency, nor does it assist in accounting for determining whether the President is unable in the absence of a Vice President. Finally, the 1947 Act does not address vulnerabilities occurring near presidential elections.

Addressing potential criticisms of Cabinet succession, Amar observed the concern that the presidency is not an appointed position and only elected individuals should hold the office. In response to this concern, the professor pointed to the Twenty-Fifth Amendment's confirmation process for determining the qualifications of a nominee. In like fashion, he suggested that Congress create a new Cabinet position, Assistant Vice President or Second Vice President. To increase the democratic mandate of this individual, the presidential nominee could publicly announce before the November elections who this second in line would be.

In Amar's view, this new Cabinet position would solve the constitutional problems, as the Assistant Vice President would be an "officer" and there would be no bumping problem. He concluded by alluding to his 1994 testimony, wherein he detailed solutions to the problems of vice-presidential disability and more fully addressed the windows of vulnerability surrounding presidential elections.

The next witness was John C. Fortier, Executive Director of the Continuity of Government Commission and a Research Associate at the American Enterprise Institute. Fortier began by praising Republican Senator Mike DeWine's leadership with regard to the passage of S. 148, which placed the Secretary of Homeland Security just after the "big four" Cabinet members.* Moving to the Presidential Succession Act, he proceeded to describe a number of areas where the current system needs improvement.

First, there is the possibility that the entire line of succession could be killed in an attack on Washington. If this happened there would be no clear individual who would assume the presidency. As a fix to this potentiality, Fortier suggested, noting the overlap with Professor Amar's recommendation, that the President be allowed to nominate four or five individuals who reside primarily outside the Washington area who would be approved by Congress in the normal confirmation process. These

---

* Ultimately, the Secretary of Homeland Security was placed after the Secretary of Veterans Affairs following the tradition of ordering the line of succession after the Speaker and the President pro tempore by creation of Cabinet position. *See* Vacancies in Offices of Both President and Vice President: Officers Eligible to Act, Pub. L. No. 80-199, 61 Stat. 380 (codified as amended at 3 U.S.C. § 19 (2006).

individuals could be sitting governors, former Presidents, or Cabinet members. They would regularly participate in security briefings, enabling them to serve if such a need arose.

Fortier next addressed the difficulties with having legislators in the line of succession. Like others, he generally agreed that having Members of Congress in the line of succession presents potential pitfalls. However, there is one instance in which he recommended they remain as potential successors: the situation in which an election controversy is not resolved prior to the January 20 inauguration. In such a situation, it would be better to have a recently elected Speaker of the House act as President than a member of the previous administration's Cabinet. Fortier distinguished this scenario from others in that it falls under the "failure to qualify" provisions of the Twentieth Amendment, which does not have the "Officer" language of the Succession Clause of Article II.

An inauguration of a new President is a particularly sensitive time, in Fortier's view. Not only are almost all high-ranking individuals present, but many of the outgoing Cabinet members have already resigned, leaving only Acting Secretaries potentially in the line of succession. To address this problem, Fortier suggested three solutions. First, it should be custom that the outgoing President nominate the Cabinet members of the new President prior to January 20 so that they could be in place at the time of inauguration. Second, it should be made clear that Acting Secretaries are not in the line of succession. Last, Congress potentially has its own continuity problems, which it should resolve.

M. Miller Baker, a partner at the law firm McDermott, Will and Emery, was the third witness. His testimony repeated the critiques of the bumping provision and the resignation requirement of the 1947 Act. Another problem in his view was that the succession statute as it stands does not provide for "a more senior Cabinet successor that was temporarily unable to act to assume the Acting Presidency from a more junior Cabinet member that assumed the Acting Presidency."[7] This could create a situation in which the more junior Cabinet member would hesitate to act, hoping to avoid any accusations of usurping power. Baker imagined a situation in which Secretary of State Colin Powell was temporarily unavailable and wondered if Treasury Secretary Paul O'Neill would have assumed the Acting Presidency, precluding Powell from serving.

Continuing with the problems more junior-ranking Cabinet members present, Baker suggested that not only the Speaker of the House and the President pro tempore be removed from the line of succession but also all members of the Cabinet with the exception of the Secretary of State, the Secretary of the Treasury, the Secretary of Defense, the Attorney General, and the Secretary of Homeland Security. In his view, no one contemplated Cabinet members such as the Secretary of Veterans Affairs or Secretary of Agriculture acting as President, especially in a crisis, which is the only situation during which such a need could arise.

Baker's testimony concluded with his suggestion that Congress consider creating additional Cabinet positions solely for the purpose of succession, largely mirroring Mr. Fortier's own recommendation.

Professor Howard M. Wasserman of Florida International University next addressed the committee. First, he observed that the panelists so far had agreed on two points: that the succession statute is seriously flawed and that the events of September 11 had made those flaws particularly evident. Further, he expressed general agreement that a Cabinet line of succession is preferable, as it does not pose partisan concerns, questions of democratic legitimacy, or separation-of-powers problems. However, unlike previous witnesses, Wasserman argued that there is a place for legislators in the line of succession, that they should be placed after the Cabinet members. The logic for this is that the line of succession should be expanded as had been suggested in adding an Assistant Vice President. Also, if sufficient members of Congress survived an attack, they would be able to select a Speaker or President pro tempore without delay who could then act as President.

Wasserman suggested providing for a special election, noting that the 1792 Act contained elections in the case of a double vacancy in the presidency. A special election should occur within six months, giving the public time to mourn and recover while allowing the necessary arrangements to be made to hold such an election. This special election would enable the nation to move past the tragedy.

Democratic Senator Russell D. Feingold of Wisconsin spoke briefly before Chairman Lott proceeded to question the witnesses. In his first question, Senator Lott sought clarification as to why President Harry S. Truman, in proposing the current (1947) succession statute, insisted on having legislators in the line of succession. In his answer, Amar pointed to Truman's skepticism over an unelected official's assuming the office of the presidency. Still, in Truman's original proposal he included arrangements for a special election. This suggests that he did not conceive of legislators' serving as Acting President until the next presidential election. Amar again reminded the committee that the Twenty-Fifth Amendment provides legitimacy for the Vice President by having a special nomination and confirmation process. Noting that the Vice President is not directly elected, he added that were a candidate for President also to designate his second in line, that individual would have some popular legitimacy through the election process.

Chairman Lott then questioned the usefulness of an Assistant Vice President, as the position would have no real responsibilities. He also queried whether the problems identified by the witnesses could be addressed by statute or if they would require a constitutional amendment. Addressing the second question, Amar noted that a statute could fix these problems. Turning to the question of the Assistant Vice President, Amar clarified that the point of the position is that this individual would be physically outside the immediate Washington area and would therefore be less likely to be killed or injured during an attack. In response, Senator Lott wondered if some Cabinet member could be regularly stationed outside the capital. This suggestion appeared acceptable to Amar, though it is unclear which Cabinet member would serve in such a capacity.

Baker was not as convinced that the succession problems could be fixed by simple statute. Though agreeing that some difficulties could be addressed through legislation, he noted that under the Twenty-Fifth Amendment, one of the first duties of an Acting President would be to nominate a Vice President. He said that it was unclear whether an Acting President can select a Vice President, as would happen when the Speaker acts as President in the instance of a vice-presidential vacancy. This problem could not be addressed by statute, he added. Baker also suggested that a constitutional amendment might be necessary to validate the creation of an office of Assistant Vice President. (See Postscript to this chapter.)

Joining in, Fortier agreed with Amar that legislative solutions could be found for many of the discussed problems. He then observed that the original draft of the Twenty-Fifth Amendment removed Congress from the line of succession and that the Cabinet would serve in determining the inability of a President. He expressed a desire to see these two provisions returned, presumably through another amendment.

Senator Cornyn next asked what would happen if both the President and Vice President were disabled. Would presidential power just pass to the next in line? He also asked if there should be some objective standard in determining disability. Wasserman suggested that an objective standard might be useful, though one is not provided by the Twenty-Fifth Amendment. He added that if both the President and the Vice President were disabled, the Speaker of the House would become Acting President. This is why, in his view, the line of succession should remain within the executive branch, since the Speaker might be from another party.

Democratic Senator Christopher J. Dodd of Connecticut joined the debate, briefly detailing the history of the succession statutes and returning the discussion to whether Truman's logic for the change was indeed sound. Amar suggested that the subsequent passage of the Twenty-Fifth Amendment, with a President nominating his successor with the approval of a special confirmation process, effectively repudiated Truman's argument that the executive should not choose his own successor.

Next, Senator Lott asked the panel why in the present succession statute the Speaker is second in line whereas in the 1792 Act the President pro tempore was third and the Speaker fourth. Fortier noted that the President pro tempore in 1792 was not the position it is today, held by the longest-serving member of the majority party. Still, Truman felt that the Speaker was the appropriate individual as he is first elected in his own district and then elected to the Speakership by the majority of the House. Amar countered that the Speaker presents a problem in that the House of Representative is not a continuing body like the Senate and there have historically been long periods where there was no Speaker.

Senator Dodd then moved the inquiry into the possibility of having non-Cabinet members, such as sitting governors, in the line of succession, wondering how such an arrangement would work. Baker suggested that a provision could be developed to handle this possibility and opined that the state governors be left to the discretion of the President.

Senators Cornyn and DeWine expressed concern regarding the wisdom of holding special elections. In their view, doing so would merely add uncertainty at a time when certainty is needed. Further, a special election could very well disenfranchise military voters. Amar argued that there is a necessary tradeoff with special elections as they do provide democratic legitimacy. In his view much of this was solved by the Twenty-Fifth Amendment, providing the President with the ability to nominate a Vice President. However, the further down the line of succession one goes, the less legitimacy such individual would have to act as President.

With this, the two chairmen thanked the participants and adjourned the hearing.

House Hearings

On October 6, 2004, the House of Representatives held a hearing on the Presidential Succession Act. The Judiciary Committee's Subcommittee on the Constitution invited four witnesses to speak. As at the Senate hearing, Akhil Amar and M. Miller Baker provided testimony. Thomas H. Neale, from the Congressional Research Service of the Library of Congress, and Democratic Representative Brad Sherman of California also testified.

Republican Representative Steve Chabot of Ohio, a committee chair, began briefly outlining the history of the three succession acts. Before introducing the individual witnesses, he identified three of the major critiques of the present 1947 Succession Act: the bumping provision, the geographical concentration of the line of succession, and the possibility of a change in party control. The witnesses then followed.

Neale, who testified first, noted that the issue of presidential succession was largely a settled matter before the terrorist attacks of September 11 and that those events made evident and pressing some of the gaps, oversights, and difficulties with the current succession law.

Referring to the first oversight as mostly a matter of "housekeeping," Neale noted that since September 11, the Department of Homeland Security had been created with a corresponding new Cabinet member, the Secretary of Homeland Security. The question presented was where the Secretary should be placed in the succession order. Although traditionally a new Cabinet member would be placed at the end of the line, at the time of the hearing the Senate had passed a bill altering the tradition with the Secretary of Homeland Security following the Attorney General. Neale then identified questions regarding the statute as it presently exists. The question of whether members of the legislature are "officers" in the sense used in Article II was contrasted with the more "political or perhaps philosophical question: should the offices in the line . . . be elected Members of the House and Senate . . . or should we return the Succession Act of 1866 and put appointed Cabinet Officers [back into the line of succession]."[8] The third question was in regard to the bumping provision of the present Act. Finally, the resignation requirement, specifically focusing on cabinet members, was examined.

The events of September 11 brought other matters to the forefront. Neale observed that many have speculated about the possible problems of an attack on Washington, D.C., and that some have proposed legislation to remedy this matter. Additional suggestions have been made about addressing pre-inaugural Cabinet nominations. His testimony concluded with a brief acknowledgment of the lengthy election process.

Amar next addressed the committee. He referred to his testimony before the Senate the year before and his 1994 testimony reiterating his points made then.

Also a participant in the 2003 Senate hearings, M. Miller Baker was the third witness. Returning to many of his suggestions from his Senate testimony, he added that the present succession law should be changed to remove the bumping provision as it currently exists. However, it ought to allow what he referred to as "good bumping," whereby if a more senior Cabinet member is inaccessible another could act but later would need to step aside when the senior secretary became available.

Representative Sherman began, noting that he had been working on this matter since 2000. The issue, in his view, could be solved without a constitutional amendment. In the legislation he proposed, he identified two goals: "First, continuity. When the voters select a philosophy to govern the Executive Branch of the Government, that philosophy should govern that branch for the four year period. Second, legitimacy. We should always have one President who has undisputed rights to that office."[9]

Focusing first on continuity, Representative Sherman referred to the assassination of President Abraham Lincoln, whose conspirators planned also to kill Vice President Andrew Johnson and Secretary of State William H. Seward. Given the events of September 11, he said, we can only expect a repeat of such a conspiracy. Further, he suggested the fear of a change in policy could be equally devastating. Noting that without Nixon's ability to promptly appoint Ford as Vice President, he might have clung to power with impeachment and removal potentially tainted by the partisan hint that Democrat Carl Albert, the House Speaker, would act as or become President.

He also stated that the line of succession must provide legitimacy. The current succession act, he observed, fails in this regard, providing various examples of how under the present system different individuals have conceivable claims to the presidency.

Representative Sherman then summarized the legislation he would sponsor to address the problems he had presented.[10] There then followed questions by committee members. Baker observed that there might be constitutional problems with including governors in the line of succession in that their choice may conflict with state laws. Still, he added that it would be possible to "federalize a State governor, as the commander in chief of the State's National Guard, as a Federal officer,"[11] which would conceivably remove the "officer" question requirement. Amar returned to the problem of an attack on the capital being potentially solved by his proposal to have an Assistant Vice President. Comparing it to the designated hitter in baseball, Amar said this individual would provide reassurance and protection to the line of succession. He then referred to the one part of the Sherman proposal allowing for succession through the legislature, acknowledging his confidence that in such a unique instance individuals would likely forgo the question of the constitutionality of legislative succession.

In the course of the give and take with Amar, Democratic Representative Jerrold L. Nadler of New York sought to clarify the meaning of "not available," noting that one need not be in Washington to be able to act. As an example he noted that Vice President Lyndon B. Johnson was in Dallas when he was sworn in following the assassination of President John F. Kennedy. However, responded Baker, at the time of the attempted assassination of President Ronald Reagan, Vice President George H.W. Bush was without effective communication with the White House. Clarifying his question, Representative Nadler added that if the would-be successor were unavailable, who would make the decision to go to the next in line of succession? Baker suggested that the Federal Emergency Management Agency (FEMA) has procedures and that the Office of Legal Counsel has advisory opinions on the matter. Amar suggested that the Acting Presidency theoretically devolves on the person next in line until it is ascertained that it does not. Other instances could be addressed through a previously determined person who could act by proxy, Amar said.

Changing the focus of discussion, Representative King questioned whether the concerns over the bumping provision were really a difficulty and if just the status of the presidency itself would not cause potential challengers to refrain from questioning the legitimacy of the Acting President. Representative Sherman suggested that with sufficient support, an individual who felt he or she was wrongfully denied the position might be inclined to challenge. Joining in, Baker clarified that under the Succession Clause one does not become President but only acts as President. For this reason, he believed, bumping may be constitutionally permissible. He did, however, acknowledge that the precedent of President John Tyler's succession to the presidency in 1841 suggests otherwise. Still, he said, this was made constitutionally unquestionable only by Section 1 of the Twenty-Fifth Amendment and would not necessarily apply to statutory succession.

Turning to Amar, Representative King questioned his preference of having appointed Cabinet members serve as Acting President over elected members of Congress. Amar responded that that was precisely the concern Truman had had when he supported what became the 1947 Act. However, he said, the 1947 Act predated the Twenty-Fifth Amendment, which sets the model whereby the successor is chosen by the President. Neither Gerald R. Ford nor Nelson A. Rockefeller was elected to the offices of the President and Vice President, respectively. Furthermore, the elected official model favored by Truman, Amar added, does not allow the transfer of power back and forth between President and Vice President, as does the Twenty-Fifth Amendment, in a case of temporary inability. The vice presidency has become a position that works closely with the President, no longer primarily a presiding officer of the Senate. Representative Sherman agreed, adding that the Speaker and the President pro tempore are elected solely by members of their respective bodies and not chosen for national leadership. Referring to the 1972 election, he said if the people voted for Richard M. Nixon and eventually saw Carl Albert act as President that would not be acceptable. The debate was concluded without resolution, the time having expired.

REVIEW OF CONGRESSIONAL PROPOSALS

Representative Brad Sherman has proposed no fewer than eight proposals affecting the presidency. Two of these proposals have been constitutional amendments, with the remaining addressing continuing concerns regarding the perceived problems with the 1947 Presidential Succession Act.

Representative Sherman's first bill, introduced on February 27, 2002, was H. R. 3816, the Presidential Succession Act of 2002. The proposal sought to account for problems with potential party changes in the current succession law specifying legislators as potential successors. As with the current law, the individual first following the President and Vice President would come from the House of Representatives. In such a case, the President would designate either the Speaker of the House or the Minority Leader as the successor. This would prevent the possibility in the present law that the Speaker may represent another party. The procedures for this would involve the President's notifying in writing the Clerk of the House of Representatives as to the designation of the Speaker or the Minority Leader as the successor.

As with the 1947 Act, the next individual in the line of succession would come from the Senate. The method for designation ostensibly tracks the procedures proposed for the House, in this case the notification of the designated individual to serve going to the Secretary of the Senate. However, the proposed act strays from the current law in fully removing the President pro tempore from the line of succession. Instead, the President would designate either the Senate Majority Leader or the Senate Minority Leader.

Representative Sherman's proposal provides that succession by the designated member of the House or the Senate would not be rendered ineffective by the end of a presidential term. The Act does not remove the bumping provision of Section 19(d)(2) of the current law. The resignation requirement also remains in the proposal. Further, after the legislature, succession goes to the Cabinet, in the order of the creation of the positions, as in the 1947 law. Finally, if the President does not designate the House or Senate member to succeed, the proposed act defaults to the present line of succession with the Speaker of the House following the Vice President. However, in the case of the Senate, the Majority Leader follows the Speaker in the line of succession. H. R. 3816 was referred to the House Subcommittee on the Constitution. No further action was taken.

On July 15, 2003, Representative Sherman presented H. R. 2749, the Presidential Succession Act of 2003. This proposed act keeps the substantive changes from the 2002 proposal with its allowance that the President may choose which leader of either House of Congress would serve as successor in case the President and the Vice President were not able to carry out the powers and duties of the office. This proposal also adds that the Acting President "shall promptly nominate a Vice President upon any vacancy of the office of the Vice President." The most significant change in the proposed 2003 Act is the removal of the bumping provision of Subsection 2(d) of the 1947 Act. Finally, whereas the 2002 proposal struck and added text to the 1947 Act, the 2003 Act replaces the entirety of the current law. This may, in part, clarify some of the drafting in the 2002 proposal.

H. R. 5390, the Presidential Succession Act of 2004, introduced on November 18, 2004, is the most substantial revision to the succession provisions proposed by Representative Sherman. The first major alteration in the line of succession is that the proposed 2004 Act replaces the legislative line of succession with a Cabinet line of succession. In order to ensure that the Cabinet member succeeding is from the current administration, the proposal requires that the individual who would succeed to the presidency have been nominated by the President whom he or she replaces. Likewise, if the Vice President succeeds to the presidency, his or her Cabinet appointments would be considered in the line of succession. U.S. ambassadors to the United Nations, the United Kingdom, France, Russia, and China would follow the Cabinet members in the line of succession. In the case that neither Cabinet members nor listed ambassadors are able to serve, the Act provides for a legislative line of succession. As with the 2002 and 2003 Acts, the President would designate the Majority or Minority Leaders as the successors. H. R. 5390 adds a provision whereby the President-elect would designate which congressional members would be in the line of succession following inauguration.

The proposed Presidential Succession Act of 2004 also provides for pre-inaugural scenarios wherein both the President-elect and the Vice President–elect are dead or permanently incapacitated. The proposed act allows for a Cabinet member or above-listed ambassador appointed by the outgoing President to be considered in the succession list, if the appointment was suggested by the President-elect or the President-elect approves the appointment by notifying the Clerk of the House of Representative or Secretary of the Senate. H. R. 5390 facilitates the pre-inaugural arrangements through a Sense of Congress. Prior to January 20 the Sense of Congress would be that the President-elect would suggest nominees to the sitting President, these nominees would be submitted to the Senate, and the Senate would confirm the individuals to begin service immediately upon the President's inauguration.

In the event that at inauguration neither a President nor a Vice President has been elected or the executive offices are vacant because of failure to qualify, the Speaker of the House would serve as Acting President. If the Speaker fails to qualify, the Majority Leader of the Senate would become Acting President.* Since the Acting President's tenure is assumed to be temporary, he or she would not be permitted to nominate a Vice President. Accordingly, if a vacancy resulted from either inability or failure to qualify, the Acting President would serve until the cause of the vacancy is removed. As with the previous proposals, any successor would need to resign his or her current post.

The fourth proposed legislation by Representative Sherman to alter the line of succession, the Presidential Succession Act of 2005, H. R. 1943, scales back significantly from the previous proposals. Like the 2004 Act, it adds ambassadors to the line of succession. In doing so, it requires that the ambassadors added to the list of successors be eligible for the office of the President as provided by the Constitution, that they be appointed with the advice and consent of the Senate, and that they not be under impeachment by the House of Representatives while succeeding to the presidency. H. R. 1943 leaves intact the legislative succession of the current law. The 2005 proposal also makes a series of conforming changes such as replacing "act as President" with "serve as Acting President" conceivably for purposes of clarification.

The proposed Presidential Succession Act of 2005 attempts to address many of the gaps in the current succession system through a number of statements reflected in a Sense of Congress resolution. These are divided into two categories, the first addressing the votes of electors and the second dealing with the continuity of government and transitions between presidential administrations.

In addressing the period before the electors meet and cast votes for the President and the Vice President, the legislation recommends that before the end of the party conventions the President and Vice President designate whom the electors should vote for in the case both nominees die or are permanently incapacitated. If the presidential nominee dies or is permanently incapacitated for President but the vice-presidential nominee is not, the electors should cast ballots for the vice-presidential nominee as President. If the vice-presidential nominee dies or is permanently incapacitated, the electors should vote for his nominee for Vice President. In the event that both nominees for the President or Vice President are dead or permanently incapacitated, the designees for each respective position would receive the votes of the electors. Finally, the Act recommends that the political parties should establish rules that would facilitate these procedures.

The suggested Sense of Congress resolution pertaining to continuity of government and smooth transitions begins by listing a number of congressional findings.

---

* The Act does not seem to contemplate other reasons why the Speaker of the House would not be able to serve.

Of note is the expression that terrorists should not be able to change the party in power by an act of terrorism. Referencing the National Commission on Terrorist Attacks Upon the United States, the Resolution states that Congress finds that national security appointments should assume their position as soon as possible. Moving to the Sense of Congress, it recommends that the outgoing President consider the nominees of the President-elect for positions that are in the line of succession. If the President nominates the incoming President's nominees, the Senate, to secure continuity of government, should conduct a confirmation hearing before the inauguration, and the outgoing President should deliver the commissions to those nominees approved by the Senate on January 20 before the inauguration ceremony.

The proposed Presidential Succession Act of 2005 ultimately was referred to the House Subcommittee on the Constitution, and no further action was taken. On January 17, 2007, Representative Sherman introduced H. R. 540, the Presidential Succession Act of 2007. This proposal is nearly identical to the 2005 Act. The only difference is that the Secretary of Homeland Security is added to the line of succession as a result of the creation and filling of that Cabinet position.

Most recently, on December 17, 2010, Representative Sherman proposed H. R. 6557, the Presidential Succession Act of 2010. The bill essentially returns to the 2003 proposal providing the President with the ability to determine which House and Senate leaders would be in the line of succession. It adds to the 2003 proposal the Sense of Congress language that was included in the two most recent alterations to the line of succession submissions by Representative Sherman. Of note, the latest bill adds language requiring that the various notifications given by the President be made publicly available.

Representative Sherman's leadership in the area of presidential succession ensures that when Congress is ready to adopt changes, there will be a rich legislative record to consider.

POSTSCRIPT

The 1975 Hearings before the Senate Subcommittee on Constitutional Amendments, on the Implementation of Section 2 of the Twenty-Fifth Amendment, make clear that Congress understood that in situations involving dual vacancies in the presidential and vice-presidential offices a statutory successor, such as the Speaker, has the power to exercise the appointing power of Section 2 to fill a vacancy in the vice presidency. See Hearing transcript at pages 147–49, 152–53, in which references are made to where in the legislative history in 1964 and 1965 that subject was treated. Moreover, George Reedy testified in 1975 that there is no limitation on the authority of a statutory successor acting as President contained in Article II, Section 1, Clause 6. Id. 148. See the testimony of then–Assistant Attorney General Antonin Scalia, 47–67.

15

Symposia, Scholarship, and Commissions

... Any ambiguities concerning presidential succession and any flaws in the rules governing succession have the capacity to lead to national disaster ... sitting in the audience during the Symposium and listening to the papers presented here, I was struck by how many gaps there are in our current system and what dangers those gaps pose. ...

DEAN WILLIAM MICHAEL TREANOR[1]

The Twenty-Fifth Amendment has enjoyed tremendous popularity, if one is to judge by the media depictions of the Amendment with different subplots, and the books, articles, magazine features, and newspaper articles regarding it. Its presence in the Constitution as highlighted by the appointments of Gerald R. Ford and Nelson A. Rockefeller, and its relationship to the nation's well-being and security have contributed strongly to the attention it has received. In terms of that attention, the number of serious efforts that have been made to improve the system of presidential succession by commissions, academic institutions, and a bipartisan continuity-in-government commission is striking. A summary of some of these follows.

MILLER COMMISSION

In 1985, a Commission on Presidential Disability was appointed by the White Burkett Miller Center of Public Affairs at the University of Virginia to review the country's experience with the Twenty-Fifth Amendment and to examine important issues regarding presidential health. It was chaired by former U.S. Attorney General Herbert Brownell and former Senator Birch Bayh. They were joined by a vice chair and ten Commission members, including Chief Justice Warren E. Burger. They were assisted in their work by a small but able staff, met in approximately six working sessions, and received a number of presentations. Among those who shared perspectives with them was Fred Fielding, who related his experiences with the Twenty-Fifth Amendment during the presidency of Ronald Reagan. The Commission's final report, issued in 1988, was drafted by Chalmers M. Roberts, a former reporter for the *Washington Post*.* The report is a highly thoughtful document in explaining the provisions of the Twenty-Fifth Amendment and advancing recommendations for its use. In the Introduction to its report, the Commission noted that "under most circumstances, the 25th amendment is clear, simple and easily implemented" but "some of the amendment's provisions, however, are designed to respond to extremely complicated circumstances and could prove most difficult to implement." To assist in the task of implementation, the Commission advanced many suggestions with respect to the disability provisions of the Amendment.

With respect to Section 3, it said that "it should be possible to identify in advance a fairly wide range of circumstances where the President should almost automatically invoke Section 3." One situation involves elective surgery where "general anesthesia, narcotics, or other drugs that alter cerebral function will be used." It added that "a similar case involves a debilitating disease or physical malfunction." It reasoned that the President in all such situations "should accept the inevitability of temporarily transferring power to the Vice President beyond the immediate hours in the operating room, or even in the hospital." In borderline cases, it said, the President should "take the precaution of using Section 3 and designate the Vice President as Acting President." It reasoned that "the more the provision is used by succeeding Presidents, the more routine it becomes and the less sense of crisis there will be at home and abroad." On the continued viability of letter agreements such as those that existed prior to the Twenty-Fifth Amendment, the Commission said it believed "that such delegations no longer are appropriate" and would be "inconsistent with the 25th amendment." The Commission also questioned whether the "expressed authority of Section 3 carries with it implicit power to anticipate in advance when that power will be exercised," finding persuasive the argument that "Section 4 provides the exclusive means for determining presidential inability once the President loses the capacity to make that determination for himself." The Commission said that the "history of the Amendment indicates that its framers intended to create a mechanism that would supersede those prior strategies, and they did not intend either to repudiate or merely to supplement the earlier arrangements."†

---

* White Burkett Miller Center, Report on Presidential Disability and the Twenty-Fifth Amendment, 148 (Kenneth W. Thompson, ed. 1988).
† *Id., See* the multivolume work of the Miller Center entitled "Papers on Presidential Disability and the Twenty Fifth Amendment" (University Press of America 1988, 1991, 1996, and 1997). These papers are invaluable for the student of the subject, containing many thoughtful essays and reflection pieces by doctors, scholars, experienced political observers, and distinguished servants of the public.

With respect to Section 4, the Commission offered its view that, even though the use of the Cabinet may not be optimal, "it is unlikely that any other body would be free of difficulties or receive as much political acceptance." As for the implementation of the "such other body" provision of Section 4, it noted in its report that Chief Justice Burger, as Chief Justice Earl Warren before him, was of the view that no member of the Supreme Court should be involved in any deliberations of Congress on the Amendment. The Commission said that it considers it "essential to keep the judicial function separate lest, in a situation perhaps now unimaginable, the Supreme Court might be called to rule on some application of the 25th Amendment." As for Section 4 invocations, the Commission encouraged the involvement of the President's spouse and chief of staff and said that "it is obvious that the presidential physician would be a critical person should Section 4 ever have to be considered."

In speaking of disability situations generally, the Commission said that the Chief Executive's "worldwide prestige has given rise to extraordinary public expectations about the American President's ability to cope with a sudden national emergency or world crisis." It added that "preserving the American public's respect for the capacity and dependability of the American presidency is an important reason for not deliberately permitting an official crisis." In short, it said that "this Amendment must be utilized whenever necessary as a natural ingredient in the government process." The Commission recommended a number of useful steps to ensure successful implementation.

1. The general public should be better informed about the Twenty-Fifth Amendment. Discussions by presidential candidates are important to increasing awareness.

2. The President should make use of the Twenty-Fifth Amendment a regular process of government and should not be reluctant to use it. The likelihood of instability and crises is reduced the more routine the use of the Amendment becomes.

3. The President should not attempt to reclaim his powers under the Amendment until his full mental capacity has returned.

4. Between Election Day and Inauguration Day, the President-elect, the chief of staff, the President's counsel, the White House physician, the Vice President–elect, and the President's spouse should discuss the Amendment and devise plans of action for all medical contingencies.

5. Written guidelines should be developed by each administration for three different medical contingencies: an emergency, a planned procedure, and treatment of chronic ailments.

6. The role of the White House physician should be increased. The physician should be consulted constantly during a President's term for his or her input and knowledge of the President's health.

7. The White House staff must be apprised of its critical position when disability issues arise. It should not try to govern by itself and it must deal with the public in an open and honest manner.

As previously noted, the Miller Commission recommendations prompted the George H.W. Bush Administration to conduct the April 18, 1989 meeting and subsequent April 28 press briefing,* and these recommendations have been drawn on by succeeding presidential administrations for planning purposes.[†]

THE WORKING GROUP ON PRESIDENTIAL DISABILITY:
THE JIMMY CARTER CENTER

In 1993, the historian Arthur S. Link, biographer of President Woodrow Wilson, past president of the American Historical Association, and co-author of the *History of the American Neurological Society*, asked former President Jimmy Carter if he would host and participate in a program dedicated to the issue of the Twenty-Fifth Amendment and the question of presidential disability.[2] President Carter acceded to the request, and a panel known as the Working Group on Presidential Disability was formed, consisting of approximately fifty individuals, mainly medical experts but including some presidential historians, political scientists, and public commentators.[‡3] The prime motivating factor for Link and the group was in response to what they believed had been the insufficient attention the Miller Commission had given the diagnosis of disability.[4] Specifically, the group felt that the disability provisions of Section 4 required a "second hard look" before the Miller Commission's findings could be accepted, that "everyone would do the right and wise thing in the event of a medical crisis[.]"[5] The group first convened at the Carter Center of Emory University in Atlanta, Georgia, on January 26–28, 1995.[6]

In his opening address, President Carter explained that during his presidency, there "was no ordinary way to ascertain whether or not I was incapacitated, or when the transfer of authority would be made."[7] He said that it is the inclination of a President's subordinates to hide from the public the extent of any inabilities from which the President might suffer.[8] To combat this, Carter said, there needed to be a specific obligation to release the facts.[9] Additionally, he said that in the case of presidential inability the opinion of the White House physician should not be

---

*Chapter 13, *supra*.

† Senator Birch Bayh stated at the 2010 Fordham presidential succession program, "I had a . . . conversation with Valerie Jarrett at the White House . . . who said I could announce . . . that the Obama Administration has a very comprehensive contingency plan. Hopefully, we never have to use it." Transcript of Symposium, *Panel and Response on Interpreting Ambiguities in Current Constitutional Arrangements*, at 71 (Apr. 16, 2010). See note pp. 239–40, *infra*.

‡ Though invited, the author was initially unable to participate.

solely relied upon. He suggested that the physician be supported by an "official . . . consultation group that would work with the White House physician to make the final decision."[10]

In a discussion following his address, President Carter clarified that it would ultimately be for the Cabinet and the Vice President to declare the President disabled.[11] However, he continued to hold to his view that the White House physician should serve as "a spokesperson" and, with the help of a consultative group, present a mandatory report to the Cabinet and the Vice President when an issue of disability arises.[12] In response to a question as to how he would have reacted to an evaluation of his mental ability to function, he said that he might have been willing to submit to such an evaluation but other Presidents might not.[13] In his view, Presidents should be required by law to have an annual physical examination and have the results made public but he noted that this may not reveal cases of mental incapacity unless such mental incapacity had previously come to light.[14]

Much of the focus of the Carter Center presentations and discussion groups centered on what could be learned from the diagnosis of presidential disability from historical precedents, specifically those of Wilson, Franklin Delano Roosevelt, and Dwight D. Eisenhower. The overall tenor of the program can be divined from the titles of the presentations—"The Twenty-Fifth Amendment and Its Achilles Heel"; "Sudden Incapacitation"; "Neurological Disorders"; "Behavioral Disorders"; "The Medical Heritage of President Franklin D. Roosevelt"; "Maintaining the President's Health—President Wilson"; "The Spouse's View"; "Taking Care of the President"; "The President's Physician"; and "The Public's Right to Know."

The Specific Presentations

The title of Professor Richard E. Neustadt's *Achilles Heel* presentation alluded to Section 4 of the Amendment, which he considered a misguided attempt to decide what future generations should do in the event of a temporary disability of the President. That decision, according to Neustadt, should be best left to the people "on the ground" at the time. The three issues of his concern were what he coined "The Three Delicacies": personal, professional, and constitutional.[15] The personal delicacy dealt with the patient as the President and the idea of medical issues forming into political issues.[16] If the President were able to choose his own physician, he suggested, he would be able to pick an individual who would allow his medical issues to be swept under the rug, a physician "who would heed, not only his desire not to know, but also his presumable desire that nobody else learn."[17] The second delicacy involved doctor–patient relations, touching on questions such as "how much do you tell the President about his condition, whether he wants to know or not," and "how pushy should you be about medical examinations."[18] He framed the problem of confidentiality in terms of what the President can expect to keep private versus what information, if any at all, a doctor can rightfully release to the public and what information the public has a "right to know."[19] His primary concern regarding Section 4 was that in the event of a controversy, there would be, in effect, two Presidents—an Acting President and an elected President both with claims to the office for the twenty-one days in which Congress had to determine the outcome. He asked what would be the effect on the office if the Acting President received a majority of Congress but not the requisite two-thirds vote? The Constitution should in his view have been left alone in the Section 4 area,[20] with the solution to the problem being an agreement between the President and the Vice President prior to inauguration in which they formulate procedures and specify a particular medical authority whose opinion would be binding in the event of disability. Such an agreement would be modeled on the letters between Eisenhower and Richard M. Nixon and between John F. Kennedy and Lyndon B. Johnson. Neustadt said that the "such other body" language of Section 4 was also troubling because it would remove the Cabinet as a collaborator of the Vice President, thereby robbing him of the political legitimacy a united Cabinet would confer. This would leave the decision to the Vice President and, Neustadt assumes, some medical commission, which in turn would increase the likelihood of the decision's appearing to the public as constituting some sort of usurpation.

Following this presentation there was a discussion as to when and under what circumstances a physician is obliged to release information of a medical danger to the public. If a doctor is responsible to the public, the question was raised as to whether information would be withheld. This tension would be a constant throughout the meetings of the Working Group, as detailed in the rich volume produced after the conferences.

Dr. Herbert L. Adams recounted in *Sudden Incapacitation* the immediate aftermath of the attempted assassination of President Reagan and the decision not to invoke the Amendment even though Reagan clearly was incapacitated. Abrams ascribed the inaction regarding invocation of the Amendment as follows: to the ignorance, caution, concern, and arrogance of those around the President.* He proposed that guidelines for invocation of the Amendment be promulgated in order to increase its use. For example, the required use of general anesthesia on the President, or a heart attack or a stroke, he said, are the types of instances that should automatically trigger a temporary transfer of power. In addition, Abrams was of the opinion that the President, the Vice President, and the staff at some point should review the succession procedures and the Twenty-Fifth Amendment during or shortly after the election

---

* *See* HERBERT L. ABRAMS, "THE PRESIDENT HAS BEEN SHOT": CONFUSION, DISABILITY, AND THE 25TH AMENDMENT IN THE AFTERMATH OF THE ATTEMPTED ASSASSINATION OF PRESIDENT RONALD REAGAN (W.W. Norton & Co., 1992).

period. Abrams ended his presentation by introducing what may have been the biggest issue before the group, the lack of a definite meaning of the word "inability."[21]

The next presentation, *Neurological Disorders* by James Toole, discussed how, even though a presidential campaign is grueling, candidates are elected either with preexisting medical conditions or develop such conditions while in office. To illustrate, Toole advocated having candidates subject themselves to "physical, neurological, and psychiatric examinations, which would be made public, the purpose of which would not be to eliminate candidates but to disseminate the relevant facts about their health and the prognosis of any serious chronic disorder."[22] Dr. Burton J. Lee, the physician to President George H.W. Bush, explained that the administration "did have a plan in place to establish disability, to establish impairment, and to implement the Twenty-Fifth Amendment."[23] In his opinion, the physician to the President should be the one to establish disability and impairment, proposing that the position have the same status as that of legal counsel or economist. He stated that "if you bureaucratize his job and layer it with an assortment of people he has to deal with, you are going to make the decision making improper, you are slowing it down, and you are going to bring it down to the lowest common denominator. . . . When you add layers of bureaucracy you prevent government from working."[24]

Following the presentations by Toole and Lee, a discussion ensued concerning President George H.W. Bush and a jumbled statement he made to the press. Lee explained that Bush had a "very obscure . . . syndrome" that ran in the Bush family that includes "left-handedness, exceptional intelligence, dyslexic problems, exceptional athletic ability . . . ."[25] Bush, Lee went on, was challenged in public speaking and had all his life a peculiar speech pattern. Lee then stated that Abrams's attempt to connect Bush's hyperactivity to a thyroid disorder was incorrect. He said that he had known Bush since their school days at Andover and he had always suffered from hyperactivity. Abrams responded that hyperthyroidism could have a profound impact on the decision making of people who suffer from it. As with the handling of the endocrine episode of hyperthyroidism that occurred in 1991, Lee observed that the physician to the President was in the best position to know of any impairment and to choose the most appropriate doctors when an event arises to handle it.[26]

In *Behavioral Disorders*, Dr. Jerrold Post posited that it was not the severe illnesses such as stroke or heart failure that raised the "potential for political distortion of medical diagnosis and treatment." Rather, these illnesses would be exposed by the glare of the media; however, "the insidious illness, the subtle disability, not readily obvious . . . is the most problematic for the political system."[27] The onset of other, particularly mental, illnesses may not be noticed by colleagues, or even by the President's physician, who in any event will accord great deference to the leader. "If the leader and his inner circle ignore how much the illness is compromising his decision making and effectiveness and carefully orchestrate his public appearances, the presence or degree of the disability can be significantly obscured."[28] In addition, "because of the collective need for the leader to be seen as wise, decisive, and in control, illnesses which affect the leader's mental processes and/or emotional reactions are especially threatening to his political followers."[29] The example of Senator Thomas F. Eagleton of Missouri in the 1972 presidential campaign and that of Governor Michael Dukakis of Massachusetts in 1988, who had to defend himself against a rumor that he had been treated for depression following an election loss, highlight the cost resulting from the public stigma toward mental illness. Post stated that the White House has been no stranger to illnesses of an undiagnosed nature; however, "one of the difficulties with mental illness in the White House is discriminating between transient emotional reactions or situation-appropriate reactions and mental illness." He made references to President Calvin Coolidge's depression following the death of his son, Lyndon Johnson's paranoia as reported on by Robert Goodwin in the *New York Times*, Nixon's alleged heavy drinking during Watergate, and Kennedy's supposed amphetamine use. Additionally, Post explained that "substance abuse in political office is a particularly troublesome problem," alcohol being the biggest culprit.[30] Post continued on to address acute organic illnesses, such as Alzheimer's or dementia, and in general the deterioration of mental functioning that occurs with advancing age.[31] Citing more modern examples, Post quoted from the book *Landslide: The Unmaking of a President*,* which recounts an episode when White House Chief of Staff Howard Baker in the absence of medical participation decided that he considered President Reagan to be "up to the job" in the face of rumors he was "at the brink of being physically and mentally incapable of carrying out his responsibilities."[32] Post ended his presentation by citing a recommendation made by Abrams that there be seven types of situations that should automatically trigger use of the Twenty-Fifth Amendment, two of which are any planned surgical procedures that require general anesthesia, and the use of psychoactive drugs in any significant amount. Post felt, however, that instead of the Twenty-Fifth Amendment, what should be triggered is "active consideration of the temporary invocation of the Twenty-Fifth."[33]

Dr. Hugh E. Evans's *The Medical Heritage of President FDR* offered new facts uncovered regarding FDR's health. Evans said that "official reassurances about the President's health represent the primacy of the physicians' political and military judgment over their medical knowledge and responsibility. Even if their opinions were correct, it raises profound questions about their accountability."[34] Evans then explained his review of FDR's four inaugural addresses and his last speech to a joint session of

---

* *See* Jane Mayer & Doyle McManus, Landslide: The Unmaking of a President, 1984–88 (Boston: Houghton Mifflin, 1988).

Congress. Evans said that none of the speeches reflected neurological disease and that based on the speeches there was "no basis on which the disability provisions of the Twenty-Fifth Amendment (had it then existed) should have been invoked."[35] He concluded that there should be "annual medical exams of the incumbent president, vice president, and the two persons next in succession, [which] would alert both the 'patients,' their colleagues in government, and the public to potential problems."[36]

In the discussion following Evans's presentation, the issues of doctor–patient confidentiality and the public's "right to know" surfaced once again. The moderator, Professor Edwin M. Yoder, put the issues into context. He explained that in complex situations, important decisions will be made by a "handful of trusted people who have an intimate relationship" with the President, and it is when those complex situations occur that there is a greater insistence on the public's knowing the truth.[37] The tension in this type of situation, Yoder said, can lead to two different results. The first direction would be toward the creation of an absolute standard of care or pathway and an attempt to eliminate an individual physician's judgment in diagnosing health issues. The second result would be that the "trusted subordinates will manipulate or massage, and to some degree prevaricate about, the gravity of the impairment."[38] The question was then addressed as to what the President can expect from his physician about his health in terms of confidentiality, especially when it is determined that there is a serious situation such as depression. Dr. Jerry Wiener of George Washington Univerity said it is when the decision is made that the patient represents a danger to himself or others that actions must be taken. Professor Yoder, in response, raised the idea of "implied consent on the part of the person who presents himself or herself for election to public office to waive privacy expectation."[39] Dr. Lawrence C. Mohr strongly disagreed, explaining that the President does have a fundamental right to privacy and if a dangerous situation arises, then it should be dealt with by the proper authorities with due process of law.[40]

In *Maintaining the President's Health—President Wilson* or *The Tragedy of Woodrow Wilson*, Arthur Link retold the story of President Wilson's stroke and disability and its effect on the failure to secure ratification of the Versailles Treaty. The *Spouse's View* presentation by Katy Hariger built on the theme of the Wilson tragedy to discuss the role of the spouse, which creates "the problem of the influence of someone not held accountable in the political process."[41] Hariger proposed that the First Lady be given acknowledgment through law,[42] indicating that she would be influential in helping to persuade a President to relinquish his duties under Section 3 of the Amendment in the event of disabling illness.

The *White House Physician* by Mohr and *The President's Physician* by Dr. Daniel Ruge focused on the nature of White House care—the choice of White House physician and the functioning of the medical unit within the White House. Mohr stated that "it is very important that every White House physician be thoroughly familiar with the provisions of the Twenty-Fifth Amendment and give considerable thought to its implementation." He stressed how within the George H.W. Bush administration a detailed plan for implementing the provisions of the Twenty-Fifth Amendment under every conceivable circumstance was developed so that the President's approval as to how to deal with a situation could be gotten before the situation actually presented itself.[43] Mohr said that "if the President decides to release information it should be done through a straightforward written statement issued through the White House press office," simultaneously satisfying the public's right to know and doctor–patient confidentiality.[44] Additionally, Ruge stated, "the physician to the President should never decide alone" if there is "an incapacity of a chronic nature" and that it is best for the physician to be able to choose other physicians to help him or her who are familiar with dealing with the particular situation occurring.[45]

Finally, in *The Public's Right to Know*, Thomas Wicker, author and journalist, discussed the health crises of Presidents from Eisenhower to George H.W. Bush. While he believed the public has a right to know about the President's health, he recognized that such information could cause severe harm to the President's political career and therefore the press does not have a right to "find out everything by any means they can."[46] He concluded, "I don't believe that, in the final analysis, this body, or the body that Senator Bayh once headed, or any other body, can *insure* a total, truthful disclosure of the President's health with everybody's interests safeguarded in a fair and just manner, so that no one can charge that there has been some kind of cover-up."[47] He proposed using Section 2 of the Twenty-Fifth amendment and making the President run alone for office and, once sworn into office, nominate an individual to be the Vice President. Wicker recognized this would require a constitutional amendment, but it would ensure, through extensive congressional hearings, that more would be learned about the vice-presidential nominee who could at some point in time serve as a future President.[48]

Concluding Presentations for and Against Reform

The Carter Center meetings concluded with two presentations both for and against reform, followed by a discussion period. Dr. Bert E. Park presented the pro-reform position, while the historian Stephen E. Ambrose presented the anti-reform position. Park argued that while the Twenty-Fifth Amendment gave the Vice President (with the Cabinet) the power to determine whether the President is disabled, "precisely from *whom* the [Vice President] obtains the necessary medical facts to pass judgment should the President not declare his own disability was all but ignored by the Amendment's sponsors, not to mention subsequent scholars." In contrast, Park proposed "a simple and straightforward" way of providing for this but noted that disability has two stages: first impairment and then whether the impairment means the President is disabled as regards his functions. Park stated that "incumbent Presidents were medically impaired in the medical sense and disabled in the constitutional sense" on eight separate occasions in the twentieth century alone. However, "given the potential conflict for the presidential physician between duty to public and to the patient, this individual cannot (and should not) bear the burden of determining disability alone." He then suggested that the American Medical Association's "Guides to the Evaluation of Permanent Impairment" might be used to determine presidential impairment as they have been for determining disability in CEOs and others.

Park suggested that there be formed "a group of consultants skilled in the determination of impairment to pass judgment on the President's state of health, in conjunction with the White House physician, should the need arise." This group would be formed by a concurrent congressional resolution. Park further proposed the exact composition of this group of "impairment specialists"—seven physicians consisting of two neurosurgeons, two internists, two psychiatrists, and the White House physician. In advocating for such a group, he expressed his view that impairment is a medical decision alone but that judging disability has a political component. "The findings of a prospectively chosen team of impartial consultants, with no political ax to grind, would be of immeasurable benefit to a Vice President, who otherwise might be accused of usurping power." In contrast, any group formed under the "such other body" language of Section 4 of the Amendment would suffer because its members would not have been chosen prospectively but rather at "the eleventh hour, when disagreement has already arisen." Park also responded to objections to the formation of such a panel by former Attorney General Brownell on the grounds that continuing scrutiny of presidential health was an affront to the dignity of the presidency. Park cited the precedent, among others, that the Federal Aviation Administration required that pilots undergo yearly examinations.

Stephen Ambrose's anti-reform position could be summed up thus—that not all problems can be solved through legislation and that "the Twenty-Fifth Amendment provides a good base to operate from." Nonetheless, Ambrose agreed with some of the other panelists that the office of White House physician should be strengthened and candidates' medical records should be made available, which Eisenhower had done in 1956 to reassure the public. Ambrose suggested that the "such other body" provision of Section 4 could be made up of former Presidents: "I don't know whom I would trust more than [George H.W.] Bush, Carter, and Ford to serve as 'such other body' to make a decision." In reviewing the history of presidential disability, Ambrose paid particular attention to the Eisenhower experience, specifically noting that after Ike's stroke in 1955 the "word was out that the President was talking gibberish." "No less a person than [the journalist] Walter Lippmann called for his resignation,"[49] and even Eisenhower's aides were frightened by the President's insistence on going back to work. Finally, in response to the idea of a medical panel empowered under the "such other body" provision,

proposed that the Council of the Institute of Medicine of the National Academy of Sciences could put together a list of candidates for the panel of consultants and the executive branch could choose from that list.[60] Abrams explained that such a panel would serve as a support system for the President's physician and assure "the President, the Vice President, and the cabinet that if they make the political determination of disability, it is going to be based on evidence of impairment that will be expert, dispassionate, objective, and unencumbered by any conflict of interest."[61] He was supported in his proposals by others in the Working Group.

Others opposed such a standing group. Dr. Wiener was particularly concerned about the predetermination of the consultants, stating, "I really do believe that the physician to the President must have the option of choosing consultants appropriate to specific circumstances."[62] Dr. Mohr said that having such a group would severely deviate from "the normal course of clinical practice" and that one of the greatest challenges, if perhaps not the greatest challenge, of a White House physician is to "maintain a normal medical practice environment in this otherwise very abnormal atmosphere of the White House." Mohr stated that there is no authority for the creation of such a group and that if such a group were formed, there would be the question of what authority it would have. Professor Robert Gilbert observed that the creation of a standing group would counteract everything the Working Group had done in that it had agreed that the White House physician would appoint consultants as needed and would represent those consultants. Gilbert opposed the idea of such a group and also acknowledged that there "are times when public disclosure is not in the public interest" and that this proposed group would "represent alternate sources of information, and everyone would be speaking rather than one person."[63] Drs. Frank Wood and Joseph English both expressed concerns with the role that the Institute of Medicine would play in this process. While Wood stated that the Institute would be put "in an extraconstitutional position of authority," English said that by accepting such a responsibility, the Institute would be participating in "something of a political process."* Senator Bayh had the final word, noting that throughout history it has been made apparent that Congress would be opposed to such a committee and that it would not be in the conferees' best interest to support something that Congress has voted against.[64]

At the end of the discussion, the Working Group voted on whether to adopt the proposed appendix for a formalized group. The proposition fell in a vote of five "for" and twenty-five "against."

---

* James F. Toole & Robert J. Joynt, Presidential Disability: Papers, Discussions, and Recommendations on the Twenty-Fifth Amendment and Issues of Inability and Disability Among Presidents of the United States 488 (U. Rochester Press, 2001).

After deliberation and voting, the Working Group produced nine final recommendations, accompanied by commentary. Those nine recommendations are as follows:

1. The Twenty-Fifth Amendment is a powerful instrument which delineates the circumstances and methods for succession and transfer of the power of the presidency. It does not require revision or augmentation by another constitutional amendment. However, guidelines are needed to ensure its effective implementation.

2. The Twenty-Fifth Amendment has not been invoked in some circumstances envisioned by its founders. When substantial concern about the ability of the President to discharge the powers and duties of office arises, transfer of power under provisions of the Twenty-Fifth Amendment should be considered.

3. A formal contingency plan for the implementation of the Amendment should be in place before the inauguration of every President.

4. Determination of presidential impairment is a medical judgment based upon evaluation and tests. Close associates, family, and consultants can provide valuable information which contribute to this medical judgment.

5. The determination of presidential inability is a political judgment to be made by constitutional officials.

6. The President should appoint a physician, civil or military, to be senior physician in the White House and to assume responsibility for his or her medical care, direct the military medical unit, and be the source of medical disclosure when considering imminent or existing impairment according to the provisions of the Twenty-Fifth Amendment.

7. In evaluating the medical condition of the President, the senior physician in the White House should make use of the best consultants in relevant fields.

8. Balancing the right of the public to be informed regarding presidential illness with the President's right to confidentiality presents dilemmas. While the senior physician to the President is the best source of information about the medical condition of the President, it is the responsibility of the President or designees to make accurate disclosure to the public.

9. The Twenty-Fifth Amendment provides a remarkably flexible framework for the determination of presidential inability and the implementation of

the transfer of powers. Its provisions should be more widely publicized and its use destigmatized.*

However, a minority opinion was written by Professor Joel Goldstein, Senator Bayh, and the author regarding recommendation 4 and the commentary discussing "presidential impairment." The first concern we had was that "the distinction between 'presidential impairment' and 'presidential inability' is not likely to be understood by the public or media, particularly if not considered in conjunction with recommendation 5."[65] The second issue was the fact that recommendations 4 and 5 together created a "dual track approach" in determining presidential inability. Recommendation 4 states that the determination of presidential impairment is a medical judgment, while recommendation 5 states that presidential inability is a political judgment. This, we thought, gives the "impression of two 'determinations' with equal weight when, in fact, the Constitution stipulates one."[66] Our group stated that the determination of presidential inability is one that is left solely up to constitutional decision makers and that "the legislative history surrounding the adoption of the Twenty-Fifth Amendment makes clear that its framers intended that constitutional decision makers would solicit appropriate medical advice."[67] Additionally, the group opined that the idea of "determination of presidential impairment" implies that the medical role "will be limited to a single 'determination'" when in fact doctors are continually involved in advising and offering medical advice to constitutional decision makers. We also did not approve of the idea of a formal determination of presidential impairment, fearing that such a determination if made and leaked to the public would imply that the President was unable to perform his duties. We said that "this would have the effect either of compromising his or her ability to lead or of forcing the constitutional decision makers to a decision they otherwise might not make."[68]

CONTINUITY OF GOVERNMENT COMMISSION REPORT— THE PRESIDENCY

The Continuity in Government Commission was formed shortly after the events of September 11, 2001, thanks to the leadership of individuals like Norman Ornstein of the American Enterprise Institute (AEI), Thomas Mann of the Brooklings Institution, and John Fortier of AEI. They researched and wrote about continuity issues and were dedicated, with others, to ensuring that all branches of the federal government functioned after a catastrophic attack. The bipartisan Continuity

---

* The recommendations are discussed with commentary in JAMES F. TOOLE & ROBERT J. JOYNT, PRESIDENTIAL DISABILITY: PAPERS, DISCUSSIONS, AND RECOMMENDATIONS ON THE TWENTY-FIFTH AMENDMENT AND ISSUES OF INABILITY AND DISABILITY AMONG PRESIDENTS OF THE UNITED STATES 527–36 (U. Rochester Press, 2001)

Commission that was born after September 11 was funded by the Carnegie Corporation of New York, the William and Flora Hewlett Foundation, the John D. and Catherine T. MacArthur Foundation, and the David and Lucille Packard Foundation.

Former Presidents Jimmy Carter and Gerald Ford served as honorary cochairmen of the Commission; and Lloyd Cutler, counsel to Presidents Carter and Clinton, and former Senator Alan K. Simpson of Wyoming served as co-chairmen. The members of the Commission were distinguished Americans: Professor Philip Chase Bobbitt of Texas Law School; Kenneth M. Duberstein, Chief of Staff for President Reagan; former House Speaker Thomas Foley of Washington state; Professor Charles Fried of Harvard Law School; former House Speaker Newt Gingrich of Georgia; former Deputy Attorney General of the United States Jamie S. Gorelick; former U.S. Attorney General Nicholas deB. Katzenbach; Second Circuit Court of Appeals Judge Robert A. Katzman; former U.S. Secretary of Labor Lynn Martin; former House Minority Leader Robert H. Michel of Illinois; former White House Chief of Staff Leon Panetta; and former Secretary of Health and Human Services Donna E. Shalala. The Commission undertook to study continuity in each of the three branches of the federal government. In 2003 it issued its first major report, involving the Congress, entitled "Preserving Our Institutions." On July 2, 2009, it issued its second report, dealing with the presidency, entitled "Presidential Succession."* The author was privileged to be a member of the panel who was asked to comment on the report, which he did.

In its report, the Commission said, "If the [September 11] attack had been more horrible, we might not have been able to respond so effectively." The report begins with the nightmarish scenario of a terrorist attack during a State of the Union address. This attack kills or injures most individuals in the line of succession. The narrative displays the various problems with the current line of succession, with low-level Cabinet members rising to the presidency, the bumping of such individuals by legislative members, and more general ambiguities in the chain of command resulting from a catastrophic event.

The Commission then details the history and particular constitutional and statutory provisions governing presidential succession. In doing this, the report identifies six major problems with the present succession system. First, all the individuals in the line of succession are based in Washington, D.C. An attack on the Capitol, such as during a State of the Union address, could conceivably wipe out any potential successor to the presidency. Second, the presence of congressional leaders in the line of succession provides both constitutional and political difficul-

---

* See CONTINUITY OF GOV'T COMM'N, PRESERVING OUR INSTITUTIONS: THE CONTINUITY OF THE PRESIDENCY (2009), *available at* http://www.bookings.edu/research/reports/2000/07/06-continuity -of-government.

ties. Third, the current order of Cabinet succession, based on the date of creation of Cabinet office, fails to account for which Cabinet members are best qualified to act as President in the event of a catastrophe. Further, the current succession law allows for acting Cabinet secretaries to be potential successors. The fifth problem is that the current system does not address transfers of power from an incapacitated President to individuals in the line of succession if the Vice President cannot serve. Related to this, the resignation of Cabinet members is required only by statute and may hinder a smooth transition of power. Finally, the report identifies inauguration and pre-inauguration periods as times that are precarious to presidential succession.

In addressing the first problem, as Fortier noted in his earlier Senate testimony, the Commission suggests the creation of four or five federal offices to which the President would appoint individuals and the Senate would confirm. Likely candidates would include governors and former Presidents. These officers for the line of succession would presumably reside outside of Washington, D.C., eliminating the potential that a catastrophic attack could wipe out the entire line of succession.

Agreeing with most critics of the present succession system, the report recommends that legislators be removed from the line of succession. Legislators are elected by members of the state or district they represent; this limited form of representation does not overcome the problems that legislative successors present. First, there is the continuing concern as to the constitutionality of legislators in the line of succession. Both the "officer" question and the bumping provision* have been subjects of repeated debate. Removing legislators would eliminate this problem. Also, concerns over the possibility of power switching from one party to the other would end. Finally, the resignation requirement would become a non-issue; no longer would there be the worry as to whether the legislator would be willing to resign, losing his or her position, in order to serve as Acting President.

Even if congressional members are not removed from the line of succession, the present system should still be altered, according to the Continuity Commission: The bumping provision ought to be removed. Also, it suggests that the President pro tempore should be replaced by the Senate Majority Leader. Congressional leaders should be included in the line of succession only in cases of permanent vacancy of the presidency. The report concludes its examination of legislative succession by noting that problems in the continuity of the legislature must be addressed in order for legislators to be safely in the line of succession.

The third proposal in the report recommends implementing special elections. If in the first two years of an administration the offices of both the President and Vice President become vacant, Congress should provide for special elections within

---

* *See* Chapter 3.

five months of the vacancies. In the absence of such special election, the interim successor would serve out the remainder of the term.

Assuming that legislators are removed from the line of succession, the report determines that the order of succession should be changed. Only the "big four" department heads—Secretary of State, Secretary of Defense, Attorney General, and Secretary of the Treasury—should be included. The rest of the line of succession should be replaced by the four or five new officers residing outside the Washington, D.C., area.

The fifth proposal would remove acting secretaries from the line of succession. The Commission treats this largely as a matter of statutory clarification. Still, it determines that such individuals should not ascend to the presidency.

The report recommends that Congress can provide under which procedures lower-level officials would serve as Acting President. Even where Congress may not have the authority, it could still provide guidance. Further, if the Cabinet is unavailable to the Vice President, hindering the invocation of Section 4, Congress should clarify the "other body" provision of the Twenty-Fifth Amendment.

The Commission's last recommendation addresses the inaugural and pre-inaugural dangers. In order to ensure a smooth transition of power, it believes, there should be pre-inauguration nominations and confirmation by the Senate of individuals in the line of succession. Second, the period between when the Electoral College meets and Congress's certification of the results should be shortened.* Last, political parties should provide for the possible death of candidates prior to the meeting of the Electoral College.

Despite the bipartisan nature of the Commission and the seriousness and thoughtfulness of its proposals, Congress has found no need to act on any of its recommendations. This has been of great disappointment to its members, as described at the Fordham University School of Law's Presidential Succession Conference in 2010.†

FORDHAM UNIVERSITY SCHOOL OF LAW PRESIDENTIAL SUCCESSION CONFERENCE

In April 2010, Fordham University School of Law hosted a symposium to address the adequacy of our current system of presidential succession in the modern context.[69] The speakers were individuals who have personal experience dealing with presidential succession as well as leading academics and commentators in the

---

*The electors vote in December, forty-one days after the people vote in November for the electors, and Congress meets to count and declare the votes on the following January 6 under current federal law.
† The *Fordham Law Review* and the school's library have on file a transcript of the proceedings held on April 16 and 17, 2010, referred to in this edition as the "Transcript of the Fordham 2010 Conference."

field.* They addressed the reality that in an age of terrorism and weapons of mass destruction, the possibility of succession's proceeding past the Vice President is a serious concern. Two major topics emerged throughout the symposium: first, the constitutionality and policy implications of having legislators in the current line of succession, and, second, the ambiguities surrounding disability scenarios. Implicit in the discussions was the critical and important role of the Vice President, without whom a disability determination becomes precarious.

The symposium's discussion served as a call to action, as a result of which a group of faculty and students formed the Presidential Succession Clinic at Fordham Law School to develop a set of comprehensive recommendations to strengthen and safeguard succession in the modern era. A summary of these recommendations, as well as the principles and ideas discussed at the symposium, follows.

Symposium Discussion

Constitutionality of Presidential Succession Statutes   Despite a widespread view among academics that legislative succession is unconstitutional,[70] the Constitution is not without its ambiguities on the subject.

Professor James E. Fleming approached the discussion as a "constitutional theory generalist" in addition to considering the political feasibility of reform.[71] He concluded that neither separation of powers nor the "Officer" requirement in Article II, Section 1, Clause 6 of the Constitution precluded legislative succession.[72]

He defended the constitutionality of the 1947 Act based on his perspective on separation of powers. He noted that there are two approaches to separation of powers. One view is "formalistic, categorical, and hermetic,"[73] while the other is "functionalistic, flexible, and pragmatic."[74] According to the latter approach, Fleming argued, separation of powers does not mean "a system of pure 'separation of powers,'" but instead a system of 'separated *institutions* sharing powers.'"[75] He suggested "considerable deference concerning the constitutionality of practices,

---

* Participating in the two-day symposium were then–Dean of Fordham Law, William Michael Treanor (now Dean of Georgetown University Law Center); Senator Birch Bayh; Fred F. Fielding; Benton Becker; Professor Akhil Amar (of Yale Law School); Professor Joel K. Goldstein (of Saint Louis School of Law); Professor James E. Fleming (of Boston University School of Law); Dr. John C. Fortier and Dr. Norman Ornstein (Senior Counsel to the Continuity in Governing Commission); Professor Edward B. Foley (of Ohio State University Moritz College of Law); Professor Robert E. Gilbert (of Northeastern University School of Law); Professor Rose McDermott (of Brown University); Dr. William F. Baker, former president of Educational Broadcasting Corporation; and Professor Robert Kaczorowski of Fordham Law School. Senator Bayh's presence at the symposium provided an unparalleled contribution to the discussions, as did those of Fred Fielding and Benton Becker, who supplied a thorough historical account of their experiences with the Twenty-Fifth Amendment—Fielding as counsel to Presidents Nixon, Reagan, and George W. Bush, and Becker as counsel to President Ford when he was going through his vice-presidential confirmation hearings.

like legislative succession, that have been in place since the early years of our constitutional system."[76]

Professor Goldstein noted that most discussion has focused on textual and "originalist" interpretations of the Constitution, approaches that yield inconclusive outcomes.[77] In contrast, structural arguments are more useful in solving the problem. Accordingly, Goldstein concluded he was unable to deem a legislative line of succession or a Cabinet line of succession always unconstitutional.*[78]

Further, Goldstein stated that "[l]ongstanding practice regarding institutional arrangements helps shape constitutional meaning[,] and legislative succession commands substantial support. . . ."[79] Thus, there is "no constitutional infirmity in legislative succession."[80] Yet Fleming conceded that those who do not share his and Goldstein's view on separation of powers find the "very idea of legislative succession to the [p]residency repugnant to their formalistic, hermetic vision."[81]

Goldstein also addressed the early history of the "Officer" provision accounting for Madison's, Hamilton's, and Washington's views.†[82]

The Speaker of the House and the Senate President pro tempore, he pointed out, were referred to elsewhere in the Constitution‡ by the term "Officer."[83] Thus, the "textual and originalist arguments strike me [Goldstein] as inconclusive, particularly when one considers that they did not persuade a contemporaneous Congress and President."[84] Fleming argued that the Constitution "should make sense as a matter of ordinary understanding"[85] so that the term "Officer" means simply one who holds an office.[86] However, Professor Akhil Amar noted that there are sharp distinctions in the Constitution regarding legislative and executive officers.[87] Goldstein reasoned that if legislators are "Officers" in the constitutional sense, then legislative succession resembles a parliamentary form of government because each House of Congress can choose who may act as President.[88] Amar made note of this as well.[89] However, the Constitution emphatically rejects a parliamentary form of government.[90] Goldstein pointed to the fact that the Electoral College chooses the President and, unless impeached, the President is free of congressional intrusion.[91] Further, if a legislator retains his or her seat in Congress and serves as Acting President, then that person will be removable by his or her constituents and his or her respective House of Congress.[92]

The rejection of parliamentary government, the participants reasoned, is further buttressed by the existence of the Incompatibility Clause, which prohibits members of the legislative branch from simultaneously serving in the executive branch.[93] The

---

* Joel Goldstein does, however, note that no serious argument has ever been posed that Cabinet succession is unconstitutional. Joel K. Goldstein, *Taking from the Twenty-Fifth Amendment: Lessons in Ensuring Presidential Continuity*, 79 FORDHAM l. REV. 959, 1019 (2010).

† *See* Chapter 3 and corresponding discussion there.

‡ *See* U.S. CONST. art I, § 2, cl. 5 and U.S. CONST. art I, § 3, cl. 5.

1947 Act does require the Speaker of the House and the President pro tempore of the Senate to resign before assuming the powers and duties of the presidency.[94] Goldstein noted, however, that a legislator who resigned may no longer be an "Officer" as envisioned by the Constitution and would not then be able to act as President. On the other hand, should he not resign, said Officer acting as President would run afoul of the Incompatibility Clause.[95]

Goldstein then took account of both the Twentieth Amendment and the Twenty-Fifth Amendment. The Twenty-Fifth Amendment has added certain values to the constitutional framework of presidential succession.[96] The need for "a smooth succession of a new leader who was conversant with the activities of the executive branch" is implicit in the Twenty-Fifth Amendment.[97] Legislative succession would frustrate that implicit value because of the possibilities of party discontinuity, the inability of a legislative leader to effectively "play the understudy role,"[98] and the lack of a close relationship between a legislative leader and other individuals within the executive branch.[99] Goldstein added that another value implicit in the Twenty-Fifth Amendment is the desire to have disability determinations initiated in the executive branch, based on the participants in that determination having a close relationship with the President.[100]

In arguing that the Amendment has added constitutional values to presidential succession, Amar also referred to what he called apostolic succession.[101] He explained that the nation as a whole voted for a certain party and policy and that it should have leaders who can trace their grant of authority back to the original President for whom the people voted.[102] As support for this proposition, Amar noted that the Twenty-fifth Amendment recognizes a President's ability to hand-pick his Vice President, pursuant to Section 2.[103] Such a value is not consistent with legislative succession but wholly consistent with Cabinet succession.[104]

Moving to the Twentieth Amendment, Goldstein noted that in a failure-to-qualify scenario, Congress has the power to name the "person" who shall act as President and that this language is broader than the term "Officer" contained in Article II, Section 1, Clause 6[105] of the Constitution.* However, he contended that the same structural arguments would apply in a failure-to-qualify situation.[106] Yet, without a President-elect or a Vice President–elect, unless the election was won by a President running for a second term, succession to Acting President by members of the previous Cabinet may run afoul of values such as party continuity, democratic pedigree, and electoral accountability.[107] Legislative succession is likely the only type of succession that makes practical sense in the failure-to-qualify scenario.[108] Thus, he reasoned that structural arguments should either give way in

---

* This a view that Professor Amar also holds. Akhil Reed Amar, *Applications and Implications of the Twenty-Fifth Amendment*, 47 HOUS. L. REV. 1 (2010).

certain specific scenarios, such as failure to qualify, or serve as mere considerations instead of imposing absolute limits.[109]

Fleming echoed President Harry S. Truman's original arguments for the 1947 Act that the Speaker of the House enjoys the third-highest democratic pedigree in our system of government.[110] Fleming noted this at the symposium, but he also spoke to the fact that today people are more accepting of the President's ability to name his own successor, which erodes Truman's earlier reasoning in this regard.[111]

However, Amar noted that the 1947 Succession Act is inconsistent with the deepest themes of the Twenty-Fifth Amendment.[112] Undercutting Truman's rationale is the Amendment's provision for the President to pick his own successor.[113] A President picks his Vice President, thus his successor, when selecting a running mate and pursuant to Section 2 of the Twenty-Fifth Amendment during times of vice-presidential vacancy.[114] Senator Bayh noted the irony in Truman's position: He ascended to the presidency only because President Franklin D. Roosevelt picked him as a running mate. If a presidential candidate can pick his successor, why shouldn't the President be able to do so?[115]

Goldstein elaborated on some of the specific implications of legislative succession and the possibility of cross-party succession. Through legislative succession a successor can be a political opponent whose presence in the line of succession would disrupt continuity and disability determinations and cause overall conflict with the principles inherent in the Twenty-Fifth Amendment.[116] However, Goldstein noted that Cabinet succession is not free from policy concerns. Some may view the Cabinet as lacking a democratic pedigree, especially considering their confirmations by the Senate are not as detailed or as scrutinized as Section 2 confirmations for Vice President, nor are they confirmed by both Houses of Congress as nominated Vice President are.[117] In addition, the President may try to avoid disability determinations under Section 4 of the Twenty-Fifth Amendment by firing Cabinet members who support the conclusion that he is disabled.[118] Accordingly, Goldstein acknowledged that legislators do not serve at the will of the President and therefore provide advantages in the context of a Section 4 scenario.[119]

Another troubling aspect of legislative succession, as noted by Goldstein and Amar, is the incentive it creates for delaying a Vice President's confirmation under Section 2 of the Twenty-Fifth Amendment.[120] Addressing this, Benton Becker spoke to the 1973 confirmation of then-Representative Ford as Vice President.[121] Becker recounted that Speaker Carl Albert was cooperative in the confirmation process and anxious to personally move down the line of succession, once more becoming second in line instead of first, upon the confirmation of Representative Ford.[122] However, the partisan nature of Washington, D.C., Becker said, revives old concerns that a legislator might delay the confirmation of a Vice President under Section 2 in order to increase his or her chances of attaining the White House.[123] Becker stated that "it would seem to me a far greater likelihood [today] for pure partisanship controlling an unfavorable and unfair result by delaying the nomination [for Vice President]."[124]

Goldstein made note of three other policy considerations regarding legislative succession. He believes that succession by the Senate President pro tempore is problematic.[125] This becomes apparent when one considers the advanced age at which some members of the Senate serve in this honorific post.[126] To this point, Ornstein, in discussing the difficulty of gaining support for reform, mentioned that Senator Robert Byrd "actually did express some interest in giving up the position of third in line of succession, understanding that somebody* at his age would not be an appropriate person to occupy the White House."[127] Additionally, Goldstein observed that the current line of succession is concentrated in Washington, D.C., a fact that does not take into account the possibility of a mass catastrophe† scenario.[128] Given the heightened possibility of one incident's throwing Washington into chaos, "[t]he current long line was drafted in a formulaic manner that was not sensitive to its fundamental mission, to produce an able Acting President following some mass catastrophe."[129]

Senator Bayh spoke of policy considerations regarding appropriate successors. He believed that there are better reasons to remove legislators from the line of succession than a purely technical argument regarding the constitutionality of someone as an "Officer."[130] He specifically mentioned that whiplash, the back and forth possible with legislative succession trumping Cabinet succession, and continuity of policy are real concerns.[131] Linking this to Gerald Ford's nomination as Vice President, he observed that the people voted in 1972 for four years of Nixon and, thus, Senator Bayh found himself, despite personal political leanings, supporting Gerald Ford and opposing Nelson Rockefeller because he did not feel that Rockefeller would provide continuity of policy.[132]

Embracing the idea of structuring a line of succession to promote continuity and protect against whiplash, Amar spoke to the odd incentives our current system creates for political assassinations and regime change. Assassinations and regime change are

> the risk[s] that we run when some deranged assassin or terrorist organization gets it into his head or their heads to effect a regime change by simultaneously attacking the President and the Vice President, and shifting executive power from the folks that we did elect and the policy continuity that we were expecting to perhaps the exact opposite of the political spectrum.‡

---

* Byrd was President pro tempore from 1989 to 1995, 2001 to 2003, and 2007 to 2010. He was ninety-two years old when his service ended by death.

† To be noted is that on September 11, 2001, Flight 93, which crashed in Pennsylvania, was believed to be headed for the White House or the Capitol.

‡ Symposium, Interpreting ambiguities, note on pp. 239–40, supra, at 58.

As support for this proposition he noted the desire for regime and policy change that may have motivated both the assassins of Presidents Abraham Lincoln and James A. Garfield.*

Why Is the Vice President So Important? Who Decides Disability?

Beyond legislative succession, the subject of presidential inability was addressed at the symposium. The Vice President has a distinct and necessary role in disability determinations. Therefore, any time the country is without a Vice President, it risks entering into the line of succession contained in the 1947 statute, with all its ambiguities and uncertainties. Plainly, Sections 3 and 4 cannot be implemented without a Vice President.[133] Section 2 of the Twenty-Fifth Amendment was drafted in order to ensure that the country has the benefit of a Vice President at all times.[134] Yet the Amendment does not provide a mechanism to declare the Vice President disabled.[135] The determination of a vice-presidential disability is critical in the following situations: a vice-presidential disability followed by a presidential death, and the concurrent disabilities of the President and Vice President. There are similar scenarios involving the disability of an Acting President serving as a result of the implementation of the statutory line of succession.[136] Without a vice-presidential disability determination process, the country risks being without an able Vice President, a situation that could potentially grind the succession process to a halt.

Before the adoption of the Twenty-Fifth Amendment, there was no way of determining a presidential disability. In the symposium the author referred to the argument of Ruth Silva on contingent grants of power that later, along with the opinion of Attorney General Brownell, informed the formal opinion of Attorney General Robert F. Kennedy.[137] Silva wrote that based on the theory of contingent grants of power, the individual who is to become the Acting President has the power and authority to determine the existence of a presidential disability.[138] Kennedy's opinion, based on the same principle, stated that "[t]he large majority [wa]s of the view that the Vice President, or other 'officer' designated by law to act as President[,] has the authority under the Constitution to decide when inability exists."[139] Based on these authorities and a survey of case law, the author concluded that "as the 1947 Act mentions no person or entity . . . other than the successor as holding the succession power . . . the 'officer' designated by law to act as President under the 1947 Act is granted the sole discretion to determine whether inability exists."[140]

Even though the Twenty-Fifth Amendment places that determination in the power of the Vice President and the Cabinet, the question remains unsettled as to who can decide that a disability exists without an able Vice President or in the event of vice-presidential vacancy. Brownell's opinion, mentioned earlier, rejected

* Id. at 58–59.

Congress's ability to determine presidential disability but left open the question in the event of a double disability or vacancy.[141]

Noting the power granted to Congress to create a line of succession in Article II, the author is of the view that Congress has the ability to legislate in this area under the necessary and proper provision of Article, 1 Sec. 8, Clause 18 of the Constitution.[142] Goldstein and Amar agreed with this view, believing that Congress possesses the power to legislate in a manner consistent with Sections 3 and 4 of the Twenty-Fifth Amendment.[143] Legislation is necessary because the individual next in the line of succession, under the contingent grants of power theory, would enjoy unfettered discretion as to disability determinations, whereas the Vice President is restricted by the Cabinet under Section 4 of the Twenty-Fifth Amendment.[144] In recognizing the ability of Congress to legislate provisions similar to Sections 3 and 4, Goldstein recognized that without legislation, there is no legal procedure for the President to pass his powers and duties to anyone other than the Vice President.[145] Goldstein noted, and the author agrees, that without such provisions, the President might be able to enter into letter agreements similar to those that have existed since their first use under President Eisenhower.[146] Ultimately, the President should not be impeded in his or her ability to turn over the powers and duties of the presidency in the event of an inability.[147] The President should be encouraged to pass the powers and duties of office when doing so is necessary.[148] Legislation could also cover the determination of a vice-presidential inability.[149]

Much of the symposium focused on what situations, circumstances, and facts constitute a disability. The author observed that most of the debates surrounding the drafting and enactment of the Twenty-Fifth Amendment focused on physical and mental disability.[150] Even still, uncertainty remains with regard to which situations can constitute an inability. Multiple speakers addressed the inabilities throughout the history of the country.[151] Professor Gilbert canvassed an extensive list of Presidents who suffered physiological illnesses while in office.* The sheer expanse of this list suggests that "physiological illness has been a close companion to the American presidency."[152] However, the focus of the symposium largely was on nonphysiological disabilities.

Gilbert chronicled the psychological illness of three important Presidents: Franklin Pierce, Abraham Lincoln, and Calvin Coolidge.[153] Throughout the discussion it was apparent that psychological illness is difficult to assess. It is even more difficult to predict the effects of such a malady.

Gilbert highlighted how "difficult it would have been for both physicians and public officials to examine the Pierce, Coolidge, and Lincoln experiences *in private*

---

* His list included George Washington, John Adams, James Madison, James Monroe, Andrew Jackson, William Henry Harrison, Zachary Taylor, Abraham Lincoln, James A. Garfield, Chester A. Arthur, Grover Cleveland, William McKinley, Woodrow Wilson, Warren G. Harding, Franklin Delano Roosevelt, Dwight D. Eisenhower, John F. Kennedy, Lyndon B. Johnson, and Ronald Reagan.

and then try to decide in which cases, if any, Section 4 of the Twenty-Fifth Amendment should [have been] invoked" if the Twenty-Fifth Amendment had existed during their presidencies.[154] As Gilbert noted, the difficulty lies in knowing that Pierce and Coolidge should have or might have justifiably been found unable to perform as President. Yet, invoking Section 4 "in Lincoln's case would have been wholly unjustified and extraordinarily unwise."[155] Gilbert asked the following question: "Even given a diagnosis of depression, schizophrenia, or paranoia, for example, how depressed, schizophrenic, or paranoid must a President be before Section 4 of the Twenty-Fifth Amendment should be invoked?"[156] Mental illness was thought to be covered under the Twenty-Fifth Amendment,[157] but given that "the line between mental illness and normalcy tends to be indefinite . . . viewed not as an absolute but as a continuum,"[158] the determination is rather difficult. This problem is highlighted, Professor Rose McDermott of Brown University said, by the fact that "psychiatrists fail to diagnose 70 percent of patients who have depressive syndromes" and "90 percent of the time[,] primary-care physicians don't see the problem that exists."[159]

Building off of this discussion, McDermott spoke about the role of genetics in presidential succession. She questioned whether genetic vulnerability can be thought of as a presidential inability and whether such vulnerability must manifest itself before a President is determined to be disabled.[160] She discussed the troubles of Abraham Lincoln, Woodrow Wilson, and John F. Kennedy.[161] Still, given the history of our Presidents, McDermott questioned whether Presidents should be screened for genetic susceptibilities and, if so, how to best handle that situation in the political environment.[162] She also spoke to the possibility of screening for desirable characteristics in a President.[163] Senator Bayh later responded to this by stating that our bio-accomplishments are impressive and frightening. It was his impression that such information has to be handled carefully and that it may be better not to have this type of information about a President at all.[164]

Other Concerns ELECTIONS Professors Nathan L. Colvin and Edward B. Foley also contributed to the symposium through their discussion of election law.[165] They recounted the Tilden–Hayes 1876 election dispute and drew important connections to the 2000 election, which led to the *Bush v. Gore*[166] decision.

Two potential gaps in pre-inaugural succession were identified by the panelists. The first concerns a candidate who dies before the counting of the electoral votes.*[167] I noted that there is authority to support the proposition that once the electoral

---

* Dr. John C. Fortier also discussed gaps in the pre-inaugural time frame, as well as gaps that exist during inauguration and during a disputed election. Transcript of Fordham Law Review Program, *Panel and Response: Gaps in Electoral, Transition and Confirmation Processes*, at 21–37 (Apr. 17, 2010). See note, pp. 239–40, *supra*.

votes are cast a candidate becomes the President-elect or the Vice President–elect, yet others dissent from that view.[168] Second, a real gap in presidential succession exists when a candidate has died after the election but before even the casting of electoral votes.[169] Senator Bayh voiced the opinion that in such a situation, presidential electors are "perfectly free to cast [votes] for John Brown if they want to, or Wayne Morris—Ronald Reagan, at one time."[170] He further expanded on that thought, noting that "[t]he question [then] is which slate of electors Congress accepts, which goes back to the old Tilden–Hayes situation."[171] These pre-inaugural gaps remain in the current system of presidential succession.

Solutions Proposed at the Symposium   Throughout the symposium the speakers advanced many solutions for the gaps that remain in the system of presidential succession.

LINE OF SUCCESSION   The line of succession can be amended in various ways to reflect the constitutional or policy considerations deemed most important. Goldstein proposed a legislative–Cabinet line of succession, as we currently have, but that maintains party continuity by inserting into the line of succession the leaders of the President's party in the House and Senate.[172] Fleming, who acknowledged that Congress is unlikely to remove itself from the line of succession, agreed with this proposal.[173] Goldstein also proposed specifically designating these legislators as "officers" to further mitigate some of the constitutional issues.[174] Expanding on these ideas, Fleming proposed the creation of a "vice Vice President" or a body of successors.[175] He envisioned the vice Vice President as a former President or former Vice President.[176] The body of successors could comprise individuals designated as "officers" and would include governors or statesmen such as Colin Powell.[177] In either case, Fleming would construct the line of succession so that the Vice President or the body of successors would be placed before the Cabinet members.[178] Senator Bayh expressed his opinion that placing a former President in a competitive position within the executive branch would cause a great deal of trouble.[179] Professor Goldstein was also against the idea of a vice Vice President. Goldstein put forth the fact that since Walter F. Mondale's vice presidency, the office has become a "constructive, contributing, [and] growing office" and that a vice Vice President would risk compromising that growth.[180]

Further, Goldstein proposed including officers situated or domiciled outside of Washington, D.C., as well as Cabinet members knowledgeable about security issues in order to protect the line of succession in a mass catastrophe scenario.[181] The officers outside of Washington could be ambassadors, according to Goldstein's proposal, and they would be placed later in the line of succession than the Cabinet members selected for their knowledge about security matters.[182]

Additionally, the legislative–Cabinet succession proposed by Goldstein would allow for succession by a legislator in a failure-to-qualify scenario, although Goldstein would require that the legislator be from the same party as the President-elect or Vice President–elect in the failure-to-qualify scenario where there is a double death, disability, or vacancy.[183] In the situation where there was no President-elect or Vice President–elect, then there is no party continuity to maintain and Professor Goldstein posited that this may be a compelling situation for a special election.[184]

Fleming proposed conducting a special election in all succession scenarios, outside of the Vice President succeeding to the presidency, in order to make all succession to the presidency temporary.[185] Dr. Fortier also made note that the Continuity of Government Commission recommended special elections and particularly in situations where a full term awaits the Acting President.[186] During the symposium the author expressed a different view on the subject of special elections, noting that they would be clouded by difficult policy questions, constitutional concerns, and practical and logistical nightmares.[187]

DISABILITY DETERMINATIONS   At the symposium the author proposed a federal statute allowing for succession procedures in those situations where a Vice President cannot act.[188] Others agreed with this proposal. In the absence of a statute, Goldstein noted that letter agreements could be used and that such instruments would informally allow determinations to be made.*[189]

Gilbert proposed the addition of a mental health specialist to the White House medical staff.[190] In support of this proposal, he said that the medical staff would not be specifically attached to the President so that such an addition would avoid fanfare.[191]

ELECTORAL COLLEGE   Finally, there was the suggestion of the abolition of the Electoral College. This would simplify, but not cure, all presidential succession issues regarding the election.[192] Professors Colvin and Foley gave support to creating "some other neutral or bipartisan body" as the arbiter of election disputes, rather than the current system in place under the Electoral Commission Act.[193]

FORDHAM CLINIC ON PRESIDENTIAL SUCCESSION

At the suggestion of Dean Treanor and as a result of the call to action at the symposium, the author established a clinical seminar for the fall and spring terms of the 2010–11 school year to have students explore recommendations to secure and strengthen the system of presidential succession. The author was joined by Professors Dora Galacatos and Nicole A. Gordon.†

---

* See Chapter 13, pp. 203–4 and the letter composed by Vice President Richard Cheney.
† The participants of the clinic seminar, authors of the report, and crafters of the recommendations for reform were Carina Bergal, Rosana Escobar Brown, Christopher Fell, Francisco A. Pardo, Erin M.

Together, we selected nine Fordham Law students to participate in the clinic.[*] Guided by Professor Galacatos, Professor Gordon, and the author, the students examined a broad range of proposals for changing the presidential succession system and extrapolated the intended and unintended political, social, and practical consequences of such recommendations in detailed and nuanced analyses. They also examined the gaps that exist in the current succession process. The gaps were divided into contingencies for which the law provides some direction and those on which the law is silent. The students then prioritized the gaps in order of urgency with attention to the practical and political realities of achieving change.[†]

Finally, the seminar developed a set of recommendations designed to address the gaps and deficiencies in the succession framework. The recommendations were designed to be nonpartisan, constitutionally sound, and practical. They are embodied in a report published in the *Fordham Law Review*.[‡]

In making recommendations for reform, the students were guided by five values: adherence to the Constitution, certainty and predictability in the transition of leadership, legitimacy of a presidential successor in the eyes of the public, party continuity, and depth in qualifications of a possible successor. Consistent with these goals, the students opted not to propose a constitutional amendment, understanding the extreme difficulty of pressing for change in this manner. Instead, the recommendations focused on statutory change, exercise of executive and personal powers, and amendment of political party and Congressional rules.

Line of Succession

The students noted that as a matter of policy, inclusion of legislative members in the line of succession presents concerns, including violation of the doctrine of separation of powers, the possibility of a sudden and complete shift in party control of the executive branch, and conflicts of interest in instances of impeachment or removal of the President. On the other hand, inclusion of executive officers raises questions about Cabinet members' qualifications to serve as Acting President.

Sullivan, Patrick Sweeney, Jennie R. Tricomi, Daniel J. Tyrrell, and Elnaz Zarrini, all now graduates of the Law School.

[*] Professor Galacatos is Executive Director at Fordham Law School's Center for Social Justice; Professor Gordon is a former chair of the New York State Bar Association Federal Constitution Committee and former executive director of the New York City Campaign Finance Board.

[†] In addition, the seminar interviewed seven experts and practitioners on presidential succession, including Senator Birch Bayh; Justin Cooper, Oval Office Assistant to President Bill Clinton; Fred F. Fielding; John C. Fortier; Joel K. Goldstein; Frances Fragos Townsend, Assistant to President George W. Bush for Homeland Security and Counterterrorism and his National Continuity Director; and Benton Becker. They made available their extensive knowledge and insight to aid the students in arriving at a comprehensive understanding of the system of presidential succession.

[‡] 81 Fordham L. Rev. 1, 60–63 (2012).

Therefore, given the various concerns—constitutional and otherwise—about the inclusion of legislative leaders, the seminar recommended a return to the executive line of succession as provided for in the 1886 Succession Act. Failing adoption of this recommendation, the seminar recommended an exclusively Cabinet line of succession for cases of presidential inability in order to facilitate a voluntary transfer of presidential power when circumstances require it and to mitigate disruption in legislative leadership.[194]

Further, the seminar recommended legislative confirmation of whether acting secretaries are included in the line of succession, and, if they are not, either remove them from the line or, alternatively, amend the 1947 Act so that they can assume the powers and duties of the presidency in the order of the departments' creation, but only after succession has passed through all of the Cabinet Secretaries.

Presidential and Vice-Presidential Inability

Although the Twenty-Fifth Amendment has resolved several important presidential succession issues, the students were concerned that neither the Amendment nor the 1947 Act addresses threats to presidential continuity posed in certain circumstances by a presidential or vice-presidential inability. These include inability of a President when there is a vacancy in the office of Vice President, dual inability of a President and Vice President, inability of a Vice President, and inability of an Acting President. The clinic recommended that the following steps be taken.

Statutory Action:

Acknowledge that the President or Acting President, upon declaration of his own inability, can transfer his powers voluntarily to the next in the line of succession in instances of vice-presidential inability or vacancy.

Authorize the person next in the line of succession after the Vice President, together with a majority of the Cabinet, to declare the inability of the President or Acting President in instances of vice-presidential inability or vacancy.

Executive Contingency Planning:

The President or Acting President should prepare a prospective executive declaration of inability at the beginning of his service in which he would define the situations that in his view would render him unable to discharge the powers and duties of the presidency in the future and provide that the declaration go into effect based upon a review process set out by the President or Acting President.

The Vice President should prepare a prospective executive declaration of inability at the beginning of his service in which he would define the situations that in his view would render him unable to discharge the powers and duties of the vice presidency in the future and provide that the declaration be self-executing, based upon a clearance mechanism as directed by the Vice President.[195]

Pre-Inaugural Period

The current system of pre-inaugural presidential succession is governed by a legal framework based on constitutional provisions, federal and state statutes, and political party rules. The students found that this system contains gaps that threaten continuity of government in the context of succession to the presidency for the political parties to adopt prior to the inauguration. They arrived at the following recommendations:

- In the event of the death or resignation of a presidential candidate before the political party conventions, require the parties to hold an open meeting to decide which replacement candidate(s) will receive the delegates' votes.
- In the event of the death or resignation of a presidential nominee between the political party conventions and the general election, require the parties to either hold an open meeting to select a replacement candidate or recall the convention delegates.
- During the period between the general election and the meeting of the Electoral College, provide that the vice presidential candidate replaces a deceased or resigned presidential candidate of the same ticket and that the candidate's party issue recommendations to the presidential electors as to a new candidate for the office of Vice President.

Second, the clinic suggested one change to congressional rules and procedures that would help avert confusion and opportunities for political maneuvering, thus strengthening the presidential succession system:

- In the event of the death or resignation of a presidential or vice-presidential candidate between the meeting of the Electoral College and the counting and declaration of the Electoral College votes by Congress, require Congress to count votes cast for a candidate if he was alive at the time of the Electoral College vote.

Finally, the clinic addressed the lack of an institutionalized process for nominating Cabinet members during the transition between presidential administrations so as to maintain a line of succession. The clinic advanced the following recommendation to address this concern:

During the period between the counting and declaration of Electoral College votes by Congress and Inauguration Day, the outgoing President should consider promptly nominating any Cabinet nominees the President-elect submits to him, and Congress should confirm as many nominees as possible prior to Inauguration Day, consistent with the proper discharge of Congress's advice and consent responsibility. One or more newly confirmed Cabinet Secretaries should remain at a secure location outside of Washington, D.C., on Inauguration Day. This recommendation is particularly important in the case of an exclusively executive line of succession, as the clinic recommends.[196]

Reflections on Modifying the System of Presidential Succession

Although the clinic advanced preferred recommendations, its participants recognized the obstacles to modifying the current system of presidential succession. In light of this reality, the clinic made a range of proposals that provide decisionmakers with different options to consider. It was, and remains, the sincere hope of the clinic that the nation's leaders implement necessary changes in the name of national security, continuity of government, and the common good.

16

Representation of the Twenty-Fifth Amendment in Popular Culture

The whole notion of the 25th Amendment is that the institution matters more than the man. Bartlet's decision was even more self-sacrificing because he willingly gave power to his opposition.

STEVE ATWOOD, "Dogs of War," *The West Wing*[1]

One way of ascertaining changes that *might* need to be addressed in the area of presidential succession is through exploring popular culture. Media, most particularly through theater and television, provide a lens on what populates the collective imagination of the public.[2] As William Baker said in his fascinating article "Presidential Succession Scenarios in Popular Culture and History and the Need for Reform," "[b]y looking at the issue of presidential succession through the lens of the popular imagination, we can begin to see what in the nation's laws needs changing."[3]

The media offers several depictions of when the Twenty-Fifth Amendment is perceived to apply. Examples include: What would happen if the President were killed in a nuclear attack (*Jericho*[4] and *By Dawn's Early Light*[5]), a natural disaster (*The Day After Tomorrow*[6]), or even an alien invasion (*Mars Attacks!*[7])?[8] Other plotlines feature Vice Presidents or other officials staging a *coup d'état* to overthrow the President.[9] The following themes have been entertained by popular culture as problems in presidential succession.

VICE-PRESIDENTIAL VACANCY

A recent trend in television series is to depict what the public views as "gaps" in the field of presidential succession. For example, the inability provisions of the Twenty-Fifth Amendment cannot be invoked if there is a vacancy in the vice presidency. In addition, there is no framework for determining if the Vice President is disabled during a presidential disability.[10] The difficulty in these scenarios is that under Section 1, when the President is removed from office or has died or resigned, "the Vice President shall become President";[11] and if the President cannot declare his own inability, the Vice President and a majority of other principal officers can do so.[12] Therefore the absence of a Vice President could create difficulties in succession events.[13] This gap has been illustrated in two television series, *The West Wing* and *Commander in Chief*.[14]

In the last episode of season four of *The West Wing*, terrorists kidnap the daughter of fictional President Josiah Bartlet on the eve of her college graduation, leaving the President seriously distraught.[15] Shortly after, terrorists send the White House a ransom letter, requesting that prisoners of war be released and that the President announce on television that the United States will abandon its military presence in the fictional Middle Eastern country of Qumar.[16] Given the intense conflict of interest, and to blunt the bargaining power of the kidnappers, President Bartlet temporarily transfers his presidential powers by invoking Section 3[17] of the Twenty-Fifth Amendment.[18]

However, the vice presidency is vacant because of a recent scandal, leaving no Vice President to discharge President Bartlet's powers and duties under the Constitution.[19] Accordingly, President Bartlet assembles the Cabinet members in a private room and receives their consent to make Speaker of the House Glen Walken the Acting President.[20] Although President Bartlet acknowledges that the Twenty-Fifth Amendment does not require the consent of the Cabinet, he wanted the Cabinent's consent so the administration could work squarely behind the Acting President.[21] President Bartlet then signs a letter relinquishing presidential power.[22] Since the Constitution prohibits a member of Congress from holding concurrently a civil office, Speaker Walken resigns from Congress, and is sworn in as Acting President by the Chief Justice.[23]

A number of issues arise from this scenario. First, there was no Vice President to discharge President Bartlet's powers under the Twenty-Fifth Amendment. Therefore some scholars argue the President should have invoked the Succession Act of 1947, which dictates that the Speaker of the House will become President, not Section 3 of the Twenty-Fifth Amendment.[24] The show's writers seemingly reasoned that the President invoked Section 3 of the Twenty-Fifth Amendment, since his personal situation left him unable to serve.[25] In a later episode when the President's daughter is rescued from her kidnappers, President Bartlet reclaims his powers by notifying congressional leaders in the manner required by Section 3 of the Twenty-Fifth Amendment.[26] However, since the Twenty-Fifth Amendment does not apply to this situation, because there was no Vice President, there is no requirement of notice to Congress.[27] Instead, he could have simply resumed his powers under the Presidential Succession Act, which provides that the Acting President shall act as President *only* until the President's disability has been removed.[28] Although the notice provisions of the Twenty-Fifth Amendment only apply to the Vice President, and not to statutory successors, the use of such measures would be good practice. The Fordham Law School Presidential Succession Clinic offers statutory steps for accomplishing this practice, as do scholars in the field.

Another issue this situation makes evident is that neither the Twenty-Fifth Amendment nor the Succession Act of 1947 clearly define what "inability" means.[29] Tom Rozinski, a political science professor at Touro College, argues that "inability" means only physical or mental illness, not a conflict of interest.[30] This *West Wing* episode highlights but does not address whether a President can declare himself "unable to serve" as a result of a personal tragedy or a conflict of interest.[31] The legislative history of the Amendment reflects that "inability" was not limited only to cases of physical and mental disability. The history reflects that inability would extend to such occurrences as a kidnapping of a President, a failure of communication, and circumstances rendering him incapable of discharging his powers and duties.*

Furthermore, if there is a vacancy in the vice presidency and the Speaker of the House becomes Acting President, the issue arises that House Speakers are often from the opposing party of the President.[32] In *The West Wing*, this is exactly what occurs. President Bartlet hands over his presidential powers to Speaker Walken, who is the most powerful Republican in the country.[33] While White House officials commend this act of patriotism by the President, Cabinet members also express concern about the chaos that could result if the President and Acting President gave contradictory orders.[34] Thus, some argue that the new President should be of the same party as the former President, to preserve continuity of policy.[35] Professor Akhil Reed Amar echoes this argument, commenting that if both the President and the Vice President are unavailable, presidential power should flow to some other federal "officer" named by law.[36] He suggests that the framers of the Constitution clearly had in mind that a Cabinet officer, one who had been chosen by the President himself, would assume the discharge of powers and duties of the office.[37]

---

* See discussion of the reach of the term in Chapter 14, *infra*, noting that one way to achieve party continuity is to have a member of the president's cabinet designated next in line; yet, the Speaker of the House is also elected, which may provide a more democratic choice. However, this chaos and political confusion are avoided in *The West Wing* when President Bartlet later reclaims his powers. See Baker, endnote 2, at 839.

Yet the Succession Act of 1947 places the Speaker of the House, followed by the President pro tempore of the Senate, ahead of the Cabinet officers.[38] In his article, Baker makes similar arguments.[39]

The gap of a vice-presidential vacancy also appears in the 2005 television show *Commander in Chief*. Here, fictional Vice President Mackenzie Allen becomes the first female President of the United States.[40] There is a vice-presidential vacancy when her Vice President, Warren Keaton, resigns because of a conflict of interest with the Speaker of the House, Nathan Templeton.* Templeton is of the opposing political party and publicly reveals his contentions with President Allen.†

In the show's plot, President Allen is disabled for a short period when her appendix bursts, and she requires a four-hour surgery.[41] Before President Allen is taken to the emergency room, she invokes the Twenty-Fifth Amendment.[42] President Allen calls her Chief of Staff, Jim Gardner, to notify the President pro tempore of the Senate that he would take over until she recovers from surgery.[43] Although the Succession Act dictates that Speaker Templeton is next in the constitutional line of succession, President Allen assumes the Speaker would not invoke this right, because he would have to resign from Congress to assume the office of Acting President.[44] When the power-hungry Speaker Templeton is asked to sign a waiver to swear in the Senate President pro tempore, he surprisingly decides to assume the presidential powers himself.[45] President Allen, furious and appalled, calls to warn Speaker Templeton that she could undo anything he does when she resumes office.[46] Templeton does not heed her warnings and engages in policies that he knows President Allen would not support. For example, Templeton ends a current airline strike, something the President would have never done.[47]

The *Commander in Chief* episode raises issues similar to the *West Wing* episode. First, President Allen's relinquishing of her powers fell outside the scope of the Amendment and would have been governed by the Succession Act of 1947.[48] Second, there is again the concern of the conflict that arises when the Speaker of the House of an opposing party temporarily replaces a disabled President.[49] The last issue this episode prompts is: Is there a way to ensure that the country has a Vice President at all times?[50] This idea is reflected in Section 2 of the Twenty-Fifth Amendment.[51] However, the process required to fill a vice-presidential vacancy

---

* *Commander in Chief: Pilot* (ABC television broadcast September 27, 2005). Speaker Templeton learns of some damaging personal information about Warren Keaton, Allen's Vice President. Templeton withholds the information, however, with an understanding that General Keaton would return the favor. When Templeton later asks Vice President Keaton for political favors that conflict with President Allen's decisions, Vice President Keaton sees no other option than to give his resignation to the President.

† The information concerned Keaton's deceased daughter, who was a medical doctor and single mother. *Commander in Chief: First Scandal* (ABC television broadcast November 8, 2005).

takes a few months based on precedents; thus, there will inevitably be a period of time when the office is vacant.[52] In order to maintain a short lived vice-presidential vacancy, the American Bar Association recommends the use of joint hearings by both Houses of Congress to fill a vacancy under section 2.[53]

PRESIDENT'S INABILITY DECLARED BY VICE PRESIDENT AND CABINET MEMBERS

Another recurring theme is found in the depiction of Section 4 of the Amendment.[54] The issue is, what factors qualify when a Vice President and Cabinet members declare an inability? This is exemplified in the television series *24*, when a conflict arose between the President and the Vice President.[55] In the second season, fictional President David Palmer receives a tape recording of a conversation between a terrorist and three high-ranking officials of Middle Eastern countries regarding the making of a bomb.[56] President Palmer refuses to order a military strike against the countries until he has proof that the recording is genuine.[57] The Cabinet believes that the President is acting "irrationally" because of his cautious response to an impending terrorist attack, and they perceive his inaction as a sign of weakness.[58] The Vice President and Chief of Staff decide it would be best for the American people if the President were removed from power.[59] A majority of the Cabinet and the Vice President vote to relieve President Palmer of his presidential powers by invoking Section 4 of the Twenty-Fifth Amendment.[60] The Vice President, Jim Prescott, is then sworn in as Acting President and orders the military strikes against the three Middle Eastern countries.[61] However, just hours later, it is discovered that the recording is indeed a forgery.* Vice President Prescott and the Cabinet officers rescind their earlier vote, and President Palmer resumes his powers.[62]

This scenario raises various questions. One is, does irrational behavior constitute inability, and if so, what factors constitute irrational behavior? [63] Section 4 of the Amendment does not define when the President is "unable to discharge his powers."[64] However in *24*, just a few hours after the President's removal, when the recording was discovered to be a forgery, the Vice President and Cabinet members rescinded their earlier vote.[65] It appears that the writers in *24* interpreted the disability clause in Section 4 of the Twenty-Fifth Amendment to be so broad that the concept would encompass even political and policy disagreements. They also chose not to include in the plot the following requirements of the Twenty-Fifth Amendment: The Vice President and a majority of the President's Cabinet are impowered, only by use of a written declaration of inability sent to the President

---

* The recording was fabricated by European and American businessmen to wage war with the Middle East, in order to benefit from increasing oil prices.

pro tempore and Speaker, to remove the President from the discharge of his powers and duties; and that the President may resume his powers and duties unless the Vice President and Cabinet restate, within four days of the President's recovery statement, a written declaration that the President has a continuing inability. The four days need not run their course, however, if the Vice President and Cabinet agree to the President's immediate resumption of his powers and duties. As for the taking of the presidential oath by the Vice President in a case of inability, it is suggested by this author that he need not do so, as provided in the plot, because his oath as Vice President covers his succession duty as an Acting President, while remaining in his office as Vice President. The President does not lose his office during a period of inability but only cedes its powers and duties to the Vice President for the inability's duration.*

Another portrayal of the Vice President and Cabinet officers' deciding presidential disability is seen in the movie *Air Force One*.[66] The film's opening scene is in Moscow, Russia. Fictional United States President James Marshall gives a speech at a state dinner, announcing that the United States will no longer negotiate with terrorists. The President's speech follows a controversial turn of events, where General Ivan Radek, a dictator of a terrorist regime in the former Soviet Republic of Kazakhstan, is captured with the help of the United States. After the dinner, President Marshall leaves Moscow and boards *Air Force One* to return to the United States, along with the First Lady and their daughter, many of his Cabinet members, and advisors.[†] However, six members of Radek's regime disguise themselves as Russian television crew members, and board and hijack the plane, seeking to hold the President hostage until Radek is released. Agents manage to safely secure President Marshall in an escape pod, which is an emergency vessel attached to the plane, and which the hijackers are unable to access. Yet the hijackers take control of the plane and head for Kazakhstan, in hope of forcing Radek's release.

The leader of the hijackers, Ivan Korshunov, holds the First Lady and the daughter hostage, as well as other Cabinet officers. He calls the Vice President, Kathryn Bennett, and threatens to kill hostages until the dictator, General Ivan Radek, is released. In the meantime, the President escapes the pod, and enters back into the plane to save his family and the other hostages. He enables almost all of the hostages to escape via the parachutes on the plane, and succeeds in killing almost all of Korshunov's men. However, when Korshunov, who still holds the First Lady and First Daughter hostage in a separate area of the plane, threatens to kill the First Daughter, the distressed President agrees to release Radek. Eventually, President Marshall kills Korshunov himself and regains control of the plane. Radek is

---

* See Chapter 8, *supra*, p. 114 n. 62.
† *Air Force One* is the official air traffic control call sign of any U.S. Air Force aircraft transporting the President of the United States.

also fatally shot before his release, and President Marshall lands safely and is re-united with his family.

The constitutional issue in this scenario is the inability of the President's staff in the United States to know if he is "disabled" or not.[67] There were two different opinions in the film. The Secretary of Defense argued that the President was still able to discharge his duties, under the National Security Act of 1947.* On the other hand, the Attorney General claimed that since the President's family was being held hostage, and the President himself may have been held hostage to force the release of a terrorist leader, he was in the same position as if he suffered a stroke, and was thus disabled. The rationale was that President Marshall would be acting not as the President, but as a father and husband, and thus in his duress, would be "disabled" under the Twenty-Fifth Amendment. A majority of the Cabinet agreed with the Attorney General and voted to discharge the President of his duties and swear in Vice President Bennett as Acting President. However, right before Vice President Bennett is sworn in as Acting President, invoking Section 4 of the Twenty-Fifth Amendment, Bennett hesitates to remove the President from power, because she is uncertain of the President's situation and does not want to appear to be usurping power. The issue is resolved, however, when President Marshall lands safely. Thus, an issue that arises is under what circumstances can the Vice President and Cabinet officers declare the President to be disabled, especially if the President is unable to dispute this declaration.

CONCLUSION

Other themes have been depicted in popular culture in books, movies, television shows, and even video games.[68] One theme that arises is who is in the order of the constitutional line of succession. In the movie *2012*, the President and Vice President die, and the Speaker of the House is missing.[69] The Chief of Staff appoints himself Acting President. However, under the Presidential Succession Act of 1947, the President pro tempore of the Senate is actually next in the constitutional line of succession. Another theme depicted in popular culture is seen in the book *Full Disclosure* by William Safire.[70] In *Full Disclosure,* the President is blinded by an assassination attempt while at a summit meeting in the former Soviet Union.[71] The Cabinet and the Vice President try to unseat him by invoking Section 4 of the Twenty-Fifth Amendment, believing he is unable to discharge the duties of President. However, the President survives the Cabinet vote. Ironically, the President and Vice President both resign, and the Speaker of the House rises to the Presidency.

---

* The Act, signed into law on July 26, 1947, created a number of enduring structures: a National Security Council (NSC) to coordinate policy, consisting of the President, Vice President, Secretary of State, and the newly created Secretary of Defense; a Department of Defense, including a statutory Joint Chiefs of Staff (JCS); and a Central Intelligence Agency (CIA).

These brief summaries of media depictions of the Twenty-Fifth Amendment certainly raise possibilities that inhere in the Amendment and in a system of government by the people and for the people. People with power, as Madison noted in the *Federalist* and as America's experience with self-governance bears out, are capable of abusing and misusing power and making mistakes in its exercise. The Twenty-Fifth Amendment, as with respect to the impeaching article and other provisions of the Constitution, is grist for misunderstandings, rampant speculations, and conspiracy theories even when carefully and properly applied by the people invested with constitutional power. All of this makes important the media's fascination with Twenty-Fifth Amendment plots, since at their root they educate, inform, and focus on outcomes in a wide range of contingencies that could happen, even in a country anchored on the rule of law.

As this book goes to press, the movie *White House Down* by Columbia Pictures was making the rounds. Its story involves a President who becomes unavailable, leading to a transfer of power to his Vice President whose plane is then shot down by a corrupt security system surrounding our highest officers. Behind it all in the plot was the Speaker of the House of Representatives, who sought the presidential office under the line of succession in order to keep in place the military-industrial complex established in the Middle East. Fortunately, in the plot the President returns and the Speaker is arrested. May such an outcome be always the result for people who wrongly seek such a use of power.

An Evaluation

17

Appraisal

On the brief record of the 25th Amendment, it has served the nation well under extraordinary and unforeseen circumstances.

JAMES RESTON, November 1, 1974[1]

In any appraisal of the Twenty-Fifth Amendment, one must start with the function it played in shaping the extraordinary events of 1973 and 1974. As Representative Peter W. Rodino stated at the 1975 review hearings on the Twenty-Fifth Amendment before the Senate Subcommittee on Constitutional Amendments:

> Had there been no amendment, not only would the Nixon and Agnew resignations still have left the nation without a nationally elected executive, but the uncertainty and partisan divisions which would have been inherent in the operation of the succession statutes might have threatened the very constitutional process which ultimately preserved our institutions. Or, barring that, they might have rendered any "new administration" wholly unable to govern.
>
> The 25th Amendment permitted the constitutional process to proceed in such a way that the American people could have confidence that no one sought partisan advantage.*

---

* See *Hearing on the First Implementation of Section Two of the Twenty-Fifth Amendment Before the Subcomm. on Constitutional Amendments of the Senate Comm. on the Judiciary*, 94th Cong. 34–35 (1975). In its report the subcommittee noted:

> There was general agreement that without the 25th Amendment it would have been much more difficult for President Nixon to resign, thus forcing the country through a prolonged and divisive impeachment trial. In addition the character of the entire investigative process

When charges of criminal wrongdoing were leveled against Vice President Spiro T. Agnew, the option of resignation was viable partially because there existed a mechanism under which a new Vice President could be selected from the same party as that of the President. Had the Amendment not been operative, it is quite possible that significant pressure against resignation might have developed because a resignation would have placed a member of the opposition party at the head of the line of succession. With the Amendment in place, however, the President, Vice President, and Attorney General were able to consider whether a resignation was in the national interest without having to worry about a lack of executive continuity should something happen to the President during the remainder of his term.

The existence of the Amendment also assisted the country in passing through one of its greatest tests: impeachment proceedings against a President. Since the Amendment had operated to replace a Republican Vice President with another Republican Vice President, Congress was able to deal with the question of impeachment in the following months with the knowledge that it could not be charged with attempting to install its Speaker as President and thereby turn over control of the executive to a different political party. This is to be contrasted with the situation in 1868, when impeachment proceedings were brought against President Andrew Johnson. Then the President pro tempore of the Senate, Benjamin Wade, who stood first in the line of succession, participated in the impeachment proceedings in the Senate, and voted in favor of Johnson's removal from office.* Wade's participation in that proceeding was widely criticized at the time and was one of the factors that led Congress in 1886 to remove the President pro tempore and the Speaker from the line of succession.

But in 1974, because of the Twenty-Fifth Amendment, President Richard M. Nixon was able to resign without having to surrender his party's control of the White House. Had the Republicans lost the White House instead of having two of their leaders serve out the existing term, the consequences to the party itself might well have been devastating. Indeed, the resignations of both of its national leaders, without an opportunity for two other members of the party to restore credibility to the federal government, might have operated to prevent the Republicans from being an effective force in national politics for a substantial period of

---

of the House Judiciary Committee investigation might well have been changed, increasing political motivation and decreasing the objective pursuit of what was in the national interest.

Report of the Subcomm. on Constitutional Amendments of the Senate Comm. on the Judiciary, 94th Cong., 1st Sess., A Review of the Implementation of Section 2 of the 25th Amendment, 3 (Comm. Print 1975). The subcommittee concluded that no change in the Amendment was warranted.

* It is reported that at the time he cast his vote, Wade had already selected his Cabinet. Donald Young, *American Roulette: The History and Dilemma of the Vice Presidency* 82 (1972); Lately Thomas, *The First President Johnson* 595 (1968).

time and, it may be argued, might even have led to a disintegration of the party at all levels of government.

Finally, upon Nixon's resignation, the Amendment made it possible for the country to enjoy a swift, orderly, and undisputed transfer of executive power. Gerald R. Ford was immediately recognized as the new President, a fact that served as a unifying and stabilizing force throughout the country. Indeed, the acceptance accorded Ford is a great tribute to the American system.

As to the first applications of the Amendment, I note the following: The Amendment has been applied six times: Section 1, when Gerald Ford became President; Section 2, when Vice President Agnew and President Nixon resigned from office; and Section 3, when Presidents underwent surgery under general anesthesia. The exercise of Section 3 was raised as a possibility on two other occasions involving a medical issue but was not pursued either time because it was determined that general anesthesia would not be administered to the President. Section 4 was raised as a possibility at least twice during the presidency of Ronald Reagan.

I now turn more specifically to the sections of the Amendment.

SECTION I

Section 1 was used for the first time on August 9, 1974, when Gerald Ford took the presidential oath of office after Nixon resigned as President. The President's resignation was effective at noon, and moments later the oath was administered by the Chief Justice of the United States, Warren E. Burger, in the East Room of the White House before members of the Cabinet, Congress, and family and friends. The Chief Justice asked, "Mr. Vice President, are you ready to take the oath of office as President?" and then proceeded to administer it as Ford placed his right hand on a Bible. President Ford delivered brief inaugural remarks, stating:

> The oath that I have taken is the same oath that was taken by George Washington and by every President under the Constitution. But I assume the Presidency under extraordinary circumstances never before experienced by Americans. . . .
>
> I am acutely aware that you have not elected me as your President by your ballots, and so I ask you to confirm me as your President with your prayers. . . .
>
> . . . If you have not chosen me by secret ballot, neither have I gained office by any secret promises. I have not campaigned either for the Presidency or the Vice Presidency. I have not subscribed to any partisan platform. I am indebted to no man, and only to one woman—my dear wife—as I begin this very difficult job.
>
> I have not sought this enormous responsibility. . . . I will be the President of all the people.

He then added, "Our long national nightmare is over. Our Constitution works. Our great Republic is a government of laws and not of men. Here, the people rule."[2] He asked for prayers for his predecessor that he might find peace. Ford then proceeded to the Oval Office to begin his work as President. In the early evening of August 12, 1974, he appeared before a joint session of Congress for the first time as President, noting that there was a lot of work to be done and that he was a "man of the people."

In becoming President for the rest of Nixon's term, Ford continued the precedent set by John Tyler, but not by virtue of Tyler's rejection of the title "Acting President" and claim to the office of President based on his reading of Article II, Section 1, Clause 6 of the Constitution. Instead, Ford did so under Section 1 of the Twenty-Fifth Amendment, which gives explicit constitutional recognition to the Tyler precedent. Though the circumstances surrounding Ford's becoming President were traumatic for the nation, he discharged his responsibility with fidelity to the Constitution and with dignity.

SECTION 2

Section 2 was first used following the resignation of Spiro Agnew as Vice President on October 10, 1973. Two days later, Nixon nominated Ford to replace Agnew. He was confirmed on November 27, 1973, by a vote of 92–3 in the Senate and on December 6 by a vote of 387–35 in the House. Almost immediately thereafter, he was administered the oath of office by the Chief Justice of the United States, Warren E. Burger, in the chamber of the House of Representatives before a joint session of Congress. He delivered a speech in which he vowed equal justice for all and loyalty to President Nixon.

Less than a year later, Section 2 was exercised again after the resignation of President Nixon and the assumption of the presidency by Ford, which left a vacancy in the vice presidency. Nixon resigned on August 9, Ford immediately became President, and eleven days later, on August 20, nominated Nelson A. Rockefeller to be his Vice President. Rockefeller was confirmed by the Senate (90–7) and by the House of Representatives (287–128) on December 19, 1974. Following the House vote, Rockefeller was sworn in as Vice President in the Senate chamber by Chief Justice Burger. He gave brief remarks of gratitude and expressed his commitment to addressing the nation's challenges.

Against the backdrop of the circumstances under which the Twenty-Fifth Amendment had to operate, the conclusion is inescapable that the process worked exceedingly well in the selection of two Vice Presidents. Ford's selection was the smoother and speedier of the two* and seems to have been the result of a grand

---

* From nomination to confirmation, a period of 57 days elapsed, in contrast to 121 days in the case of Rockefeller.

compromise. Congressional leaders made it clear that Congress did not want the President to nominate a person then considered a potential Republican presidential candidate in 1976,* and Nixon undoubtedly wanted to avoid a stiff, bruising confirmation battle and to restore credibility to his administration, lest there be further damage to his efforts to avoid impeachment. It is not clear whether he was also motivated by a belief that the installation as Vice President of a person who had never been considered for the presidency would provide an impediment to impeachment. In any event, Gerald Ford came to be viewed by both the President and Congress as the ideal nominee under the circumstances. Although he was a relative stranger to large segments of the country and had never been a serious candidate for high national office, Ford was well known to and respected by the bodies that had to approve his nomination, and he possessed the much-desired qualities of openness and integrity.†

In the case of the Rockefeller selection, since the nominee enjoyed a preeminent position in his party and possessed the experience and ability to be an outstanding Vice President, his nomination by Ford measured up to the high standards intended by the Twenty-Fifth Amendment in the selection of a Vice President. As Clifton Daniel of the *New York Times* observed, the Amendment enabled the President to nominate "one of the most experienced public officials in America" without "regard to the usual political considerations that prevail in a national political convention and a Presidential election."[3]

Although it is risky to generalize, the selections of Ford and Rockefeller indicate that a lame duck President may have difficulty filling a vice-presidential vacancy with a potential candidate for President, while a President eligible for reelection may have an easier time with the nomination of a national figure. Yet both selections suggest that public opinion and the press can be counted on to guard against any potential for political abuse that exists under the Amendment. These forces contributed significantly to the thorough inquiries to which Ford and Rockefeller were subjected and influenced Congress not to extract from Ford a pledge with respect to running for President in 1976, not to defer action on Ford's nomination pending completion of the Nixon impeachment inquiry, and not to drag out Rockefeller's confirmation for decision by a new Congress.

Chairman Rodino of the House Judiciary Committee put it succinctly: "I think it is unquestionable that without section 2 of the 25th amendment, this Nation might not have endured nearly so well the ordeal of its recent constitutional crisis."

---

* *N.Y. Times*, Oct. 12, 1973, at 28.
† Ford's counsel, Benton Becker, said that Ford was under consideration at the 1968 convention as Nixon's running mate.

SECTION 3

The three applications of Section 3—in 1985, 2002, and 2007—were all faithful to the Constitution in terms of procedure, with a President who was about to undergo general anesthesia signing a letter addressed to the President pro tempore and Speaker declaring when he commenced his surgery, his inability, and the transfer of presidential authority to the Vice President. Following each surgery, the President signed another letter addressed to the legislative leaders resuming his powers and duties. While Section 3 was executed on these occasions in accordance with Section 3 of the Twenty-Fifth Amendment, its first use by President Reagan in 1985 was fudged, prompting Senator Birch Bayh later to ask the President's counsel, Fred Fielding: "Fred, how did you ever let the President send a letter like that at the time? . . ." Fielding said, "This is the only thing we could get him to sign."[*]

The failure to invoke the inability provisions of the Amendment in 1981 has been the subject of debate. Professor Joel Goldstein has not been alone in stating that President Reagan

> was clearly unable to discharge his powers and duties from the time he was wounded and rapidly losing blood until some time after he came out of surgery. Moreover, the Twenty-fifth Amendment vests constitutional power in the Vice President and principal heads of the executive departments, not in a triumvirate of White House aides accountable to the President. The Twenty-fifth Amendment should have been invoked.[†]

Goldstein is certainly correct as to where the power is, but, as he notes later in his *Fordham Law Review* article, there were many extenuating circumstances. These included the unavailability of succession precedents and policies to draw on, a lack of familiarity by presidential aides and members of the Cabinet with the succession provisions of the Constitution and statutory law, the difficulty of communicating with Vice President George H.W. Bush, and the suddenness of the shooting and attendant uncertainty as to the President's condition. Upon Vice President Bush's return from Texas that evening, there appears to have been a discussion of the use of Section 4 of the Twenty-Fifth Amendment. Fielding has said, "The decision was made that it should not be [invoked]. The next morning the President was alert, writing notes to people. He met and conducted some minor official tasks, with the cameras being there to show that the President was working. The Vice President met with the senior staff and oversaw routine business."[‡]

---

[*] Birch Bayh, Interview, *A Modern Father of Our Constitution: An Interview with Former Senator Birch Bayh*, 79 FORDHAM L. REV. 781, 797 (2010).
[†] Joel Goldstein, *Taking from the Twenty-Fifth Amendment: Lessons in Ensuring Presidential Continuity*, 79 FORDHAM L. REV. 959, 977–78 (2010).
[‡] John D. Feerick, *Presidential Succession and Inability: Before and After the Twenty-Fifth Amendment*, 79 FORDHAM L. REV. 907, 928 (2010).

Several years later, when President Reagan underwent surgery for removal of a cancerous tumor, he transferred power to the Vice President but quickly reclaimed his powers and duties upon regaining consciousness. He disclaimed having used the Twenty-Fifth Amendment, though following all of its provisions, but he later acknowledged having actually exercised Section 3. This ambiguous use of the Amendment is not likely to recur given Reagan's admission, the later uses of Section 3 by President George W. Bush, and the employment of the recommendations of the Miller Commission by presidential administrations since 1989. These later events have paved the way for a more routinized use of the Amendment as contemplated by its authors, but it is not at all certain that a President dealing with an inability will rush to transfer presidential authority.

Fred F. Fielding, a most knowledgeable student of the subject of presidential inability, described in detail his eyewitness account of the aftermath of the Reagan shooting at the *Fordham Law Review*'s April 2010 symposium:

> Upon word of the shooting and that the President had actually been hit, I called the National Security Adviser and we started to assemble people in the Situation Room, which is, of course, the secure facility within the White House complex. . . .
>
> The group that gathered in the Situation Room that day consisted of ten or more individuals, people leaving and coming at various points. It wasn't a full Cabinet meeting, but rather an ad hoc assembly of people. . . .
>
> . . . .
>
> The scene in the Situation Room, if I could try to describe it, was obviously apprehensive, but it wasn't harried or frantic. Again, go back to context. The people that were in the room were professionals. The Cabinet had only recently been assembled. These were people that had come from different backgrounds. Some people came from the President's California retinue and his governor's team. Others were former Nixon Administration officials. Some were brand new to the whole thing. In all fairness, this was a roomful of strangers who really operated fairly well together under these circumstances.
>
> While no one approached me or the Attorney General with any requests for papers sufficient to exercise Section 3 or 4 of the Twenty-Fifth Amendment during the time I was there, I had earlier prepared such papers. I had them with me in draft, for both Section 3 and Section 4 coverage.
>
> . . . .
>
> As we all know, the Twenty-Fifth Amendment was not invoked on March 30. I have read that during that tense afternoon the draft Sections 3 and 4 letters were pulled from my hands and sealed in a safe. It's not so. But think how silly that sounds. It wasn't a great secret that the Twenty-Fifth

Amendment was in play, if you will. To say that suddenly things were pulled and put in a safe sounds very silly.

It is true that we were informed that the bullet had been removed from the President's lung after surgery, and an hour later, we were informed that doctors were very confident of a full recovery. That news quelled any further thoughts or discussion about invoking the Twenty-Fifth Amendment until the Vice President returned. He was en route back. Of course, once he got back, he met with us, in an expanded group in the Situation Room. The group of us—the Attorney General, I, the Chief of Staff, and Secretary [of Defense] Weinberger, but not the Secretary of State—went into the Vice President's office. There we discussed whether Section 4 should be invoked, at that point. The decision was made that it should not be. The next morning the President was alert. He was joking, writing notes to people. He met and conducted some very minor official tasks, with the cameras being there to show that the President was working. The Vice President met with the senior staff and oversaw routine business.

Some have contended that the Twenty-Fifth Amendment should still have been under consideration in the course of the ensuing days. The President recovered gradually and underwent additional procedures. People presumably were talking about Section 4, or a prompting by the President to engage in Section 3. But if the amendment hadn't been triggered on the day of the shooting, hadn't been triggered that evening, it certainly was not going to be willingly engaged, absent a change in the President's health, by the mere virtue of his understandably reduced schedule. The world had been told he was recovering, and, thankfully, that's what turned out to be the case.[4]

Addressing Fielding, I said:

You put a question as to the role of counsel in dealing with the President. I think you said that you had wondered about that. The only comment I have is, remembering all the discussions that surrounded Section 3 and carefully thinking about it at the time and studying the comments, that section was designed to give the President maximum flexibility in a situation involving inability. If the President, in making that choice with the people he was discussing it with, was comfortable with the choice, that's his call, in my opinion. . . .

Fielding replied, "Your counsel agrees."*

---

* See generally Fred F. Fielding, An Eyewitness Account of Executive "Inability," 79 FORDHAM L. REV. 823 (2010).

SECTION 4

Section 4 of the Twenty-Fifth Amendment, while its use was raised as a possibility on two occasions, has never been acted on, and if it becomes necessary to do so, it makes clear that both the Vice President and a majority of the heads of the executive departments are entrusted with the roles of decision makers. The papers delivered by Professors Robert E. Gilbert and Rose McDermott at the Fordham program of 2010 indicate that a case of psychological disability will be a harrowing experience for the nation. However this may be, those closest to the President will be important to the effective consideration and possible execution of Section 4 in such circumstances. President Dwight D. Eisenhower, though not faced with such a disability, laid out one approach when he said in a memorandum accompanying his letter agreement with Vice President Nixon in February 1958:

> There is only one final thought I would like to add. If any disability of mine, in the judgment of any group of distinguished medical authorities that you might assemble, finally become[s] of a permanent character, I would, of course, accept their decision and promptly resign my position. But if I were not able to do so, and the same group of consultants would so state, then you would take over not only the powers and duties but the perquisites of the presidency, including the White House itself. In temporary cases of my "inability," we agree that you should act for the necessary period in your capacity as Vice president and, additionally, as "Acting president."*

There is no reason a President could not do something similar through a prospective declaration of either inability or resignation prepared at the beginning of his administration, as suggested by the Fordham presidential succession clinic, as a safeguard, and as appears already to be in place as a result of the pioneering work of Fred Fielding when he served as White House counsel to President Reagan. To be sure, the recommendations of the Miller Center at the University of Virginia calling for more advance Twenty-Fifth Amendment planning among family, doctors, and aides close to the President, as well as the Vice President, have better equipped the nation for handling all forms of disability. President George H.W. Bush served the nation well when he held a press conference at the beginning of his term to inform the public of his contingency planning.

President Eisenhower set a special benchmark of the responsibility of a President to his country in the area of presidential disability by his actions in 1958.

---

* Dwight D. Eisenhower, *Personal and Secret: To Richard Milhous Nixon, 5 February 1958, in* THE PAPERS OF DWIGHT DAVID EISENHOWER 556 (Louis Galambos & Daun van Ee eds.), available at http://www.eisenhowermemorial.org/presidential-papers/second-term/documents/566.cfm.

PROPOSALS FOR REFORM

There have been many proposals over the past forty-five years to change the system of presidential succession.[5] These proposals range from outright abolition of both the vice presidency and the Twenty-Fifth Amendment[6] to modification of the system to provide for a special presidential election upon the succession of a Vice President.

In the years following the ratification of the Amendment, the historian Arthur Schlesinger and others have supported the abolition of the vice presidency and the adoption of a procedure for a speedy presidential election whenever a vacancy occurs in the presidency, with the Secretary of State acting as President in the interim.[7] They have argued that the use of appointed leaders is not consistent with our democracy and the principle of government by the people. Said Senator Edward Kennedy, "I believe the campaign trail is the surest road to choose a President who will be an effective national leader in foreign and domestic policy."[8]

In 1975, Senator John O. Pastore of Rhode Island proposed a constitutional amendment that would require a special election for President and Vice President whenever an appointed Vice President succeeds to the presidency and more than twelve months remain in the presidential term.[9] At the time he presented his proposal Pastore argued that, should the nation be governed by an appointed President and Vice President, it will no longer "be democratically governed" and "a constitutional crisis will occur."[10] Under Pastore's proposal, an appointed Vice President who succeeds to the presidency would be prohibited from invoking the procedures of Section 2 to nominate a new Vice President. Instead, the Speaker of the House would act as Vice President* during the special election period while continuing to discharge his duties as Speaker. He would not, however, have the vice-presidential duty of serving as President of the Senate. In the event of a need to cast a tie-breaking vote in the Senate, Pastore's proposal provided for the Secretary of State to discharge that duty. Pastore's proposal also specified that the President and Vice President who are elected in a special election serve only the remainder of the established term.

It also has been proposed that whenever a vacancy occurs in the vice presidency, it should be filled by a special election open to candidates of both parties.[11] Another variation is to limit the election to candidates of the President's party. Still others propose that the presidential succession statute of 1947 be amended to provide for a special presidential election whenever simultaneous vacancies exist in the offices of President and Vice President.[12] Some of these legislative proposals have the Speaker serving as President in the interim, while another approach is for

---

* In addition to his constitutional duties of succeeding to the presidency, presiding over the Senate, and participating in a declaration of presidential inability, the Vice President is a statutory member of the National Security Council and, by custom, a member of the Cabinet.

† See supra Chapter 14.

the House Minority Leader to serve in that capacity if his party had occupied the White House as a result of the most recent presidential election.[13]

Other proposals include removing the presiding offers of Congress entirely from the line of succession in favor of a straight Cabinet line; requiring a President's nomination under Section 2 of the Twenty-Fifth Amendment to be submitted to a popular referendum for approval or disapproval; convening the most recent Electoral College to select a Vice President whenever an elected or appointed Vice President succeeds to the presidency; convening the most recent Electoral College to select a new President and Vice President whenever both offices become vacant or an appointed Vice President succeeds to the presidency; and electing two Vice Presidents in the regular quadrennial election.[14]

Senator Robert Griffin of Michigan,[15] Tom Wicker of the *New York Times*, and others advanced the interesting idea that only candidates for the presidency should run in our regular quadrennial election and that, after taking office, a new President should nominate a person for Vice President under the procedures of the Twenty-Fifth Amendment. In advancing this idea, Wicker stated:

> The fact is that Presidents dictate their choices for Vice President with ruthless disregard of any but political qualifications, and political conventions approve them with no "inquisition" at all. The further fact is that no Vice President is really elected by the people or their electors; he is an appendage to their Presidential choice.[16]

Comments on proposals relating to the Twenty-Fifth Amendment follow.

SECTION 2

President Ford suggested that Section 2 of the Twenty-Fifth Amendment be amended to provide specific time limits within which a President must nominate and Congress must confirm or reject a nominee.[17] Implementing such limits for filling vice-presidential vacancies is undesirable. Neither the President nor the Congress should be straitjacketed in discharging their responsibilities. The period of time required for the rendering of a congressional judgment obviously will vary from nominee to nominee. Some nominees will be better known than others and require less time for Congress to render its judgment. Others may require a great deal of time because of the need to study charges made during the confirmation process. The time period also will be influenced by the press of other congressional business. Furthermore, the existence of time limits could present legal difficulties if they were exceeded.

If, in view of the long delay in confirming Nelson Rockefeller, a time limit on confirmation were deemed necessary, the better course of action would be to provide for it in the rules of both Houses rather than in a new constitutional amendment. Congress, I believe, has the power to so provide in its rules in discharging its responsibilities under the Twenty-Fifth Amendment; still, it should be noted that the authors of the Amendment rejected the use of time limits, supporting an argument that time limits might be unconstitutional. One advantage of dealing with them by congressional rules is that Congress would have the flexibility to change any limit that it found to be too short or too long. To freeze limits in the Constitution would require another constitutional amendment to change them—unless, of course, the amendment gave Congress the power to change the specified limits.

The Twenty-Fifth Amendment reflects an intent that there be a President and Vice President at all times, so when a vacancy occurs Congress must act with reasonable dispatch to fill it. A time limit was rejected as was the insertion in the Amendment of the word "immediately."

But none of this is intended to suggest that Congress should not render its judgment on a vice-presidential nomination with reasonable dispatch. The time involved in passing judgment on Rockefeller's nomination could have been shortened had Congress accepted a recommendation, made in July 1974 by a Special Committee of the American Bar Association, that a single joint hearing be held in order to pass on vice-presidential nominations. The ABA noted that a "joint inquiry not only would eliminate duplication of effort but would tend to increase the effectiveness of the inquiry, since the resources of both Houses would be combined, coordinated and utilized to best advantage."[18] Although the Twenty-Fifth Amendment requires each House to vote separately, Congress has the power, by making appropriate changes in its rules, to use a joint hearing to probe a candidate's qualifications. In fact, there was considerable support for such an idea following Agnew's resignation,* but it appears that political considerations killed the proposal. A review of the record of the Ford and Rockefeller confirmation hearings reveals considerable duplication of effort. Both committees drew on the same investigatory arms of government, heard many of the same witnesses, and covered many of the same matters. Although each committee served as a check on the other, and matters were dealt with by one which were not covered by the other, the record does not indicate that these advantages of dual hearings outweigh the advantages of a single hearing. After all, nominees for the U.S. Supreme Court, the Cabinet, and other key posts are subject to one hearing. Of course, if there were to be a single joint hearing in the selection of a Vice President, the committee should be large enough to have representation from both parties geographically and ideologically.

Although some consider the idea of any hearings on the qualifications of vice-presidential nominees to be unseemly and demeaning,[19] many experiences under-

---

* Indeed, during the hearings before the Senate Committee on Rules and Administration, Chairman Cannon expressed his personal preference for a joint hearing. *Hearings on Nomination of Gerald R. Ford of Michigan to be Vice President of the United States Before the Senate Committee on Rules and Administration*, 93rd Cong. 149–50 (1973). Chairman Rodino expressed a contrary view during the 1975 review hearings on the Twenty-Fifth Amendment before the Subcommittee on Constitutional Amendments.

score the desirability of thorough scrutiny of candidates for high office and positions in the executive and judicial branches of government. The exhaustive inquiries into the nominations of Ford and Rockefeller came at a time when the integrity of all public officials was being questioned. Hence, one useful by-product of the hearings was to emphasize the high standards of conduct expected of persons who aspire to the presidency and vice presidency. It is interesting that, because of these hearings, the suggestion has been made that all Vice Presidents be chosen under the procedures of Section 2.[20] If there is a need for greater scrutiny in the pre-nomination period for vice-presidential nominees, the political parties should improve their own selection procedures. To assign this function to Congress after Inauguration Day would divert the attention of a new President at a time when it is essential that his team be intact and that he be developing the policies and programs of his administration, and it would create an unavoidable period during which there would be no Vice President.

As for the suggestion that a President under the threat of impeachment not be permitted to nominate a successor, such a limitation in Section 2 seems unnecessary. In the first place, the Constitution reflects the policy that until he is impeached and removed, the President has the obligation to discharge his duties. Indeed, the framers specifically rejected a proposal under which the President would be suspended from exercising his powers and duties upon his impeachment by the House of Representatives. Second, Congress shares with the President the power of selecting a new Vice President. If a particular nomination is improper, Congress can and ought to reject it. Third, the acceptance of Gerald Ford as President, despite his nomination by a President whose removal was a distinct possibility at the time the nomination was made, shows that the process can work properly in the face of a threatened impeachment. Finally, to include such a limitation in Section 2 might invite impeachment resolutions against a President at a time of a vice-presidential vacancy.

The further criticism of the Amendment on the grounds that it sets no standards for the selection of a Vice President is unfair. It cannot be expected to prescribe more than the procedures for handling a vacancy. Nowhere does the Constitution set any standards by which to judge a person's ability to perform in office. The absence of standards obviously means that it is left to the President and to Congress to make their own judgments, utilizing whatever tests and historical perspectives they feel are appropriate.* Congress and the President share an independent responsibil-

---

* It should be pointed out, however, that the debates surrounding the adoption of the Twenty-Fifth Amendment repeatedly speak of the President's being permitted to nominate a person of his own political party and ideology who might carry on the mandate of the prior presidential election. Indeed, Senator Bayh, father of the Twenty-Fifth Amendment, voted against the confirmation of Nelson Rockefeller because he would have implemented different policies, were he to become President. *See* Birch Bayh, Interview, *A Modern Father of Our Constitution: An Interview with Former Senator Birch Bayh*, 79 FORDHAM L. REV. 781 (2010). It may be argued that a Congress dissatisfied with the ideology

ity to ensure that only persons qualified to be President are chosen as Vice President. In my opinion, the executive and legislative branches discharged their responsibilities well in the first implementations of the Twenty-Fifth Amendment.

DEFINING INABILITY

Another suggestion made with respect to the Twenty-Fifth Amendment, which is not new, involves clarifying the meaning of the term "inability." Some critics feel that Congress should strive to revise the Amendment or, alternatively, enact a statute that would delineate exactly what situations should lead to an invocation of Sections 3 and 4 of the Amendment. On this issue, Dr. Herbert L. Abrams in his book has developed a set of guidelines to "serve as a coherent and rational list of the settings in which invocation must be considered."[21] Some of these conditions are: minor surgical procedures that require general anesthesia, major surgery, the use of psychoactive drugs in significant amounts, serious illness, and the diagnosis of a progressive, mentally disabling condition.[22] According to Abrams, it is important for Presidents to resort to Section 3 under the appropriate circumstances. He finds it equally important, however, that Section 3 not be overused, stating that its use should be "limited to circumstances in which the president's ability to make or communicate rational decisions has been compromised."[23]

It's been recalled that the terms "unable" and "inability" were purposely not defined in the Amendment. It was reasoned that any attempt to define such terms ran the risk of not including every contingency that could give rise to a presidential inability. It was also felt that a detailed definition could lead to problems of interpretation at a time of an inability crisis, when the country could least afford debate and controversy. According to the authors of the Amendment, "[T]he word 'inability' and the word 'unable' as used in [Section 4] . . . , which refer to an impairment of the President's faculties, mean that he is unable either to make or communicate his decisions as to his own competency to execute the powers and duties of his office."[24] Precisely for the reasons that the authors did not draft the Amendment more rigidly, Congress should not attempt to foresee and provide for all instances in which a President may become disabled. An attempt by Congress to exercise greater control over the process prescribed by Sections 3 and 4 would clash with the philosophy expressed throughout the Amendment. The Amendment provides a broad grant of power and discretion to be used appropriately by the President, Vice President, and Cabinet. It sets up procedures that are weighted heavily in favor of the President. This scheme reflects the striking of many compromises,

---

of the President should not require a different philosophy from a vice-presidential nominee, because that would change the last election mandate and to some extent add to the American system the British "vote of no confidence."

leaving little room for congressional interference without another constitutional amendment.

ENHANCING THE ROLE OF THE WHITE HOUSE PHYSICIAN

Some have recommended an increased role for the White House physician in more detail than the Miller Commission. Dr. Abrams has suggested an expanded and carefully defined role for the White House physician during the invocation process of Section 4* so that medical information upon which any finding of inability must rest will be properly considered.[25] Abrams recommends a protocol that would take into account the White House physician's responsibility to serve both the President and the nation. He would among other things empower the physician to send letters to the appropriate officials recommending invocation of the Twenty-Fifth Amendment when the President becomes incapacitated and is unable to invoke Section 3. He also would allow the physician to consult with experts to review the President's medical condition if the physician believes the President is disabled but refuses to invoke Section 3. If the experts concur with the physician's opinion, Abrams recommends that the physician "be empowered to inform the president that he will send letters indicating his opinion to the vice-president, the members of the cabinet, and the chief of staff."[26]

According to Abrams, it is paradoxical that the person responsible for the President's health does not have a major role in informing the pertinent officials about the extent of a presidential disability and assessing the need for a transfer of power.[27] Though he recognizes the doctrine of doctor/patient confidentiality, he says that "[b]reaching the president's confidence on the grounds of national interest is essential, if the alternative is to allow a disabled president to retain authority."[28] Abrams's recommendations weight the physician's duties more heavily on the side of national interests than on the side of doctor/patient confidentiality limitations.

As for the suggestion that the White House physician be given a formal role in a case of presidential inability, I do not think this is necessary or desirable. First, there must be the highest level of confidence between the President and those who serve him (or her) medically, a confidence that promotes a full exchange of information. Both the President and the nation benefit from such an exchange. To introduce

---

* Section 4 provides that if the Vice President and a majority of the Cabinet (or other body designated by Congress) transmit letters to congressional leaders declaring the President disabled, the Vice President will become Acting President. The President will resume his office when he transmits letters to the congressional leaders indicating his ability to do so, unless the Vice President and a majority of the Cabinet (or other body designated by Congress) transmit letters to the leaders stating the contrary within four days. If the latter occurs, the President will still resume his powers unless, within twenty-one days, Congress determines, by a two-thirds vote of both Houses, that the President is still unable to discharge the powers and duties of the presidency. U.S. Const. amend. XXV, § 4.

into that relationship formal reporting obligations by medical personnel to third parties irrespective of presidential wishes could prevent the development of the kind of bond that should exist between a doctor and patient. This is not to say that there might not be circumstances where conscience and ethics require action by a doctor in the public interest without a patient's consent. For my part, I would leave that to the circumstances of a particular moment rather than require it as a matter of law.

A second reason for not enlarging the responsibility of the White House physician by statute to provide for a specific role of initiating a question of presidential inability stems from the Amendment itself. It needs to be emphasized that the Amendment gives the Vice President and Cabinet (or such other bodies established by law) the primary role in the process and implicitly requires them to secure such information, medical and otherwise, as may be necessary to make an informed decision. Medical information obviously will be important in many cases.* They should seek it from all those with knowledge of the facts. This should include the President's family and staff as well as medical specialists who may be attending the President. The White House physician may not be in the best position to judge the President's condition, depending on the nature of the medical situation. Those closest to the President should be expected to cooperate with any Twenty-Fifth Amendment inquiry made by the Cabinet and Vice President. Were they not to do so, their refusal would be a factor to be considered in the determination of the existence of an inability under the Amendment.

The confrontation hypothesized above involving the doctor's withholding relevant information should not occur if the President follows the guidelines suggested by the Miller Commission. To be sure, there may be situations in which activation of Section 4 is a possibility and the President's condition is such that communication is not possible. To best prepare for such circumstances, each President should authorize the White House physician and those closest to him (or her) to cooperate fully with any Twenty-Fifth Amendment inquiry undertaken by the Cabinet and Vice President. Such an inquiry would likely have the full backing of the American public, in the glare of modern communications technology, making it exceedingly difficult for those around the President to thwart the inquiry.

I recognize that the general approach suggested here leaves open the possibility of a President's keeping secret his or her actual inability. I am not persuaded, however, that formalizing the role of the White House physician eliminates that possibility entirely either. Such formalization also has the potential of harming the presidency in some situations by creating debate and controversy prematurely and by trivializing the President's health.

---

* A kidnapping is an example of one where it may be irrelevant. For other examples, see *infra,* pp. 197–202.

MODIFYING SECTION 4

As for the suggestion that Section 4 be modified because Vice Presidents may use the Amendment to usurp the powers of the presidency, such a fear is unwarranted. Historically, Vice Presidents have been very hesitant to exercise what power they may have or to appear disloyal to the President. The circumspection of Vice President Nixon during President Eisenhower's illnesses demonstrates this fact, as does the cautious behavior of Vice President Bush in the aftermath of the assassination attempt on President Reagan and at the time of his colon surgery. Vice Presidents, of course, are ultimately accountable, not only to the President, but also to the people who elect them. Surely, they will be hesitant to take action that will make them appear self-aggrandizing or disruptive, especially if they hold higher political aspirations. In addition, in an egregious case, the Vice President would be subject to impeachment. Therefore, fears that Section 4 provides a Vice President with the opportunity to usurp the presidency, even temporarily, are unfounded and do not justify a modification of the Twenty-Fifth Amendment.[29]

REPEALING THE AMENDMENT

On July 22, 1991, Henry B. Gonzalez, a member of the House of Representatives from Texas, introduced a joint resolution to repeal the Twenty-Fifth Amendment.[30] Gonzalez submitted the same resolution in many Congresses to follow.[31] According to Gonzalez, "The fatal flaw in the bill [which later became the Twenty-Fifth Amendment] is the almost unchecked ease with which the President can be removed by either an unscrupulous or mistaken subordinate."[32] In support of his 1991 efforts, he stated his belief that "[t]he incentives for blind ambition to govern actions under the disability clause of the 25th Amendment are stronger now than ever before" because of the rise of the imperial presidency in this country.[33] Gonzalez's proposal has received no congressional attention to date.

CONCLUDING REFLECTIONS
ON TWENTY-FIFTH AMENDMENT PROPOSALS

None of the above is to say that changes in the operation of the Twenty-Fifth Amendment are not justified. As the Miller Commission usefully suggested, invocation of the Amendment should be planned for. Such planning should be carefully developed early in each administration, based on medical, political, and constitutional considerations. To its credit, the George H.W. Bush administration acted upon the Miller Commission's recommendations by adopting specific guidelines to enable it to handle future instances of presidential inability effectively. By adopting specific guidelines, the Bush administration properly recognized the need to prepare for cases of presidential inability. This is a healthy precedent for future Presidents.

Such an approach best serves the Twenty-Fifth Amendment's goal of providing a framework for succession and for defining inability without unduly binding the hands of those officials who may have to confront those incidents.

PROPOSALS ON THE VICE PRESIDENCY AND SPECIAL ELECTIONS

Abolition of the Vice Presidency

The suggestion to abolish the vice presidency is an old chestnut that, if accepted, would substantially change our system of presidential succession. While the vice presidency has been an object of scorn and satire throughout its history, the office has contributed significantly to the stability and continuity of our government in difficult circumstances. Under the system of vice-presidential succession to the presidency, we have had only peaceful transfers of presidential authority. Moreover, since World War II the occupants of the vice presidency have provided useful assistance to our Presidents in the discharge of their responsibilities.

Abolishing the vice presidency and providing for a Speaker or Secretary of State to act temporarily as President in the event of a presidential vacancy could seriously undermine the stability and continuity of our government. Possibly neither would possess the constitutional qualifications for President or have been chosen for his or her ability to serve as President. But even if they should possess the qualifications, it is doubtful whether either would be recognized as a true President since they would occupy the White House only as caretakers—that is, until a President and Vice President could be chosen in a special election. It is also questionable whether a caretaker could deal effectively with Congress or exercise any real leadership domestically. Foreign leaders too might be encouraged to defer dealing with a caretaker while awaiting the election of a President. Furthermore, it could happen that the caretaker might be of a different party from the most recent President, so that his succession would lack continuity with the administration of the President he replaced. As Senator Frank Moss of Utah observed about John F. Kennedy's assassination:

> Consider what could have happened had the next man in line of succession been a man of opposite political persuasion. At best he would have had only secondhand information on Kennedy policies, and he could have been hostile to them. There would have been the turmoil of an immediate Cabinet shuffle, and changes in other appointive positions in the Government. We would have been taking the risk of a slowdown in Government business, and perhaps a breakdown which would have taken all of our capabilities to master. I do not believe that world order in the age of the atom, the supersonic flight, and instant communications can tolerate that sort of leadership strain in the most powerful country in the world.

And even had the man next in line for the Presidential succession after the Kennedy assassination been a man of similar political faith in the legislative body, the takeover could not have been as untroubled and smooth. A legislative officer, engrossed as he is in business on Capitol Hill, cannot know as much about the business of the executive branch as does the Vice President who is constantly participating in it.[34]

In contrast, a person chosen as a potential presidential successor under the Twenty-Fifth Amendment will necessarily possess the constitutional qualifications and will have been judged on his or her ability to serve as President. Section 2 of the Twenty-Fifth Amendment also assures continuity of party and administration.

The abolition of the vice presidency also would vitiate the presidential inability provisions of the Twenty-Fifth Amendment that depend on the availability of a Vice President. The Amendment embodies a number of checks and balances designed to protect the President. One such check is that a President's Cabinet, or any body established by Congress, has no power to declare a President disabled without the concurrence of the Vice President. Obviously, substituting in effect the Secretary of State or Speaker for the Vice President would remove this important check and possibly impair the independence of the presidency.

Furthermore, abolishing the office of an elected Vice President in favor of the Speaker's or the Secretary of State's acting temporarily as President in the event of a vacancy would substantially increase the likelihood of persons not elected nationally serving as President. Although Speakers reach their position in Congress by choice of the majority party in the House of Representatives, they are elected to Congress by the voters of but one of the 435 congressional districts in the country and in no way are chosen because of their qualifications as a presidential prospect. The Secretary of State, on the other hand, may never have been elected to any public office. When Harry S. Truman succeeded to the presidency, the presence of Secretary of State Edward R. Stettinius Jr. at the head of the line of succession brought sharp criticism, since he had never been elected to a public office and lacked the type of political experience necessary for the presidency. As a consequence, Stettinius was forced to resign as Secretary of State. A Vice President, however, enjoys a nationwide popular base. Although a vice-presidential candidate is closely tied to his party's presidential candidate, the people elect the Vice President, realizing that he may succeed to the presidency during the ensuing term. Furthermore, a Vice President usually possesses before his election, or acquires while serving as Vice President, the type of governmental and political experience necessary for dealing effectively with Congress in the event of his succession to the presidency. A Vice President, by virtue of his relationship with the President and Congress, is best able to prepare himself for possible succession to the presidency and to make any such succession truly effective. The record of vice-presidential successions, especially in the twentieth century, demonstrates the wisdom of the framers in establishing an office of Vice President.

SPECIAL ELECTION FOR PRESIDENT AND VICE PRESIDENT

The proposals to abolish the vice presidency or to provide for a presidential election for a new President and Vice President whenever a Vice President succeeds to the presidency would change important principles that have operated throughout our experience with presidential succession—those of the stability and continuity of the elected President's four-year term.

A leading advocate of abolishing the vice presidency, the late historian Arthur Schlesinger Jr., emphasized the importance of continuity in urging that the Speakers, because they might be of the opposition party, not act as President during the period of a special election. A change in party control, said Schlesinger, "would be a graver infringement of the democratic principle than the provisional service of an appointed officer as acting President." He added, "Fidelity to the results of the last election and to the requirements of continuity in policy creates, it seems to me, an irresistible argument for returning the line of provisional descent to the executive branch."*[35] It may be observed that this was the rationale used to support the procedures of Section 2 of the Twenty-Fifth Amendment.

The present system of vice-presidential succession assures that a President's party will continue to occupy the presidency for the full four years, thus respecting the four-year electoral mandate, which is a fundamental part of our existing system.†
Procedures for a special presidential election could lend weight to efforts to force an unpopular President from office. Indeed, it is noteworthy that some of those who advocate this proposal believe the Constitution should provide specifically for a special election whenever Congress finds that the President has lost popular confidence.[36]

Another objection to a special presidential election system is that the triggering events (e.g., death of a President and Vice President) might not be conducive to the holding of a special election. As the journalist Max Lerner noted:

> The death, resignation or impeachment of a President is bound to be a scarring event or part of a scarring process. It is a tense, even a tragic, moment. It isn't a good time to hold a presidential convention and election

---

* In its 1975 report, the Subcommittee on Constitutional Amendments stated, "In effect, the Amendment helps insure that the popular mandate from the previous election will be continued throughout the regular four-year term. More rapid changes in policy would tend to promote instability as well as prevent a fair appraisal and evaluation of policies of the political party which had won the previous election." *Id.* 2.

† In a statement to the Senate Judiciary Committee in 1964, Senator Eugene J. McCarthy stated, "The succession law should respect the mandate of the people, who vote not only for a man but also, in a broad way, for his party and his program. The elevation of a leader of another party in midterm is undesirable in principle and could have most unfortunate practical effects." *Hearings on Presidential Inability and Vacancies in the Office of Vice President Before the Subcomm. on Constitutional Amendments of the Senate Comm. on the Judiciary,* 88th Cong. 208 (1964).

campaign, with all their polarizing impact. It is best at that moment to have someone ready and able to act, who has been chosen for the succession and whom the people have come to accept in that role.[37]

James Reston observed that when a "thunderclap of history suddenly carries away a President, either by death or forced resignation," there is a need for "reflection, calm and unity—three qualities seldom present in Presidential elections."[38] Though it may be argued that after a Watergate type of crisis an election might be desirable for its cleansing effects, it is of dubious wisdom to hold one immediately after the assassination or death of a President.* To date, our experiences with presidential succession do not indicate that an election is necessary to furnish a mandate to govern.

The extant proposals for a special election gloss over numerous practical problems. They ignore, for example, such questions as whether a special election would entail the present six-month system of primaries and conventions, followed by a two-month period of post-convention campaigning, and then followed a two-month period of casting, counting, and certifying the votes and declaring the winners. The suggestion of a special election within a period of two or three months disregards a salient feature of the American presidential election system—namely, the importance of a significant pre-convention testing period for candidates to develop and be scrutinized by the people. Donald R. Matthews of the Brookings Institution noted:

> The process that culminates in the popular choice of a president begins years before election day, and a long sequence of events determines the alternatives from which the voters choose. . . . How, and how well, the preliminary screening process works is thus at least as important as what happens on election day. . . .[39]

Under a quick presidential election procedure there is a serious risk that the type of candidates who are now produced might not emerge and that establishment leaders would be given inordinate power in the selection process. Former party candidates, incumbents, and persons of wealth would have a distinct advantage, while newer candidates would have practically no opportunity to develop.† But

---

* In speaking of the widespread remorse and the great outpouring of intense public feeling caused by President Kennedy's assassination, Professor Fred I. Greenstein observed:

> Historical accounts make it clear that at least since the death of Lincoln, every presidential death in office—those of Roosevelt, McKinley, Garfield, and even Harding—have produced similar public responses. Something in presidential incumbency itself evidently has been responsible for these reactions since the deaths of other public figures, including ex-Presidents, were by no means as emotionally moving to such large numbers of citizens.

Choosing the President 124 (Barber ed., 1974).

† Another area in need of analysis is the financing of a special election. In order to compete effectively in any election, candidates generally need time to raise money to cover their campaign costs. Obviously, a special election collapsed into a short period of time would put poorer and less-known candidates at a considerable disadvantage.

bringing into play the present system of nomination and election of a President in a special presidential election process would mean that during the interim period of almost a year the presidency would be occupied by a caretaker, with the possible consequences noted earlier in this chapter.

Another objection is that, under some of the special election proposals, we could have as many as four elections in as many years.* Such a circumstance would leave little time for governing. This remote possibility becomes less remote under the proposal calling for a special presidential election every time an elected Vice President succeeds to the presidency.

Pastore's Special Election Proposal

The proposal advanced by Senator Pastore would institutionalize the caretaker presidency, since a Vice President selected under the Twenty-Fifth Amendment would not become President for the rest of the term but only until a special election is held. Under such circumstances it is questionable whether a succeeding appointed Vice President would be capable of providing effective leadership. And yet it is precisely at such a time, after the loss of the elected President and Vice President, that strong leadership is necessary.

By requiring a special election if more than one year remains in the term, Pastore's proposal entails such impractical situations as the specially elected President and Vice President running immediately again. In fact, two presidential elections could take place in the same year. To illustrate: If a vacancy were to occur late in the third year of a term, the special election cycle would be triggered shortly before the regular quadrennial process is to begin. Such a situation would be confusing and make little sense. Even if the proposal provided that two years must remain in the term before a special election would take place, the following possibility is left open: If the vacancy should occur late in the second year of a term, the special election would take place in the third year and then be followed shortly by the regular quadrennial election in the fourth year. Only a double vacancy occurring in the first year of a term or early in the second year would not be followed on its heels by another presidential election.

The designation under Pastore's proposal of the Speaker of the House of Representatives to act as Vice President in the period preceding a special election would have the additional disadvantage of blending the legislative and executive branches in an undesirable relationship. The Speaker would be placed in an untenable

---

* That is, two regular quadrennial elections plus two special elections. For example, if the principle of vice-presidential succession for the rest of the term were scrapped, the death, resignation, or removal of a President would immediately trigger a special election. Similarly, if one of these events occurred during the tenure of the next President, another special election would take place. At the end of the four-year period that began with the first President, there would be a regular election unless the specially elected President and Vice President were selected for a four-year period.

position if, as Acting Vice President, he or she should participate in the executive decision-making processes of the Cabinet and National Security Council and then, as a member of Congress, participate in the legislative process with respect to executive decisions. The problem would be exacerbated if the Speaker were a member of a different party. The designation of the Speaker as Acting Vice President would also violate the design of the presidential inability features of the Twenty-Fifth Amendment, which contemplate a Vice President of the same party as the President. A President who became disabled and wished to declare his own inability under the procedures of Section 3 might hesitate to do so if the Speaker, unlike the Vice President a person not of the President's choosing, were a member of the other party. Further, the mechanism of Section 4 for declaring a President disabled is premised on the existence of a Vice President of the President's party, in part to prevent Congress from assigning to itself a decision to declare a President disabled. Yet, if the Speaker were the Acting Vice President, Congress, by virtue of its power under Section 4 to replace the Cabinet as the body to function with the Vice President, would be in a position during the interim period to determine a case of inability involving the caretaker.

Finally, since Senator Pastore's proposal would deprive a Vice President of a major part of his existing constitutional function,* it could discourage able persons from accepting a vice-presidential nomination under Section 2. There also might be a tendency for less emphasis to be given in the selection process to a nominee's presidential qualifications since his tenure would be of a caretaker nature.

Statutory Special Election Proposals

The suggestion to amend the 1947 succession law to provide for a special election in the event of double vacancies in the offices of President and Vice President is impractical and dangerous. The matter of a special election is so clouded with uncertainty and controversy that serious questions would be raised after simultaneous vacancies regarding the legitimacy of such a transfer of presidential power, a matter about which there should be absolute certainty. One of the hallmarks of our presidential succession system has been the swift, smooth, unquestioned, and undisputed manner by which presidential power has been transferred whenever a vacancy has occurred in the presidency.

With respect to this proposal, one must start with the question of whether Congress has the power to pass such a law. Though there is evidence that the framers of the Constitution left open in Article II the possibility of a special election, the existence of congressional power to establish such a system has been disputed by a number of constitutional scholars as well as by members of Congress during past discussions of our succession laws.[40] Indeed, in 1867, the House Judiciary

---

* That is, upon succession, serving as President for the rest of the term.

Committee felt there was no such power, although the same committee reached a different conclusion in 1945.[41] One of the principal architects of the 1947 succession law, Senator Burton K. Wheeler of Montana, expressed strong reservations about the constitutionality of a special election law. Others felt that holding such an election would not be practical. As a consequence, the proposal was rejected in the deliberations leading to the 1947 law, and the principle was established that when the Speaker or the President pro tempore acts as President, he does so for the remainder of the President's term (except in a case of inability or failure to qualify).

But even if there were such legislative power, there is the question of the elected President's tenure. Since the Constitution provides only for a four-year term for an elected President and Vice President commencing on January 20, it is unclear whether Congress has the power to provide that a specially elected President and Vice President serve only for the duration of the existing term, which was the basis of the special election proposal advanced during the deliberations on the 1947 law. In view of the provision of Article II that an elected President "shall hold his Office during the term of four years," it is hard to see how Congress could by statute prescribe a shorter term. If Congress were to recognize a four-year term for a specially elected President and Vice President, the present cycle of concurrent presidential and congressional elections would be changed.*

A further question exists concerning the election of a Vice President in a special presidential election. By virtue of the Twelfth Amendment, a President and Vice President are always elected together. Yet the Twenty-Fifth Amendment prescribes a procedure for filling a vice-presidential vacancy. Therefore, it may be argued that whenever a statutory successor acts as President, he is under an obligation to exercise the constitutional power to nominate a Vice President under Section 2 of the Twenty-Fifth Amendment who, when confirmed, would serve out his predecessor's term. Therefore, the argument goes, the availability of the Twenty-Fifth Amendment procedure would preclude the election of a Vice President in a special presidential election.

Special Election for Vice President

The suggestion for filling a vice-presidential vacancy by means of a special vice-presidential election ignores certain practical considerations. If, as has been suggested, the election were open to candidates of both parties, it would be possible for a Vice President to be elected from the opposite party or from a wing of the President's party that is openly antagonistic to him. This possibility would be extremely harmful to the office of President because it would set up a potentially

---

* Of course, a special presidential election could be held at the mid-term congressional elections. For proponents of this approach, see John D. Feerick, *The Vice-Presidency and the Problems of Presidential Succession and Inability*, 32 FORDHAM L. REV. 484 & n.164 (1964).

divisive force within the executive branch. Our two national officers might find themselves at odds on many issues and competing for public attention, thereby contributing to ineffective executive leadership. Indeed, a Vice President of another party or one incompatible with the President might have nothing to do but stir up trouble.

Furthermore, a special election for Vice President would involve changes in Article II, in the Twelfth and Twentieth amendments, and in constitutions and election laws. It would present complicated problems on the nature of the election process—such as whether candidates for Vice President would run in state primaries, be nominated by a national convention, and then campaign for a period of time prior to Election Day. But were there such a cycle, the new Vice President might well enter office with a mandate quite different from that of the President, who would have been chosen at an earlier time. As long as we continue our present system of presidential and vice-presidential candidates running as a team, there seems little justification for a special election for Vice President.

Use of the Most Recent Electoral College

The use of the most recent Electoral College would also introduce problems. There would be little, if any, opportunity for the electors to scrutinize candidates for Vice President, with all the risks the absence of scrutiny entails. Even if they had investigatory powers at their disposal, the electors would be largely unknown and unaccountable to the public. Since their meeting would not be preceded by an election, they would be without any popular mandate in choosing a Vice President. This would vest in a body generally viewed as being without discretionary authority a considerable amount of discretion. Such circumstances could produce a situation in which a majority of the electors would be unable to agree on one candidate. Indeed, the special election and Electoral College proposals for filling a vice-presidential vacancy would increase the risk of having to resort to the present procedure of the Twelfth Amendment involving the Senate only, since such an election likely would encourage a number of candidates to get into the field, with the resultant possibility of no one's winning a majority of the electoral votes. It would be ironic if, after providing for a special vice-presidential election, the selection had to be made by Congress anyway, and by only one body of the Congress at that.

CONCLUDING REFLECTIONS

In the final analysis, there is an insufficient historical track record to justify a revision of the Twenty-Fifth Amendment. On the contrary, the Amendment, as noted, worked quite well in handling the presidential succession crises of 1973 and 1974. It is true, on the other hand, that the Amendment did not work as it was intended in 1981 and 1985. In my opinion, these failures do not reflect a basic weakness in the Amendment, as they were born out of procedural and political considerations.

Additionally, criticisms of the Reagan administration's failure to invoke the Twenty-Fifth Amendment have helped ensure, in my view, that if similar incidents occur, the Amendment will be invoked. These incidents, as evidenced by steps taken by the George H.W. Bush administration and the exercise of Section 3 by President George W. Bush, have paved the way for the invocation of the Amendment whenever a President is disabled through the use of anesthesia or otherwise seriously challenged by issues of inability.

It is worth remembering that the enduring brilliance of the U.S. Constitution is due in no small part to trust—the trust that people have in the Constitution and in the system of government arising from it, in the men and women who govern under it, and ultimately in the people who rule themselves through it.

Finally, it is helpful to recall that from 1789 until 1967, the nation, for all practical purposes, operated without any constitutional provisions governing cases of presidential inability. The establishment of such provisions was rendered exceedingly difficult because of the widespread divergence of opinion on the way to deal with such cases. After great debate and consideration and many compromises, a widespread consensus developed that the Amendment met the nation's needs; at the same time, it was recognized that it was not perfect and did not cover every contingency. As Walter Lippman said of the Amendment, "I[t] is . . . a great deal better than an endless search for . . . the absolutely perfect solution which will never be found, and . . . is not necessary."[42]

18

Recommendations

In the end, in dealing with so fundamental a structure as succession to the Presidency, the best guide is the maxim if there is no need to change, there is need not to change.

PAUL A. FREUND, March 11, 1975[1]

In early writings, first for the *Fordham Law Review* in 1963 and 1964, and then in *From Failing Hands*, this author took aim at laying out ideas on the subject of presidential inability and the vice presidency. Before arriving at these views, I considered political arrangements in colonial America, the succession provisions of the early state constitutions, the debates at the Constitutional Convention of 1787 and in the state ratifying conventions, and then the enormous history that developed in the area of presidential inability and with respect to the vice presidency. I benefited greatly from the congressional debates and hearings on matters of presidential succession in the period from 1881 to 1963, the approaches taken by the Eisenhower and Kennedy administrations in addressing the issue of presidential inability, and the enormous scholarship that occurred in these fields as reflected in books, law review and newspaper articles, and most especially in the pioneering work of Ruth Silva. I studied the succession approaches of other nations with respect to their executives and the arrangements adopted in each of the fifty states for the handling of succession to the office of governor. *From Failing Hands* sets forth the results of my research and provided my recommendations and supporting reasoning. The publication of the book in 1965 was before the Twenty-Fifth Amendment was acted on in Congress, leading to an effort by me to complete the journey begun in 1961, upon my law school graduation, by undertaking a treatise on the Amendment itself, resulting in the 1976 publication of *The Twenty-Fifth Amendment: Its Complete History and Applications*.

It seemed to me from the beginning that the determination of presidential inability belonged in the executive branch. I believe this is important in protecting the term of four years to which the President has been elected by the people. I believe it important to the principle of separation of powers that is at the foundation of the U.S. Constitution. I therefore supported the approaches of S. J. Res. 139 and the American Bar Association consensus on presidential inability and vice-presidential vacancy and gave supporting testimony at the initial hearings of the Senate Subcommittee on Constitutional Amendments, chaired by Senator Birch Bayh. I strongly pressed the point of separation of powers, undoubtedly influenced by a paper I wrote on the subject as a student at Fordham College.

Beyond presidential inability and vice-presidential vacancy reform, I urged a reexamination of the statutory line of succession, noting the legal objections by many scholars and the framers of the Constitution as to the placement of legislative officers in the line and the threat to the principle of party continuity wherein leaders of Congress were in a political party different from the President's. I also suggested lengthening the line of succession, improving the process of choosing Vice Presidents, and dealing with contingencies, such as death and disability, that might occur in the pre-inaugural period. I was pleased to participate in a program on vice-presidential selection sponsored by the *Fordham Law Review* in 1976, where many good ideas were discussed, and another program by the *Fordham Law Review* in 2010, entitled "The Adequacy of the Presidential Succession System in the 21st Century: Filling the Gaps and Clarifying the Ambiguities in Constitutional and Extra-constitutional Arrangements." Following the program, I was asked by Dean William Treanor to serve as one of three professors in a presidential succession clinic that, after a year of detailed and exhaustive study, has offered many recommendations for improvements in the system. Suffice it to say, I am in almost total agreement with those recommendations. The nine law students in the clinic, of different backgrounds and political party affiliations, felt strongly that legislative leaders should not be in the line at all. Their point of view has strong scholarly support behind it. This writer was originally of that persuasion (for legal and policy reasons) but now can see no reform, which is long overdue, of the succession law of 1947 occurring, if the price involves the removal of the legislative officers entirely from the line of succession. The Fordham Law School presidential succession clinic report[*] has given us a twenty-first-century reform agenda worthy of serious consideration.[*]

---

* See pages 249–53, *supra*, of the report, where its recommendations are laid out and thoroughly discussed. This author could accept, however, unlike the students, retaining legislators in the line of succession, provided they were the leaders of the President's party, also a continuation of Acting Secretaries, provided they are placed at the end of the statutory line, as their continuation furnishes an additional "security blanket" in case of a mass catastrophe. *See* John D. Feerick, *A Response to Akhil*

While the author, along with the Fordham Law Clinic, believes that no change in the Twenty-Fifth Amendment ought to be made, quite clearly changes in the operation of the Amendment are justified. As the Miller Commission usefully suggested, invocations of the Amendment should be planned for. Such planning should be carefully developed early in each administration, based on medical, political, and constitutional considerations. To its credit, the administration of George H.W. Bush acted upon the Miller Commission's recommendations by adopting specific guidelines to enable it to handle future instances of presidential inability effectively. By adopting specific guidelines, the Bush administration properly recognized the need to prepare for cases of presidential inability. Subsequent presidential administrations have built on this precedent. Fred Fielding noted that

> one of the first things I did when I became Counsel to President Reagan was to put my staff to work on preparing a book, it was going to be a comprehensive book. It was really kind of an emergency manual, which detailed every possible scenario that we could think of for presidential inability or even vice presidential inability.[2]

Fielding said he always carried the book with him and kept one in his White House safe. It was passed on to the next administration. He added, "I was delighted when I went back into the White House this last time, to see that book not only exists, but it's very nicely bound, and it's not only in the Counsel's office, but it's in every emergency facility and permanently in *Air Force One* and *Air Force Two*."[3] This is a healthy precedent for future Presidents. Such planning best serves the Twenty-Fifth Amendment's goal of providing a framework for succession and inability without unduly binding the hands of those officials who may have to confront those incidents.

The swift manner by which presidential power has been transferred upon the deaths in office of eight Presidents and the resignation of one President has demonstrated the stability and continuity of our government. In every case the succession has been peaceful, and no question has been raised as to the legitimacy of the successor's occupancy of the White House.* Since the presidency is such a vital part of the structure of our government, there must never be any doubt about the adequacy of the country's laws on election and succession to that office. In the history of our country the absence of procedures for dealing with cases of presidential inability had proved to be a great deficiency in the system, and the devising

---

Reed Amar's Address on Applications and Implications of the Twenty-Fifth Amendment, 47 Hous. L. Rev. 41, 61–64 (2010).
* But see Tyler's claim to be President and not Vice President acting as President. *Supra*, Chapter 1.

of an effective system of succession beyond the vice presidency a recurrent problem. The adoption and re-adoption of succession statutes, often based on the personalities of the people occupying the particular offices at the time, and the growth in the importance of the vice presidency had underscored the need for a better approach to situations involving the loss of a President or Vice President and the accompanying vacancy in the vice presidency.

After long and great study, the Twenty-Fifth Amendment was adopted to remedy these demonstrated needs and deficiencies. The Amendment was the result of a conscious effort by its drafters to create a general and flexible framework for succession to the presidency. It is designed to respect and preserve the separation of powers among the branches of government and to allow the officials who confront succession crises to address them with discretion and as the circumstances and the times warrant. The Amendment does not presume to prescribe binding, narrowly tailored rules for the resolution of often unpredictable situations that might arise far in the future.

Nothing in the record to date indicates that there is a superior remedy for dealing with the complex problems involved. The Amendment deals with these problems practically, in a manner consistent with the principle of separation of powers, and in a way that protects the office of President and ensures stability and continuity in the event of succession.* It gives the decisive role only to those in whom the American people most likely would have confidence. It involves only persons who have been elected by the people or approved by their chosen representatives, and it embodies checks on all concerned—the President, Vice President, Cabinet, and Congress. Thus, under the inability procedures of the Amendment, neither the Vice President nor the Cabinet can declare a President disabled without the concurrence of the other, and if a President disagrees with their declaration, he is in a position to have the dispute resolved by Congress in accordance with procedures weighted heavily in his favor. Similarly, under the vice-presidential vacancy procedures of the Amendment, a President's nomination requires approval by both Houses of Congress, so that each House has a check on the other.

Therefore, in the consideration of any change in the Twenty-Fifth Amendment, attention must be given to the interrelationship of its provisions, and to the fact

---

* Senator John L. McClellan of Arkansas appropriately noted during the 1965 Senate debates:

> To cope with the problems of Presidential inability and vacancies in the Office of the Vice President, we must provide means for orderly transition of Executive power in a manner that respects the separation of powers concept and maintains the safeguards of our traditional checks and balances system. Finally, any such provision must have the confidence and support of our people if it is to accomplish the desired results.

111 CONG. REC. 3275 (1965).

that history provides examples of new rules' producing unexpected and undesirable results. As Sidney Hyman, a noted authority on the presidency, once observed, "Every constitutional system must pay some price in weakness for the element of strength it has. Not everything is [solvable]. Not everything can be controlled by law."[4]

Appendixes

Appendix A*

Section-by-Section Development of the Twenty-Fifth Amendment

SECTION I

As Introduced in the Senate in 1963 and 1964

SECTION 1. In case of the removal of the President from office, or of his death or resignation, the Vice President shall become President for the unexpired portion of the then current term. Within a period of thirty days thereafter, the new President shall nominate a Vice President who shall take office upon confirmation by both Houses of Congress by a majority of those present and voting.

As Passed by the Senate in 1964

SECTION 1. In case of the removal of the President from office or of his death or resignation, the Vice President shall become President.

As Passed by the Senate in February 1965

SECTION 1. In case of the removal of the President from office or of his death or resignation, the Vice President shall become President.

---

* The history recorded relates to S. J. Res. 139, S. J. Res. 1 and H. J. Res. 1, but there are derivatives, including S. J. Res. 161 (1958), S. J. Res. 19 (1961), and H. J. Res. 529 (1961). *See generally* 17 Rec. Ass'n B. City N.Y. 185 (1962). Not included in the history contained in this Appendix A are the provisions of the Conference Committee report, dated June 23, 1965, because the report essentially became the final form of the then-proposed amendment. See Chapter 6, *infra*.

As Passed by the House in April 1965

SECTION 1. In case of the removal of the President from office or of his death or resignation, the Vice President shall become President.

Final Form

SECTION 1. In case of the removal of the President from office or of his death or resignation, the Vice President shall become President.

SECTION 2

As Introduced in the Senate in 1963 and 1964

SEC. 2. In case of the removal of the Vice President from office, or of his death or resignation, the President, within a period of thirty days thereafter, shall nominate a Vice President who shall take office upon confirmation by both Houses of Congress by a majority vote of those present and voting.

As Passed by the Senate in 1964

SEC. 2. Whenever there is a vacancy in the office of the Vice President, the President shall nominate a Vice President who shall take office upon confirmation by a majority vote of both Houses of Congress.

As Passed by the Senate in February 1965

SEC. 2. Whenever there is a vacancy in the office of the Vice President, the President shall nominate a Vice President who shall take office upon confirmation by a majority vote of both Houses of Congress.

As Passed by the House in April 1965

SEC. 2. Whenever there is a vacancy in the office of the Vice President, the President shall nominate a Vice President who shall take office upon confirmation by a majority vote of both Houses of Congress.

Final Form

SEC. 2. Whenever there is a vacancy in the office of the Vice President, the President shall nominate a Vice President who shall take office upon confirmation by a majority vote of both Houses of Congress.

SECTION 3

As Introduced in the Senate in 1963 and 1964

SEC. 3. If the President shall declare in writing that he is unable to discharge the powers and duties of his office, such powers and duties shall be discharged by the Vice President as Acting President.

As Passed by the Senate in 1964

SEC. 3. If the President declares in writing that he is unable to discharge the powers and duties of his office, such powers and duties shall be discharged by the Vice President as Acting President.

As Passed by the Senate in February 1965

SEC. 3. Whenever the President transmits to the President of the Senate and the Speaker of the House of Representatives his written declaration that he is unable to discharge the powers and duties of his office, such powers and duties shall be discharged by the Vice President as Acting President.

As Passed by the House in April 1965

SEC. 3. Whenever the President transmits to the President pro tempore of the Senate and the Speaker of the House of Representatives his written declaration that he is unable to discharge the powers and duties of his office, and until he transmits a written declaration to the contrary, such powers and duties shall be discharged by the Vice President as Acting President.

Final Form

SEC. 3. Whenever the President transmits to the President pro tempore of the Senate and the Speaker of the House of Representatives his written declaration that he is unable to discharge the powers and duties of his office, and until he transmits to them a written declaration to the contrary, such powers and duties shall be discharged by the Vice President as Acting President.

SECTION 4

As Introduced in the Senate in 1963 and 1964

SEC. 4. If the President does not so declare, the Vice President, if satisfied that such inability exists, shall, upon the written approval of a majority of the heads of the executive departments in office, assume the discharge of the powers and duties as Acting President.

As Passed by the Senate in 1964

SEC. 4. If the President does not so declare, and the Vice President with the written concurrence of a majority of the heads of the executive departments or such other body as Congress may by law provide, transmits to the Congress his written declaration that the President is unable to discharge the powers and duties of his office, the Vice President shall immediately assume the powers and duties of the office as Acting President.

As Passed by the Senate in February 1965

SEC. 4. Whenever the Vice President, and a majority of the principal officers of the executive departments or such other body as Congress may by law provide, transmit to the President of the Senate and the Speaker of the House of Representatives their written declaration that the President is unable to discharge the powers and duties of his office, the Vice President shall immediately assume the powers and duties of the office as Acting President.

As Passed by the House in April 1965

SEC. 4. Whenever the Vice President and a majority of the principal officers of the executive departments, or such other body as Congress may by law provide, transmit to the President pro tempore of the Senate and the Speaker of the House of Representatives their written declaration that the President is unable to discharge the powers and duties of his office, the Vice President shall immediately assume the powers and duties of the office as Acting President.

Thereafter, when the President transmits to the President pro tempore of the Senate and the Speaker of the House of Representatives his written declaration that no inability exists, he shall resume the powers and duties of his office unless the Vice President and a majority of the principal officers of the executive departments, or such other body as Congress may by law provide, transmit within two days to the President pro tempore of the Senate and the Speaker of the House of Representatives their written declaration that the President is unable to discharge the powers and duties of his office. Thereupon Congress shall decide the issue, assembling within forty-eight hours for that purpose if not in session. If the Congress, within ten days after the receipt of the written declaration of the Vice President and a majority of the principal officers of the executive departments, or such other body as Congress may by law provide, determines by two-thirds vote of both Houses that the President is unable to discharge the powers and duties of the office, the Vice President shall continue to discharge the same as Acting President; otherwise, the President shall resume the powers and duties of his office.

Final Form

Sec. 4. Whenever the Vice President and a majority of either the principal officers of the executive departments or of such other body as Congress may by law provide, transmit to the President pro tempore of the Senate and the Speaker of the House of Representatives their written declaration that the President is unable to discharge the powers and duties of his office, the Vice President shall immediately assume the powers and duties of the office as Acting President.

Thereafter, when the President transmits to the President pro tempore of the Senate and the Speaker of the House of Representatives his written declaration that no inability exists, he shall resume the powers and duties of his office unless the Vice President and a majority of either the principal officers of the executive department or of such other body as Congress may by law provide, transmit within four days to the President pro tempore of the Senate and the Speaker of the House of Representatives their written declaration that the President is unable to discharge the powers and duties of his office. Thereupon Congress shall decide the issue, assembling within forty-eight hours for that purpose if not in session. If the Congress, within twenty-one days after receipt of the latter written declaration, or, if Congress is not in session, within twenty-one days after Congress is required to assemble, determines by two-thirds vote of both Houses that the President is unable to discharge the powers and duties of his office, the Vice President shall continue to discharge the same as Acting President; otherwise, the President shall resume the powers and duties of his office.

SECTION 5

As Introduced in the Senate in 1963 and 1964

Sec. 5. Whenever the President makes public announcement in writing that his inability has terminated, he shall resume the discharge of the powers and duties of his office on the seventh day after making such announcement, or at such earlier time after such announcement as he and the Vice President may determine. But if the Vice President, with the written approval of a majority of the heads of executive departments in office at the time of such announcement, transmits to the Congress his written declaration that in his opinion the President's inability has not terminated, the Congress shall thereupon consider the issue. If the Congress is not then in session, it shall assemble in special session on the call of the Vice President. If the Congress determines by concurrent resolution, adopted with the approval of two-thirds of the Members present in each House, that the inability of the President has not terminated, thereupon, notwithstanding any further announcement by the President, the Vice President shall discharge such powers and duties as Acting President until the occurrence of the earliest of the following events: (1) the Acting President proclaims that the President's inability has ended, (2) the Congress determines by concurrent resolution, adopted with the approval of a majority of the Members present in each House, that the President's inability has ended, or (3) the President's term ends.

As Passed by the Senate in 1964

SEC. 5. Whenever the President transmits to the Congress his written declaration that no inability exists, he shall resume the powers and duties of his office unless the Vice President, with the written concurrence of a majority of the heads of the executive departments or such other body as Congress may by law provide, transmits within two days to the Congress his written declaration that the President is unable to discharge the powers and duties of his office. Thereupon Congress shall immediately decide the issue. If the Congress determines by two-thirds vote of both Houses that the President is unable to discharge the powers and duties of the office, the Vice President shall continue to discharge the same as Acting President; otherwise the President shall resume the powers and duties of his office.

As Passed by the Senate in February 1965

SEC. 5. Whenever the President transmits to the President of the Senate and the Speaker of the House of Representatives his written declaration that no inability exists, he shall resume the powers and duties of his office unless the Vice President, with the written concurrence of a majority of the principal officers of the executive departments or such other body as Congress may by law provide, transmits within seven days to the President of the Senate and the Speaker of the House of Representatives their written declaration that the President is unable to discharge the powers and duties of his office. Thereupon Congress shall immediately proceed to decide the issue. If the Congress determines by two-thirds vote of both Houses that the President is unable to discharge the powers and duties of the office, the Vice President shall continue to discharge the same as Acting President; otherwise the President shall resume the powers and duties of his office.

SECTION 6

As Introduced in the Senate in 1963 and 1964

SEC. 6 (a)(1) If, by reason of death, resignation, removal from office, inability, or failure to qualify, there is neither a President nor Vice President to discharge the powers and duties of the office of the President, then the officer of the United States who is highest on list, and who is not under disability to discharge the powers and duties of the office of President, shall act as President: Secretary of State, Secretary of Treasury, Secretary of Defense, Attorney General, Postmaster General, Secretary of Interior, Secretary of Agriculture, Secretary of Commerce, Secretary of Labor, Secretary of Health, Education and Welfare, and such other heads of executive departments as may be established hereafter and in order of their establishment.

(2) The same rule shall apply in the case of the death, resignation, removal from office, or inability of an individual acting as President under this section.

(3) To qualify under this section, an individual must have been appointed, by and with the advice and consent of the Senate, prior to the time of the death, resignation, removal from office, or inability of the President and Vice President, and must not be under impeachment by the House of Representatives at the time the powers and duties of the office of President devolve upon him.

(b) In case of the death, resignation, or removal of both the President and Vice President, his successor shall be President until the expiration of the then current presidential term. In case of the inability of the President and Vice President to discharge the powers and duties of the office of President, his successor, as designated in this section, shall be subject to the provisions of sections 3, 4, and 5 of this article as if he were a Vice President acting in case of disability of the President.

(c) The taking of the oath of office by an individual specified in the list of paragraph (1) of subsection (a) shall be held to constitute his resignation from the office by virtue of the holding of which he qualifies to act as President.

(d) During the period that any individual acts as President under this section, his compensation shall be at the rate then provided by law in the case of the President.

SECTION 7

As Introduced in the Senate in 1963 and 1964

SEC. 7. This article shall be inoperative unless it shall have been ratified as an amendment to the Constitution by the legislature of three-fourths of the several States within seven years from the date of its submission.

Appendix B

Constitutional Provisions on Succession

TWENTY-FIFTH AMENDMENT

SECTION 1. In case of the removal of the President from office or of his death or resignation, the Vice President shall become President.

SEC. 2. Whenever there is a vacancy in the office of the Vice President, the President shall nominate a Vice President who shall take office upon confirmation by a majority vote of both Houses of Congress.

SEC. 3. Whenever the President transmits to the President pro tempore of the Senate and the Speaker of the House of Representatives his written declaration that he is unable to discharge the powers and duties of his office, and until he transmits to them a written declaration to the contrary, such powers and duties shall be discharged by the Vice President as Acting President.

SEC. 4. Whenever the Vice President and a majority of either the principal officers of the executive departments or of such other body as Congress may by law provide, transmit to the President pro tempore of the Senate and the Speaker of the House of Representatives their written declaration that the President is unable to discharge the powers and duties of his office, the Vice President shall immediately assume the powers and duties of the office as Acting President.

Thereafter, when the President transmits to the President pro tempore of the Senate and the Speaker of the House of Representatives his written declaration that no inability exists, he shall resume the powers and duties of his office unless the Vice President and a majority of either the principal officers of the executive department or of such other body as Congress may by law provide, transmit within four days to the President pro tempore of the Senate and the Speaker of the House of Representatives their written declaration that the President is unable to discharge the powers and duties of his office. Thereupon Congress shall decide the issue, assembling within forty-eight hours for that purpose if not in session. If the Congress, within twenty-one days after receipt of the latter written declaration, or, if Congress is not in session, within twenty-one days after Congress is required to assemble, determines by two-thirds vote of both Houses that the President is unable to discharge the powers and duties of his office, the Vice President shall continue to discharge the same as Acting President; otherwise, the President shall resume the powers and duties of his office.

TWENTIETH AMENDMENT

SECTION 1. The terms of the President and Vice President shall end at noon on the 20th day of January, and the terms of Senators and Representatives at noon on the 3d day of January, of the years in which such terms would have ended if this article had not been ratified; and the terms of their successors shall then begin.

SEC. 2. The Congress shall assemble at least once in every year, and such meeting shall begin at noon on the 3d day of January, unless they shall by law appoint a different day.

SEC. 3. If, at the time fixed for the beginning of the term of the President, the President elect shall have died, the Vice President elect shall become President. If a President shall not have been chosen before the time fixed for the beginning of his term, or if the President elect shall have failed to qualify, then the Vice President elect shall act as President until a President shall have qualified; and the Congress may by law provide for the case wherein neither a President elect nor a Vice President elect shall have qualified, declaring who shall then act as President, or the manner in which one who is to act shall be selected, and such person shall act accordingly until a President or Vice President shall have qualified.

SEC. 4. The Congress may by law provide for the case of the death of any of the persons from whom the House of Representatives may choose a President whenever the right of choice shall have devolved upon them, and for the case of the death of any of the persons from whom the Senate may choose a Vice President whenever the right of choice shall have devolved upon them.

SEC. 5. Sections 1 and 2 shall take effect on the 15th day of October following the ratification of this article.

SEC. 6. This article shall be inoperative unless it shall have been ratified as an amendment to the Constitution by the legislatures of three-fourths of the several States within seven years from the date of its submission.

TWELFTH AMENDMENT

The Electors shall meet in their respective states, and vote by ballot for President and Vice-President, one of whom, at least, shall not be an inhabitant of the same state with themselves; they shall name in their ballots the person voted for as President, and in distinct ballots the person voted for as Vice-President, and they shall make distinct lists of all persons voted for as President, and of all persons voted for as Vice-President and of the number of votes for each, which lists they shall sign and certify, and transmit sealed to the seat of the government of the United States, directed to the President of the Senate;

The President of the Senate shall, in the presence of the Senate and House of Representatives, open all the certificates and the votes shall then be counted;

The person having the greatest number of votes for President, shall be the President, if such number be a majority of the whole number of Electors appointed; and if no person have such majority, then from the persons having the highest numbers not exceeding three on the list of those voted for as President, the House of Representatives shall choose immediately, by ballot, the President. But in choosing the President, the votes shall be taken by states, the representation from each state having one vote; a quorum for this purpose shall consist of a member or members from two-thirds of the states, and a majority of all the states shall be necessary to a choice. And if the House of Representatives shall not choose a President whenever the right of choice shall devolve upon them, before the fourth day of March next following, then the Vice-President shall act as President, as in the case of the death or other constitutional disability of the President;

The person having the greatest number of votes as Vice-President, shall be the Vice-President, if such number be a majority of the whole number of Electors appointed, and if no person have a majority, then from the two highest numbers on the list, the Senate shall choose the Vice-President; a quorum for the purpose shall consist of two-thirds of the whole number of Senators, and a majority of the whole number shall be necessary to a choice. But no person constitutionally ineligible to the office of President shall be eligible to that of Vice President of the United States.

ARTICLE II, SECTION I, CLAUSE 6

In Case of the Removal of the President from Office, or of his Death, Resignation, or Inability to discharge the Powers and Duties of the said Office, the Same shall devolve on the Vice President, and the Congress may by Law provide for the Case of Removal, Death, Resignation or Inability, both of the President and Vice President, declaring what Officer shall then act as President, and such Officer shall act accordingly, until the Disability be removed, or a President shall be elected.

Appendix C

Statutory Succession Laws

ACT OF JULY 18, 1947, AS AMENDED

(a) (1) If, by reason of death, resignation, removal from office, inability, or failure to qualify, there is neither a President nor Vice-President to discharge the powers and duties of the office of President, then the Speaker of the House of Representatives shall, upon his resignation as Speaker and as Representative in Congress, act as President.

(2) The same rule shall apply in the case of the death, resignation, removal from office, or inability of an individual acting as President under this subsection.

(b) If, at the time when under subsection (a) of this section a Speaker is to begin the discharge of the powers and duties of the office of President, there is no Speaker, or the Speaker fails to qualify as Acting President, then the President *pro tempore* of the Senate shall, upon his resignation as President pro tempore and as Senator, act as President.

(c) An individual acting as President under subsection (a) or subsection (b) of this section shall continue to act until the expiration of the then current presidential term, except that—

(1) If his discharge of the powers and duties of the office is founded in whole or in part on the failure of both the President-elect and the Vice-President-elect to qualify, then he shall act only until a President or Vice President qualifies; and

(2) If his discharge of the powers and duties of the office is founded in whole or in part on the inability of the President or Vice-President, then he shall act only until the removal of the disability of one of such individuals.

(d) (1) If, by reason of death, resignation, removal from office, inability, or failure to qualify, there is no President *pro tempore* to act as President under subsection

(b) of this section, then the officer of the United States who is highest on the following list, and who is not under disability to discharge the powers and duties of the office of President shall act as President: Secretary of State, Secretary of the Treasury, Secretary of Defense, Attorney General, Secretary of the Interior, Secretary of Agriculture, Secretary of Commerce, Secretary of Labor, Secretary of Health and Human Services, Secretary of Housing and Urban Development, Secretary of Transportation, Secretary of Energy, Secretary of Education, Secretary of Veterans Affairs, Secretary of Homeland Security.

(2) An individual acting as President under this subsection shall continue so to do until the expiration of the then current presidential term, but not after a qualified and prior-entitled individual is able to act, except that the removal of the disability of an individual higher on the list contained in paragraph (1) of this subsection or the ability to qualify on the part of an individual higher on such list shall not terminate his service.

(3) The taking of the oath of office by an individual specified in the list in paragraph (1) of this subsection shall be held to constitute his resignation from the office by virtue of the holding of which he qualifies to act as President.

(e) Subsections (a), (b), and (d) of this section shall apply only to such officers as are eligible to the office of President under the Constitution. Subsection (d) of this section shall apply only to officers appointed, by and with the advice and consent of the Senate, prior to the time of the death, resignation, removal from office, inability, or failure to qualify, of the President *pro tempore*, and only to officers not under impeachment by the House of Representatives at the time the powers and duties of the office of President devolve upon them.

(f) During the period that any individual acts as President under this section, his compensation shall be at the rate then provided by law in the case of the President.

ACT OF JANUARY 19, 1886

SEC. 1. *Be it enacted by the Senate and House of Representatives of the United States of America in Congress assembled*, That in case of removal, death, resignation, or inability of both the President and Vice-President of the United States, the Secretary of State, or if there be none, or in case of his removal, death, resignation, or inability, then the Secretary of the Treasury, or if there be none, or in case of his removal, death, resignation, or inability, then the Secretary of War, or if there be none, or in case of his removal, death, resignation, or inability, then the Attorney-General, or if there be none, or in case of his removal, death, resignation, or inability, then the Postmaster-General, or if there be none, or in case of his removal, death, resignation, or inability, then the Secretary of the Navy, or if there be none, or in case of his removal, death, resignation, or inability, then the Secretary of the Interior, shall act as President until the disability of the President or Vice-President is removed or a President shall be elected: *Provided*, That whenever the powers and duties of the office of President of the United States shall devolve upon any of the persons named herein, if Congress be not then in session, or if it would not meet in accordance with law within twenty days thereafter, it shall be the duty of the person upon whom said powers and duties shall devolve to issue a proclamation convening Congress in extraordinary session, giving twenty days' notice of the time of meeting.

SEC. 2. That the preceding section shall only be held to describe and apply to such officers as shall have been appointed by the advice and consent of the Senate to the offices therein named, and such as are eligible to the office of President under the Constitution, and not under impeachment by the House of Representatives of the United States at the time the powers and duties of the office shall devolve upon them respectively.

SEC. 3. That sections one hundred and forty-six, one hundred and forty-seven, one hundred and forty-eight, one hundred and forty-nine, and one hundred and fifty of the Revised Statutes are hereby repealed.

ACT OF MARCH 1, 1792

SEC. 9. *And be it further enacted*, That in case of removal, death, resignation or inability both of the President and Vice President of the United States, the President of the Senate pro tempore, and in case there shall be no President of the Senate [pro tempore], then the Speaker of the House of Representatives, for the time being shall act as President of the United States until the disability be removed or a President shall be elected.

SEC. 10. *And be it further enacted*, That whenever the offices of President and Vice President shall both become vacant, the Secretary of State shall forthwith cause a notification thereof to be made to the executive of every state, and shall also cause the same to be published in at least one of the newspapers printed in each state, specifying that electors of the President of the United States shall be appointed or chosen in the several states within thirty-four days preceding the first Wednesday in December then next ensuing: *Provided*, There shall be the space of two months between the date of such notification and the said first Wednesday in December, but if there shall not be the space of two months between the date of such notification and the first Wednesday in December; and if the term for which the President and Vice President last in office were elected shall not expire on the third day of March next ensuing, then the Secretary of State shall specify in the notification that the electors shall be appointed or chosen within thirty-four days preceding the first Wednesday in December in the year next ensuing, within which time the electors shall accordingly be appointed or chosen, and the electors shall meet and give their votes on the first Wednesday in December, and the proceedings and duties of the said electors and others shall be pursuant to the directions prescribed in this act.

Appendix D
Presidential and Vice-Presidential Vacancies

Presidential Vacancies

President	Term for Which Elected	Date of Vacancy	Vice President Who Succeeded	Date Oath Taken	Length of Unexpired Term[a] Years	Months	Days
1. William H. Harrison	March 4, 1841–45	April 4, 1841	John Tyler	April 6, 1841	3	11	0
2. Zachary Taylor	March 4, 1849–53	July 9, 1850	Millard Fillmore	July 10, 1850	2	7	23
3. Abraham Lincoln[b]	March 4, 1865–69	April 15, 1865	Andrew Johnson	April 15, 1865	3	10	17
4. James A. Garfield[b]	March 4, 1881–85	September 19, 1881	Chester A. Arthur	September 20, 1881 and September 22, 1881	3	5	13
5. William McKinley[b]	March 4, 1901–5	September 14, 1901	Theodore Roosevelt	September 14, 1901	3	5	18
6. Warren G. Harding	March 4, 1921–25	August 2, 1923	Calvin Coolidge	August 3, 1923 and August 21, 1923	1	7	2
7. Franklin D. Roosevelt	January 20, 1945–49	April 12, 1945	Harry S. Truman	April 12, 1945	3	9	8
8. John F. Kennedy[b]	January 20, 1961–65	November 22, 1963	Lyndon B. Johnson	November 22, 1963	1	1	29
9. Richard M. Nixon	January 20, 1973–77	August 9, 1974	Gerald R. Ford	August 9, 1974	2	5	11
TOTAL:					26	3	28

a. The computation is based on the dates of the President's death or resignation.

b. Presidents who were assassinated; the other Presidents died in office, except Richard Nixon, who resigned.

Vice-Presidential Vacancies

Vice President	Period for Which Chosen	Termination of Service[a]	Reason for Termination	Length of Vacancy		
				Years	Months	DAYS
1. George Clinton	March 4, 1809–13	April 20, 1812	Death		10	12
2. Elbridge Gerry	March 4, 1813–17	November 23, 1814	Death	2	3	9
3. John C. Calhoun	March 4, 1829–33	December 28, 1832	Resignation		2	4
4. John Tyler	March 4, 1841–45	April 4, 1841	Succession	3	11	0
5. Millard Fillmore	March 4, 1849–53	July 9, 1850	Succession	2	7	23
6. William R. King	March 4, 1853–57	April 18, 1853	Death	3	10	14
7. Andrew Johnson	March 4, 1865–69	April 15, 1865	Succession	3	10	17
8. Henry Wilson	March 4, 1873–77	November 22, 1875	Death	1	3	10
9. Chester A. Arthur	March 4, 1881–85	September 19, 1881	Succession	3	5	13
10. Thomas A. Hendricks	March 4, 1885–89	November 25, 1885	Death	3	3	7
11. Garrett A. Hobart	March 4, 1897–1901	November 21, 1899	Death	1	3	11
12. Theodore Roosevelt	March 4, 1901–5	September 14, 1901	Succession	3	5	18
13. James S. Sherman	March 4, 1909–13	October 30, 1912	Death		4	5
14. Calvin Coolidge	March 4, 1921–25	August 2, 1923	Succession	1	7	2
15. Harry S. Truman	January 20, 1945–49	April 12, 1945	Succession	3	9	8
16. Lyndon B. Johnson	January 20, 1961–65	November 22, 1963	Succession	1	1	29
17. Spiro T. Agnew	January 20, 1973–77	October 10, 1973	Resignation		1	26
18. Gerald R. Ford	December 6, 1973–77	August 9, 1974	Succession		4	10
TOTAL				37	9	1

a. In the case of a Vice President who succeeded to the presidency, the date of the President's death or resignation is treated as the date of termination.

Appendix E

Times During Which the Speaker, the President pro tempore, or Both Were from a Party Different from the President's

Congress	President and Party[a]	Speaker and Party[a]	President Pro Tempore and Party[a]
20th, 1827–1829	John Quincy Adams—C(DR)	Andrew Stevenson—J	Samuel Smith—J
28th, 1843–1845	John Tyler—W	John W. Jones—D	Willie P. Mangum—W
30th, 1847–1849	James K. Polk—D	Robert C. Winthrop—W	David R. Atchison—W
31st, 1849–1851	Zachary Taylor } W Millard Fillmore	Howell Cobb—D	David R. Atchison—W William R. King—D
32nd, 1851–1853	Millard Fillmore—W	Linn Boyd—D	William R. King—D David R. Atchison—W
34th, 1853–1857	Franklin Pierce—D	Nathaniel P. Banks—R	Jesse D. Bright—D Charles E. Stuart—D James M. Mason—D
36th, 1859–1861	James Buchanan—D	William Pennington—R	Benjamin Fitzpatrick—D Jesse D. Bright—D Solomon Foot—R
44th, 1875–1877	Ulysses S. Grant—R	Michael C. Kerr—D Samuel J. Randall—D	Thomas W. Ferry—R
45th, 1877–1879	Rutherford B. Hayes—R	Samuel J. Randall—D	Thomas W. Ferry—R
46th, 1879–1881	Rutherford B. Hayes—R	Samuel J. Randall—D	Allen G. Thurman—D
48th, 1883–1885	Chester A. Arthur—R	John G. Carlisle—D	George F. Edmunds—R
49th, 1885–1887	Grover Cleveland—D	John G. Carlisle—D	John Sherman—R

(Continued)

Congress	President and Party[a]	Speaker and Party[a]	President Pro Tempore and Party[a]
50th, 1887–1889	Grover Cleveland—D	John G. Carlisle—D	John J. Ingalls—R
52nd, 1891–1893	Benjamin Harrison—R	Charles F. Crisp—D	Charles F. Monderson—R
54th, 1895–1897	Grover Cleveland—D	Thomas B. Reed—R	William P. Frye—R
62nd, 1911–1913	William H. Taft—R	Champ Clark—D	William P. Frye—R
			Charles Curtis—R
			Augustus O. Bacon—R
			Jacob H. Gallinger—R
			Henry Cabot Lodge—R
			Frank B. Brandegee—R
66th, 1919–1921	Woodrow Wilson—D	Frederick H. Gillett—R	Albert B. Cummins—R
72nd, 1931–1933	Herbert C. Hoover—R	John Nance Garner—D	George H. Moses—R
80th, 1947–1949	Harry S. Truman—D	Joseph Martin, Jr.—R	Arthur H. Vandenberg—R
84th, 1955–1957	Dwight D. Eisenhower—R	Sam Rayburn—D	Walter F. George—D
85th, 1957–1959	Dwight D. Eisenhower—R	Sam Rayburn—D	Carl Hayden—D
86th, 1959–1961	Dwight D. Eisenhower—R	Sam Rayburn—D	Carl Hayden—D
91st, 1969–1971	Richard M. Nixon—R	John W. McCormack—D	Richard B. Russell—D
92nd, 1971–1973	Richard M. Nixon—R	Carl B. Albert—D	Allen J. Ellender—D
			James O. Eastland—D
93rd, 1973–1975	Richard M. Nixon—R	Carl B. Albert—D	James O. Eastland—D
94th, 1975–1977	Gerald R. Ford—R	Carl B. Albert—D	James O. Eastland—D
97th, 1981–1983	Ronald Reagan—R	Thomas P. O'Neill Jr.—D	Strom Thurmond—R
98th, 1983–1985	Ronald Reagan—R	Thomas P. O'Neill Jr.—D	
99th, 1985–1987	Ronald Reagan—R	Thomas P. O'Neill Jr.—D	Strom Thurmond—R
100th, 1987–1989	Ronald Reagan—R	James Wright—D	John C. Stennis—D
101st, 1989–1991	George H.W. Bush—R	Thomas S. Foley—D	Robert C. Byrd—D
102nd, 1991–1993	George H.W. Bush—R	Thomas S. Foley—D	Robert C. Byrd—D
104th, 1995–1997	William J. Clinton—D	Newt Gingrich—R	Strom Thurmond—R
105th, 1997–1999	William J. Clinton—D	Newt Gingrich—R	Strom Thurmond—R
106th, 1997–1999	William J. Clinton—D	Dennis Hastert—R	Strom Thurmond—R
107th, 2001–2003	William J. Clinton—D	Dennis Hastert—R	Robert Byrd—D
			Strom Thurmond—R[b]
110th, 2007–2009	George W. Bush—R	Nancy Pelosi—D	Robert Byrd—D
112th, 2011–2013	Barack Obama—D	John Boehner—R	Daniel Inouye—D

a. The party abbreviations are as follows: C—Coalition; D—Democratic; DR—Democratic—Republican; J—Jacksonian; R—Republican; W—Whig.

b. When the Congress began, the Senate was divided 50-50. Because the Vice President's tie-breaking vote would change control from Democrats to Republicans on January 20, the Senate elected Byrd to serve until noon and Thurmond to serve from noon on January 20. Control changed again from June 6, 2001, when Jim Jeffords left the Republican Party and Byrd was once again elected President pro tempore.

Appendix F

Rule Number 9 of the Republican Party*

FILLING VACANCIES IN NOMINATIONS

(a) The Republican National Committee is hereby authorized and empowered to fill any and all vacancies which may occur by reason of death, declination, or otherwise of the Republican candidate for President of the United States or the Republican candidate for Vice President of the United States, as nominated by the national convention, or the Republican National Committee may reconvene the national convention for the purpose of filling any such vacancies.

(b) In voting under this rule, the Republican National Committee members representing any state shall be entitled to cast the same number of votes as said state was entitled to cast at the national convention.

(c) In the event that the members of the Republican National Committee from any state shall not be in agreement in the casting of votes hereunder, the votes of such state shall be divided equally, including fractional votes, among the members of the Republican National Committee present or voting by proxy.

(d) No candidate shall be chosen to fill any such vacancy except upon receiving a majority of the votes entitled to be cast in the election.

* As adopted by the 2008 Republican National Convention, September 1, 2008, and amended by the Republican National Committee on August 6, 2010. REPUBLICAN NAT'L COMM., THE RULES OF THE REPUBLICAN PARTY, AS ADOPTED BY THE 2008 REPUBLICAN NATIONAL CONVENTION SEPTEMBER 1, 2008, AND AMENDED BY THE REPUBLICAN NATIONAL COMMITTEE ON AUGUST 6, 2010 (2010), *available at* http://www.gop.com/images/legal/2008_RULES_Adopted.pdf.

Appendix G
Selected Sections of the Charter and Bylaws of the Democratic Party

THE CHARTER*

Article 3—Democratic National Committee

SECTION 1. The Democratic National Committee shall have general responsibility for the affairs of the Democratic Party between National Conventions, subject to the provisions of this Charter and to the resolutions or other actions of the National Convention. This responsibility shall include:

. . .

(c) filling vacancies in the nominations for the office of President and Vice President. . . .

Article 9—General Provisions

SECTION 8. To assure that the Democratic nominee for the office of President of the United States is selected by a fair and equitable process, the Democratic National Committee may adopt such statements of policy as it deems appropriate with respect to the timing of Presidential nominating processes and shall work with state Parties to accomplish the objectives of such statements.

SECTION 12. All meetings of the Democratic National Committee, the Executive Committee, and all other official Party committees, commissions and bodies shall be open to the public, and votes shall not be taken by secret ballot.

* DEMOCRATIC NAT'L COMM., THE CHARTER & THE BYLAWS OF THE DEMOCRATIC PARTY OF THE UNITED STATES 3 (2010), *available at* http://www.democrats.org/files/misc/pdf/Charter_and_Bylaws _8_20_10.php (Article III, Section 1(c)).

THE BYLAWS

Article 2—Democratic National Committee

SECTION 8. Attendance and Quorum and Voting.

. . .

(g) Proxy voting shall be permitted. Proxies may be either general or limited and either instructed or uninstructed. All proxies shall be in writing and transferable if so specified. No DNC member may at any one time hold or exercise proxies for more than one other DNC member; provided, however, that proxy voting shall not be permitted in voting to fill a vacancy on the National ticket.

Appendix H

Letter from President Lyndon B. Johnson
to House Speaker John W. McCormack

The following is a letter from President Lyndon B. Johnson to Speaker John W. McCormack, dated December 23, 1963, accompanied by an eleven-page memorandum with four pages of attachments, dated December 4, 1963, written by Assistant Attorney General Norbert A. Schlei, entitled *Agreement Between the President and the Speaker of the House as to Procedures in the Event of Presidential Inability.**

* Letter, President Johnson to Speaker John W. McCormack, 12/23/63, Ex FG 1 WHCF, Box 9, LBJ Library.

THE WHITE HOUSE
WASHINGTON

EXECUTIVE
FG1
FG 412
FE 4-1
FE 4-2

December 23, 1963

Dear Mr. Speaker: *John W. McCormack*

Confirming our oral agreement regarding the
procedures to be followed in the event of my
inability to exercise the powers and duties of the
Presidency, I am reducing the agreement to
writing and would appreciate your signing the
original of this letter and returning it to me for
safekeeping in the Presidential files. Enclosed
for your use is a signed duplicate original. The
terms of the agreement are as follows:

1. In the event of inability, the President would --
if possible -- so inform the Speaker of the House,
and the Speaker of the House would serve as Acting
President, exercising the powers and duties of the
Office until the inability had ended.

2. In the event of an inability which would prevent
the President from communicating with the Speaker
of the House, the Speaker of the House, after such
consultation as seems to him appropriate under the
circumstances, would decide upon the devolution of
the powers and duties of the Office and would serve
as Acting President until the inability had ended.

3. The President, in either event, would determine
when the inability had ended and at that time would
resume the full exercise of the powers and duties of
the Office.

Page 1 of 2 pages.

-2-

4. After being informed by the President of his inability or, in the event of an inability which would prevent the President from communicating with the Speaker of the House, after the latter satisfies himself that such inability exists, the Speaker of the House will resign as Speaker and as Representative in Congress before undertaking to act as President.

Sincerely,

Honorable John W. McCormack
Speaker of the House of Representatives
Washington, D. C.

Agreed: _____   Date: _____

Page 2 of 2 pages.

Department of Justice
Washington

MEMORANDUM

DEC 4 1963

Re: Agreement Between the President and the
Speaker of the House as to Procedures
in the Event of Presidential Inability.

The question has been asked whether President Johnson
and Speaker of the House McCormack may enter into an understanding on presidential inability similar to the agreements
entered into by President Eisenhower and Vice President
Nixon on March 3, 1958, 1/ and by the late President Kennedy
and then Vice President Johnson on August 10, 1961. 2/ For
the reasons set forth hereafter, it is concluded that such
an agreement would be consistent with the Constitution and
the Presidential Succession Act of 1947 (3 U.S.C. 19), which
is set out in full in Appendix 1 hereto.

However, the provisions of the Act require any officer
after the Vice President in the line of succession to resign
from his office before undertaking to act as President. 3/
The Speaker must resign both "as Speaker and as Representative
in Congress" (3 U.S.C. 19(a)(2)). The President pro tempore
of the Senate must resign both as such President "and as
Senator" (3 U.S.C. 19(b)). Consequently, in the event that
the President's inability appears to be of a temporary
nature, the Speaker may well hesitate to undertake to act
as President. 4/ If he is willing to commit himself in
advance to resigning and acting as President, regardless of

1/ Public Papers of the President, Dwight D. Eisenhower,
   1958, p. 196.
2/ Public Papers of the President, John F. Kennedy, 1961,
   p. 561.
3/ The resignation of a cabinet member in the line of
   succession is effectuated by taking the oath of office
   as Acting President. 3 U.S.C. 19(d)(3).
4/ In response to the suggestion that it would be unfair
   to require the Speaker or the President pro tempore to
   resign in such circumstances, Senator Wherry, floor

(Cont'd)

the expected duration of any Presidential inability to act,
an agreement between the President and the Speaker can be
made in language identical with the Eisenhower-Nixon and
Kennedy-Johnson agreements except for an additional provision to the effect that the Speaker will resign in the event
that a Presidential inability to act occurs. Such a proposed memorandum of understanding between the President and
the Speaker is attached hereto as Appendix 2.

If the Speaker is unwilling so to commit himself, it
may be appropriate to consider entering into a more elaborate
agreement between the President, the Speaker, the President

4/ (Cont'd)
manager of the bill, made two somewhat contradictory arguments. First he contended that any future Speaker will
have been put on notice that, as part of the responsibilities
of office, he "may be called upon in time of emergency, even
for a temporary period, to act as President, and that in
order to qualify it will be necessary for him to resign."
In the same vein the Senator added:
    ". . .[W]hen any officer of the United States, partic-
    ularly an elective one, is called upon during an emergency
    to act as President, there should be no hesitation or
    doubt on his part as to his duty.
    "The honor of being President of the United States,
    even for a temporary period, is sufficient, but, in
    addition, there is the duty that everyone holds to
    serve his country in time of emergency wherever he is
    called to serve." 93 Cong. Rec. 7711-7712.
However, Senator Wherry also said that if the President
suffered from merely a temporary disability the Speaker
would probably not resign. "* * * [N]o doubt if the occasion did present itself, it would be in the case of permanent disability or death." Id. 7775. "* * * [T]he result
would be that at least in the judgment of the Speaker * * *
there would be no doubt about the permanent disability of
the person then in Office." Id. 7779.

-2-

pro tempore of the Senate and at least the next officer in
the line of succession, the Secretary of State, to provide
that the latter will act as President in the event of the
occurrence of what appears to be only a temporary disability
of the President. Before discussing the content of such an
agreement, I will discuss briefly the constitutionality and
background of the Presidential Succession Act and agreements
such as those under consideration.

I

Article II, section 1, clause 6 of the Constitution
reads as follows:

"In Case of the Removal of the President from
Office, or of his Death, Resignation, or Inability
to discharge the Powers and Duties of the said
Office, the Same shall devolve on the Vice President, and the Congress may by Law provide for the
Case of Removal, Death, Resignation or Inability,
both of the President and Vice President, declaring
what Officer shall then act as President, and such
Officer shall act accordingly, until the Disability
be removed, or a President shall be elected."

Pursuant to this provision, Congress enacted the Presidential
Succession Act of July 18, 1947 (P.L. 199, 80th Cong., 1st
Sess., 3 U.S.C. 19). 5/ When this proposal was before the

5/ The Presidential Succession Act was enacted by Congress
in 1947 in response to a plea by President Truman that the
Speaker of the House of Representatives should be first in
the order of succession in case of the removal, death,
resignation, or inability to act, of both the President and
Vice President. President Truman expressed the belief that
the Speaker is elected not only in his own district, but
also is elected as presiding officer of the House by votes
of the representatives of all the people of the country, and
therefore "his selection, next to that of the President and
Vice President, can most accurately be said to stem from the

(Cont'd)

Congress, the then Acting Attorney General, Douglas W.
McGregor, expressed the opinion that it was constitutional,
and the House Committee on the Judiciary concurred in this
conclusion. House Rept. No. 817, 80th Cong., 1st Sess.,
p. 4 (1947). Apparently Congress in enacting this proposal
into law accepted those views as a proper construction of
Article II, section 1, clause 6 of the Constitution. Those
views seem to me to be clearly correct. 6/

_____

5/ (Cont'd)
people themselves." H. Rept. No. 817, 80th Cong., 1st
Sess., p. 3 (1947). In preferring the Speaker as first
in line after the Vice President, President Truman gave
as reasons that a new House is elected every two years,
always at the same time as the President and Vice President,
and is usually in agreement politically with the Chief
Executive. Id. Therefore it was likely that the views
of the Speaker of the House would be in sympathy with the
views of a majority of the people. 93 Cong. Rec. 8623,
July 10, 1947.
6/ The constitutional problem emphasized during the
consideration of the 1947 proposal was whether the Speaker
of the House and the President pro tempore were "Officers"
within the meaning of Article II, section 1, clause 6 of
the Constitution. In concluding that these members of the
Congress were such "Officers," the Acting Attorney General
and the House Judiciary Committee relied heavily on Lamar
v. United States, 241 U.S. 102, 112-113 (1916), and the
fact that the succession law of 1792 designated the President pro tempore and the Speaker of the House as successors
to the Presidency. "This law [of 1792] represents a construction of Article II by an early Congress, whose views
of the Constitution have long been regarded as authoritative,
and reflects a long-continued acquiescence in such a construction." H. Rept. 817, supra, p. 4.

-4-

to the agreement that his inability was likely to endure
for a considerable period or, in the event that he were
unable so to advise them, the Speaker determined that
this was so, the same steps would be followed as provided
in the attached agreement, i.e., the Speaker would resign
and act as President. If there were no Speaker, the
President pro tempore would resign and act as President.
3 U.S.C. 19(c) provides that once the Speaker or the
President pro tempore resigns to act as President he
cannot be replaced by a newly elected and qualified
Speaker. He continues to act until the expiration of
the current Presidential term or until the termination
of the disability of the President or the Vice President.

The agreement would also provide, however, that if
the President advised the other parties to the agreement
that his disability was apt to endure for less than a
specified period -- perhaps fifteen days or less -- or,
in the event that he was unable to advise them, the
individual eligible to succeed him (either the Speaker
of the House or, if there were none, the President pro
tempore) should determine that this was so, neither the
Speaker nor the President pro tempore would resign.
Rather, they would continue in office and the Secretary
of State would act as President. The agreement could
provide that the Secretary would act as President for the
period of disability or for a specified period after which,
if the President's disability continued, the Speaker or
President pro tempore would resign and act as President.
As in the prior understandings, the parties would agree
under all circumstances to accept the President's judgment
as to whether his disability has terminated.

The only noteworthy legal problem presented by such
an agreement relates to the termination of the Secretary's
service in a situation where the President's disability
first appears to be temporary, so that the Secretary of

-9-

State undertakes to act, but thereafter appears to be permanent or endures for a considerable period of time. Although the answer would not be entirely clear in the absence of some determinative provision in the agreement, it appears that in these circumstances either the Speaker or the President pro tempore, simply by resigning from office, could displace the Secretary as Acting President.

In this connection it should be noted that there is a significant difference between 3 U.S.C. 19(c), which deals with retention of the Acting Presidency by the Speaker and the President pro tempore, and 3 U.S.C. 19(d)(2), which deals with the retention of the office by a cabinet member. The former provision states clearly that the Speaker or President pro tempore, once he undertakes to act, shall continue to do so until the President's disability is removed or the term ends. The latter provision, in contrast, states that a cabinet member shall not continue to act as President "after a qualified and prior-entitled individual [other than another cabinet member] is able to act." It would seem clear that upon resigning from his office in Congress an otherwise qualified Speaker or President pro tempore "is able to act." Conceivably it could be argued that, in context, "able to act" refers only to physical inability. However, in view of the legislative history indicating a clear understanding that the Congressional officers in the line of succession would not be obliged to serve if they did not choose to resign, and in view of the contrastingly clear language of 3 U.S.C. 19(c), I am satisfied that the less limiting interpretation is the correct one.

In any event, the understanding could resolve the problem. For example, it could provide that after it becomes clear that the President's disability is permanent or after a stated period of time has elapsed, the Secretary of State would resign as Acting President unless requested not to do so by the Speaker and President pro tempore. If the Secretary resigned, it would then be clear beyond argument under the provisions of the Succession Act that the Speaker could succeed him as Acting President. 3 U.S.C. 19(a)(2). The understanding could obligate him to do so. Contrariwise, the agreement could provide that, in order to avoid having four individuals act as President during one term, neither the Speaker nor the President pro tempore would undertake to act as President once the initial determination were made that the President's disability was likely to be of short duration.

The foregoing description of a possible understanding underscores some of the complexities of the situation and possible steps which could be taken to meet them. Other means of meeting them can undoubtedly be developed, and we would, of course, be pleased to explore them further to whatever extent is desired.

Norbert A. Schlei
Assistant Attorney General
Office of Legal Counsel

Attachments

-11-

APPENDIX 1

Presidential Succession Act
(3 U.S.C. 19)

§ 19. Vacancy in offices of both President and Vice President; officers eligible to act.

(a)(1) If, by reason of death, resignation, removal from office, inability, or failure to qualify, there is neither a President nor Vice President to discharge the powers and duties of the office of President, then the Speaker of the House of Representatives shall, upon his resignation as Speaker and as Representative in Congress, act as President.

(2) The same rule shall apply in the case of the death, resignation, removal from office, or inability of an individual acting as President under this subsection.

(b) If, at the time when under subsection (a) of this section a Speaker is to begin the discharge of the powers and duties of the office of President, there is no Speaker, or the Speaker fails to qualify as Acting President, then the President pro tempore of the Senate shall, upon his resignation as President pro tempore and as Senator, act as President.

(c) An individual acting as President under subsection (a) or subsection (b) of this section shall continue to act until the expiration of the then current Presidential term, except that --

(1) if his discharge of the powers and duties of the office is founded in whole or in part on the failure of both the President-elect and the Vice-President-elect to qualify, then he shall act only until a President or Vice President qualifies; and

(2) if his discharge of the powers and duties of the office is founded in whole or in part on the

inability of the President or Vice President, then he
shall act only until the removal of the disability of
one of such individuals.

(d)(1) If, by reason of death, resignation, removal
from office, inability, or failure to qualify, there is no
President pro tempore to act as President under subsection
(b) of this section, then the officer of the United States
who is highest on the following list, and who is not under
disability to discharge the powers and duties of the office
of President shall act as President: Secretary of State,
Secretary of the Treasury, Secretary of Defense, Attorney
General, Postmaster General, Secretary of the Interior,
Secretary of Agriculture, Secretary of Commerce, Secretary
of Labor.

(2) An individual acting as President under this subsection shall continue so to do until the expiration of the
then current Presidential term, but not after a qualified
and prior-entitled individual is able to act, except that
the removal of the disability of an individual higher on the
list contained in paragraph (1) of this subsection or the
ability to qualify on the part of an individual higher on
such list shall not terminate his service.

(3) The taking of the oath of office by an individual
specified in the list in paragraph (1) of this subsection
shall be held to constitute his resignation from the office
by virtue of the holding of which he qualifies to act as
President.

(e) Subsections (a), (b), and (d) of this section shall
apply only to such officers as are eligible to the office of
President under the Constitution. Subsection (d) of this
section shall apply only to officers appointed, by and with
the advice and consent of the Senate, prior to the time of
the death, resignation, removal from office, inability, or
failure to qualify, of the President pro tempore, and only
to officers not under impeachment by the House of Representatives at the time the powers and duties of the office

-2-

of President devolve upon them.

(f) During the period that any individual acts as President under this section, his compensation shall be at the rate then provided by law in the case of the President.

-3-

APPENDIX 2

"December ____, 1963

"The President and Speaker of the House John W.
McCormack have this day agreed that the following procedures are in accord with the purposes and provisions
of Article 2, Section 1 of the Constitution, dealing with
presidential inability. They believe that these procedures, which are intended to apply to themselves only,
are in no sense outside or contrary to the Constitution
but are consistent with its present provisions and implement its clear intent.

"1. In the event of inability, the President would
-- if possible -- so inform the Speaker of the House, and
the Speaker of the House would serve as Acting President,
exercising the powers and duties of the Office until the
inability had ended.

"2. In the event of an inability which would prevent the President from communicating with the Speaker of
the House, the Speaker of the House, after such consultation as seems to him appropriate under the circumstances,
would decide upon the devolution of the powers and duties
of the Office and would serve as Acting President until
the inability had ended.

"3. The President, in either event, would determine
when the inability had ended and at that time would resume
the full exercise of the powers and duties of the Office.

"4. After being informed by the President of his
inability or, in the event of an inability which would
prevent the President from communicating with the Speaker
of the House, after the latter satisfies himself that
such inability exists, the Speaker of the House will
resign as Speaker and as Representative in Congress before undertaking to act as President."

Appendix I

Schedule of Gerald Ford for August 9, 1974

OFFICE OF THE VICE PRESIDENT
·WASHINGTON·

THE VICE PRESIDENT'S SCHEDULE

Friday, August 9, 1974

+   +   +   +   +   +   +   +   +   +   +   +

8:15 am	Secretary of State Kissinger	OEOB
9:45	Presidential Take-off	White House Lawn
11:45	Swearing-in Ceremony	White House East Room

+   +   +   +   +   +   +   +   +   +   +   +

THE PRESIDENT'S SCHEDULE

After Ceremony	Meeting with Congressional Leadership in attendance at swearing-in ceremony	Cabinet Room
	Meeting with Senior White House Staff	Roosevelt Room
2:00 pm	Economic Conference	Cabinet Room
	Chairman Burns	
	Secretary Simons	
	Counselor Rush	
	Chairman Stein	
	Director Ash	
	Chairman designee Greenspan	
	R.T. Hartmann	
	L. W. Seidman	
	William Scranton	
2:20-2:25	NATO Ambassadors	Roosevelt Room
2:45	Japanese Ambassador	Sec's WH Office
3:15	USSR Ambassador	Sec's WH Office
4:00	Middle East Ambassadors	Roosevelt Room
4:45	Peoples Republic of China Ambassador	Sec's WH Office
5:00	General Lawson	Oval Office
5:15	Latin American Ambassadors (optional)	Roosevelt Room

OFFICE OF THE VICE PRESIDENT

WASHINGTON

THE PRESIDENT'S SCHEDULE

Friday, August 9, 1974 - page 2

| 5:30 | Meeting with Presidential Transition Staff | Cabinet Room |

John Brynes
Senator Robert Griffin / - twient alden.
Bryce Harlow
R.T. Hartmann
Jack Marsh
Rogers Morton
Donald Rumsfeld
William Scranton
L.W. Seidman
Jerry terHorst ✓
Clay Whitehead
— William Whyte —

| 6:00 | Israel Ambassador | Sec's WH Office |
| 6:30 | Vietnam Ambassador | Sec's WH Office |

To Benton Becker with appreciation and admiration for his effective and skilful service in the tough days in August and September 1974. You earned your presence in the Oval Office on August 9th

Gerald R. Ford

Appendix J

Twenty-Fifth Amendment Memo
Prepared for President Gerald R. Ford

The following is a nine-page memorandum and option paper dated August 21, 1975, which is on file at the presidential library of Gerald Ford and was prepared by his staff for his review, but there is no record of any subsequent action or discussion. The document also indicates that there was a verbal disability agreement between Nixon and Ford (see second paragraph, page 4).

THE WHITE HOUSE
WASHINGTON

August 21, 1975

MEMORANDUM FOR: THE PRESIDENT

THROUGH: RODERICK M. HILLS

FROM: BOBBIE GREENE KILBERG ^{BGK}

SUBJECT: 25th Amendment

25th Amendment Provisions

The 25th Amendment provides for Presidential succession in the case of
removal, resignation, or death of a President and stipulates the procedures for determining both the existence of Presidential incapacity and
the termination of that state of incapacity.

Section 1 of the Amendment specifies that in the case of the death or resignation of the President or his removal from office, the Vice President shall
become President. Section 2 states that if there is a vacancy in the office
of the Vice President, the President shall nominate a Vice President who
would take office upon being confirmed by a majority vote of both houses of
Congress.

Section 3 provides for a Presidential declaration of incapacity. Under this
Section, the President transmits a written statement to the President pro
tempore of the Senate and the Speaker of the House of Representatives
declaring that he is unable to discharge the powers and duties of his office.
Upon that action, the Vice President becomes Acting President, discharging
the powers and duties of the office of the President, until such time as the
President transmits to the President pro tempore of the Senate and the
Speaker of the House a written declaration that he has regained his ability
to execute the responsibilities of his office. The President then resumes
the powers and duties of his office.

Page 2

Section 4 provides for a situation in which the President either is unable or unwilling to declare his own incapacity. In such a case, the Vice President and a majority of the Secretaries of the Executive Departments, or such other body as Congress may by law provide, 1/ can transmit to the President pro tempore of the Senate and the Speaker of the House their written declaration that the President is unable to discharge the powers and duties of his office. Upon this occurrence, the Vice President immediately assumes the powers and duties of the office as Acting President. The President can regain his authority by transmitting a written declaration to the President pro tempore and the Speaker of the House that no incapacity exists. He then resumes his powers and duties unless the Vice President and a majority of the Executive Department Secretaries transmit within four days to the President pro tempore of the Senate and the Speaker of the House their written declaration that the President remains unable to discharge the responsibilities of his office. In that event, the Congress must decide the issue, with the requirement that it assemble within 48 hours for that purpose if it is not in session. A decision must be reached within 21 days after receipt of the written declaration or the date of assembly when Congress is not in session. If Congress determines by a two-thirds vote of both houses that the President is unable to discharge the powers and duties of his office, the Vice President shall continue to discharge those duties as Acting President. If the Congress does not vote by two-thirds of each house, the President shall resume the powers and duties of his office.

Implementation of the 25th Amendment

The 25th Amendment was ratified on February 10, 1967. Its provisions have been utilized twice, once upon your nomination and confirmation as Vice President and once upon your succession to the Presidency upon President Nixon's resignation. Despite the fact that the 25th Amendment was in effect during the last two years of Lyndon Johnson's Presidency, there is no record of his modifying the written agreement on incapacity between himself and Vice President Humphrey to reflect the provisions of the Amendment.

1/ The Congress has not provided by legislation for any other system.

Page 3

As a result of President Eisenhower's heart attack in 1955 and his ileitis attack during the start of his second term, the President and Vice President Nixon reached an agreement on the temporary devolution of Presidential authority in the event of an inability rendering the President incapable of exercising the powers and duties of his office. This agreement was in effect during President Eisenhower's stroke in 1957, and its existence was not made publicly known until a written agreement was released in March, 1958.

Following the Eisenhower example, President Kennedy and Vice President Johnson signed an incapacity agreement which was publicly released in August, 1961. President Johnson and Speaker of the House McCormick signed an agreement in December, 1963, and President Johnson and Vice President Humphrey signed an agreement in January, 1965. The Johnson/McCormick agreement was not made public, and the Johnson/Humphrey agreement was not publicly released until the President's gall bladder operation in October, 1965. All the written agreements, attached at Tab A, were identical. President Kennedy, however, in his accompanying press release, specifically stated that he and the Vice President had agreed on the wisdom of Cabinet concurrence in and Attorney General legal support for the incapacity judgment.

The principal difference between the aforementioned agreements and the 25th Amendment is that the agreements made no provision for resolving a dispute between the President and Vice President on the question of incapacity. Rather, as one would expect in any voluntary agreement signed by a President, control over determination of the existence of incapacity rested solely with the President, as long as he could communicate, and control over termination of the incapacity rested solely with the President, even if it was the Vice President who had declared the existence of the incapacity due to the President's inability to communicate at that time.

The pre-25th Amendment agreements were written in order to circumvent Constitutional ambiguity and thus overcome Vice Presidential reluctance to exercise the Presidential power necessary to preserve continuity in executive leadership. There were a number of inadequacies with relying solely on the operation of a personal agreement between a President and Vice President: (1) it only applied to the terms of office of the signatories; (2) it did not carry the force of law and could be challenged; and (3) it

Page 4

authorized the Vice President to act without the protection of unequivocal
Constitutional authority.   This uncertainty and the very serious implication of a Vice Presidential assumption of Presidential power were the
focus of arguments in favor of a Constitutional amendment.

Since the ratification of the 25th Amendment, there is no record of written
agreements between a President and Vice President. None can be found for
President Nixon and Vice President Agnew. According to Bill Casselman,
there was a verbal agreement on incapacity and succession between you and
President Nixon, but it was not committed to writing. There also is no
written agreement between you and Vice President Rockefeller.

Issues

There are a number of issues which can be of concern in relation to the
25th Amendment:

(1) Under Section 3, when a President voluntarily declares his own inability
to govern, he alone has the power to declare that the inability no longer exists. There is no recourse under the Amendment for the Vice President,
the Cabinet Secretaries, or the Congress to block his resumption of power
by disagreeing with the termination of that inability.

(2) Under Section 4, when a President is either unable or unwilling to declare his own incapacity, what standards must the Vice President and a
majority of the Cabinet Secretaries use to make their determination that
the President is unable to discharge the powers and duties of his office?
The legislative history of the Amendment does not provide guidance in this
area.

(3) Must the incapacity of the President be physical or mental or can it
result from outside events, e.g., a mechanical inability to communicate?
The legislative history is not clear on this point. The issue of disability
which is neither mental nor physical was only mentioned in passing a few
times during the Committee hearings and was never focused on. However,
there is nothing to preclude a President and Vice President from voluntarily
entering into a written agreement which would include provisions for dealing
with a non-mental and non-physical disability.

(4) Under Section 4, Congress has 21 days in which to make a determination on the continuation or termination of Presidential incapacity, if the President did not himself declare the original incapacity and the Vice President and a majority of the Cabinet Secretaries disagree with the President's declaration of an end to his incapacity. Who governs during this period? The legislative history of the Amendment indicates that the Vice President continues to exercise the powers and duties of the office of the President during the 4-day period for transmittal of an objection to resumption of power by the President and during the 21-day period in which Congress must act. However, during both those periods of time, it would be very difficult to avoid a feeling of serious uncertainty and this atmosphere could be debilitating to the exercise of executive leadership.

(5) Under Section 4, if the Congress votes that the Presidential incapacity is continuing, may the President ask for another vote at any time by resubmitting his written declaration that no inability exists? According to the legislative history, the answer would seem to be in the affirmative.

(6) Under Section 4, the Amendment requires a majority vote of the Congress for Vice Presidential confirmation; the vote of the Vice President and a majority of the Cabinet Secretaries to declare Presidential incapacity when the President is unable or unwilling to declare his own incapacity; and the vote of the Vice President and a majority of the Cabinet Secretaries, together with a two-thirds vote of the Congress, to prevent the President, on the grounds of continuing incapacity, from resuming the powers and duties of his office.

Are these votes to be based on the body's total membership or only on those present and voting, a quorum being present? In voting on your confirmation as Vice President, the Congress interpreted a majority vote as requiring a simple majority of those present and voting. In his 1965 testimony before both the House Judiciary Committee and the Senate Judiciary Committee, Subcommittee on Constitutional Amendments, Attorney General Nicholas deB. Katzenbach stated that the votes required by the Amendment were based on those present and voting, a quorum being present. He asserted that this interpretation was consistent with long standing precedent. Both the House and Senate Committee Reports support that view. In specific reference to the two-thirds vote of Congress required under Section 4, both Reports

Page 6

note that this vote is in conformity with the Constitutional provision on impeachments. That provision provides for a two-thirds vote in the Senate of those members present. Given the legislative history and legal precedents, a challenge to this interpretation would have very little, if any, chance of prevailing.

Presidential/Vice Presidential Written Agreement

A written agreement between you and Vice President Rockefeller might be beneficial for two reasons: (1) to clarify for your own operating procedures the ambiguities raised by some of the provisions of the 25th Amendment; and (2) if you should choose to release the agreement, to educate the public and foreign nations as to the procedures that will be followed to insure continuity of executive leadership during a period of Presidential incapacity. Such an agreement should list the procedures provided for in the Amendment, emphasizing the specific powers of the President, Vice President, Cabinet Secretaries and Congress in relation to incapacity, and should set standards for the Vice President and Cabinet Secretaries to follow pursuant to Section 4 in the event that the President is unable or unwilling to declare his own incapacity. In establishing such standards, the agreement would define, to the extent possible, what constitutes an incapacity. The agreements written prior to the 25th Amendment did not attempt to define incapacity, but they also did not provide for Vice Presidential disagreement with the President over the issue of incapacity. Since the ratification of the 25th Amendment allows for a Vice Presidential and Cabinet Secretarial challenge to the President, it is prudent in our opinion to provide a written Presidential/ Vice Presidential agreement on the subject.

Recommendations

It is the recommendation of the Counsel's Office that you and Vice President Rockefeller sign a written agreement on incapacity.

Approve _____

Disapprove _____

Comment _____

Page 7

If you approve the signing of a written agreement, the Counsel's Office recommends that the following be included in that agreement:

(1) Description of Section 3 of the 25th Amendment which provides that when the President has declared himself incapacitated, the Vice President discharges the duties and powers of the office of the President until such time as the President declares an end to his incapacity. It would be emphasized that in the case of a voluntary incapacity declaration by the President, the President alone has the authority to determine its end and his ability to resume the powers and duties of his office.

Approve _____

Disapprove _____

Comment _____

(2) Description of provisions in Section 4 of the Amendment for action by the Vice President and a majority of the Cabinet Secretaries in the event that the President either is unable or unwilling to declare his own incapacity; and, in such a case, for a challenge by the Vice President and a majority of the Cabinet Secretaries to the President's declaration that his incapacity is terminated and for a two-thirds vote by the Congress on that issue. It would be emphasized that the Vice President assumes the duties and powers of the office of the President immediately upon transmittal to the President pro tempore of the Senate and the Speaker of the House of a written declaration by the Vice President and a majority of the Cabinet Secretaries that the President is unable to discharge his powers and duties. It further would be emphasized that the Vice President would continue to execute all the powers and duties of the office of the President during both the transmittal period and the 21-day period provided for Congressional action.

Approve _____

Disapprove _____

Comment _____

Page 8

(3) Statement that the President retains the legal right to resubmit at any time his written declaration that no incapacity exists.

Approve _____

Disapprove _____

Comment _____

(4) Establishment of the level of severity which physical or mental illness must attain in order to constitute an inability to govern. This standard and others related to it would define incapacity and would be written after discussions with Dr. Lukash, other medical experts, and the appropriate Presidential advisers.

Approve _____

Disapprove _____

Comment _____

(5) Statement that the definition of incapacity includes disabilities that are neither mental nor physical in nature and provision of a list of examples, such as a mechanical failure of communications with Air Force One for a period of "x" hours. The list would be developed in discussions with the appropriate Presidential advisers and technical experts.

Approve _____

Disapprove _____

Comment _____

It is the recommendation of the Counsel's Office that this written agreement not contain any statement about the method of counting Cabinet Secretarial and Congressional votes, i.e., whether it is based on total membership or on those present and voting, a quorum being present. This question was

Page 9

settled with sufficient specificity in the legislative history of the Amendment.
Its review in the agreement would serve no purpose and would be inappropriate,
especially if it was viewed as an encroachment on Congressional procedures.

Approve _____

Disapprove _____

Comment _____

It is the recommendation of the Counsel's Office that you release to the public
the written agreement on incapacity between you and Vice President Rockefeller.
The release of the agreement would educate the public and foreign nations as
to the procedures that would be followed to insure continuity of executive leadership during a period of Presidential incapacity and to insure the return of that
leadership to the President at the termination of his incapacity. In doing so,
it would help both you and the Vice President to act in a manner that preserved
the public trust.

Approve _____

Disapprove _____

Comment _____

Attachments

Notes

1. Presidential Inability

1. *The Records of the Federal Convention of 1787* 427 (Farrand ed., 1911 & 1937).

2. For a summary of the colonial experience, see J. Feerick, *From Failing Hands* 23–38 (1965).

3. U.S. Const. art. II, § 1, cl. 6.

4. For the constitutional convention and post-convention history of the succession clause, see *From Failing Hands* 39–56.

5. I. Brant, *James Madison, Commander in Chief, 1812–1836*, 184 (1961).

6. *Id.*

7. *Id.* at 187.

8. *Id.*

9. *Id.*

10. *Id.* at 188.

11. *Id.* at 210.

12. *Id.* at 219–20.

13. *See From Failing Hands* 91–92.

14. J. Richardson, *A Compilation of the Messages and Papers of the Presidents, 1789–1902* 31–34 (1907).

15. H. Fraser, *Democracy in the Making* 160 (1938); R. Morgan, *A Whig Embattled: The Presidency under John Tyler* 59 & n.8 (1954).

16. R. Silva, *Presidential Succession* 15–16 & n.8 (1951).

17. 10 Cong. Globe, 27th Cong., 1st Sess. 3–5 (1841).

18. *Id.* at 5.

19. *See generally From Failing Hands* 117–39.

20. *Id.* at 124.

21. R. Caldwell, *James A. Garfield: Party Chieftain* 355 (1931).

22. T. Reeves, *Gentleman Boss: The Life of Chester Alan Arthur* 238–43 (1975).

23. *Is It the End, N.Y. Times*, Aug. 27, 1881 at 4.

24. *Id.* July 8, 1881 at 1.

25. Reeves, *supra* note 22, at 244–45; G. Howe, *Chester A. Arthur: A Quarter-Century of Machine Politics* 153 (1934).

26. Brownell, *Presidential Disability: The Need for a Constitutional Amendment*, 68 Yale L. J. 189, 193–94 (1958).

27. *See From Failing Hands* 133–39.

28. Reeves, *supra* note 22, at 247, 253.

29. Richardson, *supra* note 14, at 65.

30. Reeves, *supra* note 22, at 317–18.

31. *Id.* at 358–59.

32. *Id.* at 360.

33. *Id.* at 370.

34. *Id.* at 373–74.

35. *See From Failing Hands* 147–51; *see also* Matthew Algeo, *The President Is a Sick Man* (2011). This book provides a fresh perspective on the secret operation that Cleveland endured in 1893 and the great lengths taken to conceal his inability. Algeo's account emphasizes how Cleveland and his inner circle successfully deceived the public, the media, and even the senior figures in the Cleveland administration, deception that was all the more shocking in light of Cleveland's famous maxim "Whatever you do, tell the truth." Algeo observes that it was Cleveland's reputation for honesty that allowed him to deceive the people of the United States in such a spectacular fashion.

36. *See* Algeo, at 15.

37. *Id.* at 17.

38. *Id.* at 40; Cleveland, a "sound money man," blamed the bleak economic situation on the Sherman Silver Purchase Act, which had been passed in 1890 and which caused the nation's gold supply to dwindle drastically at a time when other nations were returning to the gold standard. By forcing the U.S. government to buy a large quantity of silver every month and issue a commensurate amount of banknotes that could be redeemed either for silver or gold, the act resulted in widespread inflation—inflation that Cleveland believed could be addressed only by the act's repeal. *Id.* 11–13.

39. *Id.* at 6. This diagnosis would, in fact, prove to be incorrect. Tests conducted on the tumor in the 1980s showed that Cleveland actually had an extremely rare, nonmetastic form of cancer called verrucous carcinoma, not squamous cell carcinoma. This may explain why the operation was successful in preventing a recurrence of the cancer. The study also marveled at the speed of the *Oneida* operation, pointing out that even today such an operation would take a "substantial number of

hours." *Id.* at 225–26 (quoting John Brooks, Horatio T. Enterline, & Gonzalo E. Aponte, *The Final Diagnosis of President Cleveland's Lesion*, Transactions & Studies of the College of Physicians of Philadelphia [March 1980]).

40. *Id.* at 53–54.

41. *Id.* at 54.

42. *Id.*

43. *Id.* at 81, 83.

44. *Id.* at 55.

45. *Id.* at 79.

46. *Id.*

47. *Id.* at 79, 87.

48. *Id.* at 89.

49. *Id.* at 92.

50. *Id.* at 93.

51. *Id.* at 108.

52. *Id.*

53. *Id.* at 114.

54. *Id.* at 94.

55. *Id.* at 144–45 (quoting E. J. Edwards, *The President: A Very Sick Man*, Philadelphia Press (Aug. 29, 1893)).

56. *Id.* at 160.

57. *See From Failing Hands* 149.

58. A. Nevins, *Grover Cleveland: A Study in Courage* 533 (1962).

59. *Id.* at 214.

60. W. Keen, *The Surgical Operations on President Cleveland in 1893*, 190 The Saturday Evening Post (Sept. 22, 1917) at 55.

61. *See From Failing Hands* 156–57.

62. *See id.* at 162–80. *See generally* G. Smith, *When the Cheering Stopped: The Last Years of Woodrow Wilson* (1964).

63. Hearings on Presidential Inability and Vacancies in the Office of Vice President Before the Subcomm. on Constitutional Amendments of the Senate Comm. on the Judiciary, 88th Cong., 2d Sess. 112 (1964) (quoting historian John M. Blum).

64. H. Eaton, *Presidential Timber: A History of Nominating Conventions, 1868–1960* 244–45 (1964).

65. J. Tumulty, *Woodrow Wilson as I Know Him* 443–44 (1921).

66. *The Cabinet Diaries of Josephus Daniels: 1913–1921* 445 (Cronon ed., 1963).

67. CBS Reports, The Crisis of Presidential Succession (January 8, 1964) (remarks of Arthur Krock).

68. E. Wilson, *My Memoir* 290 (1939).

69. *See From Failing Hands* 173.

70. Tumulty, *supra* note 65, at 445.

71. *See From Failing Hands* 179.

72. *Id.* at 184.

73. See J. Bishop, *FDR's Last Year* ix–x (1974); W. Manchester, *The Glory and the Dream* 321–27 (1973).

74. *See* Bishop at 10.

75. *Id.* at 130.

76. D. Acheson, *Present at the Creation* 103 (1969).

77. J. Gunther, *Roosevelt in Retrospect: A Profile in History* 28–29 (1950).

78. Bishop, *supra* note 73, at 295–96.

79. E. Stettinius, *Roosevelt and the Russians: The Yalta Conference* 25 (1949); Bishop 295–96.

80. *See From Failing Hands* 199–201.

81. Giangress and Moore, *Dear Harry: Truman's Mailroom, 1945–1953,* 466 (1999).

82. *Id.* at 211–29.

83. *N.Y. Times,* Sept. 26, 1955 at 1.

84. *Nixon Meets Top Officials; Ruling on Powers Deferred; Cabinet Officers Talk with Nixon,* Sept. 28, 1955 at 1.

85. S. Adams, *Firsthand Report: The Story of the Eisenhower Administration* 186–87 (1961).

86. D. Eisenhower, *The White House Years: Mandate for Change* 540 (1963).

87. R. Donovan, *Eisenhower: The Inside Story* 373 (1956).

88. Eisenhower, *supra* note 86, at 538.

89. *Id.* at 541.

90. E. Benson, *Cross Fire: The Eight Years with Eisenhower* 282 (1962).

91. Adams, *supra* note 84, at 192.

92. Eisenhower, *supra* note 86, at 545.

93. *CBS Reports, The Crisis of Presidential Succession* (January 8, 1964).

94. R. Nixon, *Six Crises* 143 (1962).

95. *N.Y. Times,* June 10, 1956 at 60.

96. Nixon, *supra* note 94, at 168.

97. *From Failing Hands* 225–26.

98. Adams, *supra* note 85, at 200.

99. *Id.* at 200–1.

100. Nixon, *supra* note 94, at 177.

101. *N.Y. Times,* Nov. 23, 1963 at 7.

2. Vice-Presidential Vacancy

1. *The Works of John Adams* 460 (Adams ed., 1856).

2. *See* Feerick, *The Electoral College: Why It Was Created,* 54 A.B.A.J. 249, 250–52 (1968).

3. J. Elliot, *The Debates in the Several State Conventions on the Adoption of the Federal Constitution* 493 (2d ed. 1836).

4. See *The Records of the Federal Convention of 1787* 625 (Farrand ed., 1911 & 1937); 2 Farrand 186.

5. *Id.* at 427.

6. *Id.* at 493–95.

7. *Id.* at 536–37.

8. *Id.* at 537.

9. *Id.*

10. *Id.*

11. See Field, *The Vice-Presidency of the United States*, 56 American L. Rev. 365, 369–72 (1922).

12. *The Federalist and Other Constitutional Papers* 628 (Scott ed., 1894).

13. See Feerick, *From Failing Hands* 55–56 (1965).

14. *The Federalist* No. 68 at 456 (Ford ed., 1898).

15. 1 Stat. 23, *see*, for a discussion of the subject, From Failing Hands p. 6. See H. B. Learned, *The Vice-President's Oath of Office*, 104 Nation 248 (1917); *see also* Feerick, *The Vice-Presidency and the Problems of Presidential Succession and Inability*, 32 Fordham L. Rev. 457, 462 & n. 31 (1964).

16. See N. Pierce, *The People's President* 60–61, 71 (1968); *see also* Feerick, *The Electoral College—Why It Ought to Be Abolished*, 37 Fordham L. Rev. 1, 17 (1968).

17. Pierce, *supra note* 16, at 65–71.

18. See *From Failing Hands* 74–75.

19. *Id.* at 66.

20. 1 Annals of Cong. 672 (1789) (Joseph Gales ed., 1789).

21. *Id.* at 674.

22. W. Maclay: *The Journal of William Maclay* 2 (1927).

23. 8 Annals of Cong. 144 (1803); *see From Failing Hands* 72–75. For an analysis of the effect of the amendment, see Wilmerding, *The Vice Presidency*, 68 Pol. Sci. Q. 17, 29–31 (1953).

24. 8 Annals of Cong. 84, 682 (1803). On April 12, 1808, Senator James Hillhouse of Connecticut proposed an amendment to abolish the office altogether, *id* at 81, note 10 Annals of Cong. 357 (1808).

25. E. Waugh, *Second Consul* 50 (1956).

26. See L. Hatch, *A History of the Vice-Presidency of the United States* 419 (Shoup ed., 1934); Learned, *The President's Cabinet* (1912); Paullin, *The Vice-President and the Cabinet*, 29 Am. Hist. Rev. 496, 498 & nn. 13 & 14 (1924).

27. *See generally*, M. Dorman, *The Second Man* (1968); M. Harwood, *In the Shadow of Presidents: The American Vice-Presidency and Succession System* (1966). For the outstanding modern day text of the vice presidency, see Joel K. Goldstein, *The Modern American Vice Presidency: The Transformation of a Political Institution* (1982).

3. Succession Beyond the Vice Presidency

1. *See* John Feerick, *From Failing Hands* 23–38 (1965).

2. *The Records of the Federal Convention of 1787* 499, 535 (Farrand ed., 1911 & 1937).

3. *See* J. Elliot, *The Debates in the Several State Conventions on the Adoption of the Federal Constitution* 487–88 (2d ed. 1836).

4. *See From Failing Hands* 57–62.

5. 2 Annals of Cong. 1854 (1862).

6. *Id.* at 1865.

7. 3 Annals of Cong. 281 (1791).

8. *Id.* at 282.

9. *Id.* at 281.

10. *Id.* at 282.

11. *See From Failing Hands* 59–60.

12. 1 Stat. 240.

13. *Writings of James Madison* 95 & n. 1 (Hunt ed., 1906).

14. *Id.* at 95–96.

15. *See From Failing Hands* 140–46.

16. 8 Annals of Cong. 2245–416 (1798–99).

17. *See From Failing Hands* 144–45.

18. 14 Cong. Rec. 689 (1882).

19. 17 Cong. Rec. 250 (1885).

20. 24 Stat. 1.

21. *See* Charles S. Hamlin, *The Presidential Succession Act of 1886*, 18 Harv. L. Rev. 182, 191 (1905).

22. *See From Failing Hands* 204–10.

23. H. Truman, *Memoirs*, Vol. I, *Year of Decisions* 23 (1955).

24. *Id.* at 326.

25. H. Truman, Special Message to the Congress on the Succession to the Presidency, June 19, 1945, *Public Papers of the Presidents of the Untied States* 129 (1961); 91 Cong. Rec. 6272 (1945).

26. H. R. 3587, 79th Cong. (1st Sess. 1945).

27. 91 Cong. Rec. 7010–22 (1945).

28. 241 U. S. 103 (1916).

29. 91 Cong. Rec. 7017 (1945).

30. *Id.* at 7013.

31. S. 564, 80th Cong., 1st Sess. (1947).

32. *See From Failing Hands* 207–08; 93 Cong. Rec. 7767–70 (1947).

33. 93 Cong. Rec. 7781 (1947).

34. *Id.* at 7783–84.

35. 3 U.S.C. § 19 (1964), as amended, 3 U.S.C. § 19 (1970).

36. 93 Cong. Rec. 8022, 8626, 7696 (1947); 91 Cong. Rec. 7009 (1945).

37. See 93 Cong. Rec. 7772 (1947); 91 Cong. Rec. 7026 (1945); *see also* Feerick, *The Vice-Presidency and the Problems of Presidential Succession and Inability*, 32 Fordham L. Rev. 482–83 & n. 159 (1964).

38. 111 Cong. Rec. 7967 (1965).

39. N. Y. *Herald-Tribune*, Dec. 12, 1963 at 1.

40. J. F. terHorst, *Gerald Ford and the Future of the Presidency* 145 (1974).

4. Early Steps to Solve the Inability Problem

1. *Hearings on Presidential Inability Before the Subcomm. on Constitutional Amendments of the Senate Comm. on the Judiciary*, 88th Cong. 10 (1963) (statement of Senator Estes Kefauver).

2. *See* John Feerick, *From Failing Hands* 133–35 (1965).

3. 13 Cong. Rec. 124, 142–43, 191–93 (1881).

4. Feerick, *supra* note 2, at 179.

5. *Id.* at 238.

6. Staff of H. Comm. on the Judiciary, 84th Cong., Presidential Inability: Analysis of Replies to a Questionaire and Testimony at a Hearing on Presidential Inability 4, 49 (Comm. Print 1957).

7. Staff of H. Comm. on the Judiciary, 84th Cong., Presidential Inability: Analysis of Replies to a Questionaire and Testimony at Hearing on Presidential Inability 4, 49 (Comm. Print 1957).

8. *Hearings Before the Special Comm. on Study of Presidential Inability of the House Comm. on the Judiciary*, 84th Cong. 3–6 (1956).

9. *Hearings Before the Special Subcomm. on Study of Presidential Inability of the House Comm. on the Judiciary*, 85th Cong. 7–8 (1957).

10. *Hearings Before the Special Subcomm. on Study of Presidential Inability of the House Comm. on the Judiciary*, 85th Cong. 29 (1957) (statement of Representative Kenneth B. Keating).

11. *Hearings Before the Special Subcomm. on Study of Presidential Inability of the House Comm. on the Judiciary*, 85th Cong. 29–30 (1957) (statement of Attorney General Herbert Brownell).

12. Harry S. Truman, *Truman Proposes a Panel on a President's Disability*, N.Y. Times, June 24, 1957 at 1, 14.

13. *Hearings on Presidential Inability Before the Subcomm. on Constitutional Amendments of the Senate Comm. on the Judiciary*, 85th Cong. 1 (1958).

14. Feerick, *supra* note 2, at 241–42.

15. *CBS Reports: The Crisis of Presidential Succession* (CBS television broadcast January, 1964).

16. Press Release, White House (March 3, 1958). See Nixon, *Six Crises* 178–80.

17. Feerick, *supra* note 2, at 229n. As to the Johnson-Humphrey understanding, it does not appear from the files at the LBJ Library that there was ever a fully executed letter between them. In October 1965, as the President underwent gall bladder surgery, the White House issued a press release indicating that procedures such as those adopted by Eisenhower and Nixon were in effect. Public papers of Lyndon Johnson, 2 PUB. PAPERS 1043 (Oct. 5, 1965). *See* Appendix H.

18. For a good statement of the history, *see* 1963 Senate Hearings 67–70.

19. S. REP. No. 88-1382, at 18 (1964).

20. *Presidential Inability: Hearings Before the Subcomm. on Constitutional Amendments of the S. Comm. On the Judiciary*, 88th Cong. 10 (1963) (statement of Sen. Kefauver, Chairman, S. Subcomm. on Constitutional Amendments).

21. *Hearings on Presidential Inability and Vacancies in the Office of Vice President Before the Subcomm. on Constitutional Amendments of the Senate Comm. on the Judiciary*, 88th Cong. 22 (1964) (statement of Senator Kenneth B. Keating).

22. *Id.*

5. Senate Passage of S. J. Res. 139

1. *Hearings on Presidential Inability and Vacancies in the Office of Vice President Before the Subcomm. on Constitutional Amendments of the Senate Comm. on the Judiciary*, 88th Cong. 1 (1964) [hereinafter 1964 Senate Hearings] (statements of Senator Birch Bayh).

2. S. J. Res. 139, 88th Cong. (1st Sess. 1963).

3. John Feerick, *From Failing Hands* 245 (1965). The work of the ABA conference is described in detail in *id.* at 246–54. Bayh, *One Heartbeat Away* 45–50 (1968). Kirby, *A Breakthrough on Presidential Inability: The ABA Conference Consensus*, 17 Vand. L. Rev. 463 (1964).

4. *See* 1964 Senate Hearings, *supra* note 1.

5. *See, e.g., id.* at 91, 128–29, 223.

6. *Id.* at 129.

7. *Id.* at 115.

8. *Id.* at 139.

9. *Id.* at 92.

10. *Id.* at 93.

11. *Id.* at 130.

12. *Id.* at 232.

13. *Id.* at 161.

14. *Id.* at 136–37.

15. *Id.* at 71.

92. *Id.* at 22,995.

93. *Id.* at 23,001.

94. *Id.* at 23,019.

95. *Id.* at 23,061.

6. Congress Acts

1. *Hearings on Presidential Inability and Vacancies in the Office of Vice President Before the Subcomm. on Constitutional Amendments of the Senate Comm. on the Judiciary*, 89th Cong. 13 (1965) [hereinafter *1965 Senate Hearings*] (statement of President Lyndon B. Johnson).

2. 111 CONG. REC. 30 (1965).

3. 1965 Senate Hearings, *supra* note 1, at 14.

4. *Id.* at 11–12.

5. *Id.* at 11.

6. *Id.* at 10.

7. *Id.* at 29.

8. *Id.* at 26.

9. *Id.* at 27.

10. *Id.* at 28.

11. *Id.* at 18–19.

12. *Id.* at 33.

13. *Id.* at 34.

14. *Id.* at 22–23, 29.

15. *Id.* at 48.

16. *Id.* at 48–49.

17. *Id.* at 49.

18. *Id.* at 50.

19. *Id.* at 64.

20. *Id.* at 66.

21. *Id.* at 67.

22. *Id.* at 73.

23. *Id.* at 99.

24. *Id.* at 98.

25. *Id.* at 101.

26. *See* S. REP. NO. 89-66 (1965).

27. Birch Bayh, *One Heartbeat Away: Presidential Disability and Succession* 210 (1968).

28. *Id.* at 211–12.

29. S. REP. NO. 89-66, at 3 (1965).

30. *Id.*

31. 111 CONG. REC. 3253 (1965).

32. *Id.* at 3255.

33. *Id.* at 3265.

34. *Id.* at 3257.

35. *Id.* at 3268–69.

36. *Id.* at 3269.

37. *Id.* at 3270.

38. *Id.* at 3271.

39. *Id.* at 3273.

40. *Id.* at 3274.

41. *Id.*

42. *Id.* at 3276.

43. *Id.*

44. *Id.* at 3278.

45. *Id.*

46. *Id.* at 3279.

47. *Id.* at 3281.

48. *Id.* at 3275.

49. *Id.*

50. *Id.* at 3281.

51. *Id.* at 3279.

52. *Id.* at 3282.

53. Bayh, *supra* note 27, at 269.

54. 111 CONG. REC. 3283 (1965).

55. *Id.* at 3286.

56. *Hearings on Presidential Inability and Vice Presidential Vacancy Before the House Comm. on the Judiciary*, 89th Cong. 4 (1965) (statement of Representative William M. McCulloch of Ohio).

57. *Id.* at 245.

58. *Id.* at 243.

59. *Id.* at 104.

60. *Id.* at 67.

61. *Id.* at 236.

62. *Id.* at 96.

63. *Id.* at 41–42.

64. *Id.* at 5, 56–57, 77–78, 86–87.

65. *Id.* at 242.

66. *Id.* at 205.

67. *Id.* at 91.

68. *Id.* at 190.

69. *Id.* at 90–91.

70. *Id.* at 66.

71. *Id.* at 91.

72. *Id.* at 206.

73. *See* H.R. REP. No. 89-203 (1965).

74. *See supra* text pp. 89–90 ("President pro tempore of the Senate," however, was used instead of "President of the Senate," so as to make clear that the Vice President would not be the recipient of any presidential inability notices to Congress).

75. *Succession Bill Cleared for Vote; Hostile House Panel Sends Measure to the Floor*, N.Y. TIMES, Apr. 1, 1965, at 20.

76. III CONG. REC. 7936–37 (1965).

77. *Id.* at 7937.

78. *Id.* at 7936.

79. *Id.*

80. *Id.* at 7942.

81. *Id.* at 7940.

82. *Id.* at 7967.

83. *Id.* at 7955.

84. *Id.* at 7938.

85. *Id.* at 7943.

86. *Id.* at 7941.

87. *Id.*

88. *Id.* at 7944–46.

89. *Id.* at 7961.

90. *Id.* at 7932–33.

91. *Id.* at 7932.

92. *Id.* at 7960.

93. *Id.* at 7961.

94. *Id.*

95. *Id.* at 7946.

96. *Id.* at 7963.

97. *Id.*

98. *Id.* at 7950.

99. *Id.* at 7963.

100. *Id.* at 7950.

101. *Id.*

102. *Id.* at 7963–64.

103. *Id.* at 7964.

104. *Id.*

105. *Id.* at 7949.

106. *Id.* at 7958.

107. *Id.* at 7965.

108. *Id.*

109. *Id.*

110. *Id.* at 7966.

111. *Id.*

112. *Id.*

113. *Id.* at 7967.

114. *Id.*

115. *Id.*

116. *Id.* at 7968–69.

117. *See* H.R. REP. No. 89-564 (1965).

118. Conversation the author had with Larry Conrad, then chief counsel to the Senate Subcommittee on Constitutional Amendments (1965).

119. 111 CONG. REC. 15,214 (1965).

120. *Id.* at 15,380.

121. *Id.* at 15,382.

122. *Id.* at 15,381–82.

123. *Id.* at 15,382–83.

124. *Id.* at 15,384.

125. *Id.* at 15,386.

126. *Id.*

127. *Id.* at 15,387.

128. *Id.* at 15,587.

129. *Id.* at 15,588.

130. *Id.* at 15,585.

131. *Id.* at 15,594.

132. *Id.* at 15,592.

133. *Id.* at 15,591.

134. *Id.* at 15,593.

135. *Id.* at 15,389.

136. *Id.* at 15,595.

137. *Id.* at 15,596.

7. Ratification

1. Remarks at Ceremony Marking the Ratification of the Presidential Inability (25th) Amendment to the Constitution, 1 PUB. PAPERS 217–18 (Feb. 23, 1967).

2. *See generally* Birch Bayh, *One Heartbeat Away: Presidential Disability and Succession* 335–42 (1968), and the state ratification files in the Office of the General Services Administration.

3. *See* Amendment of the Constitution by the Convention Method Under Article V, American Bar Association Special Constitutional Convention Study Committee 23–30 (1974).

4. *See id.* at 32–33.

8. An Analysis of Sections 1, 2, 3, and 4 of the Amendment

1. III CONG. REC. 15,594–95 (1965) (statement of Senator Sam J. Ervin).

2. *Hearings on Presidential Inability and Vacancies in the Office of Vice President Before the Subcomm. on Constitutional Amendments of the Senate Comm. on the Judiciary,* 89th Cong. 8, 86 (1965) [hereinafter *1965 Senate Hearings*]; *Hearings on Presidential Inability and Vice Presidential Vacancy Before the House Comm. on the Judiciary,* 89th Cong. 40 (1965) [hereinafter *1965 House Hearings*]; S. REP. NO. 89-66, at 12 (1965); H.R. REP. NO. 89-203, at 12 (1965); III CONG. REC. 7942, 7953, 7955, 15378 (1965).

3. 1965 Senate Hearings 8; *Hearings on Presidential Inability and Vacancies in the Office of Vice President Before the Subcomm. on Constitutional Amendments of the Senate Comm. on the Judiciary,* 88th Cong. 68 (1964) [hereinafter *1964 Senate Hearings*]; S. REP. NO. 88-1382, at 11 (1964).

4. 1965 Senate Hearings, *supra* note 2, at 8.

5. *Id.,* at 106; 109 CONG. REC. 24,420 (1963) (Bayh).

6. S. REP. NO. 89-66, at 12 (1965).

7. The author collected this legislative history in a memorandum dated September 24, 1973, to Senator Bayh, that was reprinted in S. Doc. No. 93–42, Selected Materials on the Twenty-Fifth Amendment, 93d Cong., 1st Sess. 279–300 (1973).

8. 1965 House Hearings, *supra* note 2, at 44, 87, 196, 246; H.R. REP. NO. 89-203, at 18 (1965); III CONG. REC. 3252 (1965) (Bayh); 1964 Senate Hearings, *supra* note 3, at 68; 109 CONG. REC. 24,421 (1963) (Bayh).

9. III CONG. REC. 3253–56 (1965).

10. 1965 House Hearings, *supra* note 2, at 87, 192–93, 239, 246; III CONG. REC. 3253 (1965) (Bayh, Hruska).

11. III CONG. REC. 3253 (1965) (Bayh, Hruska).

12. 1965 House Hearings , *supra* note 2, at 77–78; III CONG. REC. 3265–68 (1965) (Dirksen).

13. III CONG. REC. 3253 (1965) (Bayh, Hruska).

14. S. REP. NO. 88-1382, at 13 (1964).

15. 1965 House Hearings, *supra* note 2, at 65–66.

16. III CONG. REC. 7955 (1965) (Rodino); 110 Cong. Rec. 22,988, 22,996, 22,999 (1964).

17. For relevant proposals, see H. J. RES. NO. 88-818 (1963); H.R. RES. NO. 88-9305, 88th Cong., 1st Sess. (1963).

18. 1965 Senate Hearings, *supra* note 2, at 62; 1964 Senate Hearings, *supra* note 3, at 4, 68, 137; 109 CONG. REC. 24,421 (1963) (Bayh).

19. 1965 Senate Hearings, *supra* note 2, at 62, 64; 1965 House Hearings, *supra* note 2, at 179; III CONG. REC. 3255, 3262 (1965); 1964 Senate Hearings, *supra* note 3, at 4, 226; S. REP. NO. 88-1382, at 13 (1964); 110 CONG. REC. 22,988 (1964) (Ervin); 109 CONG. REC. 24,421 (1963) (Bayh). One of the reasons for the rejection of the

proposal that Congress select a new Vice President was that it might not ensure a member of the same party as the President's. 1964 Senate Hearings, *supra* note 3, at 28, 89.

20. 1965 Senate Hearings, *supra* note 2, at 11, 106; S. REP. NO. 89-66, at 15 (1965); H.R. REP. NO. 89-203, at 15 (1965); 111 CONG. REC. 3255 (Bayh), 3262 (Fong) (1965); 1964 Senate Hearings, *supra* note 3, at 4, 60, 121, 138; S. REP. NO. 88-1382, at 13 (1964); 110 CONG. REC. 22,988 (Bayh), 22,994 (Fong), 23,060 (Bayh) (1964).

21. 1965 House Hearings, *supra* note 2, at 210; 1964 Senate Hearings, *supra* note 3, at 130–31.

22. 1965 House Hearings, *supra* note 2, at 50, 54; 1964 Senate Hearings, *supra* note 3, at 62, 205.

23. 1965 House Hearings, *supra* note 2, at 89, 92; 111 CONG. REC. 3275 (1965) (Bayh); 1964 Senate Hearings, *supra* note 3, at 68.

24. 1965 House Hearings, *supra* note 2, at 256; 1964 Senate Hearings, *supra* note 3, at 39, 62, 81, 218; 110 CONG. REC. 22,996 (1964) (Monroney).

25. 1965 House Hearings, *supra* note 2, at 45, 49, 89.

26. 1965 Senate Hearings, *supra* note 2, at 11; 1965 House Hearings, *supra* note 2, at 179; 111 CONG. REC. 3255–56 (1965) (Ervin); 1964 Senate Hearings, *supra* note 3, at 60; 110 CONG. REC. 22,994 (Bible), 22,996 (Bayh) (1964).

27. 1965 House Hearings, *supra* note 2, at 45; 111 CONG. REC. 7955 (1965) (Rodino).

28. 111 CONG. REC. 7951 (Mathias), 7960 (Poff) (1965).

29. 1965 House Hearings, *supra* note 2, at 49, 78.

30. 1965 Senate Hearings, *supra* note 2, at 102; 1965 House Hearings, *supra* note 2, at 48; 111 CONG. REC. 3281 (Ervin), 7960 (Poff) (1965); 110 CONG. REC. 22,995 (1964) (Bayh).

31. 1965 House Hearings, *supra* note 2, at 47, 49–50; 111 CONG. REC. 3281–82 (Bass), 7961 (Rogers) (1965).

32. 1965 House Hearings, *supra* note 2, at 45, 49, 89.

33. 1965 House Hearings, *supra* note 2, at 50.

34. 111 CONG. REC. 3252 (Bayh), 7949 (Cohelan), 7953 (Bennett), 7960 (Celler) (1965).

35. 1965 Senate Hearings, *supra* note 2, at 64; 1965 House Hearings, *supra* note 2, at 66; 111 CONG. REC. 7962 (Lindsay) (1965); 1964 Senate Hearings, *supra* note 3, at 229.

36. 1965 House Hearings, *supra* note 2, at 47; 111 CONG. REC. 3275 (1965) (Bayh); 1964 Senate Hearings 226; 110 CONG. REC. 22,988 (Bayh), 22,996 (Bayh), 22,999 (Church) (1964).

37. 111 CONG. REC. 7955 (1965). An almost identical view had been expressed earlier by Senator Bayh. 110 CONG. REC. 22,987 (1964).

38. 1965 House Hearings, *supra* note 2, at 65–66.

39. See pp. 93–94, *supra*.

40. *E.g.*, U.S. Const. art. V; *See Missouri Pac. Ry. Co., v. State of Kansas*, 248 U.S. 276 (1919).

41. 1965 Senate Hearings, *supra* note 2, at 10, 52, 64; 1965 House Hearings, *supra* note 2, at 45, 60, 95–96, 101, 106; 111 Cong. Rec. 7944–46 (1965).

42. 1965 Senate Hearings, *supra* note 2, at 19.

43. 1965 House Hearings, *supra* note 2, at 48–49; S. Rep. No. 89-66, at 14 (1965); H.R. Rep. No. 89-203, at 14 (1965).

44. 1965 Senate Hearings, *supra* note 2, at 18. This question was raised after Vice President Spiro Agnew's resignation, when Ronald Reagan was being mentioned as President Nixon's possible vice-presidential choice. Wallace Turners, *Choice of Reagan Called Unlikely; Constitutional Question and Nixon's Coolness Cited by Some Observers Interpretation Given Reagan Not Told*, N.Y. Times, Oct. 11, 1973 at 35.

45. 1965 House Hearings, *supra* note 2, at 208.

46. 111 Cong. Rec. 7953 (1965) (Gilbert); 1964 Senate Hearings, *supra* note 3, at 224–32; *Hearings on Presidential Inability Before the Subcomm. on Constitutional Amendments of the Senate Comm. on the Judiciary*, 88th Cong. 33, 38 (1963) [hereinafter *1963 Senate Hearings*].

47. 111 Cong. Rec. 7938 (Celler), 7941 (Poff) (1965).

48. 1965 Senate Hearings, *supra* note 2, at 20; 1965 House Hearings, *supra* note 2, at 40; 1964 Senate Hearings, *supra* note 3, at 215; 1963 Senate Hearings, *supra* note 46, at 49, 106 & n. 44.

49. *E.g.*, 1964 Senate Hearings, *supra* note 3, at 60; 1963 Senate Hearings, *supra* note 46, at 106 & n. 44; *see* Ruth C. Silva, *Presidential Succession* 171 (1951).

50. 111 Cong. Rec. 1946–47 (1965) (McClory).

51. 1965 House Hearings, *supra* note 2, at 179.

52. 111 Cong. Rec. 7958 (1965).

53. 1965 Senate Hearings, *supra* note 2, at 9, 20, 64–65; 1965 House Hearings, *supra* note 2, at 40; 111 Cong. Rec. 3265, 7941 (Poff), 7946–47 (McClory), 7955 (Rodino) (1965); 1964 Senate Hearings, *supra* note 3, at 136; 1963 Senate Hearings, *supra* note 46, at 22.

54. 1965 House Hearings, *supra* note 2, at 240.

55. 1965 Senate Hearings, *supra* note 2, at 20–21, 64–65; 1965 House Hearings, *supra* note 2, at 96–99, 240.

56. 1965 House Hearings, *supra* note 2, at 99.

57. Williams, An Alternative: Taking the Twenty-Fifth, National Review 476 (1974). *See* John D. Feerick, *The Way of the 25th*, N.Y. Times, Dec. 13, 1973 at 47. *See also infra* chapter 10 notes 25–28.

58. 1965 House Hearings, *supra* note 2, at 264–65; S. Rep. No. 89-66, at 3 (1965); H.R. Rep. No. 89-203, at 2 (1965); III Cong. Rec. 7938 (Celler), 7941 (Poff), 7943 (Horton), 7953 (Gilbert), 7956 (Randall), 15,214 (Poff), 15,378 (Bayh) (1965). There was confusion early in the legislative history on whether a President who had voluntarily declared his own inability nevertheless was subject to the challenge procedures of Section 4 (then Section 5). Compare 1965 House Hearings, *supra* note 2, at 41–42, 99, with III Cong. Rec. 3252–53 (Bayh), 3271 (Bayh) (1965). The House amendment to Section 3 eliminated this doubt. III Cong. Rec. 15,214 (1965).

59. III Cong. Rec. 7941 (1965) (Poff).

60. See S. Rep. No. 89-66, at 2 (1965) for an excellent summary of the congressional intent regarding written declarations.

61. III Cong. Rec. 3270 (1965) (Saltonstall).

62. 1964 Senate Hearings, *supra* note 3, at 215, 232; 1965 House Hearings, *supra* note 2, at 87. *But see* III Cong. Rec. 7950 (1965) (Moore). To be noted is that when Vice President Bush acted as President in 1985 and Vice President Cheney in 2002 and 2007 they did not take the presidential oath of office.

63. 1965 House Hearings, *supra* note 2, at 88.

64. III Cong. Rec. 3253 (1965) (Hruska, Bayh); 1965 House Hearings, *supra* note 2, at 77–78, 193.

65. 1965 Senate Hearings, *supra* note 2, at 9; III Cong. Rec. 3254 (Bayh), 3282–83, 7938 (Celler), 15,380 (Kennedy) (1965); 1964 Senate Hearings, *supra* note 3, at 44; 109 Cong. Rec. 24,421 (1963).

66. III Cong. Rec. 3256 (Ervin), 7941 (Poff), 7947 (McClory), 15,593 (Bayh) (1965).

67. 1965 House Hearings, *supra* note 2, at 141; III Cong. Rec. 3265 (Carlson), 3271 (Bayh), 7938 (Celler) (1965).

68. III Cong. Rec. 3282 (1965).

69. *Id.* at 15,381.

70. *Id.* at 7941.

71. *Id.* at 3282–83 (Hart); 1964 Senate Hearings, *supra* note 3, at 25.

72. III Cong. Rec. 3283 (1965).

73. *Id.* at 7938 (Celler).

74. *Id.* at 7938 (Waggonner), 7941 (Poff), 7944–45 (Whitener), 7952, 7954 (Gilbert).

75. 1965 House Hearings, *supra* note 2, at 52, 61.

76. H.R. Rep. No. 89-203, at 3 (1965).

77. III Cong. Rec. 3284 (1965) (Hart).

78. *Id.* at 15,380.

79. *Id.* (Kennedy), 15,382 (Kennedy), 15,385 (Javits).

80. Notes 78 and 79, *supra*; III Cong. Rec. 3284 (1965) (Bayh, Hart).

81. 1965 House Hearings, *supra* note 2, at 52, 61.

82. 1965 House Hearings, *supra* note 2, at 79–80; III CONG. REC. 15,385 (1965) (Bayh, Javits).

83. 1965 House Hearings, *supra* note 2, at 247.

84. 1965 Senate Hearings, *supra* note 2, at 65; 1965 House Hearings, *supra* note 2, at 79–80, 82.

85. 1965 House Hearings, *supra* note 2, at 40, 64–65, 87–88; III CONG. REC. 7956 (1965) (Randall).

86. III CONG. REC. 3270 (Saltonstall, Ervin), 7956 (Randall) (1965).

87. *See supra* note 85.

88. III CONG. REC. 15,214 (Poff), 15,378–79 (Bayh) (1965); S. REP. NO. 89-66, at 14 (1965); H.R. REP. NO. 89-203, at 14 (1965).

89. III CONG. REC. 3284 (Bayh), 3285 (Allot), 7939 (Celler) (1965); 1965 House Hearings, *supra* note 2, at 41, 58, 250, 253.

90. 1965 House Hearings, *supra* note 2, at 99, 107, 243; III CONG. REC. 3285 (Bayh), 15,214 (Poff) (1965). As for declarations' taking longer than four days, see 1965 House Hearings, *supra* note 2, at 242–43.

91. *See supra*, note 41; 1965 Senate Hearings, *supra* note 2, at 52, 71; III CONG. REC. 3285 (Hruska), 7944 (Whitener, Celler), 7946 (Hutchinson, Celler) (1965).

92. III CONG. REC. 7941 (Poff), 15,379 (Bayh) (1965).

93. 1965 House Hearings, *supra* note 2, at 100; III CONG. REC. 7967 (1965) (Poff, Celler).

94. 1965 House Hearings, *supra* note 2, at 100; S. REP. NO. 89-66, at 2 (1965); III CONG. REC. 3270, 7967 (Poff), 7968 (McCormack) (1965).

95. S. REP. NO. 89-66, at 2 (1965); III CONG. REC. 7968 (1965) (McCormack).

96. H.R. REP. NO. 89-564, at 4 (1965).

97. 1965 House Hearings, *supra* note 2, at 41, 58, 250, 253; III CONG. REC. 3284–85 (Lausche, Bayh), 7939 (Celler); 1964 Senate Hearings, *supra* note 3, at 130.

98. III CONG. REC. 3284 (1965) (Bayh).

99. *Id.* at 7941 (Poff).

100. *Id.*

101. III CONG. REC. 3279 (Bayh), 15,214 (Poff), 15,379 (Bayh) (1965); H.R. REP. NO. 89-564, at 4 (1965).

102. III CONG. REC. 15,379 (1965) (Bayh).

103. 1965 House Hearings, *supra* note 2, at 243.

104. S. REP. NO. 89-66, at 3 (1965); III CONG. REC. 3285 (Bayh), 15,385 (Javits, Bayh) (1965).

105. 1965 Senate Hearing, *supra* note 2, at 21–22; S. REP. NO. 89-66, at 3 (1965); III CONG. REC. 3278–79, 7939, 7954 (1965); 1964 Senate Hearings, *supra* note 3, at 119. On the question of the President asserting doctor–patient confidentiality, see 1965 House Hearings, *supra* note 2, at 143–44.

106. 1965 Senate Hearings, *supra* note 2, at 34.

107. 1965 House Hearings, *supra* note 2, at 101–02, 251 (frequent declarations).

108. 111 CONG. REC. 15,588 (Ervin) (1965). The debates, however, indicate that questions involving the constitutionality of legislation passed by Congress under Section 4 would be appropriate for judicial review. 111 Cong. Rec. 15,386 (Javits), 15,594 (Bayh) (1965).

109. 1965 Senate Hearings, *supra* note 2, at 52, 61; 1965 House Hearings, *supra* note 2, at 45, 241, 253; S. REP. NO. 89-66, at 14 (1965); 111 CONG. REC. 3257 (Bayh), 7941 (Poff), 15,380 (Bayh) (1965); 1964 Senate Hearings, *supra* note 3, at 44.

110. 111 CONG. REC. 3284 (Lausche, Bayh), 15,382 (Bayh), 15,589–92 (1965).

111. *Id.* at 3257 (Bayh), 3284 (Bayh); 1964 Senate Hearings, *supra* note 3, at 44.

112. 111 CONG. REC. 7957 (1965) (Tenzer).

113. *Id.* at 3258 (Tydings), 7941 (Poff), 15385 (Bayh).

114. *Id.* at 3258 (Tydings), 7941 (Poff).

115. 1965 House Hearings, *supra* note 2, at 254.

116. S. REP. NO. 89-66 at 3 (1965); 111 CONG. REC. 15,595 (1965) (Javits).

117. 111 CONG. REC. 15,386 (1965).

118. 111 CONG. REC. 15,379 (Bayh), 15,383–86, 15,586–96 (1965).

119. 1965 House Hearings, *supra* note 2, at 93. 111 CONG. REC. 15,383–85 (1965).

120. 1965 Senate Hearings, *supra* note 2, at 24; 1965 House Hearings, *supra* note 2, at 58, 84–85, 108; 111 CONG. REC. 7963 (Celler), 15,379 (Bayh), 15,383 (McCarthy), 15,586 (Gore) (1965).

121. 1965 Senate Hearings, *supra* note 2, at 28. A firing after a decision had been made should have no effect on that decision.

122. 1965 Senate Hearings, *supra* note 2, at 28; 111 CONG. REC. 15,590 (Gore, Ervin), 15,592 (Bayh) (1965).

123. 1965 House Hearings, *supra* note 2, at 62, 81, 88; 111 CONG. REC. 15,383 (1965).

9. The Resignation of Spiro T. Agnew

1. N.Y. TIMES, Oct. 11, 1973 at 35.

2. Mark Feldstein, *Watergate Revisited*, American Journal Review (Aug./Sept. 2004) *available at* http://www.ajr.org/article.asp?id=3735.

3. Clark Clifford, *A Government of National Unity*, N.Y. TIMES, June 4, 1973 at 35.

4. The facts set forth in this section are taken largely from issues of the *N.Y. Times* and *Wash. Post*, and from R. Cohen and J. Witcover, *A Heartbeat Away: The Investigation and Resignation of Vice President Spiro T. Agnew* (1974). For an excel-

lent summary of the events leading to the resignation, see, in particular, Naughton, *How Agnew Bartered His Office to Keep from Going to Prison*, N. Y. TIMES, Oct. 23, 1973 at 1, 36.

5. Cohen & Witcover, *supra* note 4, at 15.

6. Naughton, *supra* note 4.

7. Cohen & Witcover, *supra* note 4, at 110–11.

8. *Id.* at 133–34.

9. *Id.* at 145–46.

10. *Id.* at 159.

11. *Id.* at 192.

12. N.Y. TIMES, Aug. 23, 1973 at 1.

13. Cohen & Witcover, *supra* note 4, at 203–04.

14. 13 N.Y. TIMES, Sept. 2, 1973, at 1, 34.

15. Naughton, *supra* note 4.

16. Cohen & Witcover, *supra* note 4, at 218–19.

17. *Id.* at 223–24.

18. Naughton, *supra* note 4.

19. Cohen & Witcover, *supra* note 4, at 243.

20. *Id.* at 244.

21. *Id.* at 252–53.

22. Carl Albert, *The Most Dramatic Events of My Life*, Oklahoma State University Outreach 4–5 (Mar. 1974).

23. N.Y. TIMES, Sept. 27, 1973 at 28; N.Y. TIMES, Sept. 26, 1973 at 1, 23; Jerald F. terHorst, *Gerald Ford and the Future of the Presidency* 154 (1974).

24. N.Y. TIMES, Sept. 27, 1973 at 1.

25. N.Y. TIMES, Sept. 27, 1973 at 28.

26. *Id.*

27. N.Y. TIMES, Sept. 30, 1973 at 60.

28. Cohen & Witcover, *supra* note 4, at 277–78.

29. N.Y. TIMES, Oct. 4, 1973 at 30.

30. N.Y. TIMES, Oct. 6, 1973 at 1, 9.

31. Cohen & Witcover, *supra* note 4, at 328.

32. N.Y. TIMES, Oct. 11, 1973 at 35.

33. N.Y. TIMES, Oct. 11, 1973 at 1.

34. N.Y. TIMES, Oct. 11, 1973 at 34.

35. terHorst, *supra* note 23, at 154.

36. N.Y. TIMES, Oct. 11, 1973 at 34.

37. N.Y. TIMES, Oct. 12, 1973 at 26.

10. The Substitution of Gerald R. Ford

1. 119 CONG. REC. 39,926 (1973) (statement of Gerald R. Ford).

2. Anderson, *Congress Is Ready if Agnew Quits*, REPORTER DISPATCH, Sept. 21, 1973, at 7.

3. James M. Naughton, *Any Agnew Replacement May Face Bar on '76 Bid; Democrats Meet on Vice President Criticism from Buckley*, N.Y. TIMES, Sept. 21, 1973, at 1.

4. *Id.*

5. *Id.*

6. N.Y. TIMES, Sept. 22, 1973, at 25.

7. N.Y. TIMES, Oct. 11, 1973, at 1.

8. WASH. POST, Oct. 12, 1973, at A15.

9. Albert, Most Dramatic Events of My Life 6. Pamphlet. "Three Critical Decisions: The Most Dramatic Events of My Life" by Carl Albert. Re: Resignation of Spiro Agnew, 25th Amendment, Richard Nixon, Impeachment, and confirmation of Gerald Ford. Speech given at the Carl Albert Lecture Series at Oklahoma State University. (January 17, 1974). Carl Albert Collection Biographical Series Box and Folder Inventory Box 2, available at http://www.ou.edu/specialalbertctr/archives/albertinventory/Cabio02.htm. Accessed December 6, 2012. Speeches, 1974 F31-35: "Three Critical Decisions: The Most Dramatic Events of My Life." January 17, 1974. Address delivered under the "Carl Albert Lecture Series" at Oklahoma State University, Stillwater, Oklahoma. Carl Albert Collection Speech Series Box and Folder Inventory Box 18, available at http://www.ou.edu/specialalbertctr/archives/albertinventory/Caspch18.htm. Accessed December 6, 2012.

10. WASH. POST, Oct. 12, 1973, at A12.

11. *Id.*

12. *Id.*

13. *Id.*

14. *Id.*

15. James M. Naughton, *Any Agnew Replacement May Face Bar on '76 Bid; Democrats Meet on Vice President Criticism from Buckley*, N.Y. TIMES, Oct. 11, 1973, at 1, 33. *See also* Joel K. Goldstein, *Taking from the Twenty-Fifth Amendment: Lessons in Ensuring Presidential Continuity*, 79 FORDHAM L. REV. 959, 970 (2010).

16. N.Y. TIMES, Oct. 12, 1973, at 28; WASH. POST, Oct. 12, 1973, at A1, A15.

17. N.Y. TIMES, Oct. 12, 1973, at 28.

18. WASH. POST, Oct. 12, 1973, at A10.

19. WASH. POST, Oct. 12, 1973, at A12.

20. N.Y. TIMES, Oct. 13, 1973, at 19.

21. Jerald F. terHorst, *Gerald Ford and the Future of the Presidency* 155–56 (1974).

22. N.Y. TIMES, Oct. 13, 1973, at 19.

23. *Id.*

24. Goldstein, *supra* note 15, at 971 (2010).

25. 119 CONG. REC. 33,993–94 (1973).

26. *Id.* at 33,994 (statement of Senator Michael Mansfield, Majority Leader).

27. N.Y. TIMES, Oct. 12, 1973, at 28; WASH. POST, Oct. 12, 1973, at A1, A15.

28. 119 CONG. REC. 33,793 (1973).

29. *Id.* at 33,792–95.

30. *Id.* at 33,794 (statement of Senator Hubert Humphrey).

31. *Id.* at 33,994.

32. N.Y. TIMES, Oct. 13, 1973, at 18.

33. 119 CONG. REC. 33,998 (1973) (statement of Senator Edward W. Brooke).

34. *Id.* at 33,997 (statement of Senator Lawton Chiles).

35. *Id.* at 34,001 (statement of Senator Edward Kennedy).

36. *Id.*

37. *Id.* at 34,003 (statement of Senator Joseph R. Biden Jr.).

38. *Id.* at 34,003 (statement of Senator Marlow W. Cook).

39. *Id.* at 34,047.

40. The investigation is described in Senate Comm. on Rules and Administration, Report on Nomination of Gerald R. Ford of Michigan to be the Vice President of the United States, S. REP. NO. 93–26 (1973); *see* H.R. REP. NO. 93–695 (1973).

41. Benton Becker, *Adequacy of Current Succession Law in Light of the Constitution and Policy Considerations*, 79 FORDHAM L. REV. 897, 900 (2010).

42. Goldstein, *supra* note 15, at 971.

43. Theodore "Ted" Sorensen, *Counselor LP: A Life at the Edge of History*, 476–78 (2008). It appears from a later interview with Carl Albert that had he assumed the position of Acting President under the 1947 succession law, he would have nominated a Republican for Vice President and, upon that person's confirmation, resigned as Acting President so that Nixon's party would continue to occupy the presidency for the duration of Nixon's term. *See* Ted Gup, *Speaker Albert Was Ready to Be President*, WASH. POST, Nov. 28, 1982, at A1.

44. *Hearings on Nomination of Gerald R. Ford of Michigan to be Vice President of the United States Before the Senate Comm. on Rules and Administration*, 93d Cong. 4 (1973) (statement of Chairman Howard Cannon of Nevada).

45. *Id.* at 8 (statement of Chairman Howard Cannon of Nevada).

46. *Id.* at 114 (statement of Gerald R. Ford).

47. *Id.* at 124 (statement of Gerald R. Ford).

48. *Id.* at 41–42, 70–73 (statement of Gerald R. Ford).

49. *Id.* at 31, 40–41 (statement of Gerald R. Ford).

50. *Id.* at 18 (statement of Gerald R. Ford).

51. *Id.*

52. *Id.* at 148, 153, 159 (statement of Senator Birch Bayh).

53. *Id.* at 181.

54. *Id.* at 171 (statement of Representative Martha W. Griffiths, of Michigan).

55. *Id.* at 290–98 (statement of Representative Bella S. Abzug, of New York).

56. *Id.* at 317 (statement of Joseph L. Rauh Jr., national vice-chairman of Americans for Democratic Action).

57. *Id.* at 338 (statement of Joseph L. Rauh Jr., national vice-chairman of Americans for Democratic Action).

58. S. REP. NO. 93–26, at 97 (1973).

59. 119 CONG. REC. 38,224 (1973) (statement of Senator Edward Kennedy).

60. *Id.* at 38,217 (statement of Senator Frank Church).

61. *Id.* at 38,225 (statement of Senator John V. Tunney).

62. *Id.* at 38,213 (statement of Senator Philip Hart).

63. *Id.* at 38,218.

64. *Id.* at 38,225 (statement of Senator John V. Tunney).

65. Albert, *supra* note 9, at 8.

66. *Hearings on Nomination of Gerald R. Ford to be Vice President of the United States Before the House Comm. on the Judiciary,* 93d Cong. 2 (1973) [hereinafter *House Hearings*] (statement of Chairman Peter Rodino).

67. *Id.* at 87 (statement of Representative George E. Danielson, of California).

68. *Id.* at 236 (statement of Representative Edward Mezvinsky, of Iowa).

69. *Id.* at 251 (statement of Representative Edward P. Boland, of Massachusetts).

70. *Id.* at 621 (statement of Representative Jerome R. Waldie, of California).

71. *Id.* at 618–19, 645, 660.

72. *Id.* at 116–17, 136, 669–70.

73. *Id.* at 147.

74. *Id.* at 58, 131, 141, 586–91.

75. *Id.* at 91–97, 570–82.

76. *Id.* at 576–78.

77. Becker, *supra* note 41, at 898.

78. *House Hearings, supra* note 66, at 5 (statement of Representative J. Edward Hutchinson of Michigan).

79. *Id.* at 583–84 (statement of Gerald R. Ford).

80. *Id.* at 129–30.

81. *Id.* at 534–35.

82. *Id.* at 6, 18.

83. *Id.* at 70 (statement of Representative Robert McClory, of Illinois).

84. *Id.* at 227 (statement of Clarence Mitchell, NAACP chief lobbyist).

85. *Id.* at 179 (statement of Representative Michael J. Harrington, of Massachusetts).

86. *Id.* at 669 (statement of Chairman Peter Rodino).

87. H.R. REP. NO. 93–695, at 13 (1973).

88. *Id.* at 43. (statement of Representative Jerome R. Waldie, of California).

89. 119 CONG. REC. 39,882 (1973) (statement of Representative James G. O'Hara, of Michigan).

90. *Id.* at 39,888 (statement of Representative Robert E. Bauman, of Maryland).

91. *Id.* at 39,834, 39,869–70.

92. *Id.* at 39,838–39 (statement of Representative Samuel L. Devine, of Ohio).

93. *Id.* at 39,862 (statement of Representative Bo Ginn, of Georgia).

94. *Id.* at 39,825–26, 39,829–30, 39,833–34.

95. *Id.* at 39,878 (statement of Representative Andrew Young, of Georgia).

96. *Id.* at 39,817–18.

97. *Id.* at 39,865–66.

98. *Id.* at 39,870–71, 39,875, 39,885–86, 39,888–89.

99. *Id.* at 39,878–79.

100. *Id.* at 39,856 (statement of Representative George E. Danielson, of California).

101. *Id.* at 39,862 (statement of Representative Edward P. Boland, of Massachusetts).

102. *Id.* at 39,885–86 (statement of Representative Edward R. Roybal, of California).

103. *Id.* at 39,820–21 (statement of Representative Jerome R. Waldie, of California).

104. *Id.* at 39,825, 39,826–27, 39,829–30, 39,833, 39,840–41, 39,882.

105. *Id.* at 39,830 (statement of Representative John Conyers Jr., of Michigan).

106. *Id.* at 39,830 (statement of Representative Charles E. Wiggins, of California).

107. *Id.* at 39,842 (statement of Representative Patricia Schroeder, of Colorado).

108. *Id.* at 39,837 (statement of Representative M. Caldwell Butler, of Virginia).

109. *Id.* at 39,840 (statement of Representative Wiley Mayne, of Iowa).

110. *Id.* at 39,834 (statement of Representative Charles B. Rangel, of New York).

11. The Resignation of Richard M. Nixon and Succession of Gerald R. Ford

1. Robert Granville Caldwell, *James A. Garfield, Party Chieftain* 155 (Dodd, Mead & Company, 1931).

2. *See* J. F. terHorst, *Gerald Ford and the Future of the Presidency* 176 (1974); Donald W. Riegle Jr., *The Ford Nomination as a Way Out*, N.Y. TIMES, Nov. 29, 1973, at 43; Tom Wicker, *Nixon and Ford: In the Nation*, N.Y. Times, Dec. 7, 1973, at 41; *id.* at 1.

3. Joel K. Goldstein, *Taking from the Twenty-Fifth Amendment: Lessons in Ensuring Presidential Continuity*, 79 FORDHAM L. REV. 959, 970 (2010).

4. Benton Becker, *Adequacy of Current Succession Law in Light of the Constitution and Policy Considerations*, 79 FORDHAM L. REV. 897, 900 (2010).

5. Goldstein, *supra* note 3, at 971 ("Speaker Carl Albert worried that too speedy a confirmation might appear to reflect cronyism that would undermine Ford's legitimacy and that of the Section 2 process. The Agnew debacle made even more necessary a careful examination of Ford's record insofar as it reflected on his character.").

6. Goldstein, *supra* note 3, at 917.

7. Goldstein, *supra* note 3, at 972.

8. *Id.* (The procedure "minimized the role of partisan considerations" as it allowed for the confirmation of a Republican Vice President to line up as Nixon's successor.)

9. Becker, *supra* note 4, at 902–03 (He also noted, "The Vice President's office was in the Executive Office Building, not in the White House. They dealt with him in that fashion.").

10. Anthony Ripleys, *Ford Is Hopeful of Compromise in Tape Dispute*, N.Y. TIMES, Jan. 7, 1974, at 1, 12.

11. N.Y. TIMES, Jan. 8, 1974, at 15.

12. Philip Shabecoffs, *Ford Says 'Extreme' Wing Extends Watergate Ordeal*, N.Y. TIMES, Jan. 16, 1974, at 1.

13. *Id.*

14. Leslie Oelsners, *Sirica Court Told Erasures on Tape Came After Oct. 1*, N.Y. TIMES, Jan. 17, 1974, at 1.

15. N.Y. TIMES, Jan. 23, 1974, at 18.

16. N.Y. TIMES, Feb. 8, 1974, at 29.

17. N.Y. TIMES, Mar. 10, 1974, at 1.

18. N.Y TIMES, Mar. 31, 1974, at 1, 25.

19. *Id.* at 25.

20. N.Y. TIMES, Apr. 15, 1974, at 20.

21. N.Y. TIMES, Apr. 21, 1974, at 26.

22. N.Y. TIMES, Apr. 28, 1974, at 26.

23. N.Y. TIMES, May 3, 1974, at 27.

24. N.Y. TIMES, May 4, 1974, at 24.

25. *Id.*

26. N.Y. TIMES, June 9, 1974, at 46.

27. N.Y. TIMES, May 29, 1974, at 24.

28. N.Y. TIMES, June 26, 1974, at 1.

29. *Id.*, at 16.

30. N.Y. TIMES, Dec. 4, 1973, at 36.

31. *Id.*

32. N.Y. TIMES, Apr. 4, 1974, at 34.

33. N.Y. POST, May 17, 1974, at 10.

34. *Wilson, Nixon and the 25th*, WASH. STAR-NEWS, Apr. 8, 1974, at A10; Zbigniew Brzezinski, *A "Leave of Absence" for Mr. Nixon?*, WASH. POST, Apr. 6, 1974, at 14.

35. James J. Kilpatrick, *Private Talk with Nixon*, SAN FRANCISCO CHRONICLE, May 17, 1974, at 14.

36. Warren Weaver Jr., *Opinion by Burger; Name of President Is Left in Indictment as Co-Conspirator*, N.Y. TIMES, July 25, 1974, at 1.

37. The Staff of the New York Times, *The End of a Presidency* 60 (N.Y. Times ed. 1974).

38. *Id.*

39. *Impeachment Article 1*, N.Y. TIMES, July 28, 1974, at 1.

40. N.Y. TIMES, July 30, 1974, at 1.

41. James Naughton, *House Panel, 21 to 17, Charges Nixon with Defying Subpoenas*, N.Y. TIMES, July 31, 1974, at 1.

42. *End of a Presidency, supra* note 37, at 63–64.

43. *Id.*

44. *President's Statement About Disclosure*, N.Y. TIMES, Aug. 6, 1974, at 1.

45. N.Y. TIMES, August 7, 1974, at 19.

46. Wallace Turners, *Reagan Urges Nixon to See Congress*, N.Y. TIMES, August 7, 1974, at 1.

47. *End of a Presidency, supra* note 37, at 69–70.

48. *Id.* at 70.

49. *Id.* at 71.

50. *The Nixon Resignation*, N.Y. TIMES, Aug. 9, 1974, at 3.

51. *Id.*

52. N.Y. TIMES, Aug. 9, 1974, at 2.

53. *Transcript of Address by New President*, N.Y. TIMES, Aug. 10, 1974, at 3.

54. James M. Naughton, *The Change in Presidents: Plans Began Months Ago*, N.Y. TIMES, Aug. 26, 1974, at 1.

55. *Id.*

56. *Id.*

57. *Id.*

58. *Id.*

59. terHorst, *supra* note 2, at 189.

12. The Installation of Nelson A. Rockefeller

1. H.R. REP. NO. 93–1609, at 27 (1974) (statement of Representative Robert W. Kastenmeier).

2. N.Y. TIMES, Aug. 8, 1974, at 23.

3. N.Y. TIMES, Aug. 8, 1974, at 1.

4. N.Y. TIMES, Aug. 8, 1974, at 23.

5. N.Y. TIMES, Aug. 10, 1974, at 3.

6. N.Y. TIMES, Aug. 11, 1974, at 43.

7. N.Y. TIMES, Aug. 9, 1974, at 1, 4.

8. N.Y. TIMES, Aug. 9, 1974, at 4.

9. N.Y. TIMES, Aug. 11, 1974, at 43.

10. N.Y. TIMES, Aug. 14, 1974, at 16.

11. N.Y. TIMES, Aug. 16, 1974, at 10.

12. N.Y. TIMES, Aug. 17, 1974, at 15.

13. NEWSWEEK, Aug. 26, 1974, at 18.

14. NEWSWEEK, Aug. 26, 1974, at 19.

15. *Watergate Backwash*, N.Y. TIMES, Aug. 19, 1974, at 24.

16. NEWSWEEK, Aug. 26, 1974, at 18.

17. NEWSWEEK, Sept. 2, 1974, at 14.

18. R. W. Apple, *A Turn in G.O.P. Tide*, N.Y. TIMES, Aug. 21, 1974, at 1, 81.

19. NEWSWEEK, Sept. 2, 1974 at 15.

20. Clifton Daniel, *A Relaxed Nominee Fits Mood Sought by Ford*, N.Y. TIMES, Aug. 21, 1974, at 26.

21. *Remarks by President and Rockefeller*, N.Y. TIMES, Aug. 21, 1974, at 1.

22. John Herbers, *Ford Discloses He Expects to Ask Nomination in 76*, N.Y. TIMES, Aug. 22, 1974, at 1, 69.

23. R. W. Apple, *Rockefeller Puts Off Taking to Stump*, N.Y. TIMES, Aug. 22, 1974, at 24.

24. Linda Charlton, *Rockefeller Asserts Nixon Should Not Be Prosecuted*, N.Y. TIMES, Aug. 24, 1974, at 1.

25. Clifton Daniel, *Presidential Clemency; Ford Says He Will Decide Nixon Case After Legal Process Runs Its Course*, N.Y. TIMES, Aug. 29, 1974, at 21.

26. *Action Taken to Spare Nation and Ex-Chief, President Asserts*, N.Y. TIMES, Sept. 9, 1974, at 1.

27. Benton Becker, *Adequacy of Current Succession Law in Light of the Constitution and Policy Considerations*, 70 FORDHAM L. REV. 897 (2010). (Becker commented that Ford was "a man of great courage and guts" and his specific act of pardoning Nixon was one of "political courage." Becker also stated that he believed Ford viewed his "Profiles in Courage" award from Senator Ted Kennedy and Caroline Kennedy in 2005 as the one that "pleased him the most," since it directly related to the issuing of the pardon.)

28. *110,000 Messages Pour into Washington on Pardon*, N.Y. TIMES, Sept. 12, 1974, at 28.

29. *Nightmare Compounded*, N.Y. TIMES, Sept. 11, 1974, at 44.

30. *Support for Ford Declines Sharply; A Poll Links Drop to Pardon and Finds Disapproval for Timing of Action*, N.Y. TIMES, Sept. 12, 1974, at 1, 81.

31. *See Hearings on the Pardon of Richard M. Nixon, and Related Matters, Before the Subcomm. on Criminal Justice of the House Comm. on the Judiciary*, 93d Cong. 90–111, 148–58 (1975).

32. Linda Charlton, *Inquiry Pressed on Rockefeller; 400 F.B.I. Agents Said to Be Investigating His Fortune, Health and Other Data*, N.Y. TIMES, Sept. 5, 1974, at 19.

33. Linda Charlton, *Rockefeller Promises to Take Steps to Resolve Any Conflicts of Interest*, N.Y. TIMES, Sept. 4, 1974, at 16.

34. S. REP. NO. 93–34, at 4–5 (1974).

35. Linda Charlton, *Rockefeller to Disclose His Net Worth*, N.Y. TIMES, Sept. 12, 1974, at 24.

36. Linda Charlton, *Rockefeller Says His Assets Are Valued at $62-Million*, N.Y. TIMES, Sept. 20, 1974, at 1.

37. *Majorie Hunter*, N.Y. TIMES, Oct. 10, 1974, at 39.

38. *Id.*

39. See *Hearings on Nomination of Nelson A. Rockefeller of New York to be Vice President of the United States Before the Senate Comm. on Rules and Administration*, 93d Cong. 39–79 (1974) [hereinafter *Rockefeller Senate Hearings*].

40. *Id.* at 128.

41. *Id.* at 143.

42. *Id.* at 165.

43. *Id.* at 23.

44. *Id.* at 224.

45. *Id.* at 147.

46. *Id.* at 22–23.

47. *Id.* at 233–61.

48. *Id.* at 267–459.

49. N.Y. TIMES, Sept. 25, 1974, at 1.

50. NEWSWEEK, Oct. 7, 1974, at 46.

51. *Ford Hints at Change in '76 Election Plans*, N.Y. TIMES, Sept. 30, 1974, at 27.

52. Robert McFadden, *Rockefeller Gave Kissinger $50,000, Helped 2 Others; He Denies Any Impropriety*, N.Y. TIMES, Oct. 6, 1974, at 1, 58.

53. *Id.*

54. Linda Charlton, *Beneficiaries of Rockefeller Gifts Will Vote on His Nomination*, N.Y. TIMES, Oct. 8, 1974, at 27.

55. Linda Charlton, *Rockefeller Gifts Queried; $550,000 Went to Ronan*, N.Y. TIMES, Oct. 9, 1974, at 1, 29.

56. 120 CONG. REC. S19,171–72 (daily ed. Oct. 15, 1974) (statement of Senator Jesse Helms, of North Carolina).

57. Linda Charlton, *Rockefeller Gifts Queried; $550,000 Went to Ronan*, N.Y. TIMES, Oct. 9, 1974, at 1, 89.

58. 120 CONG. REC. S18,472 (daily ed. Oct. 8, 1974).

59. 120 CONG. REC. S18,627–28 (daily ed. Oct. 9, 1974).

60. Frank J. Prial, *Nelson and David Rockefeller Reported Principals in Secret 1968 Transit Pact*, N.Y. TIMES, Oct. 10, 1974, at 34.

61. Frank Lynn, *The Power of Rockefeller Money*, N.Y. TIMES, Oct. 9, 1974, at 30.

62. N.Y. TIMES, Oct. 10, 1974, at 1.

63. N.Y. TIMES, Oct. 10, 1974, at 38.

64. N.Y. TIMES, Oct. 10, 1974, at 46.

65. N.Y. TIMES, Oct. 10, 1974, at 1.

66. N.Y. TIMES, Oct. 22, 1974, at 1.

67. N.Y. TIMES, Oct. 10, 1974, at 34.

68. N.Y. TIMES, Oct. 17, 1974, at 27.

69. N.Y. TIMES, Oct. 11, 1974, at 1, 16.

70. N.Y. TIMES, Oct. 11, 1974, at 1, 16.

71. N.Y. TIMES, Oct. 11, 1974, at 1, 16.

72. N.Y. TIMES, Oct. 11, 1974, at 1, 1.

73. N.Y. TIMES, Oct. 12, 1974, at 1, 14.

74. N.Y. TIMES, Oct. 12, 1974, at 14.

75. N.Y. TIMES, Oct. 12, 1974, at 1, 15.

76. N.Y. TIMES, Oct. 13, 1974, at 24.

77. N.Y. TIMES, Oct. 14, 1974, at 33.

78. *Id.*

79. N.Y. TIMES, Oct. 13, 1974, at 1, 23.

80. N.Y. TIMES, Oct. 13, 1974, at 23.

81. N.Y. TIMES, Oct. 14, 1974, at 1, 38.

82. N.Y. TIMES, Oct. 15, 1974, at 1, 28.

83. N.Y. TIMES, Oct. 17, 1974, at 1.

84. N.Y. TIMES, Oct. 19, 1974, at 1, 13.

85. N.Y. TIMES, Oct. 20, 1974, at 1.

86. *Id.*

87. N.Y. TIMES, Oct. 23, 1974, at 1.

88. N.Y. TIMES, Oct. 21, 1974, at 1.

89. NEWSWEEK, Oct. 28, 1974, at 30.

90. N.Y. TIMES, Oct. 25, 1974, at 1, 36.

91. N.Y. TIMES, Oct. 29, 1974, at 1, 24.

92. Tom Wicker, *Mr. Rockefeller's Ordeal*, N.Y. TIMES, Nov. 1, 1974, at 39.

93. N.Y. TIMES, Nov. 13, 1974, at 29.

94. *Id.*

95. Rockefeller Senate Hearings, *supra* note 39, at 477.

96. *Id.* at 533.

97. *Id.* at 477.

98. *Id.* at 530–31.

99. *Id.* at 533.

100. *Id.* at 541.

101. *Id.* at 522.

102. *Id.*

103. *Id.* at 472.

104. *Id.* at 473.

105. *Id.*

106. *Id.* at 474.

107. *Id.* at 476.

108. *Id.* at 475–76, 479.

109. Tom Wicker, *Money in Office*, N.Y. TIMES, Nov. 15, 1974, at 37.

110. Rockefeller Senate Hearings, *supra* note 39, at 617.

111. *Id.* at 670–89.

112. *Id.* at 673.

113. *Id.* at 698.

114. *Id.* at 692.

115. Richard L. Madden, *President Prods Congress for Action on Rockefeller*, N.Y. TIMES, Nov. 15, 1974, at 1, 21.

116. *Ford Will Definitely Run In 1976, Nessen Reports*, N.Y. TIMES, Nov. 16, 1974, at 14.

117. Rockefeller Senate Hearings, *supra* note 39, at 710–13.

118. *Id.* at 848.

119. *Id.* at 849.

120. *Id.* at 886.

121. *Id.*

122. *Id.* at 897–98.

123. *Id.* at 887–89.

124. *Byrd Expects Senate to Confirm Rockefeller*, N.Y. TIMES, Nov. 17, 1974, at 47.

125. James M. Naughton, *Metamorphosis of Robert Byrd Continues*, N.Y. TIMES, Nov. 19, 1974, at 38.

126. Rockefeller Senate Hearings, *supra* note 39, at 930.

127. *Id.*

128. *Id.* at 930–31.

129. *Id.* at 951, 971–74.

130. *Id.* at 986.

131. *Id.* at 986–87.

132. *Id.* at 1015.

133. *Id.* at 1025.

134. *Id.* at 1025–26.

135. Linda Charlton, *Byrd and Allen Uncertain if They'll Aid Move on Floor—House Hearings Go On*, N.Y. TIMES, Nov. 23, 1974, at 1.

136. *Hearings on the Nomination of Nelson A. Rockefeller to Be Vice President of the United States Before the House Comm. on the Judiciary*, 93d Cong. 2 (1974) (statement of Peter W. Rodino, Chairman of the House Judiciary Committee).

137. *Id.* at 186–87, 197.

138. *Id.* at 65.

139. *Id.* at 169, 195.

140. *Id.* at 66–67, 164, 959–64.

141. *Id.* at 660.

142. *Id.* at 636.

143. *Id.* at 717–22.

144. *Id.* at 848–49.

145. *Id.* at 873.

146. *Id.* at 926.

147. *Id.* at 1010.

148. 120 CONG. REC. S20,783–85 (daily ed. Dec. 9, 1974).

149. 120 CONG. REC. S20,788, S20,790.

150. 120 CONG. REC. S20,801.

151. 120 CONG. REC. S20,814.

152. 120 CONG. REC. S20,814–20.

153. 120 CONG. REC. S20,978 (daily ed. Dec. 10, 1974).

154. 120 CONG. REC. S20,978–82.

155. 120 CONG. REC. S20,993.

156. H.R. REP. No. 93–1609, at 11 (1974).

157. *Id.* at 24.

158. 120 CONG. REC. H12,459–60 (daily ed. Dec. 19, 1974).

159. 120 CONG. REC. H12,367.

160. 120 CONG. REC. H12,439 (Clausen).

161. 120 CONG. REC. H12,372 (Hungate).

162. 120 CONG. REC. H12,391–92 (Crane).

163. 120 CONG. REC. H12,364 (Holtzman).

164. 120 CONG. REC. H12,370–71 (Kastenmeier).

165. 120 CONG. REC. H12,383.

166. 120 CONG. REC. S22,267–68.

167. *Exit Rockefeller: A New Equation for 1976*, Congressional Quarterly, Nov. 8, 1975, at 2366.

168. *Vice President's Letter*, N.Y. TIMES, Nov. 4, 1975, at 27.

169. Philip Shabecoff, *Rockefeller Declares 'Party Squabbles' Led to Move; Leaves Own Race Open*, N.Y. TIMES, Nov. 7, 1975, at 1, 16.

170. N.Y. TIMES, Nov. 4, 1975, at 1.

171. *Id.* at 24. *See also* Christopher Lydon, *Ford's First National Campaign: Incumbent in Role of Underdog*, N.Y. TIMES, Dec. 22, 1975, at 1.

172. 171. Philip Shabecoff, *Ford Said to Be Undisturbed by Poll Data*, N.Y. TIMES, Dec. 13, 1975, at 14 (discussing the results of a Gallup Poll showing that 40 percent of Republicans and 27 percent of independents surveyed in the period November 21–24, 1975, preferred Reagan as the Republican presidential nominee, and that 32 percent of the Republicans and 25 percent of the independents pre-

ferred Ford). *See Ford's 1975: Economy, Energy, Foreign Policy,* Congressional Quarterly, Jan. 10, 1976, at 35.

13. The Uses and Non-Uses of Section 3

1. James A. Baker III, *"Work Hard, Study . . . and Keep Out of Politics!"* 150 (2006).

2. WASH. POST, Mar. 31, 1981, at A1.

3. N.Y. TIMES, Mar. 31, 1981, at 1.

4. N.Y. TIMES, Apr. 3, 1981, at 1.

5. N.Y. TIMES, Mar. 31, 1981, at 5.

6. N.Y. TIMES, Mar. 31, 1981, at 1.

7. *Id.*

8. N.Y. TIMES, Apr. 1, 1981, Editorial, at 30.

9. N.Y. TIMES, Mar. 31, 1981, at 1.

10. WASH. POST, Mar. 31, 1981, at A1.

11. N.Y. TIMES, Mar. 31, 1981, at 1.

12. *Id.*

13. N.Y. TIMES, Apr. 1, 1981, Editorial, at 31.

14. *Papers on Presidential Disability and the Twenty-Fifth Amendment,* ed. K. Thompson, Vol. 2 at 128 n. (1991).

15. Donald T. Regan, *For the Record: From Wall Street to Washington* 169 (1988).

16. Alexander M. Haig Jr., *Caveat: Realism, Reagan, and Foreign Policy* 153 (1984).

17. Del Quentin Wilber, *Rawhide Down: The Near Assassination of Ronald Reagan,* 165–75 (2011).

18. Fred Fielding, Fordham Law Review Symposium Transcript, 16 (2010).

19. *See* Wilber, *supra* note 17, at 167.

20. Fielding, Fordham Law Review Symposium Transcript, 20.

21. Press Briefing, The White House, Mar. 30, 1981; N.Y. TIMES, Mar. 31, 1981, at 1; Haig, *supra* note 16, at 159–60.

22. *Id.*

23. Michael K. Deaver & Mickey Herskowitz, *Behind the Scenes: In Which the Author Talks About Ronald and Nancy Reagan . . . and Himself* 31 (1987).

24. Caspar Weinberger, *Fighting for Peace: Seven Critical Years in the Pentagon* 89–90 (1990).

25. *Id.,* at 90, 97.

26. Deaver, *supra* note 23, at 22.

27. *See* Wilber, *supra* note 19, at 165; Fielding Transcript, at 21.

28. Larry Speakes & Robert Pack, *Speaking Out: The Reagan Presidency from Inside the White House* 9 (1988).

29. Haig, *supra* note 16, at 157.

30. George H. W. Bush and Victor Gold, *Looking Forward: An Autobiography* 222 (1987).

31. *Id.*

32. *See* Fielding Transcript, at 21.

33. N.Y. TIMES, Apr. 1, 1981 at 20.

34. N.Y. TIMES, Apr. 25, 1981, at 1.

35. N.Y. TIMES, June 4, 1981, at B15.

36. N.Y. TIMES, May 18, 1981, at 1.

37. N.Y. TIMES, June 17, 1981, at 27.

38. Herbert L. Abrams, *"The President Has Been Shot": Confusion, Disability, and the Twenty-Fifth Amendment in the Aftermath of the Attempted Assassination of Ronald Reagan* 74 (1992) [taken from an interview with Ruge on Dec. 12, 1988].

39. N.Y. TIMES, July 13, 1985, at 1.

40. N.Y. TIMES, July 14, 1985, at 20; 131 CONG. REC. 19,008–19,009 (1985).

41. N.Y. TIMES, July 14, 1985, at 20; 131 CONG. REC. 19,009 (1985).

42. N.Y. TIMES, July 15, 1985, at 1.

43. See note 18, *supra*, at 28.

44. *See id.*, at 30.

45. *Id.*

46. N.Y. TIMES, July 24, 1985, at 1.

47. *Papers on Presidential Disability*, ed. Thompson, 129 (1991).

48. Ronald Reagan, *An American Life: Ronald Reagan* 500 (1990).

49. Nancy Reagan and William Novak, *My Turn: The Memoirs of Nancy Reagan* 274 (1989).

50. Donald T. Regan, *supra* note 15, at 8.

51. *Id.*, at 7.

52. *Id.*

53. N.Y. TIMES, Dec. 21, 1986, at 20.

54. N.Y. TIMES, May 16, 1987, at 6.

55. N.Y. TIMES, Sept. 16, 1988, at 16.

56. Jane Mayer and Doyle McManus, *Landslide: The Unmaking of the President, 1984–1988* vii–xi (1988).

57. Press Briefing, The White House, Marlin Fitzwater Apr. 28, 1989.

58. *See generally* Papers on Presidential Disability, ed. Thompson.

59. *See, e.g.,* N.Y. TIMES, May 6–May 10, May 12, 1991 and Jan. 12, 1992.

60. N.Y. TIMES, May 5, 1991, at 1.

61. N.Y. TIMES, May 6, 1991, at 1; Press Briefing, The White House, Marlin Fitzwater, May 5, 1991.

62. Press Briefing, The White House, Marlin Fitzwater, May 6, 1991.

63. WASH. POST, May 7, 1991, at A1.

64. N.Y. Times, Jan. 9, 1992, at 1.

65. Press Briefing by Mike McCurry and Dr. David Wade (Mar. 14, 1997), http://www.presidency.ucsb.edu/ws/index.php?pid=48584.

66. Press Briefing by the Physicians Attending to the President (Mar. 14, 1997), http://www.presidency.ucsb.edu/ws/index.php?pid=48596.

67. *Id.*

68. James Bennet, *Clinton knee surgery successful; President tripped tore tendon*, Denver Post, Mar. 15, 1997.

69. Press Briefing by Mike McCurry (March 15, 1997), http://www.presidency.ucsb.edu/ws/index.php?pid=48590.

70. Elisabeth Bumiller and Lawrence K. Altman, *Bush Returns to Activities After 20-Minute Procedure Finds No Polyps on His Colon*, N.Y. Times, June 30, 2002.

71. Adam R.F. Gustafson, *Presidential Inability and Subjective Meaning*, 27 Yale L. & Pol'y Rev. 459, 489 (2009) (quoting Mike Allen, *Bush Resumes Power After Test; President's Routine Colon Exam Showed No Abnormalities*, Wash. Post, June 30, 2002, at A13).

72. Bumiller & Altman, *supra* note 70.

73. *Id.*

74. *Id.*

75. Letter from President George W. Bush to the Speaker of the House of Representatives, 1 Pub. Papers 1083 (June 29, 2002); Letter from President George W. Bush to the President Pro Tempore of the Senate, 1 Pub. Papers 1084 (June 29, 2002).

76. Elizabeth Bumiller, *Bush to Undergo Colon Procedure*, N.Y. Times, June 29, 2002.

77. *Id.*

78. Gustafson, *supra* note 71, at 489 n.150.

79. Bumiller and Altman, *supra* note 70.

80. Jim Rutenberg, *Bush Has 5 Polyps Removed in Colon Cancer Screening*, N.Y. Times, July 22, 2007.

81. Gustafson, *supra* note 71 (citing Deb Riechman, *5 Polyps Removed from Bush's Colon*, Wash. Post, July 21, 2007).

82. Press Briefing by Tony Snow (July 20, 2007), http://www.presidency.ucsb.edu/ws/index.php?pid=75586

83. *What (Acting) President Cheney Did*, Wkly. Standard, Aug. 6, 2007, at 4.

84. Letter from President George W. Bush to the Speaker of the House and the President Pro Tempore of the Senate, 43 Weekly Comp. Pres. Doc. 1003 (July 21, 2007).

85. Letter from President George W. Bush to the Speaker of the House and the President Pro Tempore of the Senate, 43 Weekly Comp. Pres. Doc. 1004 (July 21, 2007).

86. N. Y. Times, *supra* note 13.

87. Rutenberg, *supra* note 80.

88. Dick Cheney, *In My Time: A Personal and Political Memoir*, 320 (2012).

14. Congressional Action

1. Richard B. Bernstein & Jerome Agel, *Amending America: If We Love the Constitution So Much, Why Do We Keep Trying to Change It?* 166 (1995).

2. *Ensuring the Continuity of the United States Government: The Presidency Before the Senate Comm. on the Judiciary, Senate Comm. on Rules and Administration* 108th Cong. 2 (2003) [hereinafter *Senate Committee*] (statement of Sen. Trent Lott, Chairman, Senate Comm. on Rules and Administration).

3. *Id.* at 4 (statement of Senator John Cornyn, of Texas).

4. *Id.*

5. U.S. CONST. art. I, § 1, cl. 6

6. *Senate Committee, supra* note 2, at 7 (statement of Prof. Akhil Amar).

7. *Senate Committee, supra* note 2, at 12 (statement of M. Miller Baker).

8. *Presidential Succession Act: Hearing Before the Subcomm. on the Constitution of the House Comm. on the Judiciary*, 108th Cong. 4–5 (2004) (statement of Thomas H. Neale).

9. *Id.* at 43 (statement of Representative Brad Sherman, of California).

10. *Id.* at 44–45.

11. *Presidential Succession Act, supra* note 8, at 52 (statement of M. Miller Baker).

15. Symposia, Scholarship, and Commissions

1. William Michael Treanor, *Introduction*, 79 FORDHAM L. REV. 775, 775–76 (2010). Dean Treanor served as dean of Fordham Law School from 2002 to 2010 and since then as dean of Georgetown Law School.

2. President Carter, Opening Address to Carter Center Program on Presidential Disability, January 26, 1995, reproduced in PRESIDENTIAL DISABILITY: PAPERS, DIS-CUSSIONS, AND RECOMMENDATIONS ON THE TWENTY-FIFTH AMENDMENT AND IS-SUES OF INABILITY AND DISABILITY AMONG PRESIDENTS OF THE UNITED STATES 16 (James F. Toole & Robert A. Joynt eds., Univ. of Rochester Press 2001).

3. PRESIDENTIAL DISABILITY: PAPERS, DISCUSSIONS, AND RECOMMENDATIONS ON THE TWENTY-FIFTH AMENDMENT AND ISSUES OF INABILITY AND DISABILITY AMONG PRESIDENTS OF THE UNITED STATES, xxx (James F. Toole & Robert A. Joynt eds., Univ. of Rochester Press 2001). ("They invited approximately fifty neurologists, internists, historians, political scientists, psychiatrists and psychologists, journalists, and men and women involved in political affairs to meet. . . .")

4. *Id.* at xxiv.

5. *Id.*

6. *See id.* at xxxiii.

7. *Id.* at 18.

8. *Id.* at 20.

9. *Id.*

10. *Id.*

11. *Id.* at 23.

12. *Id.* at 22–27.

13. *Id.* at 22.

14. *See id.* at 24–26.

15. *Id.* at 29–30.

16. *Id.*

17. *Id.* at 29.

18. *Id.* at 30.

19. *Id.*

20. *Id.* at 32.

21. *Id.* at 44.

22. *Id.* at 46.

23. *Id.* at 47.

24. *Id.* at 49.

25. *Id.* at 50.

26. *Id.* at 48–49.

27. *Id.* at 52.

28. *Id.*

29. *Id.* at 53.

30. *Id.* at 55.

31. *Id.* at 56.

32. *Id.* at 57.

33. *Id.* at 59.

34. *Id.* at 68.

35. *Id.* at 70.

36. *Id.*

37. *Id.* at 71.

38. *Id.*

39. *Id.* at 72.

40. *Id.* at 72–73.

41. *Id.* at 97.

42. *Id.* at 97–99.

43. *Id.* at 109.

44. *Id.* at 110–11.

45. *Id.* at 114–15.

46. *Id.* at 119.

47. *Id.* at 121.

48. *Id.* at 122–23.

49. *Id.* at 152.

50. *Id.* at 156.

51. *Id.*

52. *Id.* at 163.

53. *Id.* at 178.

54. *Id.* at 158.

55. *Id.* at 183.

56. *Id.* at 187.

57. *Id.* at 188.

58. *Id.* at 189.

59. *Id.* at 190.

60. *Id.* at 480–81.

61. *Id.* at 482.

62. *Id.*

63. *Id.* at 484.

64. *Id.* at 488.

65. *Id.* at 537.

66. *Id.*

67. *Id.* at 538.

68. *Id.*

69. *See* Symposium, *The Adequacy of the Presidential Succession System in the 21st Century: Filling the Gaps and Clarifying the Ambiguities in Constitutional and Extraconstitutional Arrangements*, 79 FORDHAM L. REV. 775 (2010).

70. Joel K. Goldstein, *Taking from the Twenty-Fifth Amendment: Lessons in Ensuring Presidential Continuity*, 79 FORDHAM L. REV. 959, 1019 (2010).

71. *See* James E. Fleming, *Presidential Succession: The Art of the Possible*, 79 FORDHAM L. REV. 951 (2010).

72. *Id.* at 953–54.

73. Fleming, *supra* note 71, at 953.

74. *Id.* at 954 (citation omitted).

75. *Id* at 953.

76. *Id.*

77. Goldstein, *supra* note 70, at 1020–21.

78. *Id.* at 1026–27.

79. Goldstein, *supra* note 70, at 1022.

80. Fleming, *supra* note 71, at 954.

81. *Id.* at 953.

82. Goldstein, *supra* note 70, at 1021.

83. *Id.*

84. *Id.*

85. Fleming, *supra* note 71, at 954.

86. *Id.*

87. Transcript of Symposium, *Panel & Response: Interpreting Ambiguities in Current Constitutional Arrangements*, at 41–42 (2010). See note, pp. 239–40, *supra.*

88. Goldstein, *supra* note 70, at 1022.

89. Symposium, *Interpreting Ambiguities, supra* note 87, at 74.

90. Goldstein, *supra* note 70, at 1022.

91. *Id.*

92. *Id.*

93. *Id.*

94. Presidential Succession Act of 1947, 3 U.S.C. § 19(d)(1) (2006).

95. Goldstein, *supra* note 70, at 1022.

96. *Id.* at 1025–26.

97. *Id.* at 1025.

98. *Id.* at 1026.

99. *Id.* at 1025–26.

100. *Id.* at 1026.

101. Symposium, *Interpreting Ambiguities, supra* note 87, at 75–76.

102. *Id.*

103. *Id.* at 77–78.

104. *Id.* at 78.

105. *Compare* U.S. Const. art. II, § 1, cl. 6, *with* U.S. Const. amend. XX, §3.

106. Goldstein, *supra* note 70, at 1023–24.

107. *Id.* at 1024.

108. *Id.*

109. *Id.* at 1025.

110. Fleming, *supra* note 71, at 955–56.

111. *Id.* at 955.

112. Symposium, *Interpreting Ambiguities, supra* note 87, at 44–46.

113. *Id.* at 48–49.

114. *Id.*

115. *Id.* at 61.

116. Goldstein, *supra* note 70, at 1029.

117. *Id.* at 1027.

118. *Id.*

119. Goldstein, *supra* note 70, at 1026–27.

120. Goldstein, *supra* note 70, at 1022 and note 361.

121. *See* Benton Becker, *Adequacy of Current Succession Law in Light of the Constitution and Policy Considerations*, 79 Fordham L. Rev. 897 (2010).

122. *Id.* at 905.

123. *Id.* at 904–05.

124. *Id.* at 905.

125. Goldstein, *supra* note 70, at 1029.

126. *Id.* at 1029–31.

127. Transcript of Symposium, *Panel and Response: Gaps in Electoral, Transitions and Confirmation Processes*, at 48 (Apr. 17, 2010). See note 87, *supra*.

128. Goldstein, *supra* note 70, at 1031–34.

129. *Id.* at 1032.

130. Symposium, *Interpreting Ambiguities, supra* note 87, at 55.

131. *Id.* at 87–88. Under the 1947 statute, if a Cabinet official were to serve as Acting President, he would be replaced as soon as a Speaker of the House or Senate President pro tempore was selected.

132. *Id.*

133. John D. Feerick, *Presidential Succession and Inability: Before and After the Twenty-Fifth Amendment*, 79 FORDHAM L. REV. 907, 908 (2010).

134. *Id.* at 925.

135. *Id.* at 935.

136. *Id.* at 935–36.

137. *See id.* at 913–14.

138. *Id.* at 913.

139. *Id.* at 914; *see also* United States Attorney General, *Presidential Inability*, 42 OP. ATT'Y GEN. 69 (1961).

140. Feerick, *supra* note 133, at 941–42.

141. *Id.* at 916; *see also Presidential Disability: The Need for a Constitutional Amendment*, Herbert Brownell Jr., 68 Yale L.J. 189 (1958).

142. That clause provides "To make all Laws which shall be necessary and proper for carrying into Execution the foregoing Powers, and all other Powers vested by the Constitution in the Government of the United States, or in any Department or Officer thereof." U.S. CONST. art I, § 8, cl. 18; Feerick, *supra* note 133, at 942.

143. Goldstein, *supra* note 70, at 1033. *See also* Akhil Reed Amar, *Applications and Implications of the Twenty-Fifth Amendment*, 47 HOUS. L. REV. 1, 27 (2010).

144. Feerick, *supra* note 133, at 939.

145. Goldstein, *supra* note 70, at 1033; Feerick, *supra* note 133, at 935.

146. Goldstein, *supra* note 70, at 1033.

147. Feerick, *supra* note 133, at 937–38.

148. Goldstein, *supra* note 70, at 1025.

149. *Id.* at 1033.

150. *A Modern Father of Our Constitution: An Interview with Former Senator Birch Bayh*, 79 FORDHAM L. REV. 781, 802 (2010).

151. *See* Robert E. Gilbert, *Presidential Disability and the Twenty-Fifth Amendment: The Difficulties Posed by Psychological Illness*, 79 FORDHAM L. REV. 843, 848–

70 (2010); Rose McDermott, *Extensions on the Twenty-Fifth Amendment: The Influence of Biological Factors on Assessments of Impairment*, 79 FORDHAM L. REV. 881, 890–922 (2010); Feerick, *supra* note 133, at 918–22.

152. Gilbert, *supra* note 151, at 847.

153. *Id.* at 854–74.

154. *Id.* at 871.

155. *Id.*

156. *Id.* at 873.

157. Feerick, *supra* note 133, at 926.

158. Gilbert, *supra* note 151, at 872.

159. Symposium, *Interpreting Ambiguities*, *supra* note 87, at 16.

160. McDermott, *supra* note 151, at 884–87.

161. *Id.* at 888–94.

162. *Id.* at 894–96.

163. *Id.* at 886–87.

164. *Symposium, Interpreting Ambiguities*, *supra* note 87 at 54–55.

165. Nathan L. Colvin & Edward B. Foley, *Lost Opportunity: Learning the Wrong Lesson from the Hayes–Tilden Dispute*, 79 FORDHAM L. REV. 1043, 1044 (2010).

166. *Bush v. Gore*, 531 U.S. 98 (2000).

167. *An Interview*, *supra* note 150, at 808.

168. *Id.*

169. *Id.*

170. *Id.*

171. *Id.* at 809.

172. Goldstein, *supra* note 70, at 1038–39.

173. Fleming, *supra* note 71, at 956.

174. Goldstein, *supra* note 70, at 1039.

175. Fleming, *supra* note 71, at 956–57. Professor Amar also put forth a similar idea, advocating for a vice Vice President who would basically sit and wait "in the line of succession and out of the line of fire." He discussed the possibility that former Presidents could fill this role. Amar, *supra* note 143, at 29.

176. Fleming, *supra* note 71, at 957.

177. *Id.*

178. *Id.*

179. Symposium, Panel & Response: Adequacy of Current Succession Law in Light of the Constitution and Policy Considerations, 62. Note 87, *supra*.

180. *Id.* at 59–60.

181. Goldstein, *supra* note 70, at 1039.

182. *Id.*

183. *Id.* at 1040.

184. *Id.*

185. Fleming, *supra* note 71, at 958.

186. Symposium, *Panel and Response: Gaps, supra* note 127, at 35–36.

187. Feerick, *supra* note 133, at 949.

188. *Id.* at 942; Goldstein, *supra* note 70, at 1033.

189. Goldstein, *supra* note 70, at 1033.

190. Gilbert, *supra* note 151, at 874–75.

191. *Id.*

192. *An Interview, supra* note 150, at 807; Feerick, *supra* note 133, at 946.

193. Colvin & Foley, *supra* note 165, at 1088.

194. *See Ensuring the Stability of Presidential Succession in the Modern Era: Report of the Fordham University School of Law's Clinic on Presidential Succession*, 81 FORDHAM L. REV. 1 (2012).

195. *Id* at 61–62.

196. *Id.*

16. Representation of the Twenty-Fifth Amendment in Popular Culture

1. *The West Wing: Dogs of War* (NBC television broadcast Oct. 1, 2003).

2. William F. Baker & Beth F. Fitzpatrick, *Presidential Succession Scenarios in Popular Culture and History and the Need for Reform*, 79 FORDHAM L. REV. 835, 835 (2010) (noting that the creators of television "are most responsible for what populates our collective imagination").

3. *Id.*

4. *Jericho* (CBS television series 2006–2008).

5. *By Dawn's Early Light* (HBO television series 1990).

6. THE DAY AFTER TOMORROW (20th Century Fox 2004).

7. MARS ATTACKS! (Warner Bros. Pictures 1996).

8. Baker, *supra* note 2, at 836.

9. *Id.*

10. John D. Feerick, *Presidential Succession and Inability: Before and After the Twenty-Fifth Amendment*, 79 FORDHAM L. REV. 907, 935 (2010) ("If the Vice President suffers an inability, current law offers no framework for determining that he is disabled. Further, if the Vice Presidency is vacant, or if the Vice President is disabled, the Section 4 procedures used to declare the President disabled are unavailable.").

11. *See* U.S. CONST. amend. XXV, § 1.

12. *Id.* § 4, which provides that "the President . . . shall resume the powers and duties of his office unless the Vice President and a majority of either the principal officers of the executive department or of such other body as Congress may by law provide, transmit within four days to the President pro tempore of the Senate and the Speaker of the House of Representatives their written declaration that the President is unable to discharge the powers and duties of his office."

13. Feerick, *supra* note 10, at 935–36 (providing examples such as a vice-presidential disability followed by a presidential death, concurrent vice-presidential

and presidential disability, and a vice-presidential vacancy that leaves no one to determine presidential disability).

14. *The West Wing: Twenty-Five* (NBC television broadcast May 14, 2003); *Commander in Chief: The Elephant in the Room* (ABC television broadcast May 31, 2006).

15. *The West Wing: Commencement* (NBC television broadcast May 7, 2003).

16. *Id.*

17. Section 3 states that if the President declares himself unable to discharge his powers and duties, such powers and duties shall be discharged by the Vice President as Acting President. U.S. Const amend XXX, § 3.

18. Baker, *supra* note 2, at 837.

19. *Id.*

20. *The West Wing: Twenty-Five* (NBC television broadcast May 14, 2003).

21. *Id.*

22. *Id.*

23. *Id.* See U.S. Const. Art.1, Section 6, Clause 2.

24. *See* Presidential Succession Act, 3 U.S.C. § 19(a)(1) (2006) ("If, by reason of death, resignation, removal from office, inability, or failure to qualify, there is neither President nor Vice President to discharge the powers and duties of the office of President, then the Speaker of the House of Representatives shall, upon his resignation as Speaker and as Representative in Congress, act as President"); *see also* Baker, *supra* note 2, at 837.

25. Baker, *supra* note 2, at 837.

26. *The West Wing: The Dogs of War* (NBC television broadcast Oct. 1, 2003).

27. Baker, *supra* note 2, at 837.

28. *Id.* (citing to 3 U.S.C. § 19(c)(2)).

29. Baker, *supra* note 2, at 838.

30. *Id.* (citing to Telephone Interview with Tom Rozinski, Assistant Professor, Department of Political Science, Touro College (July 21, 2010)).

31. Baker, *supra* note 2, at 838.

32. *Id.*

33. *The West Wing: Twenty-Five* (NBC television broadcast May 14, 2003).

34. *Id.*

35. *See* Thomas H. Neale, Cong. Research Serv., RL 31761, Presidential Succession: An Overview with Analysis of Legislation Proposed in the 109th Congress (June 29, 2005).

36. Akhil Reed Amar, *Applications and Implications of the Twenty-Fifth Amendment*, 47 Hous. L. Rev. 1, 27 (2010).

37. *Id.*

38. *Id.*

39. See Baker, *supra* note 2, at 838 (noting that these episodes beg the question of whether the Speaker should be next in line for the presidency at all, since House Speakers are often from the opposing party of the President.

40. *Commander in Chief: Pilot* (ABC television broadcast Sept. 27, 2005).

41. *Id.*

42. *Id.*

43. *Id.*

44. *Id.*

45. *Id.*

46. *Id.*

47. *Id.*

48. Baker, *supra* note 2, at 839; *see also supra* notes 24–28 and accompanying text.

49. *See supra notes* 32–39.

50. *See* Feerick, *supra* note 10, at 936.

51. *See* U.S. CONST. amend. XXV, § 2. ("Whenever there is a vacancy in the office of the Vice President, the President shall nominate a Vice President who shall take office upon confirmation by a majority vote of both Houses of Congress.")

52. Feerick, *supra* note 10, at 936–37.

53. *Id.*

54. *See* U.S. CONST. amend. XXV, § 4.

55. *24: Day 2* (Fox television broadcast Nov. 5, 2002).

56. *Id.*

57. *Id.*

58. *Id.*

59. *Id.*

60. *Id.*

61. *Id.*

62. *Id.*

63. *See* U.S. CONST. amend. XXV, § 4.

64. *Id.*

65. *24: Day 2* (Fox television broadcast November 5, 2002).

66. AIR FORCE ONE (Columbia Pictures 1997).

67. *See id.*

68. *See Fiction Regarding Presidential Succession*, WIKIPEDIA, http://en.wikipedia.org/wiki/Fiction_regarding_United_States_presidential_succession (last visited March 14, 2012).

69. *2012* (Columbia Pictures 2009).

70. William Safire, *Full Disclosure* (Ballantine Books, 1978). *See* John D. Feerick, *The Lawyer's Bookshelf*, N.Y.L.J., July 29, 1977, at 2 (reviewing William Safire, *Full Disclosure* (1978)).

71. *Id.*

17. Appraisal

1. N.Y. TIMES, Nov. 1, 1974, at 39.

2. *Transcript of Address by New President*, NEW YORK TIMES, Aug. 10, 1974, at 3.

3. Clifton Daniel, *Ford and 25th Amendment: Rockefeller Choice Held Free of Party Pressure*, NEW YORK TIMES, Dec. 23, 1974, at 17.

4. John D. Feerick, *Presidential Succession and Inability: Before and After the Twenty-Fifth Amendment*, 79 FORDHAM L. REV. 907, 927–28 (2010).

5. *See generally, The Twenty-Fifth Amendment*, CONG. Q., Jan. 4, 1975, at 35–36 [hereinafter *The Twenty-Fifth Amendment*]; Linda Charlton, *25th Amendment: Its Critics Say Amend or Abandon It*, N.Y. TIMES, Nov. 17, 1974 at 4; Arlen J. Large, *The 25th Amendment—An Appraisal*, WALL ST. J., Jan. 6, 1975, at 12.

6. H.R.J. Res. 124, 94th Cong. (1975) (Henry B. Gonzalez, Representative from Texas).

7. Arthur Schlesinger Jr., *Is the Vice Presidency Necessary?*, ATLANTIC MONTHLY, May 1974, at 37; Arthur Schlesinger Jr., *On the Presidential Succession*, 89 POL. SCI. Q. 475 (Fall 1974) [hereinafter Schlesinger, *Presidential Succession*]; Arthur Schlesinger, Jr., *What to Do About a Nonjob*, N.Y. TIMES, Nov. 29, 1974, at 39 [hereinafter Schlesinger, *What to Do*].

8. Edward M. Kennedy, *The Constitution and the Campaign Trail*, N.Y. TIMES, Oct. 21, 1974, at 33.

9. S.J. Res. 26, 94th Cong. (1975); S. J. Res. 172, 93rd Cong. (1973); for Senator Pastore's comments, see 120 CONG. REC. S.1370–73 (daily ed. Feb. 3, 1975); 119 CONG. REC. 37,217–19 (1973); *see also* John O. Pastore, *Special Election Best Way to Fill the Vacancies*, L.A. TIMES, Nov. 17, 1974, § 8, at 5.

10. 119 CONG. REC. 37,217 (1973).

11. Peabody, *On the Threshold of the White House*, ATLANTIC MONTHLY, July 1974, at 63.

12. H.R. 11230, 93d Cong. (1st Sess. 1973), H.R. 11243, 93d Cong. (1st Sess. 1973), H.R. 11439, 93d Cong. (1st Sess. 1973); S. 2678, 93d Cong. (1st Sess. 1973); H.R. 1714, 94th Cong. (1st Sess. 1975). *See* Kevin H. White, *For a Special Presidential Election*, N.Y. TIMES, Oct. 30, 1973, at 43; Arthur Schlesinger Jr., *Back to the Founding Fathers?*, WALL ST. J., Oct. 31, 1973, at 16; *see supra* Chapter 15.

13. *See* S. 2678, 93d Cong. (1st Sess. 1973).

14. *See The Twenty-Fifth Amendment, supra* note 5, at 35–36; H.R.J. Res. 120, 94th Cong. (1975) (popular referendum—Brinkley).

15. S.J. Res. 166, 93d Cong. (1973).

16. N.Y. TIMES, Dec. 20, 1974, at 37.

17. N.Y. TIMES, Oct. 30, 1974, at 34.

18. Report of the Special Committee on Election Reform of the American Bar Association (1974).

19. Schlesinger, *What to Do*, *supra* note 7, at 39.

20. *See supra* note 13.

21. *See* Herbert L. Abrams, *The President Has Been Shot: Confusion, Disability, and the 25th Amendment in the Aftermath of the Attempted Assassination of Ronald Reagan* 227 (W. W. Norton & Co Inc 1992).

22. *Id.* at 221–27.

23. *Id.* at 225.

24. 111 CONG. RES. 3282 (1965).

25. *Supra* note 21, at 234–36.

26. *Id.*, at 235.

27. *Id.* at 231–32.

28. *Id.* at 231.

29. For more discussion on this issue, see *supra* pp. 61–66.

30. H.R.J. Res. 310, 102d Cong. (1991); 137 CONG. REC. H5654 (daily ed. July 22, 1991).

31. H.R.J. Res. 1148, 93rd Cong. (1974); H.R.J. Res. 124, 94th Cong. (1975); H.R.J. Res. 566, 95th Cong. (1977); H.R.J. Res. 235, 96th Cong. (1979); H.R.J. Res. 204, 97th Cong. (1981); H.R.J. Res. 312, 98th Cong. (1983); H.R.J. Res. 302, 99th Cong. (1985); H.R.J. Res. 187, 100th Cong. (1987); H.R.J. Res. 73, 101st Cong. (1989).

32. 120 CONG. REC. 32,803 (1974).

33. 137 CONG. REC. H5658 (daily ed. July 22, 1991).

34. *Hearings on Presidential Inability and Vacancies in the Office of Vice President Before the Subcomm. on Constitutional Amendments of the Senate Comm. on the Judiciary*, 88th Cong. 60 (1964) (statement of Senator Frank Moss of Utah).

35. Schlesinger, *Presidential Succession*, *supra* note 7, at 89.

36. *E.g.*, Arthur M. Schlesinger, *The Imperial Presidency* 411–19 (1973).

37. N.Y. POST, Dec. 23, 1974 at 35.

38. N.Y. TIMES, Nov. 1, 1974 at 39.

39. *Perspectives on Presidential Selection* 1 (Donald Matthews ed., 1973).

40. *See* Ruth C. Silva, *Presidential Succession* 142–49 (University of Michigan Press 1951).

41. *Compare* CONG. GLOBE, 39th Cong., 2d Sess. 691 (1867), *with* H.R. REP. No. 79-829, (1945).

42. *See infra* p. 218 (quoting N.Y. Herald-Tribune, June 9, 1964 at 20).

18. Recommendations

1. *Hearing on the First Implementation of Section Two of the Twenty-Fifth Amendment Before the Subcomm. on Constitutional Amendments of the Senate Comm. on the Judiciary*, 94th Cong. 138 (1975) (statement of Professor Paul A. Freund).

2. Fred F. Fielding, *An Eyewitness Account of Executive "Inability,"* 79 FORD-HAM L. REV. 823, 828 (2010).

3. *Id.*

4. *Hearings Before the Special Comm. to Study Presidential Inability of the House Comm. on the Judiciary*, 84th Cong. 47 (1956) (statement of Sidney Hyman).

Bibliography

Books

Herbert L. Abrams, "The President Has Been Shot": Confusion, Disability, and the 25th Amendment in the Aftermath of the Attempted Assassination of Ronald Reagan (Norton, 1992).

Bruce Ackerman, Before the Next Attack: Preserving Civil Liberties in an Age of Terrorism (Yale University Press, 2006).

Spiro T. Agnew, Go Quietly . . . or Else (Morrow, 1980).

Matthew Algeo, The President Is a Sick Man (Chicago Review Press, 2011).

James A. Baker III, Work Hard, Study . . . and Keep Out of Politics! (Northwestern University Press, 2006).

Laurence I. Barrett, Gambling with History: Ronald Reagan in the White House (Doubleday, 1983).

Birch Bayh, One Heartbeat Away: Presidential Disability and Succession (Bobbs-Merrill, 1968).

Carl Bernstein & Bob Woodward, All the President's Men (Simon & Schuster, 1974).

Carl Bernstein & Bob Woodward, The Final Days (Simon & Schuster, 1976)

Richard Bernstein & Jerome Agel, Amending America (Times Books, 1993).

Jim Bishop, FDR's Last Year (Morrow, 1974).

Herbert Brownell with John P. Burke, Advising Ike: The Memoirs of Attorney General Herbert Brownell (University Press of Kansas, 1993).

Laura Bush, Spoken from the Heart (Scribner, 2011).

George Bush with Victor Gold, Looking Forward: An Autobiography (Doubleday, 1987).

George W. Bush, Decision Points (Broadway Paperbacks, 2010).

Peter Calvert, The Process of Political Succession (St. Martin's Press, 1987).

Dick Cheney, In My Time: A Personal and Political Memoir (Threshold Editions, 2011).

Ron Chernow, Washington: A Life (Penguin Press, 2010).

Richard M. Cohen & Jules Witcover, A Heartbeat Away: The Investigation and Resignation of Vice President Spiro T. Agnew (Viking, 1974).

Kenneth R. Crispell & Carlos F. Gomez, Hidden Illness in the White House (Duke University Press, 1989).

Michael K. Deaver with Mickey Herskowitz, Behind the Scenes: In Which the Author Talks About Ronald and Nancy Reagan . . . and Himself (Morrow, 1987).

Michael V. DiSalle, Second Choice: The Story of the United States Vice-Presidency and the Second Choices Who Went on to Become President (Hawthorne, 1966).

Michael Dorman, The Second Man: the Changing Role of the Vice Presidency (Delacorte, 1968).

John D. Feerick, From Failing Hands: The Story of Presidential Succession (Fordham University Press, 1965).

John D. Feerick, The Twenty-Fifth Amendment: Its Complete History and Applications (Fordham University Press, 1976).

John D. Feerick, The Twenty-Fifth Amendment: Its Complete History and Applications (Fordham University Press, 2nd ed. 1992).

Dennis M. Giangress & Kathryn Moore, Dear Harry: Truman's Mailroom, 1945–1953 (Stackpole Books, 1999).

Marlin Fitzwater, Call the Briefing! (Xlibris, 2000).

Robert E. Gilbert, The Mortal Presidency: Illness and Anguish in the White House (Fordham University Press, 1998).

Robert E. Gilbert, Managing Crisis: Presidential Disability and the Twenty-Fifth Amendment (Fordham University Press, 2000).

Joel K. Goldstein, The Modern American Vice Presidency: The Transformation of a Political Institution (Princeton University Press, 1982).

Alexander M. Haig Jr., Caveat: Realism, Reagan, and Foreign Policy. (Macmillan, 1984).

Richard H. Hansen, The Year We Had No President (University of Nebraska Press, 1962).

Michael Harwood, In the Shadow of Presidents: The American Vice-Presidency and Succession System (Lippincott, 1966).

Doris J. Jensen, Doris J. & Loretta A. Norris, The Twenty-Fifth Amendment to the United States Constitution: A Bibliography (Library of Congress Law Library, 1982).

Paul C. Light, Vice Presidential Power: Advice and Influence in the White House (The Johns Hopkins University Press, 1984).

Edward B. MacMahon & Leonard Curry, Medical Coverups in the White House (Farragut, 1987).

Connie Mariano, The White House Doctor (St. Martin's Press, 2010).

Jane Mayer & Doyle McManus, Landslide: The Unmaking of the President, 1984–1988 (Houghton Mifflin, 1988).

Rose McDermott, Presidential Leadership, Illness, and Decision Making (Cambridge University Press, 2008).

Edwin Meese III, The Heritage Guide to the Constitution (Heritage Foundation Publishing, 2005).

Candice Millard, Destiny of the Republic (Doubleday, 2011).

New York Times Staff, The End of a Presidency (Bantam Books, 1974).

Papers on Presidential Disability and the Twenty-Fifth Amendment (Kenneth W. Thompson ed., University Press of America Vol. II 1991).

Bert E. Park, The Impact of Illness on World Leaders (University of Pennsylvania Press, 1986).

Presidential Disability: Papers, Discussions, and Recommendations on the Twenty-Fifth Amendment and Issues of Inability and Disability in Presidents of the United States (James F. Toole & Robert J. Joynt eds., University of Rochester Press, 2001).

Presidential Succession: Ford, Rockefeller, and the Twenty-Fifth Amendment (Lester A. Sobel ed., Facts on File, 1975).

Dan Quayle, Standing Firm: A Vice Presidential Memoir (HarperCollins, 1994).

Nancy Reagan & William Novak. My Turn: The Memoirs of Nancy Reagan (Random House, 1989).

Ronald Reagan, An American Life: The Autobiography (Simon & Schuster, 1990).

The Records of the Federal Convention of 1787 (Max Farrand ed., Yale University Press, 1911, 1937).

GEORGE E. REEDY, THE TWILIGHT OF THE PRESIDENCY (World Publishing Company, 1970).

THOMAS C. REEVES, GENTLEMAN BOSS: THE LIFE OF CHESTER ALAN ARTHUR (Random House, 1975).

DONALD T. REGAN, FOR THE RECORD: FROM WALL STREET TO WASHINGTON (Harcourt Brace Jovanovich, 1988).

REPORT OF THE MILLER COMMISSION ON PRESIDENTIAL DISABILITY AND THE TWENTY-FIFTH AMENDMENT (White Burkett Miller Center of Public Affairs at the University of Virginia eds., University Press of America, 1988).

CONDOLEEZZA RICE, NO HIGHER HONOR (Crown Publishing Group, 2011).

CLINTON ROSSITER, 1787: THE GRAND CONVENTION (Macmillan, 1966).

DONALD RUMSFELD, KNOWN AND UNKNOWN: A MEMOIR (Penguin Group, 2011).

WILLIAM SAFIRE, FULL DISCLOSURE: A NOVEL (Doubleday, 1977).

ARTHUR M. SCHLESINGER JR., THE IMPERIAL PRESIDENCY (Houghton Mifflin, 1973).

RUTH C. SILVA, PRESIDENTIAL SUCCESSION (University of Michigan Press, 1951).

ALLAN P. SINDLER, UNCHOSEN PRESIDENTS: THE VICE-PRESIDENT AND OTHER FRUSTRATIONS OF PRESIDENTIAL SUCCESSION (University of California Press, 1986).

TED SORENSON, COUNSELOR: A LIFE AT THE EDGE OF HISTORY (HarperLuxe, 2008).

LARRY SPEAKES WITH ROBERT PACK, SPEAKING OUT: THE REAGAN PRESIDENCY FROM INSIDE THE WHITE HOUSE (Scribner, 1988).

JERALD F. terHORST, GERALD FORD AND THE FUTURE OF THE PRESIDENCY (Third Press–Viking, 1974).

CASPAR W. WEINBERGER, FIGHTING FOR PEACE: SEVEN CRITICAL YEARS IN THE PENTAGON (Warner, 1990).

THEODORE WHITE, BREACH OF FAITH: THE FALL OF RICHARD NIXON (Atheneum, 1975).

DEL QUENTIN WILBER, RAWHIDE DOWN: THE NEAR ASSASSINATION OF RONALD REAGAN (Henry Holt and Company, LLC, 2011).

JULES WITCOVER, CRAPSHOOT: ROLLING THE DICE ON THE VICE PRESIDENCY (Crown, 1992).

Congressional Materials

Analysis of the Philosophy and Public Record of Nelson A. Rockefeller, Nominee for Vice President of the United States Before the H. Comm. on the Judiciary, 93d Cong. (1974).

Axel-Lute. Checklist of Federal Documents on Watergate, Impeachment and Presidential Transition, 1973–1974. Rutgers Law Library (1975).

Celada. *Obligation on President and Congress to Fill Vice President Vacancy, in Legislative History on Application of the Twenty-Fifth Amendment to Vacancies in the Office of the Vice President Before the H. Comm. on the Judiciary*, 93d Cong. (1973).

Conference Committee. Report on Presidential Inability and Vacancies in the Office of Vice President. H.R. REP. NO. 89-564 (1965).

Debate on the Nomination of Nelson A. Rockefeller to be Vice President of the United States. H. Comm. on the Judiciary, 93d Cong. (2d Sess. 1974).

Ensuring the Continuity of the United States Government: The Presidency Before the Senate Comm. on the Judiciary, S. Comm. on Rules and Administration, 108th Cong. (2003).

John Feerick, Legislative History of Section 2 of the Twenty-Fifth Amendment, in Selected Materials on the Twenty-Fifth Amendment, S. DOC. NO. 93–42 (1973).

Hearings Before the Special Subcomm. on Study of Presidential Inability of the H. Comm. on the Judiciary, 84th Cong. (1956).

Hearings Before the Special Subcomm. on Study of Presidential Inability of the H. Comm. on the Judiciary, 85th Cong. (1957).

Hearings on Presidential Inability Before the Subcomm. on Constitutional Amendments of the S. Comm. on the Judiciary, 85th Cong. (1958).

Hearings on Presidential Inability Before the Subcomm. on Constitutional Amendments of the S. Comm. on the Judiciary, 88th Cong. (1963).

Hearings on Presidential Inability and Vacancies in the Office of Vice President Before the Subcomm. on Constitutional Amendments of the S. Comm. on the Judiciary, 88th Cong. (1964).

Hearings on Presidential Inability and Vice Presidential Vacancy Before the H. Comm. on the Judiciary, 89th Cong. (1965).

Hearings on Presidential Inability and Vacancies in the Office of Vice President Before the Subcomm. on Constitutional Amendments of the S. Comm. on the Judiciary, 89th Cong. (1965).

Hearings on Nomination of Gerald R. Ford to be Vice President of the United States Before the H. Comm. on the Judiciary, 93d Cong. (1973).

Hearings on Nomination of Gerald R. Ford of Michigan to be Vice President of the United States Before the S. Comm. on Rules and Administration, 93d Cong. (1973).

Hearings on Nomination of Nelson A. Rockefeller to be Vice President of the United States Before the H. Comm. on the Judiciary, 93d Cong. (1974).

Hearings on Nomination of Nelson A. Rockefeller of New York to be Vice President of the United States Before the S. Comm. on Rules and Administration, 93d Cong. (1974).

Hearing on the First Implementation of Section Two of the Twenty-Fifth Amendment Before the Subcomm. on Constitutional Amendments of the S. Comm. on the Judiciary, 94th Cons. (1975).

Hearings on the Pardon of Richard M. Nixon, and Related Matters, Before the Subcomm. on Criminal Justice of the H. Comm. on the Judiciary, 93d Cong. (1975).

Hearings on Presidential Succession between the Popular Election and the Inauguration: Hearing Before the Subcomm. on the Constitution of the S. Comm. on the Judiciary, 103th Cong. (1994).

H. Comm. on the Judiciary, Report on Presidential Inability and Vacancies in the Office of Vice President. H.R. REP. NO. 89-203 (1965).

H. Comm. on the Judiciary, Report on Confirmation of Gerald R. Ford as Vice President of the United States. H.R. REP. NO. 93–695 (1973).

H. Comm. on the Judiciary, Report on Confirmation of Nelson A. Rockefeller as Vice President of the United States. H.R. REP. NO. 93–1609 (1974).

How Can the Federal Political System Be Improved: A Collection of Excerpts and Bibliography Relating to the High School Debate Topic, 1974–75. S. DOC. NO. 93–79 (1974).

Legislative Analysis: Presidential Disability and Vice-Presidential Vacancies, American Enterprise Institute (Aug. 3, 1964) (Study prepared by John D. Feerick, with assistance from Emalie P. Feerick).

Legislative History on Application of the Twenty-Fifth Amendment to Vacancies in the Office of the Vice President. H. Comm. on the Judiciary, 93d Cong. (1973).

NEALE, CONG. RESEARCH SERV., RL 31761, PRESIDENTIAL SUCCESSION: AN OVERVIEW WITH ANALYSIS OF LEGISLATION PROPOSED IN THE 109TH CONGRESS (2005).

Presidential Continuity and Vice Presidential Vacancy Amendment, in Legislative History on Application of the Twenty-Fifth Amendment to Vacancies in the Office of the Vice President. H. Comm. on the Judiciary, 93d Cong. (1973).

Presidential Inability. Staff of H. Comm. on the Judiciary, 84th Cong. (Comm. Print 1956).

Presidential Inability: An Analysis of Replies to a Questionnaire and Testimony at a Hearing on Presidential Inability Before the H. Comm. on the Judiciary, 85th Cong. (Comm. Print 1957).

Presidential Succession Act: Hearing Before the Subcomm. on the Constitution of the H. Comm. on the Judiciary, 108th Cong. (2004).

Report on Nomination of Nelson A. Rockefeller of New York to be Vice President of the United States. S. REP. NO. 93–34, (1974).

Report on Presidential Inability and Vacancies in the Office of Vice President. S. REP. NO. 89-66 (1965).

Report on the Subcomm. on Constitutional Amendments of S. Comm. on the Judiciary. A Review of the Implementation of Section 2 of the 25th Amendment. 94th Cong. (Comm. Print 1975).

Selected Issues and the Positions of Nelson A. Rockefeller, Nominee for Vice President of the United States. H. Comm. on the Judiciary, 93d Cong. (1974).

Selected Materials on the Twenty-Fifth Amendment. S. Doc. No. 93–42. (1973).

S. Comm. on the Judiciary. Report on Presidential Inability and Vacancies in the Office of Vice President. S. Rep. No. 88-1382 (1964); S. Rep. No. 88-1017 (1964).

S. Comm. on Rules and Administration. Report on Nomination of Gerald R. Ford of Michigan to be the Vice President of the United States. S. Exec. Rep. No. 93–26, (1973).

Thomas H. Neale, Cong. Research Serv., RL 31761, Presidential Succession: An Overview with Analysis of Legislation Proposed in the 109th Congress (June 29, 2005).

Articles

Carl Albert, *The Most Dramatic Events of My Life,* Oklahoma State University Outreach 4 (March 1974).

Richard Albert, *The Constitutional Politics of Presidential Succession,* 39 Hofstra L. Rev. 497 (2010).

Mike Allen, *Bush Resumes Power After Test; President's Routine Colon Exam Showed No Abnormalities,* Wash. Post, June 30, 2002 at A13.

Akhil Reed Amar & Vikram David Amar, *Is the Presidential Succession Law Constitutional?* 48 Stan L. Rev. 113 (1995).

Akhil Reed Amar. *Presidents, Vice Presidents, and Death: Closing the Constitution's Succession Gap,* 48 Ark. L. Rev. 215 (1995).

Akhil Reed Amar. *Applications and Implications of the Twenty-Fifth Amendment,* 47 Hous. L. Rev. 1 (2010).

William F. Baker & Beth A. FitzPatrick. *Presidential Succession Scenarios in Popular Culture and History and the Need for Reform,* 79 Fordham L. Rev. 835 (2010).

Birch Bayh, Reflection: Remarks from Senator Birch Bayh, 79 Fordham L. Rev. 1091 (2010).

Birch Bayh, *A Modern Father of Our Constitution: An Interview with Former Senator Birch Bayh,* 79 Fordham L. Rev. 781 (2010).

Birch Bayh, *Our Greatest National Danger,* Look, Apr. 7, 1964, at 74.

Benton Becker, *Adequacy of Current Succession Law in Light of the Constitution and Policy Considerations,* 79 Fordham L. Rev. 897 (2010).

James Bennet, *Clinton Knee Surgery Successful. President Tripped. Torn Tendon,* Denver Post, Mar. 15, 1997.

Paul H. Blackman, *Presidential Disability and the Bayh Amendment*, 20 W. POL. Q. 440 (1967).

Robert A. Blattner, *Presidential Inability and Vice Presidential Vacancy*, 36 CLEVELAND BAR ASS'N JOURNAL 261 (November 1964).

Dom Bonafede, *Filling In*, NATIONAL JOURNAL, May 28, 1988 at 1445.

Borman, *Beyond the 25th Amendment*, 3 FACT 21 (1966).

William F. Brown & Americo R. Cinquegrana. *The Realities of Presidential Succession: "The Emperor Has No Clones"*, 75 GEO. L.J. 1389 (1987).

Herbert Brownell Jr., *Presidential Disability: The Need for a Constitutional Amendment*, 68 YALE L.J. 189 (1958).

Roy E. Brownell II, *Can the President Recess Appoint a Vice President*, 42 PRESIDENTIAL STUD. Q. 622 (2012).

Elisabeth Bumiller, *Bush to Undergo Colon Procedure*, N.Y. TIMES (June 29, 2002), www.nytimes.com/2002/06/29/us/bush-to-undergo-colon-procedure.html.

Elisabeth Bumiller & Lawrence K. Altman, *Bush Returns to Activities After 20-Minute Procedure Finds No Polyps on His Colon*, N.Y. TIMES (June 30, 2002), www.nytimes.com/2002/06/30/us/bush-returns-activities-after-20-minute-procedure-finds-no-polyps-his-colon.html?src=pm.

Steven G. Calabresi, *The Political Question of Presidential Succession*, 48 STAN. L. REV. 155 (1995).

Mortimer Caplin, *Presidential Disability*, NATIONAL LAW JOURNAL, Dec. 5, 1988, at 13.

CBS Reports: The Crisis of Presidential Succession (CBS television broadcast Jan. 8, 1964).

Linda Charlton, *25th Amendment: Its Critics Say Amend or Abandon It*, N.Y. TIMES, Nov. 17, 1974, at 4.

Warren Christopher, *A Special Election to Fill a Presidential Vacancy*, 30 RECORD OF THE ASS'N OF THE BAR OF THE CITY OF NEW YORK 47 (1975).

James E. Clayton, *Presidential Succession: One of the Biggest Problems*, N.Y. JOURNAL-AMERICAN, Feb. 4, 1964, at 32.

Clark Clifford, *A Government of National Unity*, N.Y. TIMES, June 4, 1973, at 35.

Nathan L. Colvin & Edward B. Foley, *Lost Opportunity: Learning the Wrong Lesson from the Hayes–Tilden Dispute*, 79 FORDHAM L. REV. 1043 (2010).

Vern Countryman, Letter to the Editor, *To Revise the 25th Amendment*, N.Y. TIMES, Apr. 9, 1975, at 42.

Walter E. Craig, *Presidential Inability and Vice Presidential Vacancy*, 1 ARIZONA BAR JOURNAL 5 (1965).

Lloyd N. Cutler, *Symposium: The Continuity of Government—Opening Remarks*, 53 CATH. U. L. REV. 943 (2004).

Clifton Daniel, *Ford and the Twenty-Fifth Amendment: Rockefeller Choice Held Free of Party Pressure*, N.Y. TIMES, Dec. 23, 1974, at 17.

Roscoe Drummond, *Congress Must Face Up Now: A Gap at Top if President Should Fall Seriously Ill*, N.Y. HERALD-TRIBUNE, Dec. 6, 1963, at 19.

Roscoe Drummond, *The Succession Debate: President's Party Is Seen Best Suited to Fill Vacancy*. N.Y. HERALD-TRIBUNE, Dec. 13, 1963, at 21.

Editorial, *N.Y. Times*, March 4, 1975 at 32.

John D. Feerick, *Filling a Vacancy in the Vice Presidency*, N.Y. L.J., Oct. 11, 1973.

John D. Feerick, *A Response to Akhil Reed Amar's Address on Applications and Implications of the Twenty-Fifth Amendment*. 47 HOUS. L. REV. 41 (2010).

John D. Feerick, *Is the Law on Presidential Succession Adequate?*, N.Y. L.J., Nov. 25, 1974, at 1.

John D. Feerick, *The Issue of Presidential Inability*, N.Y. L.J., May 15, 1974, at 1.

John D. Feerick, *Presidential Inability: The Problem and a Solution*, 50 A.B.A. JOURNAL 321 (1964).

John D. Feerick, *Presidential Succession and Inability: Before and After the Twenty-Fifth Amendment*, 79 FORDHAM L. REV. 907 (2010).

John D. Feerick, *The Problem of Presidential Inability—It Must Be Solved Now*, 36 NEW YORK STATE BAR JOURNAL 181 (1964).

John D. Feerick, *Problem of Presidential Inability—Will Congress Ever Solve It?*, 32 FORDHAM L. REV. 73 (1963).

John D. Feerick, *Proposed Amendment on Presidential Inability and Vice Presidential Vacancy*, 51 A.B.A. JOURNAL 915 (1965).

John D. Feerick, *Proposed Twenty-Fifth Amendment to the Constitution*, 34 FORD-HAM L. REV. 173 (1965).

John D. Feerick, *Ensuring the Stability of Presidential Succession in the Modern Era: Report of the Fordham University School of Law's Clinic on Presidential Succession*, 81 FORDHAM L. REV. 1 (2012) (Co-Teacher).

John D. Feerick, *The Lawyer's Bookshelf*, N.Y. L.J., July 29, 1977, at 2 (reviewing WILLIAM SAFIRE, FULL DISCLOSURE (1977).

John D. Feerick, *The Transition Was Smooth: Why Change?*, L.A. TIMES, Nov. 17, 1974, § 8 at 5.

John D. Feerick, *Vice Presidential Succession: In Support of the Bayh–Celler Plan*, 18 S.C. L. REV. 226 (1966).

John D. Feerick, *The Vice Presidency and the Problems of Presidential Succession and Inability*, 32 FORDHAM L. REV. 457 (1964).

John D. Feerick, *The Way of the 25th*, N.Y. TIMES, Dec. 13, 1973, at 47.

Mark Feldstein, *Watergate Revisited*, AMERICAN JOURNAL REVIEW (August/September 2004), www.ajr.org/article.asp?id=3735.

Jerry Finkelstein & Nelson Seitel, *Vice-President Can Oust the President*, N.Y. L.J., May 14, 1974, at 1.

James E. Fleming, *Presidential Succession: The Art of the Possible*, 79 FORDHAM L. REV. 951 (2010).

John C. Fortier & Norman J. Ornstein, *Presidential Succession and Congressional Leaders*, 53 CATH. U. L. REV. 993 (2004).

Richard D. Friedman, *Some Modest Proposals on the Vice-Presidency*, 86 MICH. L. REV. 1703 (1988).

Robert E. Gilbert, *Presidential Disability and the Twenty-Fifth Amendment: The Difficulties Posed by Psychological Illness*, 79 FORDHAM L. REV. 843 (2010).

Joel K. Goldstein, Commentary, *Akhil Reed Amar and Presidential Continuity*, 47 HOUS. L. REV. 67 (2010).

Joel K. Goldstein, *Taking from the Twenty-Fifth Amendment: Lessons in Ensuring Presidential Continuity*, 79 FORDHAM L. REV. 959 (2010).

Joel K. Goldstein, Presidential Succession and Inability: America's Inadequate Provisions (1975) (unpublished thesis, Woodrow Wilson School of Public and International Affairs, Princeton University).

Ted Gup, *Speaker Was Ready to Be President*, WASH. POST, Nov. 28, 1982, at A1.

Adam R.F. Gustafson, *Presidential Inability and Subjective Meaning*, 27 YALE L. & POL'Y REV. 459 (2009).

George D. Haimbaugh Jr., *Vice Presidential Succession: A Brief Rebuttal*, 18 S.C. L. REV. 237 (1966).

George D. Haimbaugh Jr., *Vice Presidential Succession: A Criticism of the Bayh–Celler Plan*. 17 S.C. L. Rev. 315 (1965).

Charles S. Hamlin, *The Presidential Succession Act of 1886*, 18 HARV. L. REV. 182 (1905).

Edward M. Kennedy, *The Constitution and the Campaign Trail*, N.Y. TIMES, Oct. 21, 1974, at 33.

James C. Kirby, Jr., *A Breakthrough on Presidential Inability: The ABA Conference Consensus*, 17 VAND. L. REV. 463 (1964).

Dick Kirschten, *History in the Making as Quietly as Possible as Aides Stage-Manage Postoperative News*, NATIONAL JOURNAL, July 20, 1985, at 1694.

Dick Kirschten, *Who's in Charge at the White House When a President Is Disabled?*, NATIONAL JOURNAL, Jan. 23, 1988, at 202.

Arthur Krock, *Basic Principles Emerging from the Fog*, N.Y. TIMES, Jan. 24, 1964, at 26.

Arthur Krock, *The Cart Is Getting Ahead of the Horse*, N.Y. TIMES, Dec. 12, 1963, at 38.

Arthur Krock, *The Continuum: Kennedy's Death Points Up Orderly Progression in U.S. Government*, N.Y. TIMES, Nov. 24, 1963, at 9E.

Arthur Krock, *An Object Lesson for the Critics of Congress*, N.Y. TIMES, Mar. 6, 1964, at 30.

Arthur Krock, *Solvents of an Ancient Congressional Dilemma*, N.Y. TIMES, Jan. 17, 1964, at 42.

Arthur Krock, *Succession Problem: The Death of Kennedy Again Points Up the Need to Devise Solution*, N.Y. TIMES, Dec. 8, 1963, at 9E.

Kury, *The Crisis in the Law of Presidential Succession*, 36 PENNSYLVANIA BAR ASS'N Q. 301 (1965).

Arlen J. Large, *The 25th Amendment: An Appraisal*, WALL STREET JOURNAL, Jan. 6, 1975, at 12.

David Lawrence, *The Big Succession Muddle*, WASH. EVENING STAR, Feb. 28, 1964, at A13.

David Lawrence, *Need Is Seen for a New Vice-President Right Away*, N.Y. HERALD-TRIBUNE, Dec. 13, 1963, at 21.

David Lawrence, *People's Right to Elect and the Succession Law*, N.Y. HERALD-TRIBUNE, Dec. 9, 1963, at 24.

Max Lerner, *Taking the 25th*, N.Y. POST, Dec. 23, 1974, at 35.

Letter from Paul A. Freund, Abram Chayes, & Raoul Berger to Mayor of Boston, Kevin H. White, Nov. 1, 1973. Repr. 119 Cong. Rec. 26493 (1973).

Sanford Levinson & Jack M. Balkin, *Constitutional Crisis*, 157 U. PA. L. REV. 707 (2009).

Anthony Lewis, *Presidential Disability Problem Stirs Concern*, N.Y. TIMES, Dec. 22, 1963, at 4E.

Anthony Lewis, *The 25th Amendment and Its Unanswered Questions.* N.Y. TIMES, Sept. 30, 1973, at 2.

Hans A. Linde, *Replacing a President: Rx for a 21st Century Watergate*, 43 GEO. WASH. L. REV. 384 (1975).

Walter Lippmann, *The Presidential Succession*, WASH. POST, Dec. 12, 1963, at A21.

Walter Lippmann, *Presidential Succession and Disability*, N.Y. HERALD-TRIBUNE, June 9, 1964, at 20.

Walter Lippmann, *The Problem of a Disabled President*, N.Y. HERALD-TRIBUNE, Dec. 17, 1963, at 24.

Richard P. Longaker, *Presidential Continuity: The Twenty-Fifth Amendment*, 13 UCLA L. REV. 532 (1966).

Ed Magnuson, *Six Shots at a Nation's Heart; Again, a Moment of Madness Threatens a President and Tarnishes the U.S.*, TIME MAGAZINE, Apr. 13, 1981, at 24.

John F. Manning, Response, *Not Proved: Some Lingering Questions About Legislative Succession to the Presidency*, 48 STAN. L. REV. 141 (1995).

E. Connie Mariano, *In Sickness and in Health: Medical Care for the President of the United States*, *in* MANAGING CRISIS: PRESIDENTIAL DISABILITY AND THE TWENTY-FIFTH AMENDMENT 83 (Fordham University Press, 2000).

Tom Matthews, *Reagan's Close Call*, NEWSWEEK, Apr. 13, 1981, at 34.

Rose McDermott, *Extensions on the Twenty-Fifth Amendment: The Influence of Biological Factors on Assessments of Impairment*, 79 FORDHAM L. REV. 881 (2010).

The New President, 60 A.B.A. JOURNAL 1258 (1974).

Lewis J. Paper & Raymond S. Calamaro, *Not by Honesty Alone*, N.Y. TIMES, Nov. 13, 1974, at 43.

John O. Pastore, *Special Election Best Way to Fill the Vacancies*, L.A. TIMES, Nov. 17, 1974, § 8 at 5.

Endicott Peabody, *On the Threshold of the White House*, 234 ATLANTIC MONTHLY 63 (1974).

The Presidency: Thinking about the Unthinkable, THE ECONOMIST, Jan. 19, 1985, at 24.

PRESIDENTIAL DISABILITY: PAPERS, DISCUSSIONS, AND RECOMMENDATIONS ON THE TWENTY-FIFTH AMENDMENT AND ISSUES OF INABILITY AND DISABILITY IN PRESIDENTS OF THE UNITED STATES (James F. Toole & Robert J. Joynt eds., University of Rochester Press 2001).

James Reston, *Fiddling with the 25th*, N.Y. TIMES, Nov. 1, 1974, at 39.

James Reston, *The Problem of Succession to the Presidency*, N.Y. TIMES, Dec. 6, 1963, at 34.

Deb Riechmann, *5 Polyps Removed from Bush's Colon*, ASSOCIATED PRESS, July 21, 2007, *available at* http://www.washingtonpost.com/wp-dyn/content/article/2007/07/21/AR2007072101103.html.

John P. Roche, *25th Amendment Tradition of 1787*, DAILY MAIL, Dec. 26, 1974.

Vermont Royster, *Thinking Things Over: The 25th Amendment*, WALL STREET JOURNAL, Oct. 31, 1973, at 16.

Jim Rutenberg, *Bush Has 5 Polyps Removed in Colon Cancer Test*, N.Y. TIMES (June 22, 2002), http://www.nytimes.com/2007/07/22/washington/22bush.html?scp=23&sq=rutenberg&st=nyt.

Arthur Schlesinger Jr., *Back to the Founding Fathers?*, WALL STREET JOURNAL, Oct. 31, 1973, at 16.

Arthur Schlesinger Jr., *Is the Vice Presidency Necessary?*, 233 ATLANTIC MONTHLY 37 (May 1974).

Arthur Schlesinger Jr., *On the Presidential Succession*, 89 POL. SCI. Q. 475 (1974).

Arthur Schlesinger Jr., *Taking the 25th*, N.Y. TIMES, Oct. 3, 1973, at 45.

Arthur Schlesinger Jr., *What to Do About a Nonjob*, N.Y. TIMES, Nov. 29, 1974, at 39.

Nelson Seitel, *Why the Delay on Rockefeller*, N.Y. L.J., Oct. 9, 1974, at 1.

Merril Sheils, *In My Stead*, NEWSWEEK, July 22, 1985, at 17.

Ruth D. Silva, *The Presidential Succession Act of 1947*, 47 MICH. L. REV. 451 (1949).

Godfrey Sperling Jr., *Succession: Doubts Posed*, CHRISTIAN SCIENCE MONITOR, Mar. 11, 1964, at 1.

Richard Stengel, *Who's Minding the Store? Delicate Questions Arise on the Transfer of Presidential Power*, TIME MAGAZINE, April. 12, 2005 at 24.

Symposium on the Vice Presidency: American Bar Association Special Committee on Election Reform, 45 FORDHAM L. REV. 703 (1977).

James A. Thomas Jr. & Morton Cohen, *The Drastic Remedies*, N.Y. TIMES, May 30, 1973, at 39.

The Twenty-Fifth Amendment, CONGRESSIONAL Q., Jan. 4, 1975, at 35.

Twenty-Fifth Amendment Proposals Aired in Senate Hearings: Association Position Favors No Changes, 61 A.B.A. JOURNAL 599 (1975).

The Vice Presidency: How Would a Vacancy Be Filled?, CONGRESSIONAL Q., Sept. 22, 1973, at 2499.

Seth Barrett Tillman, *The Annals of Congress, the Original Public Meaning of the Succession Clause, and the Problem of Constitutional Memory*, SOCIAL SCIENCE RESEARCH NETWORK (Feb. 14, 2011), http://ssrn.com/abstract=1524008 *or* http://dx.doi.org/10.2139/ssrn.1524008

William Michael Treanor, *Introduction to Symposium*, 79 FORDHAM L. REV. 775 (2010).

Milton Viorst, *If a President Is Disabled*, N.Y. POST, Mar. 22, 1964.

Howard M. Wasserman, *Continuity of Congress: A Play in Three Stages*, 53 CATH. U. L. REV. 949 (2004).

Tom Wicker, *Two for the 25th*, N.Y. TIMES, Dec. 20, 1974, at 37.

Tom Wicker, *Why Rush to Change the 25th?*, N.Y. TIMES, Nov. 19, 1974, at 43.

What (Acting) President Cheney Did, WKLY. STANDARD, Aug. 6, 2007, at 4.

When a President Is Disabled, WASH. POST, Apr. 30, 1989, at C6.

Kevin H. White, *For a Special Presidential Election*, N.Y. TIMES, Oct. 30, 1973, at 43.

C. Dickerman Williams, *An Alternative: Taking the Twenty-Fifth*, 26 NAT'L REV. 476 (1974).

Irving G. Williams, *The American Vice Presidency*, 689 CURRENT HISTORY 254 (1974).

Edwin M. Yoder Jr., *The "Acting President" Problem*, WASH. POST, Sept. 23, 1988, at A21.

Executive Materials

Fitzwater, Marlin. White House Press Sec'y Statement on the Health of the President George Bush (May 5, 1991) in the American Presidency Project.

Fitzwater, Marlin. White House Press Sec'y Statement on the Health of the President George Bush (May 6, 1991) in the American Presidency Project.

Johnson, Lyndon. 2 Public Papers 1043 (Oct. 5, 1965) (Press Release on Occasion of His Gall Bladder Surgery).

Kennedy, Robert F. *42 Opinions of Attorneys General* No. 5. Washington: United States Government Printing Office, 1961.

Letter, President Johnson to Speaker John W. McCormack, 12/23/63, Ex FG 1 WHCF, Box 9, LBJ Library. (Appendix H) *Letter, President Johnson to Speak John W. McCormack, 12/23/63, Ex FG 1 WHCF, Box 9, LBJ Library.* Please note, the previous underlined segment is the original citation of the document and the full document in the Johnson Library contains an 11 page memorandum authored by Assistant Attorney General Norbert A. Schlei, entitled, *Agreement Between the President and the Speaker of the House as to Procedures in the Event of Presidential Inability.*

Letter from President George W. Bush to the Speaker of the House and the President Pro Tempore of the Senate, 43 WEEKLY COMP. PRES. DOC. 1003 (July 21, 2007).

Letter from President George W. Bush to the Speaker of the House and the President Pro Tempore of the Senate, 43 WEEKLY COMP. PRES. DOC. 1004 (July 21, 2007).

Letter from President George W. Bush to the Speaker of the House of Representatives, 1 PUB. PAPERS 1083 (June 29, 2002).

Letter from President George W. Bush to the President Pro Tempore of Senate, 1 PUB. PAPERS 1084 (June 29, 2002).

Memorandum, Bobbie Greene Kilberg to President Gerald Ford, Aug. 21, 1975, copy is at the Gerald Ford Presidential Library (Appendix I).

President Carter Opening Address to Carter Center Program on Presidential Disability, Jan. 26, 1995, reproduced in *Presidential Disability: Papers, Discussions and Recommendations on the Twenty-Fifth Amendment and Issues of Inability among Presidents of the United States* 16 (James F. Toole & Robert J. Joynt eds., Univ. of Rochester Press (2001).

Press Briefing by Mike McCurry and Dr. David Wade, Mar. 14, 1997, *available at* http://www.presidency.ucsb.edu/ws/index.php?pid=48596.

Press Briefing by Tony Snow, July 20, 2007, *available at* http://www.presidency .ucsb.edu/ws/index.php?pid=75586.

Press Briefing by the Physicians Attending to the President, Mar. 14, 1997, *available at* http://www.presidency.ucsb.edu/ws/index.php?pid=48596

Press Briefing, The White House, Apr. 28, 1989.

Vice President Gerald Ford Schedule, Transitioning from Vice-Presidency to Presidency, Aug. 9, 1974, copy is at the Gerald Ford Presidential Library (Appendix I).

General Reports and Conferences

Continuity of the Government Commission, Preserving Our Institutions: The Continuity of the Presidency (2009), *available at* http://www.continuityof government.org/SecondReport.pdf

Report of the Special Committee on Election Reform of the American Bar Association (1974).

Symposium: The Adequacy of the Presidential Succession System in the 21st Century: Filling the Gaps and Clarifying the Ambiguities in Constitutional and Extraconstitutional Arrangements, Fordham Law Review, Panel & Response: Interpreting Ambiguities in Current Constitutional Arrangements Transcript, Panelists: Robert E. Gilbert, Rose McDermott, Akhil Amar, and Hon. Birch Bayh, moderated by Dr. William Baker, Apr. 16, 2010.

Symposium: The Adequacy of the Presidential Succession System in the 21st Century: Filling the Gaps and Clarifying the Ambiguities in Constitutional and Extraconstitutional Arrangements, Fordham Law Review, A Framer's Perspective: Hon. Birch Bayh, Speaking Remarks, Apr. 16, 2010.

Symposium: The Adequacy of the Presidential Succession System in the 21st Century: Filling the Gaps and Clarifying the Ambiguities in Constitutional and Extraconstitutional Arrangements, Fordham Law Review, Panel & Response: Adequacy of Current Succession Law in Light of the Constitution and Policy Considerations Transcript, Panelists: Joel K. Goldstein, John D. Feerick, Benton Becker, James E. Fleming, and Hon. Birch Bayh, moderated by Robert Kaczorowski, Apr. 16, 2010.

Symposium: The Adequacy of the Presidential Succession System in the 21st Century: Filling the Gaps and Clarifying the Ambiguities in Constitutional and Extraconstitutional Arrangements, Fordham Law Review, Keynote Speaker Fred F. Fielding, Speaking Remarks, Apr. 16, 2010. Fielding. An Eyewitness Account of Executive "Inability" 79 Fordham L. Rev. 823

Symposium: The Adequacy of the Presidential Succession System in the 21st Century: Filling the Gaps and Clarifying the Ambiguities in Constitutional and Extraconstitutional Arrangements, Fordham Law Review, Panel & Response: Gaps in Electoral, Transition & Confirmation Processes, Transcript, Panelists: Dr. John C. Fortier, Edward B. Foley, Dr. Norman Ornstein, and Hon. Birch Bayh, moderated by William Treanor, Apr. 17, 2010.

Statutes

Act effective Mar. 9 2006, Pub. L. No. 80-199, 61 Stat. 380 (codified as amended at 3 U.S.C. § 19 (2006)).

Cases

Bush v. Gore, 531 U.S. 98 (2000).

Media

2012 (Columbia Pictures 2009).

24: Day 2 (Fox television broadcast Nov. 5, 2002).

AIR FORCE ONE (Columbia Pictures 1997).

By Dawn's Early Light (HBO television series 1990).

Commander in Chief: First Scandal (ABC television broadcast Nov. 8, 2005).

Commander in Chief: Pilot (ABC television broadcast Sept. 27, 2005).

Commander in Chief: The Elephant in the Room (ABC television broadcast May 31, 2006).

Fiction Regarding Presidential Succession, WIKIPEDIA.COM, http://en.wikipedia.org/wiki/Fiction_regarding_United_States_presidential_succession (last visited Mar. 14, 2012).

Jericho (CBS television series 2006–2008).

MARS ATTACKS! (Warner Bros. Pictures 1996).

THE DAY AFTER TOMORROW (20th Century Fox 2004).

The West Wing: Commencement (NBC television broadcast May 7, 2003).

The West Wing: Twenty-Five (NBC television broadcast May 14, 2003).

The West Wing: Dogs of War (NBC television broadcast Oct. 1, 2003).

The West Wing: The West Election Day: Part 2 (NBC television broadcast Apr. 9, 2006).

Index